CHINA,
MODERNISATION AND THE GOAL OF PROSPERITY

CHINA, MODERNISATION AND THE GOAL OF PROSPERITY

Government Administration
and Economic Policy
in the late 1980s

Edited and Compiled by
KATE HANNAN
School of History, Philosophy and Politics
Macquarie University

CAMBRIDGE
UNIVERSITY PRESS

Published by the Press Syndicate of the University of Cambridge
The Pitt Building, Trumpington Street, Cambridge CB2 1RP, UK
40 West 20th Street, New York, NY 10011–4211, USA
10 Stamford Road, Oakleigh, Melbourne 3166, Australia

© Cambridge University Press 1995
First Published 1995

This book has been printed from camera–ready copy provided by the author.

Printed in Hong Kong by Colorcraft

National Library of Australia cataloguing-in-publication data

China, modernisation and the goal of prosperity
Includes index.
1. Agriculture – Economic aspects – China. 2. Investments,
Foreign – China. 3. China – Economic policy – 1976- .
4. China – Economic conditions – 1976- . 5. China – Industries.
I. Hannan, Kate.
338.951

Library of Congress cataloguing-in-publication data

China, modernisation and the goal of prosperity : government
administration and economic policy in the late 1980s / edited
and compiled by Kate Hannan : introduction by Ma Hong.
Includes index.
1. China – Economic policy – 1976- . 2. Industry and state – China.
I. Hannan, Kate.
HC426.92.C57 1995
338.951–dc20   943011
                                                                  CIP

A catalogue record for this book is available from the British Library.

ISBN 0 521 46043 3 Hardback

Contents

List of Tables and Charts	*vii*
Editor's Foreword	*ix*
Acknowledgements	*xiv*
Introduction by Ma Hong	1

SECTION I National Financial Management

1	Government Financial Regulation	15
2	Monetary Policy and Monetary System	27
3	Bonds, Stocks, Banks and Insurance	45
4	Price Reform	59
5	Taxation Policy	81

SECTION II Economic Law and the Administration of Industry

6	The Economic Legal System	91
7	Economic Planning	107
8	Administration of Industry and Commerce	123
9	Enterprise Classification and Management	137
10	Employment, Wages and Welfare	159
11	Housing, Land Use and Environmental Protection	175

SECTION III Industrial Production and Infrastructure

12 The Structure of Industry	199
13 Fixed Asset Construction	211
14 Industrial Materials and Equipment	223
15 Provision of Energy, Transport and Communication Services	237
16 The Electronics, Nuclear and Astronautical Industries	261

SECTION IV Rural Production

17 Agriculture	277
18 Township Enterprise Production	295

SECTION V Foreign Investment

19 Foreign Economic and Technical Cooperation	311
20 China's Foreign Investment Experience	319
21 Open Coastal Areas and Special Economic Zones	329

Editor's Conclusion — 337

Index — 345

List of Tables and Charts

In:1	Per Capita National Income and Consumption in Various Regions	10
1:1	Changing Composition of State Financial Revenue	17
1:2	Changing Structure of State Financial Expenditure	20
2:1	Transmission Mechanisms for Current Monetary Policy	30
2:2	Transmission Mechanisms for Future Monetary Policy	31
3:1	State Economic Construction Bonds	46
3:2	State Treasury Bonds	47
4:1	Product Pricing	63
4:2	Major Price Indices 1987	68
4:3	Major Price Indices Taking 1950 as 100	69
4:4	Changes in Price Parity of Major Agricultural and Industrial Products	70
4:5	Changes in Price Ratios Between Industrial and Agricultural Products	75
4:6	State Subsidies for Commodity Prices	79
9:1	Enterprise Type Determined According to Production Capacity	141
9:2	Number and Output of Large, Medium and Small Industrial Enterprises	142
9:3	The Position of Factory and Workshop Directors, Advisors and Groups	151
9:4	Six Channels for State Enterprise Funding	153
10:1	Changes in Money Wage of State Enterprise Workers	165
12:1	Output Value of Industry and Agriculture	201
12:2	Output Value of Light Industry Using Agricultural Materials as Raw Materials and Manufactured Goods for Production	203
12:3	Output Value of the Manufacturing, Raw Materials and Mining Industries	204
12:4	Changes in Proportion of Output Value of a Number of Important Industries	205

13:1	Investment in Fixed Assets	215
13:2	State Enterprise Investment in Capital Construction, Updating and Transformation Projects	217
13:3	State Enterprise Capital Construction Investment in Newly Built Projects, Extension and Rebuilt Projects	217
13:4	State Enterprise Investment in Productive and Non-productive Capital Construction	218
15:1	Growth of Passenger and Freight Transport	247
16:1	China's Nuclear Industry	266
16:2	Satellites Successfully Launched	271
17:1	Increase in Output of Grain and Industrial Crops	281
18:1	Funding of Township and Village Enterprise Expanded Production	298
18:2	Changes in the Structure of the Rural Economy	299
18:3	Proportion of Township and Village Enterprise Profits Used for the Support of Agricultural Production	301
18:4	Increase in Number of Workers and Staff Employed by Rural Enterprises	302
21:1	Coastal Area Output	329

Editor's Foreword

The information in this book covers the period that represents the most mature point in China's first decade of economic reform. The outline of administrative procedures and reform policy was produced from information gathered by the Chinese Academy of Social Sciences in 1987 and 1988. It is this aspect that provides a unique insight into administrative procedure, structure and policy adopted by the Chinese government during the late 1980s.

The first stage on China's road to economic reform spanned the decade 1979-1989. It began with the introduction of the programme for promoting the four modernisations and ended with the social unrest that culminated in the 'Tiananmen Incident' of June 1989. A central theme of this 1979-1989 modernisation decade was that 'prosperity' would, in time, be available to all. It was a period when, as Ma Hong states in his introduction to this book,

> *encouraging a number of people to become rich first through honest labour and legal management is [to be seen as] a powerful motive force in promoting the development of the national economy...*

The cornerstone of reform policy and its promised prosperity was development of the productive forces (a concept synonymous with the development of the national economy) and as the section titles of this book indicate, the essential policy elements involved reorganising national financial management, constructing a 'routinised' economic legal system, reforming planning and government and enterprise administrative practice and reform of industrial, agricultural and foreign investment policy, structures and administration.

This book offers a comprehensive outline of the financial policy of the late 1980s programme for reform. It is a policy that required the government to strengthen the centralised financial role played by the banking system and to employ economic levers such as credit, prices and taxation to impress planning priorities on enterprise production, while at the same time abandoning the central allocation of production funds to the enterprises. In this context, as noted in chapter two, enterprises were required to sign a contract with a bank for production funds advanced as loans. The agreed content of this legally enforceable contract was to be in accord with both central planning directives and with the ability of the enterprise to meet the repayment terms that had been set. The bank loans would be provided on credit, as a mortgage loan, a loan on guarantee or a bill discount loan. Credit loans are unsecured loans; mortgage loans are secured, with movable property required as security; loans on guarantee require the borrower to provide a guarantor who can honour the contract if the borrower is unable to meet the contract commitment (an enterprise that is a separate legal entity and has sufficient assets in its name was free to act as guarantor for another enterprise); and bill discount loans are based on legal trade in commodities. But even though these four categories were clearly established by the time this book was written, it is noted (in chapter two) that during the first decade of reform an estimated 95% of loans were issued on credit. In other words, they were unsecured.

But credit policy is not the only instrument available to government for disciplining enterprise use of funds. Pricing and taxation policy are also effective levers that can be used to ensure the primacy of national planning priorities in a reforming economy. Price can be a particularly useful device for promoting both enterprise management reform and rural production. In chapter four of this book it is noted that the price of farm and sideline products was raised to the point where the purchasing price of farm produce had risen 99% in the period 1978 to 1987. Together with the lifting of restrictions on household production and then the promotion of household sideline production, this enhanced return for farm produce made possible the rural grass-roots accumulation that in turn led to the accelerated development of the rural township industries.

China's price reform has been extensive. But it has not been without problems, nor is it complete. During the reform decade the so-called 'two-tier pricing system' or 'double-track' pricing system emerged. Under this system the price of a large proportion of raw materials remained under State control, but more importantly, it was artificially low in relation to all other products. And when the government felt itself politically unable to pass on price increases in its procurement price of raw materials—for coal or steel or for grain purchased from the agricultural sector, for example—government price subsidies were pressed into use. These subsidies were extensive and have represented a 'heavy burden' on State finances, indeed they have significantly contributed to the persistent post reform problem of State deficits. Today, the Chinese Government's ever increasing financial concerns, considerably exacerbated by the fiscal consequences of the 1989-1992 period of economic contraction have dictated that price subsidies be quickly phased out.

In the latter half of the 1980s Chinese economists and planners were arguing that 'under present conditions where price cannot be regulated smoothly, tax is a useful means for the amelioration of inequality of benefits between enterprises'. In this context taxation was recognised as a means of providing government financial revenue in the wake of policy that allowed profit to be retained at enterprise level *and* a means of economic regulation.

Reform of China's taxation system began in 1980, but even by the late 1980s this process had been only partially implemented. Simplification of the taxation administration had been widespread, but the use of taxation as a regulatory tool had not been fully developed. It was being used as a means of regulating such matters as enterprise distribution of bonus payments to workers, but it had not yet been effectively used to the extent of the far-reaching measures outlined in chapter five, that is, for purposes such as the regulation of enterprise consumption of oil or of land use.

The Chinese Communist Party's late 1980s edict that market distribution should be promoted while continuing to afford primacy to the role of planning, not only translated into the re-organisation of national financial management based on the use of economic levers, it also meant reorganising government planning and administrative procedures in relation to enterprise management. This reorganisation then formed the basis of the renewed push to promote enterprise fiscal responsibility based on relative autonomy of enterprise decision-making. Enterprise decision-making was to accord with central government guidelines, to abide by the central government priorities communicated through the conduits of credit, price and taxation policy, but it was also to be responsive to market indices. Chapter nine details the process of administrative decentralisation of production decision-making down to State enterprise level. In 1981-1982 'the Economic Responsibility System' was introduced. In 1983-1984 there was the first phase of replacing profit repatriation with tax payment and from 1984-1986 the second tax-replacing-profit stage was introduced. At the same time labour reform was also instituted. By 1986 wage payment was to be based on the principle of remuneration according to quantity and quality of work done. A system of employment of workers under labour contracts was the policy result of the adoption of this principle. As chapter ten shows this system was promoted as a way of giving enterprises, including State owned enterprises, 'flexibility in terms of their workforce'. Under this system 'the relationship between the employing enterprise and the worker is set out in the form of a contract which specifies the rights, interests and obligations of both the enterprise and the worker'. As explained in chapter ten, it is a far-reaching programme for labour reform which includes the introduction of uniform policy for the provision of worker subsidies and bonus payments and the first clear articulation of a 'job-waiting insurance system' (an unemployment insurance scheme). These are the enterprise and labour policies that now form the basis of the 1990s programme for reform.

The 1980s reform focus on the use of legally enforceable contracts promoted the need for the establishment of a 'modern' economic legal structure. The economic legal system as it is outlined in chapter six was established.

The regulatory role that the Chinese government has afforded to the legal system mirrors that expected from the use of financial economic levers. Chapter six opens with the declaration that:

> *Economic laws and regulations are effective tools through which the State protects and improves the socialist relations of production, manages the national economy and promotes the development of the productive forces..*

This makes evident the primary role afforded to State planning, but it does not canvass the extent of the role of China's legal system. The careful system for constituting national laws that is an integral part of the system has been made clear in the outline provided in chapter six, together with the organisation and procedure required for the enactment of local laws and regulations. There is also an account of the administrative form and functions of the Chinese judiciary and a discussion of the role that China's newly emerging lawyers are expected to fill. The 1986 establishment of administrative judicial courts has also been canvassed and the mediating measures that are to be taken in the case of civil matters including contract disputes between parties. Most would agree that the post reform development of China's legal system has been impressive. But if matters such as the guidelines for housing reform, land use and urban and environmental planning procedures and regulations outlined in the last chapters of section two of this book are to be effectively implemented during the 1990s, it is quite clear that the role of China's judicial system will need to be developed and extended still further.

There are a number of ways of categorising the Chinese reform process. In his introduction to this book Ma Hong has offered a categorisation of the periods of Chinese Communist Party rule which accords with the one officially introduced by Zhao Ziyang in his work report to the Thirteenth Party Congress held in October 1987. This categorisation includes China's first decade of reform in the period that is considered to be within the primary stage of socialism.

In his introduction Ma Hong argues that the primary stage of socialism is a stage that precedes a future period when 'socialist modernisation will have been accomplished'. He notes that in the late 1980s the primary stage of socialism takes the form of government economic regulation facilitated through both plan and market. It is a period when 'the State regulates the market and the market guides the enterprise'. He then argues that the 'planned commodity economy' of the late 1980s will overcome tendencies toward anarchy in production and so will overcome the problem of uneven development. It is to be recognised as an economy based on policy that will promote planned and proportionate development.

In the last half of the 1980s China's economists and planners had become increasingly concerned about disproportionate economic development. Economic problems were consistently perceived as problems resulting from uneven development and an attendant imbalance between demand and supply, the latter being recognised as the primary cause of an increasingly 'overheated' economy. Building on this analysis Chinese economists and planners argued, as they do in chapter four, that the process of economic reform has resulted in a situation where:

> *Both investment in fixed assets and funds for consumption have increased significantly and the growth of capital construction and consumption has exceeded growth expectations. This situation has made it impossible for State finances to cope. The result has been an ever-increasing financial deficit and this has been a problem solved by overdrafts from the banks. This situation inevitably led to the excessive issue of currency...*

This argument continues by noting that at the same time as both investment and consumption growth exceeded expectations, the promotion of enterprise reform 'fell behind'. It is noted that the result was the poor use of production resources, including a slow growth in labour productivity. The conclusion drawn is that this situation 'resulted in a large gap between purchasing power and the supply of commodities' and that 'under these conditions inflation is inevitable'.

By the last months of 1988 and increasingly during the first months of 1989, it was becoming clear to the Chinese leadership that economic reform introduced in the name of social stability had proved to be a two-edged sword. Reform policies had improved the living standards of the majority of the Chinese people, but over time the effects of these policies had also generated considerable social discontent. The social discontent which became increasingly evident in the first months of 1989 took the form of (i) protest over inflation (ii) open dissatisfaction with corruption and (iii) the renewal of a demand that had consistently shadowed the 1979-1989 decade of reform. This was the demand that the Party institute a programme of fundamental political reform.

Inflation had been fuelled by the over-extension of production capacity that Chinese economists and planners presented as an imbalance between supply and demand. It is a direct consequence of policies adopted during the process of economic reform. Those on fixed incomes were particularly and, it was argued, unfairly, affected by inflation. When the issue of 'corruption' arose, people used the term in the widest possible sense. 'Corruption' was used to describe incidents ranging from clear cases of nepotism and blatant profiteering at all levels of Party and government to quasi-legal and often formally legal activities pursued by government departments, enterprises (particularly economically privileged enterprises) and individuals; all of them competing for services and resources made scarce by the demands of an ever-increasing post-reform production capacity. And then there was the renewed call for the Party to initiate political reform. This call had been first nurtured by the Deng Xiaoping leadership's initial promise of redress for the injustices of the Cultural Revolution. Throughout China's first decade of reform, from 1978 when democracy had been touted as China's fifth modernisation until the events of the summer of 1989, it had taken the form of a demand for subjective decision-making. In itself, this last in the triumvirate of causes of social dissatisfaction had little clear theoretical or institutional content. But in practice, a demand for democracy based on subjective decision-making is the ultimate challenge to a Marxist-Leninist party, since the legitimacy of such a party derives from its custody and monopoly of the knowledge required to realise its articulated goal. This goal is presented as being in the best interests of those who are governed. Even without clear theoretical or institutional articulation, a demand for democracy can be recognised as a demand by the people for their subjective and effective contribution to the political decision-making process. The Chinese leadership's response to the people's 'request' for fundamental political reform was its renewed attention to Party building and to buttressing democratic centralism.

This book offers an outline of the Chinese government's administration and policy during a most interesting period. Not only was it the time when reform policy of the 1980s was at its most mature, it also immediately preceded the social upheaval of 1989: an upheaval that has focused the interest of China scholars and others on the Chinese reform process and its social and political consequences. In response to the social unrest of June 1989 the Chinese leadership altered the intended course of its reform programme. Rather than putting into practice the reform initiatives that Party Secretary Zhao Ziyang had presented to the October 1987 Thirteenth Party Congress, in the three years that followed the events of 1989 the Chinese leadership instigated a period of economic contraction accompanied by three years of Party building. Not until January 1992 did the Chinese leadership return to actively promoting the programme for economic reform that Zhao Ziyang outlined and formally presented to the Party in 1987.

This book first presents Ma Hong's own outline of his theoretical concept of China's 'primary stage of socialism' and then details the attendant economic policies and administrative structures that constituted the Chinese Communist Party's programme for reform in the late 1980s. It is these same theoretical concepts, policies and administrative structures that are now the core of the programme for reform that the Chinese leadership is instituting in the 1990s.

Kate Hannan

Acknowledgements

The information for this book was first handed to me as a pile of manila folders with rice-paper sheets in each folder. The sheets contained the extensive resource information that forms the basis of this book. The information had been collected during 1987 and 1988 by the Institute of Industrial Economics of the Chinese Academy of Social Sciences. The collection of the information was a considerable undertaking and the editing of the information that I subsequently agreed to undertake proved to be an even bigger project. By the time it had reached me much of the information that had been gathered was in a language that can only be aptly described as 'Chinglish'. If I had known then what I had agreed to do in reducing, re-writing and compiling this information I would have probably resigned immediately. But I didn't and as a result my family was asked to be very understanding. They cheerfully tolerated a distracted, often absent and often frustrated editor. Thank-you to Stewart Firth for his patience and constant encouragement and thanks to my daughters, Michelle, Kirstie and Nicole, for their support and patience over the time that it has taken me to complete this project. I would also like to thank Hans Hendrischke and Sue Folwell for their part in providing an important part of the support, funding and work required to prepare this project for publication.

I would like to thank the Centre for Chinese Political Economy at Macquarie University for partly funding the production of this book.

Introduction

by Ma Hong
Former President of the Chinese Academy of Social Sciences and Honorary Director of the Research Centre on Economic, Technological and Social Development under the State Council of the Chinese Communist Party

THE ECONOMIC CHARACTERISTICS OF CHINA'S PRIMARY STAGE OF SOCIALISM

I. CHINA IS NOW IN THE PRIMARY STAGE OF SOCIALISM

The theory that 'China is now in the primary stage of socialism' is an important concept that has two meanings. The first is that Chinese society has entered the stage of socialism and therefore it is imperative that socialism be upheld. The second is that China's socialism is still in the primary stage and therefore it is necessary to proceed via this reality and not to by-pass it.

Under the specific historical conditions of contemporary China, to believe that the Chinese people cannot take the socialist road without going through the stage of fully developed capitalism, is to take a mechanistic position on the question of the development of the socialist revolution. This is the major cognitive root of 'Right' mistakes. On the other hand, to believe that it is possible to jump over the primary stage of socialism, a period which facilitates development of the productive forces, is to take a utopian approach. This is a major cognitive root of 'Left' mistakes.

China used to be a semi-colonial, semi-feudal country. During the more than 100 years since the middle of the last century, repeated trials of strength between various political forces, repeated failures of the democratic revolution of the old type and the final victory of the new democratic revolution, have proved that the only way for China is the socialist road. But precisely because China's socialism has emerged from the womb of the semi-colonial and semi-feudal society with the productive forces lagging far behind those of the developed capitalist countries, China is destined to go through a very long primary stage of socialism. During this stage China will accomplish the industrialisation and commercialisation and socialisation and modernisation of production which many other countries have achieved under capitalist conditions.

The question to be asked is—How do things stand in China now that socialism has been developing in the country for more than three decades? On one hand, a socialist economic system based on public ownership of the means of production has been instituted, a socialist political system of people's democratic dictatorship has been established, the guiding role of Marxism in the realm of ideology has been affirmed, the country's economic strength has grown enormously, and educational, scientific and cultural undertakings have expanded considerably. On the other hand, the development of productive forces is backward and this fact determines that in the realm of productive relations the socialisation of production, which is essential for the expansion of socialist public ownership, is still at a very low level and the socialist economic system is not yet mature and well developed. This means that in the sphere of the superstructure a number of economic and cultural conditions that are necessary if we are to promote a high degree of socialist democracy are far from ripe and it also means that various decadent ideologies and the small producers' force of habit still have widespread influence in society. It is these that have at times, corrupted some Party cadres and public servants. All this shows that we still have a long way to go before we can advance beyond the primary stage of socialism.

The question then is—What is this historic stage? Is it the primary stage of socialism in China? It is not the initial phase in a general sense, a phase that every country goes through in the process of building socialism. Rather it is, in a specific sense, the special stage China must necessarily go through while building socialism under conditions of backward productive forces and an under-developed commodity economy. It will last at least 100 years from the 1950s, when the socialist transformation of private ownership of the means of production was basically accomplished, to the time when socialist modernisation will have been in the main achieved. All these years will belong to the primary stage of socialism.

The primary stage of socialism is a stage that is different from the transitional period in which the socialist economic base was not yet laid and from the stage in which socialist modernisation will have been accomplished. The principal contradiction China faces during the present stage is the contradiction between the growing material and cultural needs of the people and backward production. To resolve this principal contradiction of the present stage we must vigorously expand the commodity economy, raise labour productivity, gradually achieve the modernisation of industry, agriculture, national defence, and science and technology [the 'four modernisations'] and we must reform aspects of the relations of production and of the superstructure that are currently incompatible with the growth of the productive forces.

The above analysis is of great importance not only to the Chinese people, but also to foreign friends who show concern for China's economic development and economic reform. This is because to understand these characteristics means to having acquired an understanding of the present situation of China's production relations and productive forces. It is therefore conducive to understanding the line, principles and policies that the Chinese government has adopted at the present stage and it lays the groundwork for understanding many of the economic phenomena prevailing in present-day China.

II. COEXISTENCE OF DIFFERENT TYPES OF OWNERSHIP, WITH PUBLIC OWNERSHIP REMAINING DOMINANT

Since China introduced reform of the economic structure, substantial changes have taken place in the structure of ownership. Ownership has changed from uniform public ownership (socialist ownership by the whole people) to various forms of ownership, with socialist public ownership being dominant but where the public and private economies coexist and develop.

1. THE ECONOMY UNDER SOCIALIST PUBLIC OWNERSHIP

Socialist public ownership of the means of production was established after the Chinese Communist Party came to power. Public ownership has taken two basic forms. One form is the socialist ownership of the whole people. This form is the predominant form. It covers mineral resources, inland water resources, State-owned land, forests and other marine and land resources, as well as State enterprises, farms, commerce, banks and transport and communications enterprises. The second form is that of collective ownership by socialist labourers. This form encompasses industrial, transport and communications and building industry enterprises, banking enterprises and small retail commercial businesses. In the countryside it also includes the rural collective economy that at present is characterised by the peasant household-based contract responsibility system.

Since its establishment socialist public ownership has been gradually consolidated and developed. Practice has proved that as the basic system, socialist public ownership has promoted development of the productive forces and has been in accord with the interests of the people.

2. THE PRIVATE ECONOMY

As noted above, the private economy has subordinate status in relation to the publicly owned sector of the economy. During China's primary stage of socialism the development of the productive forces is backward and uneven. Therefore in addition to developing the socialist public economy, it is necessary, within certain limits, to develop the private economy. The economy that is under private ownership includes the individual economy of labourers, the Chinese and foreign private capitalist economy based on wage labour as well as Sino-foreign joint ventures and cooperative enterprises, part of which is publicly owned and part privately owned.

Under conditions where the socialist public economy remains predominant and where people's democratic dictatorship is practised, the economy under private ownership is in a subordinate position and has a subordinate status. It is to be recognised as a necessary and useful supplement to the socialist economy. It has been proved that the development of the private economy is conducive to making effective use of resources, expanding employment, promoting production, enlivening the market and satisfying the various needs of the people.

The development of Sino-foreign joint ventures, co-operative enterprises and wholly foreign-owned enterprises is also very important in terms of making use of resources. This market makes use of both domestic and foreign resources: and it uses both the domestic market and the international market.

The Chinese government is now enacting and improving policies and laws concerning the development of the private economy. It is doing this in an attempt to create a favourable investment climate for the development of the private economy, to protect its legitimate interests and to strengthen guidance, supervision and management of the economy. In this way it will be possible to make full use of the positive role of the private economy while limiting its negative role.

III. UNITY BETWEEN THE PLANNED ECONOMY AND THE COMMODITY ECONOMY

1. A SOCIALIST PLANNED COMMODITY ECONOMY

Long practice in various socialist countries has shown that both planned and commodity economies exist in the body of a socialist economy and that both have an intrinsic and mutually complementary role to play in a socialist economy.

A socialist economy is a planned economy and a planned economy has an objective need of socialist mass production. After the establishment of socialist public ownership of the means of production, the economic interests of various enterprises, departments and localities have been identified. This identification has then provided the basis for drafting and implementing national economic plans that reflect the interests of all people. At the same time the State has embraced the concept of a national economy and has implemented national economic plans. This has provided the necessary conditions for the maintenance of proportionate development of the national economy.

The implementation of a planned economy can overcome anarchy in production and so achieve planned and proportionate development of the national economy. It is a planned economy that can make the most effective use of manpower and the material and financial resources of a national economy and so ensure the best possible economic returns. It is also a planned economy that can adopt and popularise the advanced results of modern science and technology in a planned way and so continuously promote the development of the productive forces and it is a planned economy that can best satisfy the needs of society under existing conditions. Not to practise a planned economy would cause production to plunge into anarchy and would lead to a loss of national economic direction. It would also hinder rational development of the productive forces and damage socialist public ownership of the means of production. Therefore, in order to uphold the socialist road, it is necessary to uphold a planned economy.

The discussion immediately above deals with the intrinsic nature of the socialist economy. With regard to its extrinsic form of expression, the socialist planned commodity economy is a system that integrates planning with a market. It is in this context that several basic concepts need to be clarified. First, although the socialist commodity economy provides the possibility for society to maintain balanced growth of the national economy, it is still necessary for people to make this possibility a reality by the judicious use of two means. The first is regulation through planning combined with regulation through the market. A socialist planned commodity economy cannot develop without the growth and improvement of markets. The second is through planning that is to accord with the principle of commodity exchange and the law of value.

The form of direct economic control that relies chiefly on mandatory planning cannot meet the requirements of the development of a socialist commodity economy. Regulation through planning should never be equated with mandatory planning. The scope of mandatory planning should gradually be reduced by such means as signing contracts in accordance with the principle of exchange of equal value and the use of contracts. The State is then required to use contracts when placing orders for goods with enterprises and enterprises are required to use contracts when exchanging goods and services with one another. The State would then use indirect means to control enterprises.

Under the new economic mechanism whereby 'the State regulates the market and the market guides the enterprise', the State regulates the relations between supply and demand through economic, legal and necessary administrative means and creates a favourable economic and social environment in which enterprises are guided towards correct management decisions. Of course the attainment of this goal is an evolving process that requires the active creation of suitable conditions. It must be recognised that there is an intrinsic unity between the socialist planned commodity economy and the commodity economy. Hence it can be said that socialist economy is a planned commodity economy.

2. DEVELOPMENT OF THE SOCIALIST COMMODITY ECONOMY

Since the announcement of economic structural reform in 1978 China's socialist commodity economy has undergone enormous development.

The extent of expansion of autonomy of State-owned enterprise production in the areas of enterprise management, marketing and pricing of products, is indicated by the following. The decrease in industrial products managed in accordance with the State mandatory plan; the decrease in means of production subject to direct State allocation; decrease in the demand by enterprises for State provision of means of production; the decrease in the number of products managed in accordance with the plan of the Ministry of Commerce; and a decrease in the proportion of State-priced goods in total retail sales of consumer goods. This situation is proof that enterprises are becoming commodity producers and that the socialist whole-people-owned economy is becoming a commodity economy. In addition, the promotion of the rate of commercialisation in rural areas clearly serves to reflect the development of a rural commodity economy.

IV. CO-EXISTENCE OF DIFFERENT METHODS OF DISTRIBUTION

During the primary stage of socialism China will have an economic system based on various forms of ownership that are centred around socialist ownership of the means of production and a planned commodity economy. Various methods of distribution will then be implemented with distribution according to work done being used as the major form and other methods functioning as supplementary forms.

1. DISTRIBUTION ACCORDING TO WORK DONE

'From each according to his ability and to each according to his work' is the socialist principle of distribution that China is following.

Distribution according to work done does not mean that the labourer has access to the total product created. It is necessary to make deductions from the total social product for the requirements of the means of production and for expanded reproduction. Then it is also necessary to deduct for social funds. These funds are indispensable and include funds for administration and national defence and science and technology, education and hygiene and insurance funds. These funds are all used to satisfy the common need. The remaining social product is then deposited in individual consumption funds and is distributed by society and by the enterprise to individual labourers in accord with the amount and quality of labour that they have contributed.

Implementation of the principle of distribution in accord with work done has a positive effect. It is characterised by more work and more pay and it is favourable for mobilising labourers' enthusiasm and initiative. Distribution according to work done promotes production and improves the life of the people and is therefore favourable for consolidating the development of socialist public ownership. Moreover the implementation of this principle will serve to turn labourers into people who support themselves with their own labour.

The principle of 'from each according to his work and to each according to his work' is practised through the current system of labour remuneration. In enterprises with socialist public ownership and in some collectively owned enterprises, the basic form of labour remuneration is payment by the hour and piece-rate wages. And in addition enterprises award bonus payments to those who have rendered extra labour and they award subsidy payments to those who work under harsh conditions or who do very heavy work (such as work high above the ground, under high temperatures, deep in wells and outside in the fields). These payments act as a supplement to labour remuneration.

Prior to the economic structural reform of 1979, in enterprises with socialist collective ownership, a labour work-point system was practised. This system was later replaced by the contracted responsibility system that linked remuneration to output.

Under the traditional highly-centralised economic system the distribution of labour remuneration in enterprises with socialist whole-people ownership was done entirely in accord with State stipulations. In other words the wage standards, wage scales, type of wage and its scope and the time for production, were all set by the State. In this situation enterprises had no autonomy in terms of wage decision-making.

Currently, in enterprises with socialist collective ownership, labour remuneration is to be decided by the enterprise. But this is only the appearance. In reality there is a substantial amount of State administrative interference. Reform of the economic structure is aimed at gradually altering this situation. As a condition of abiding by State policies and decrees, enterprises with whole-people ownership may distribute their own labour remuneration, while the State exercises indirect regulation of the level of enterprise labour remuneration through economic means. This is a situation that also applies to collectively owned enterprises.

When practising the principle of distribution according to work done, China opposes both egalitarianism and great disparity between high and low income levels. The former negates the objective existence of difference among labourers while both go against the principle of distribution according to work done. The major trend in the distribution of labour remuneration is still egalitarianism and this must be overcome both ideologically and in terms of work practice. In enterprises with favourable conditions, it is necessary to actively implement the piece-work wage system and the quota wage system. This must be done in a situation where there is strict control of both quality and production quotas.

In order to correctly implement the principle of distribution according to work done, China sets great store in strengthening ideological and political work. The workers are asked to have a sense of responsibility, to correctly handle relations between the State, the collective and themselves, and to cultivate a Communist attitude towards labour.

2. OTHER METHODS OF DISTRIBUTION

During the primary stage of socialism both distribution in accord with work done and other kinds of distribution exist. The latter act to supplement the former. Enterprises float bonds to raise funds and with the emergence of share-holding, extra dividends are drawn. This means that the income of enterprise operators should include risk compensation. Meanwhile private enterprises will employ labourers in a manner that results in non-labouring income for private enterprise owners.

During the primary stage of socialism, distribution according to work done is inevitable and has become an important factor in the development and consolidation of the economy. This form of distribution is protected by law.

Policies on distribution have been worked out by the government as a means of enabling people who are good at managing enterprises to work hard and become rich earlier than others. But while making an effort to widen the gap between high and low incomes, efforts should also be made to prevent polarisation between the rich and the poor. Common prosperity should be upheld. To this end effective measures will be used to readjust excessively high individual income. Illegally gained profits and income will be strictly banned.

V. UPHOLDING COMMON PROSPERITY WHILE ENCOURAGING SOME TO BECOME RICH FIRST

1. THEORETICAL EXPLANATION

During the primary stage of socialism, encouraging a number of people to become rich first through their honest labour is a distinctive feature of China's economic system. Socialist production is aimed at promoting the common goal of prosperity and the cultural and living standards of people and with development of socialist production the common goal of prosperity will be advanced and people's lives will constantly improve.

China is a populous country and during the primary stage of socialist development the level of the development of productivity won't be high. This means that in a comparatively short period of time, the Chinese people will not be able to become rich together. Also, China's enterprises with whole-people ownership are relatively independent commodity producers with labour remuneration linked with enterprise productivity, while State enterprises practise differing forms of management. Added to this, is the situation where the level of remuneration for China's collectively owned enterprises is linked not only with enterprise productivity, but also with the level of agricultural based income that results from difference in land fertility and distance from market. It is therefore expected that during the present stage of socialism, the difference between the level of labour remuneration provided by enterprises will widen. Already in some localities economic and cultural development is very uneven. Under present circumstances it is inevitable that some people will become rich first.

Encouraging a number of people to become rich first through honest labour and legal management is a powerful motive force in promoting development of the national economy. It encourages an increase in social products and promotes the use of technology, improves management skills, increases accumulation and expands market capacity.

2. THE PRACTICE OF BECOMING RICH FIRST

The practice of a number of people of becoming rich first will take place in a situation where public ownership remains the major form of ownership and where distribution in accord with work done is the major form of distribution. This means that polarisation of the rich and the poor, as is the case in the capitalist world, will be avoided. This has been proved by policies practised since 1979.

Between 1981 and 1987 the proportion of households with per capita monthly living expenses of less than Rmb 50 decreased and in the same period the proportion of households with extremely low incomes substantially decreased. The proportion of households with per capita monthly living expenses of less than Rmb 50 decreased from 2% in 1981 to zero in 1986 and those with per capita monthly living expenses of more than Rmb 20, but less than Rmb 35, dropped from 37% to 4%. Households with per capita monthly living expenses of Rmb 35-50 rose from 42% of all households in 1981 to 47% in 1983, but dropped each year thereafter to 12% in 1987. Only the proportion of households with per capita monthly living expenses of more than Rmb 50 has increased with those having per capita monthly living expenses of Rmb 50 plus rising at the fastest rate. They rose from 6% to 71%.

In terms of per capita annual income, farmers' families showed the same trend. The proportion of families with a per capita annual income of less than Rmb 200 decreased and among these, the proportion families with a per capita annual income of less than Rmb 100 went down from 33% in 1978 to 1% in 1987; the proportion with an income of Rmb 100-150 dropped from 32% to 2%; and the proportion with an of Rmb 150-200 rose from 18% in 1978 to 27% in 1980, but fell to 5% in 1987. But the number of farming families with a per capita annual income of over Rmb 200 have increased. Those with an income of Rmb 500 rose by the largest margin. They rose from 2% in 1980 to 36% in 1987.

The above figures show that since 1979 households in both urban and rural areas have enjoyed an improved standard of living. While a number of residents have become rich earlier than others, there is a common direction of prosperity. It is expected that with the deepening of economic reform the difference in residents' income will become more marked, but that the general trend will continue to be toward a common prosperity. It is expected that there will be some irrationalities in residents' income due to an imbalance in income distribution; however, in the long term, this situation will be solved without altering the goal of common prosperity.

VI. CHINA IN THE FIRST PHASE OF INDUSTRIALISATION

1. UNDERDEVELOPED SOCIAL PRODUCTIVE FORCES

Currently China's social productive forces are not advanced and development is uneven. China's economy demonstrates a 'dualist economic' pattern typical of the first phase of industrialisation. Industrial production has been modernised, but agriculture has operated using the traditional means of manual labour. Although progress has been made in the area of agricultural modernisation and mechanisation, this area has not been sufficiently recognised as an important planning priority.

In industry, automation, mechanisation, semi-mechanisation and manual labour have existed simultaneously. Traditional industries have still occupied a dominant position and the proportion of new emerging and high-tech industries is insignificant. It is clear that it will require a fairly long period of time before this situation is changed.

Manual labour continues to be the predominant form of productive means in China's rural areas. The amount of fixed assets owned by each rural labour force is markedly lower than the fixed assets available to modern industrial enterprises and is also much lower than the fixed assets available for use in relatively modern industrial enterprises.

2. CHINA'S UNDEVELOPED COMMODITY ECONOMY

In 1987 the commodity rate of rural agricultural and sideline products was less than 60%. The degree of self-sufficiency exceeded 40%. The per capita commodity expenditure of farmers' households accounted for 64.5% of total expenditure and self-sufficient expenditure was 35.5% annually.

Meanwhile, China's industrial sector is still at the stage of developing from a product economy to a commodity economy and enterprises have not really yet become commodity producers. As far as the advanced commodity economy which requires a market system is concerned, although an ordinary consumer goods market is relatively developed, a commercial residential housing market is still in the pilot stage. A market for the basic means of consumption has not completely taken shape. A market for funds, labour force, technology and real estate still requires development. The formation of an advanced commodity economy will take some time.

3. UNEVEN DEVELOPMENT IN DIFFERENT REGIONS

China's economy has also developed unevenly. The economy in the eastern coastal regions is relatively developed, the central region is less developed and the western region is relatively underdeveloped. This situation means that changes will take place over a fairly long period of time.

In:1 PER CAPITA NATIONAL INCOME AND CONSUMPTION IN VARIOUS REGIONS*

Province	Per capita national income Absolute value Rmb	Guizhou as one	Per capita consumption Absolute value Rmb	Multiple - taking Guizhou as one
Beijing	2130	5.2	907	2.9
Tianjin	2040	5.0	816	2.6
Hebei	673	1.7	397	1.3
Shanxi	682	1.7	374	1.2
Inner Mongolia	630	1.6	446	1.4
Liaoning	1299	3.2	659	2.1
Jilin	823	2.0	570	1.8
Heilongjiang	997	2.5	564	1.8
Shanghai	3471	8.5	1109	3.5
Jiangsu	1064	2.6	526	1.7
Zhejiang	1042	2.6	530	1.7
Anhui	599	1.5	384	1.2
Fujian	627	1.7	456	1.4
Jiangxi	543	1.3	389	1.2
Shandong	770	1.9	411	1.3
Henan	540	1.3	327	1.0
Hubei	805	2.0	488	1.5
Hunan	603	1.5	402	1.3
Guangdong	897	2.2	553	1.7
Guangxi	450	1.1	339	1.1
Sichuan	515	1.3	369	1.2
Guizhou	406	1.0	317	1.0
Yunnan	453	1.1	22	1.0
Tibet	551	1.4	438	1.4
Shaanxi	531	1.3	374	1.2
Gansu	570	1.4	350	1.1
Qinghai	698	1.7	500	1.6
Ningxia	616	1.5	421	1.3
Xinjiang	740	1.8	536	1.7

* Figures are for 1986

An example of uneven development and regional inequality is the situation where in 1986, Shanghai's per capita income was 8.5 times higher than in Guizhou in the western region, while consumption in the eastern region as a whole was 3.5 times higher. It was also much higher than in Henan in the central region.

4. A LOW DEGREE OF ECONOMIC OPENING TO THE OUTSIDE WORLD

In the period since 1978 much headway has been made in the open-door policy initiated by China. But still the degree of opening to the outside world is, in comparative terms, relatively low and opening to the outside world has also been regionally uneven. Rapid progress has been made in opening up the eastern coastal region, but in other areas an export-oriented economy is yet to be formed. Many areas in the interior are still at a stage of semi-closure.

Between 1978 and 1987, although China's import and export volume registered a rapid growth, its proportion of total world import and export volume was insignificant. It was less than 2%.

In 1987 the amount of foreign capital used by the southern coastal province of Guangdong was 5,554 times higher than that used by the western region province of Gansu. Unlike the rapidly developing Guangdong economy, the Gansu economy has not opened to the outside world. Even when compared with the figure for foreign capital utilisation in Hunan Province in China's central region, the Guangdong figure was more than 300 times higher.

5. HUGE ECONOMIC AGGREGATES, LOW PER CAPITA AMOUNTS

Though China is a large country with a huge population and with an enormous fund of natural resources, its productive forces are not highly developed and the economy is unevenly developed. It is this situation that has resulted in huge economic aggregates, while on a per capita basis amounts are low. In terms of quantity, total output of China's major products is among the top in the world and yet per capita output is low. Only the output of cotton outpaces world per capita output. The output of grain and raw coal approaches world per capita output, but the output of other products still has a long way to go. Since the structural reform of the economy was initiated this situation has been changing, but it will be a long time before fundamental change has been effected.

China's present stage of development is typical of the first phase of industrialisation. Underdeveloped social productive forces, an undeveloped commodity economy and uneven economic development indicate that China is in the primary stage of socialism and the task of this stage is to vigorously develop the productive forces and the commodity economy. We must unflinchingly carry out structural reforms in the economic, political and cultural fields and we must promote socialist modernisation.

SECTION I

NATIONAL FINANCIAL MANAGEMENT

CHAPTER 1

Government Financial Regulation

I. FINANCIAL REGULATION OF THE NATIONAL ECONOMY

1. FINANCIAL POLICY

China's financial policy seeks to promote the development of the national economy. Financial policy is used to regulate a balanced national economy, to achieve a reasonable distribution of social resources and the effective utilisation of these resources and to regulate the economic interests of the State, the collective and the individual.

For almost a decade, since the Third Plenum of December 1978, China has faced the major task of improving people's livelihood and carrying out economic reform. This has meant a policy of reducing expenditures and increasing revenues. The aim of this policy is to boost the income of peasants, staff and workers.

Faced with the present financial problems of inflation, fluctuating prices and a structural dislocation of the national economy, financial policy is now intended to curb demand. Together with this policy, supply is to be improved through the use of centralised investment for the construction of energy sources and the improvement of communications.

2. IMPLEMENTATION OF FINANCIAL REGULATION

Regulation of the national economy is based on adjustment of budget revenues and expenditures. Implementation of financial policy relies on the use of the State budget, taxation, financial credit and subsidies, laws, regulations, systems and measures for the management of financial revenue and expenditures. For example, in order to broach the problem of effective social demand being larger than supply, controls are placed on institution based purchases. This means that the institutional purchase of certain commodities has now been strictly limited, especially in the case of important commodities that are in very short supply. Such a policy is seen as an effective measure of financial regulation.

(1) Financial Credit

Financial credit is then seen as a supplementary means for the regulation of the economic structure. Usually this is done through the collection of credit funds, i.e., through the issue of bonds that provide funds that are then invested in a field where the national economy is short funded.

(2) Taxation

Taxation is another means used to regulate economic activity. Regulation is achieved through tax rates that include tax reduction and exemption as a means of regulating production, distribution, exchange and consumption.

(3) Financial Subsidies

Financial subsidies are also used for economic regulation. These subsidies include price, investment, interest and loss subsidies. Price subsidies account for the greatest share of subsidies used. These subsidies assist price reform and guide micro-level investment decision-making. Price subsidies also play a substantial role in stabilising people's livelihood, but at the same time it is intended that price subsidies will be gradually reduced. This is to be done in order to reduce the negative effect of the financial burden of subsidies on the economy and in order to promote financial independence and responsibility at enterprise level.

II. STATE BUDGET

1. THE STATE BUDGET

The current State budget system is divided into three levels. These levels are composed of (i) a central level budget, (ii) a provincial (or autonomous region) level budget, and (iii) a county (or autonomous county or city) level budget.

The State level budget consists of the central budget and the general provincial budget. The provincial (autonomous region or directly administered city) budget consists of the provincial level budget and the budget of subordinate counties (cities, autonomous prefectures and autonomous counties). And the general county level budget consists of the budget of various villages (towns).

In terms of a discrete level, village (town) finance is still in the process of being established. Although this level of finance is in its initial stages, most villages (towns) still do not operate using an independent budget. This means that the current village (town) budget cannot yet be categorised as a discrete budget level, but when an operating system of village finance has been fully established, China's budget system will have four levels. The village budget would be the grassroots fourth level.

2. THE DEVELOPMENT OF STATE BUDGET REVENUE AND EXPENDITURE

In 1950 when China's first State budget was worked out, general budget revenue was Rmb 6.5 billion. In 1988 this figure was Rmb 255.5 billion. This represents a thirty-eight fold increase. In terms of general budget expenditure, there was also a thirty-eight fold increase from a 1950 figure of Rmb 6.8 billion to a 1988 figure of Rmb 263.5 billion.

(1) Change in Revenue Structure

At the beginning of the 1950s, with China's private economy accounting for a considerable proportion of the national economy, the proportion of revenue coming from the State-owned economy and the collective economy was relatively small. In 1950 it accounted for only 33.7% of general State budget revenue. By 1955 the proportion of State-owned and collective economy had grown to 77.4% and by 1957 it had climbed to 87.3%. By 1960 it reached 99%. Ninety per cent of this revenue was generated by the State-owned economy.

Since the Third Plenum of December 1978, the individual economy has been allowed to develop and the use of foreign capital has been allowed, with foreign funds being encouraged for general investment use and for the establishment of new enterprises. The growth of the individual economy (including collective town and village enterprises) and foreign capital has changed the structure of China's financial revenue. It has resulted in the proportion of revenue coming from the State-owned economy being reduced from over 90% to a little over 80%, while the proportion of revenue coming from the collective economy increased from 10% to over 16%.

As the structure of financial revenue has changed, the form of revenue has also been changing. In the period 1950-1952 the revenue directly remitted to the State by the State-owned enterprises accounted for 25.3% of general revenue. Various items of taxation accounted for 59.6%, debt revenue 5.5% and other revenue 9.6%. In 1958, after the fulfilment of the First Five-Year Plan, revenue turned over by State-owned enterprises shed 48.8%, while taxation revenue slumped to 48.3% and other revenue to only 0.8%. For the next two decades (1958-1978) approximately equal shares were maintained between revenue directly remitted to the State by State-owned enterprises and revenue raised through taxation. But since 1979, the proportion of revenue turned over by State-owned enterprises has dropped considerably and the ratio of taxation revenue raised has risen substantially. It is estimated that by 1987 taxation accounted for 91% of State financial revenue.

1:1 THE CHANGING COMPOSITION OF STATE FINANCIAL REVENUE

	Enterprise revenue (as a %)	Taxation revenue (as a %)	Debt revenue (as a %)	Other revenue (as a %)
1950	13.4	75.1	4.6	6.9
1952	31.2	53.2	5.3	10.3
1957	46.5	49.9	2.3	1.3
1962	46.6	51.7		1.7
1965	55.8	43.2		1.0
1970	57.2	42.4		0.4
1975	49.1	49.4		1.5
1978	51.0	46.3		2.7
1980	40.1	52.7	4.0	3.2
1985*	2.3	108.5	4.6	
1986	1.9	92.5	6.1	
1987	1.8	91.0	7.1	

* When State financial revenues were calculated for 1985, losses incurred by the enterprises and total price subsidies were deducted from enterprise revenue. This is why the ratio of taxation revenue was able to exceed 100. Losses and price subsidies were also deducted from 1986 and 1987 enterprise revenue.

(2) Change in Expenditure Structure

China's financial expenditure is divided into six major categories. These categories correspond with the type of expenditure. The categories are economic construction expenditure, social cultural and educational expenditure, national defence expenditure, administration management expenditure, debt expenditure and other expenditure.

(i) Economic Construction

This financial expenditure is used to improve and extend production. It includes expenditure for investment in productive fixed assets, the growth of floating funds for enterprises, support for agricultural development and funds used for boosting the State material stockpile.

(ii) Social, Cultural and Educational Expenditure

This expenditure is used to increase financial allocations for social welfare facilities. Spending includes the cost of educational projects, scientific research, cultural, sports and public health projects and the cost of social relief services.

(iii) National Defence Expenditure

This is a financial allocation used for the construction of national defence. It includes the cost of combat readiness, the cost of defence and safeguarding facilities and the cost of scientific research relevant to national defence. It also provides funds for military use.

(iv) Other Expenditure

This category covers general funds used to satisfy the development needs of the economy and to improve people's material and cultural living standard.

Currently over 80% of financial expenditure is used for development of the national economy and for the improvement of people's material and cultural living standards. The proportion of China's financial expenditure used for economic construction and for social welfare, culture and education has been steadily increasing. In 1952 this expenditure accounted for 34% of total budget expenditure and by the end of the First Five Year Plan in 1958, it had grown to 70%. At the other end of the expenditure spectrum there is the cost of administrative management. Expenditure on administrative management has been low. In most years it has accounted for only an estimated 5% of total financial expenditure.

(3) Reasons for Consecutive Years of Deficits

Since the implementation of economic reform policy, consecutive years of financial deficits have been experienced. Since 1979 a series of measures have reduced national revenue and increased expenditure. These measures were adopted as a support for economic reform. They have included:

(i) Tax Reduction and Profit Concession Measures

Tax reduction and profit concession measures have been adopted as a means of expanding the decision-making power of State-owned enterprises. They have resulted in boosting the retained proportion of profits by State-owned enterprises, while the proportion of profits turned over to national financial coffers has been sharply reduced. In 1978 the average level of State-owned enterprise retained profit was only 4.1%, but by the end of 1986 the figure had risen to 43%. In absolute figures, total profit retained by enterprises in 1979 was Rmb 8.6 billion, but by 1986 total profit retained was Rmb 57 billion.

(ii)   A Substantial Increase in the Purchasing Price of Farm and Sideline Products

This was done in the interest of supporting reform in rural areas and improving the level of peasants' income. Together with this raised purchasing price, tax reductions and exemptions were granted. These measures resulted in considerable government expenditure and a substantial reduction in State financial revenues.

(iii)   Living Subsidies for Staff and Workers

Living subsidies have improved the livelihood of urban staff and workers, but these subsidies have been continually augmented by State finance. This policy has followed in the steps of price reform. According to statistics, the subsidies for price difference that have been borne by State finance in the period from 1979 to 1986 have come to as much as Rmb 173 billion. In addition, employment has expanded and wages have increased several times over. The wages paid by the State for staff and workers have more than doubled since 1978.

(4)   In Order to Promote Economic Reform, State Expenditure was Boosted for Science, Culture, Education and Public Health

Expenditure in these fields increased from Rmb 1.9 billion in 1978 to Rmb 40.5 billion in 1987. This was an almost three-fold increase. In addition to these items, there were other measures that reduced revenues and increased expenditure. The portion of total national revenue remitted to the State in 1978 was 37%; now the State's share of national revenue has fallen to 25% and expenditure has not been correspondingly reduced. Indeed, expenditure has greatly increased. Total financial expenditure in the ten years since the introduction of economic reform has doubled that of the year prior to reform. Obviously serious difficulties have ensued. Now the Chinese government has had to adopt powerful measures in an attempt to solve this problem.

1:2 CHANGING STRUCTURE OF STATE FINANCIAL EXPENDITURE

	% allocated for capital expenditure	% spent on public health, education, culture and farm support	% spent on scientific research	% spent on defence	% spent on administration
1950	18.4	7.4	41.1		
1952	26.6	7.7	33.0	8.3	
1957	40.7	2.6	9.1	18.1	7.1
1962	18.2	6.3	22.0	18.7	7.1
1965	34.0	3.7	9.8	18.6	5.4
1970	45.9	2.4	6.7	22.4	3.9
1975	39.8	5.2	9.9	17.4	4.7
1978	40.7	6.9	10.1	15.1	4.4
1980	34.6	6.8	12.9	16.0	5.5
1985	31.3	5.4	17.0	10.3	7.7
1986	28.8	5.3	16.3	8.6	7.8
1987	25.2	5.5	16.7	8.6	8.1

Only main expenditure items have been listed in this table and so the sum of the five columns does not equal 100.

3. CONSTRUCTION AND EXAMINATION OF THE BUDGET

(1) Construction of the Budget

China's budget is worked out on a per annum basis. The financial year used for budget purposes is the calendar year of 1 January to 31 December.

The budget programme is worked out using a method described as integrating from top to bottom with from bottom to top.

In order to work out various levels of budget in line with Party policy and in order to ensure uniformity and correct implementation of financial policy, instructions for working out the budget are issued by the State Council. These instructions are issued to localities and departments each year prior to the working out of the State budget. The instructions put forward the general principle and the various policies that should be implemented when working out the budget and they note the specific requirements of various items of main revenue and expenditure. They also note the method used to work out the budget, the reporting period and the reporting programme to be followed.

The specific stipulations and specific policy targets to be used to work out the budget are mapped out by the Ministry of Finance. These in turn are based on the instructions of the State Council. Once mapped out they are despatched to localities, who, in their turn, report their suggested revenue and expenditure figures to the Ministry of Finance.

It is on the basis of the Party's requirements in relation to policy and the planned norms of the national economy and on the basis of figures provided by the different departments of the Central Authority and by the localities (provinces, autonomous regions and municipalities directly under central authority), that the Ministry of Finance maps the controlled norms for budget revenue and expenditure. These norms are then reported to the State Council for examination and approval. At the end of this process they are transmitted to the relevant departments of the central administrative authority and then down to local governments.

After receiving these transmitted norms, local governments map out the controlled norms of budget revenue and expenditure and make them known to local governments that are subordinate to them. After it receives transmitted norms the centre also maps out budget controlled norms and then transmits these norms to all subordinate enterprises and production units.

Once they have received the budget controlled norms, departments, localities and grassroots units can begin to formally work out their general budget and unit budgets. Then, after completion of the general budget and unit budgets, there is a level by level budget examination. This examination progresses level by level from the bottom to the top.

This draft budget of departments under the central authority and the draft general budget of provinces, autonomous regions and municipalities under the central authority, is finally examined by the Ministry of Finance. After repeated consultations with the departments and the provinces, autonomous regions and municipalities subordinate to the central authority, the draft State general budget is put before the State Council for examination.

(2) Examination and Approval of the State Budget

Once the State budget (that has been compiled by the Ministry of Finance) has been examined and adopted by the State Council, the Council reports to and asks for approval for the budget from the National People's Congress. The Congress then refers the budget to its Budget Committee for examination and for preparation of a budget examination report for discussion by the Congress.

The Congress adopts a resolution of approval of the State budget through discussion and based on budget approval by the National People's Congress, the State Council checks and rectifies the central budget and then checks and rectifies the local general budget. On the basis of this State Council checked and rectified budget, provincial governments and the governments of autonomous regions and municipalities directly subordinate to the central authority revise their original draft general budget and report to their level People's Congress for examination and approval. Once approval has been given, the budgets of provincial level departments and then the general budgets of subordinate counties (or cities) are checked and rectified.

The process of examination and approval for the general budget of counties (or cities) is the same as the process of examination and approval undertaken at provincial level.

4. EXECUTION OF THE STATE BUDGET

It is the State Council that is in charge of the execution of the State budget and it is local governments that are charged with the execution of the budget at their respective levels.

The Ministry of Finance, under the leadership of the State Council, is responsible for organising implementation of the central budget.

In order to effect the planned implementation of the yearly budget, governments of various levels and responsible departments and units are charged with working out seasonal plans for payment and allocation by season in accord with the yearly budget. These seasonal plans are then checked and rectified by financial departments that are on the same administrative level.

(1) Budget Revenues

Budget revenues are collected in order to ensure the positive development of production. The division of labour involved in the collection of revenue is split between the various taxation departments who organise the collection of industrial and commercial taxes and those responsible for the collection of agricultural and animal husbandry taxes.

Collection of budget revenues into the treasury can be divided into two types. First there is the collection of on the spot taxes and then there is revenue collection through centralisation. The former is used by enterprises, regardless of their level, and the latter is where enterprises do not pay tax directly to the treasury. Rather, they contribute to a centralised fund that is administered by a responsible department and then funds are paid to the treasury at the end of a fixed period. This method is seen as being useful for trades with unified accounting. It is undertaken by responsible customs and taxation offices.

Budget revenues that have been lodged in the State treasury are State budgetary funds and can only be withdrawn from the treasury by the Ministry of Finance.

(2) Budgetary Expenditure

There are two types of budget expenditure allocation. One is the allocation of funds and the other is a limited allocation of funds.

Under allocation of funds the financial department supplies a voucher of allocation in response to applications from departments and responsible units. It then authorises the payment of treasury funds. The treasury funds are then remitted to the unit's bank deposit account.

Under limited fund allocation, in reply to an application from a unit for funds, the financial department authorises set funds. It then notifies the bank where the unit has an account and the unit is then allowed to use the funds within a set time limit. The bank is charged with collating the funds actually used by the unit and under pre-set budget expenditure headings must settle with the administration's financial department by the end of each month. The financial department then takes the expenditure figure of the limited fund allocation that has been collated by the bank as the basis of general budget expenditure. It then notifies the State treasury and a lump sum is allocated to the bank. Any surplus in the limited fund allocation that has not been used by the end of the financial year is automatically cancelled by the bank (unless the financial department has allowed the use of these funds for the coming year).

(3) Budget Adjustment

In the case of changed circumstances that were unforeseen, budget adjustment can be carried out, but it must accord with legal requirements.

There are two types of budget adjustment, overall adjustment and partial adjustment. Under usual conditions, the former is a rare occurrence, while the latter occurs often.

Partial budget adjustment involves drawing from reserve funds in order to meet some temporary and urgent necessity. When, in the process of executing the budget, temporary expenses arise which have not been anticipated, but must be met, reserve funds can be drawn. At central level the drawing of reserve budget funds must have State Council's approval, while the drawing of reserve funds by localities requires government approval from the same administrative level as the level that the request has come from.

Except for special conditions, an overall balance between bank credit and the supply of goods and materials must be considered when planned budget expenditure and revenue is altered and it is also necessary that expenditure and revenue must correspond. For example, if budget revenue is effected due to State's policy, decrees or other special conditions that have arisen during budget execution, then budget expenditure must be correspondingly altered.

(4) Budget Headings

The floating use of budget headings refers to a situation where, in the process of executing the budget, surplus funds accrue under some headings while insufficient funds are available under other headings. In order to ensure the fulfilment of plans, and to avoid exceeding the general scale of original budget expenditure, surplus funds from some headings can be transferred for use under headings where funds cannot meet demand.

This floating use of funds between headings will effect the State supply plan for goods and materials, and so transfers of funds must be approved.

(5) Audit of Budget Execution

Budget audit and the audit of the final accounts is done by the People's Congress and by its Budget Committee, while day-to-day budget auditing is done by an internal supervision division of the financial department. The task of the audit is to supervise units in the strict and correct implementation of a budget and realisation of budget targets. They guard against behaviour that is damaging to financial system aims and that violates financial and economic discipline. The main task of the audit is to examine the execution of financial and economic policy by departments and units and to examine their revenue and expenditure processes. It is also intended to ensure that department and unit revenue and expenditure accords with undertaking production plans and social development plans and it is charged with ensuring that there has been no embezzlement or waste of funds.

In the case of both fund allocation and limited fund allocation, the banking system has been charged with financial supervision over funds used and the financial activities of the units. This means that the State plays a vital role in implementation of expenditure policy.

(6) Audit of Budget Revenue

This audit programme examines whether items of revenue accord with financial policy. In order to do this an examination is undertaken that looks at the question of whether the rate of progress with regard to revenue fulfilment is consistent with extent of economic growth; whether payment of revenue items into the treasury is correct in terms of both amount and time; and whether evasion of revenue payment, arrears in payments or retention of payments is evident.

The second intention of this audit programme is to examine whether the division of budget revenue at various treasury levels is correct and whether the reported amount turned over is correct. Funds retained or calculations that do not accord with budget planning are to be identified as are such issues as whether the scope of extra-budgetary funds has been extended, whether extra-budgetary fees have been raised, or if concealed revenues have acted as a 'small treasury'.

(7) Audit of Budget Expenditure

This programme consists of the following. First, examination of whether budget allocations conform with the budget that has been approved and whether the rate of fund use accords with the seasonal plan. Wrong allocations and over-expenditure are also examined. Second, whether there has been undue spending, extravagance or fraud. Items of budget expenditure by units are examined. Third, whether the budget has been supplemented or reduced and whether reserve funds have been used. Whether there have been instances of undue expense under false pretences, embezzlement or misappropriation are also investigated.

III. FINAL ACCOUNTS

Final accounts consist of central level final accounts and local general final accounts. The latter represent collection of the final accounts of provinces, autonomous regions and municipalities that are directly subordinate to the centre. These final accounts, in turn, represent collection of the final accounts of counties and cities subordinate to the province, autonomous region or centrally administered municipality.

Both central level final accounts and local general final accounts represent collection of the final accounts of units of administrative undertaking plus the final accounts of enterprises, final accounts of capital construction, the annual report of treasury, and the annual report of taxation collected by the responsible departments of the same level.

Final accounts of units of administrative undertaking are worked out by levels of government institutions together with production and implementing units, the latter including units concerned with forestry, water conservation, culture and education, public health and science. Final accounts of capital construction are worked out by State-owned enterprises and capital construction units. These include units practising the system of taking revenue to offset expenditure and those choosing to implement independent revenue and expenditure procedures.

1. PREPARATION OF FINAL ACCOUNTS

Centralised preparation of final accounts begins from the grassroots unit and proceeds from bottom to top.

In the fourth season of each year, before the preparation of final accounts for the year is begun, a measure is dispatched to localities. This measure is formulated and issued by the Ministry of Finance and is used in the preparation of the State budget.

Upon receipt of this measure local financial departments and their relevant central departments integrate the specific circumstances of the locality.

By the end of the year, grassroots units that have a unit budget are the first to prepare final accounts. They then report these accounts to the upper level in accord with the measure for preparing and reporting final accounts. The units of the upper level then report the collected unit final accounts to the responsible department and this department, in its turn, collects final accounts and prepares general final accounts.

These general final accounts of the responsible department are then reported to the financial department at the same administrative level and, in turn, provide the basis for preparation of the financial department's collection and preparation of its general final accounts. These financial department prepared general final accounts are then transmitted upward level by level.

This upward transmission of financial department general final accounts consists of county level financial departments reporting to the provincial, autonomous region or municipal financial bureau directly under central authority. These provincial, autonomous region or municipal financial departments directly subordinate to the central authority will then prepare provincial general final accounts and report to the Ministry of Finance.

2. EXAMINATION AND APPROVAL OF FINAL ACCOUNTS

After preparation, the State final accounts are sent to the State Council and to the People's Congress for examination and approval. This examination and approval of State final accounts is carried out at the same time as examination and approval of the State budget for the coming year.

After approval of the State final accounts, the State Council officially replies to the general final accounts of the provinces, autonomous regions and municipalities subordinate to the Central Authority.

IV. EXTRA-BUDGETARY FUNDS

Extra-budgetary funds are financial funds that are outside the State budget. They are categorised as independent revenue and they are managed by localities and departments in accord with the stipulations of the State financial system.

Extra-budgetary funds are funds that are supplementary to the State budget. They include additional revenue from taxation and utility fees that have not been brought into budget calculations. This revenue is uniformly controlled by local financial departments at different administrative levels. It includes monies raised by the surcharge on industrial and commercial tax, the surcharge on agricultural (animal husbandry) tax, and the surcharge on fees for urban public utilities. It also includes funds for special purpose independent use that have been drawn by State-owned enterprises and departments. These funds include production development funds, oil field maintenance fees, mine exploration and extension fees and forestry renewal funds.

Other extra-budgetary funds include enterprise income subordinate to central and local departments, for example: energy development funds for using coal to replace oil; energy funds in return for overfulfilment of oil output; port maintenance income; funds for maintaining power supply through the use of small hydropower plants; and management incomes earned by administrative and production units such as funds for road maintenance, port management, prospecting, forest cultivation, reservoir income, and garden, hostel, house and real estate management income. Income from middle and primary school tuition fees and market management income can also be included.

All funds, whether outside or within the State budget, are State financial funds, but extra-budgetary finds are a special type of funds. These funds are scattered, fragmentary and diverse. They are also funds that have a designated use and cannot be shifted into another fund category for other uses (no unit or individual ever has the power to transfer and use these funds). For example, the surcharge on agricultural (animal husbandry) tax is only to be used for public welfare undertakings in rural areas; the surcharge on urban public utilities revenue is for the construction of urban public utilities; and funds from forest cultivation are for the development of forestry projects.

Since the introduction of economic reform, the extent of the use of extra-budgetary funds has increased substantially. In 1978 extra-budgetary funds accounted for only 31% of funds used. By 1981, the figure was 59% of funds used and now this figure has reached above 80% of funds used.

The management of extra-budgetary funds has been an issue attended to by the Ministry of Finance, which, in 1983, formally issued an edict on the Trial Measures Concerning the Management of Extra-budgetary Funds. This document clearly stipulated that government departments, enterprises, and undertaking units must pay attention to planned management and financial accounting with regard to extra-budgetary funds.

It was advised that the responsible department of the county (or city) should take the revenue and expenditure plan of the extra-budgetary funds as a component part of the unit budget and that it should take the final accounts and the enterprise financial plan and have them prepared independently and then report to the financial department of the same administrative level for examination. This latter financial department would then include them as an appendix to the budget and final accounts of the county (city) level and report to the people's government for examination and approval and report to the financial department of the upper level.

At the next level, the provincial (autonomous region or municipal) financial department subordinate to central authority, would examine the revenue and expenditure plans for extra-budgetary funds. Provincial and county (city) level departments would then have collected and prepared revenue and expenditure plans for extra-budgetary funds and would add them as appendices to local budget and final accounts for report to and approval of the people's government. In turn, the people's government would report to the Ministry of Finance.

In its turn, the State Council would add the revenue and expenditure plans for extra-budgetary funds of subordinate units as an appendix to the departmental budget and this would allow extra-budgetary funds to be brought into the composite financial credit plan of each level of financial administration.

CHAPTER 2

Monetary Policy and Monetary System

I. MONETARY POLICY

1. MONETARY POLICY TARGETS

The dual targets of China's monetary policy are (i) economic development and (ii) monetary stability.

In order to catch up with the developed countries and to achieve economic modernisation, it has been necessary for China (a developing country with a poor infrastructural foundation) to maintain a relatively high rate of economic development. But at the same time, China's monetary planners have had to understand that it is important that monetary stability be maintained. Stable commodity prices and currency rates are to be recognised as vital components of 'political stability and unity' and so of sustained economic development.

Currently full employment and balance of payments have not been listed as part of the target for monetary policy. Prior to economic reform there was no theoretical acknowledgement of the possibility of unemployment in a socialist society. In practice, what followed from this lack of theoretical acknowledgement was low wages and high employment and a number of urban residents being sent to rural areas to undertake semi-self-supporting production. This meant that, superficially, unemployment was not a serious problem in China.

With the introduction of economic reform, the unemployment problem loomed larger and larger. But groaning under the heavy pressure of a very large population, the government was reluctant to make the problem of employment a target of monetary policy. Instead, it adopted other macro-policies as a means of easing the problem and as a means of avoiding the possibility of aggravating inflation.

During the period when China's economy was closed, balance of payments was not a problem, but during the period of reform, policies have been drafted that allow and promote external trade and the use of foreign capital.

In recent times there have been problems with an imbalance between social demand and supply. Faced with this situation and the attendant problem of price inflation, some economists have argued that there is a problem with the dual nature of monetary policy targets. Accordingly they have argued that monetary policy should set stabilising the currency (i.e., commodity prices) as its sole target.

2.   IMPLEMENTING MONETARY POLICY

The following means are being used for the implementation of monetary policy:

(1)   The Deposit Reserve Rate

In 1984 the People's Bank of China began to perform its role as the central bank and in this capacity instituted the system of a deposit reserve rate. It was intended that adjustment of the deposit reserve rate would be the basic tool for the implementation of monetary policy. But in 1985 and 1986 planned control still held sway and the People's Bank was simply held responsible for provision of the supply of capital needed by the special and commercial banks. In this situation plans were examined and approved by the People's Bank and before credit receipts and payments to special banks were made, planned capital had to come first from their own capital and deposits (with deduction of the sum deposited with the People's Bank in accord with the stipulations) with the remainder coming from the People's Bank in the form of loans. The result was that, in these circumstances, the deposit reserve rate did not play a significant role.

In 1987 the People's Bank stopped taking care of the special banks' capital. This meant that the deposit reserve rate now had a role to play. For example, in the last quarter of 1987 the deposit reserve rate rose from 10% to 12%, a rise that had the effect of tightening money supply.

The problem that now must be tackled is that of enforcing the situation where all special banks or other monetary organisations must hold funds that accord with the deposit reserve rate. Indeed it is illegal for these institutions to be below the deposit reserve fund rate.

(2)   The Loan Interest Rate

As noted, the bulk of loans offered by Chinese banks to enterprises are loans on credit. (Bill discount loans make up only around 1% of total loans granted.) This means that the tool used by China's monetary policy is not the discount rate but the interest rate. Nowadays the People's Bank enforces implementation of monetary policy through adjusting and directly controlling the interest rate on loans. All officially registered banks and other financial institutions must abide by the rate stipulated by the central bank. The right to use a fluctuating rate (with a ceiling of 30%) is restricted to only some collectively owned financial institutions and financial institutions in special economic zones.

The role played by the interest rate, is not however, as large as it is in other countries. This is due to the problem of making State-owned enterprises solely responsible for their gains and losses—a problem that is far from having been really solved. No significant rise in the low rate of interest is likely in the near future.

In recent years neither the interest rate on deposits nor the interest rate charged for loans have been conducive to control of scale of investment. The reason that interest rates are lower relative to other countries lies in some misunderstanding that existed prior to reform of economic structure. This misunderstanding saw income from interest payment as being exploitative in nature. Many tended to think that low interest rates reflected the superiority of socialism. Consequently, for a long period of time low interest rates remained.

But even during the last ten years of economic reform, interest rates have remained relatively low. The main reasons why interest rates have remained low, even since the introduction of economic reform, are that commodity prices are irrational and enterprise economic returns are poor. Given that for many enterprises the profit rate on funds is very low, if the interest rate was substantially raised, enterprises in their tens of thousands would certainly find the financial burden to be unbearable. Therefore the interest rate can only be gradually increased in concert with improved enterprise economic returns. But it is only when the interest rate is substantially raised that its role as a tool of monetary policy can be strengthened.

(3)   Re-Lending by the People's Bank of China

Given that the role played by interest rates is subject to restriction, the role played by the deposit reserve rate is also limited. Conditions do not allow finance adjustment through use of an open market and this means that re-lending by the People's Bank to the special and commercial banks becomes the most important monetary policy tool. Re-lending is aimed at directly controlling money supply through control of the general scope of loans advanced.

Measures taken in order to achieve the goal of monetary policy using re-lending include the People's Bank of China determining total sum of loans made each year and a policy of loans made being categorised in accord with loan period, i.e., annual loans, seasonal loans, day-to-day loans and discount loans. Annual loans are granted to the headquarters of various special banks. These represent funds that are then re-loaned to the various branches of the special banks. Seasonal loans, day-to-day loans and discount loans are granted by the People's Bank to various local branches who then re-loan the funds to special banks or other financial institutions in their respective localities.

Practice over the last few years shows that as long as the People's Bank can effectively control the central scale of lending, monetary policy expectations can be met.

In the near future, development of monetary policy will take the form of perfecting the deposit reserve fund system and the central bank lending system. Interest rates will be gradually raised to provide some interest rate flexibility and so improve economic efficiency.

As a tool of monetary policy, re-lending is meant to provide direct and overall control of the economy. But with changing conditions, interest rates will gradually take their place as a means of indirect economic control. At the same time, with cultivation of the people's tendency to invest in securities and with the development of decentralised fund pooling (especially with the development of the system of government securities insurance and the enterprise shareholding system), indirect control of market business will also become an important monetary policy tool.

2:1 TRANSMISSION MECHANISMS FOR CURRENT MONETARY POLICY

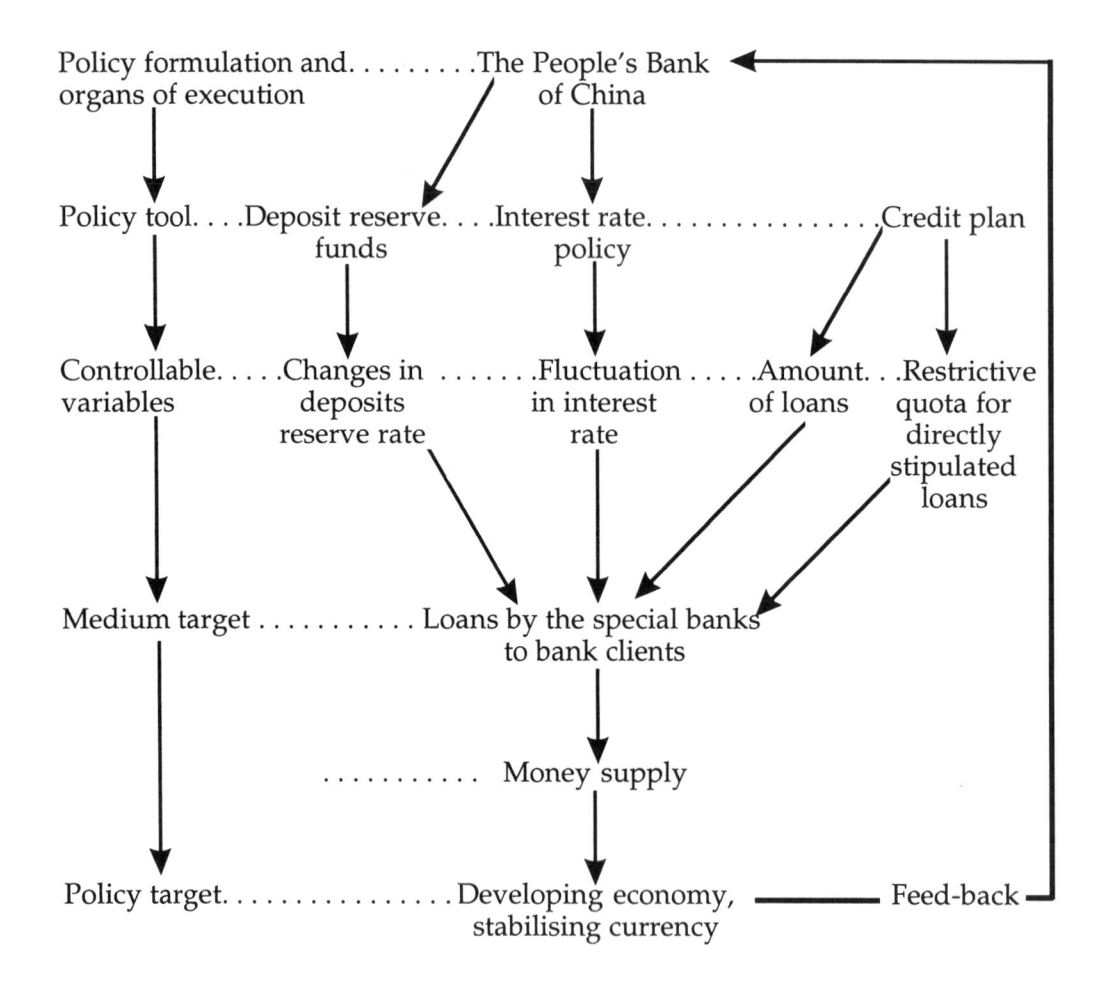

Policy formulation and........The People's Bank ◄─────────────┐
organs of execution   of China   │
        │   │   │
        ▼   ▼   │
Policy tool....Deposit reserve....Interest rate...............Credit plan
                funds   policy
        │   │   │   │   │
        ▼   ▼   ▼   ▼   ▼
Controllable....Changes in......Fluctuation.....Amount...Restrictive
variables   deposits   in interest   of loans quota for
                reserve rate   rate   directly
                                                          stipulated
                                                          loans
        │   │   │   │   │
        ▼   ▼   ▼   ▼   ▼
Medium target..........Loans by the special banks
                            to bank clients
        │   │
        │   ▼
                    ....Money supply
        │   │
        ▼   ▼
Policy target...............Developing economy, ─────── Feed-back ─┘
                            stabilising currency

2:2 TRANSMISSION MECHANISMS FOR FUTURE MONETARY POLICY

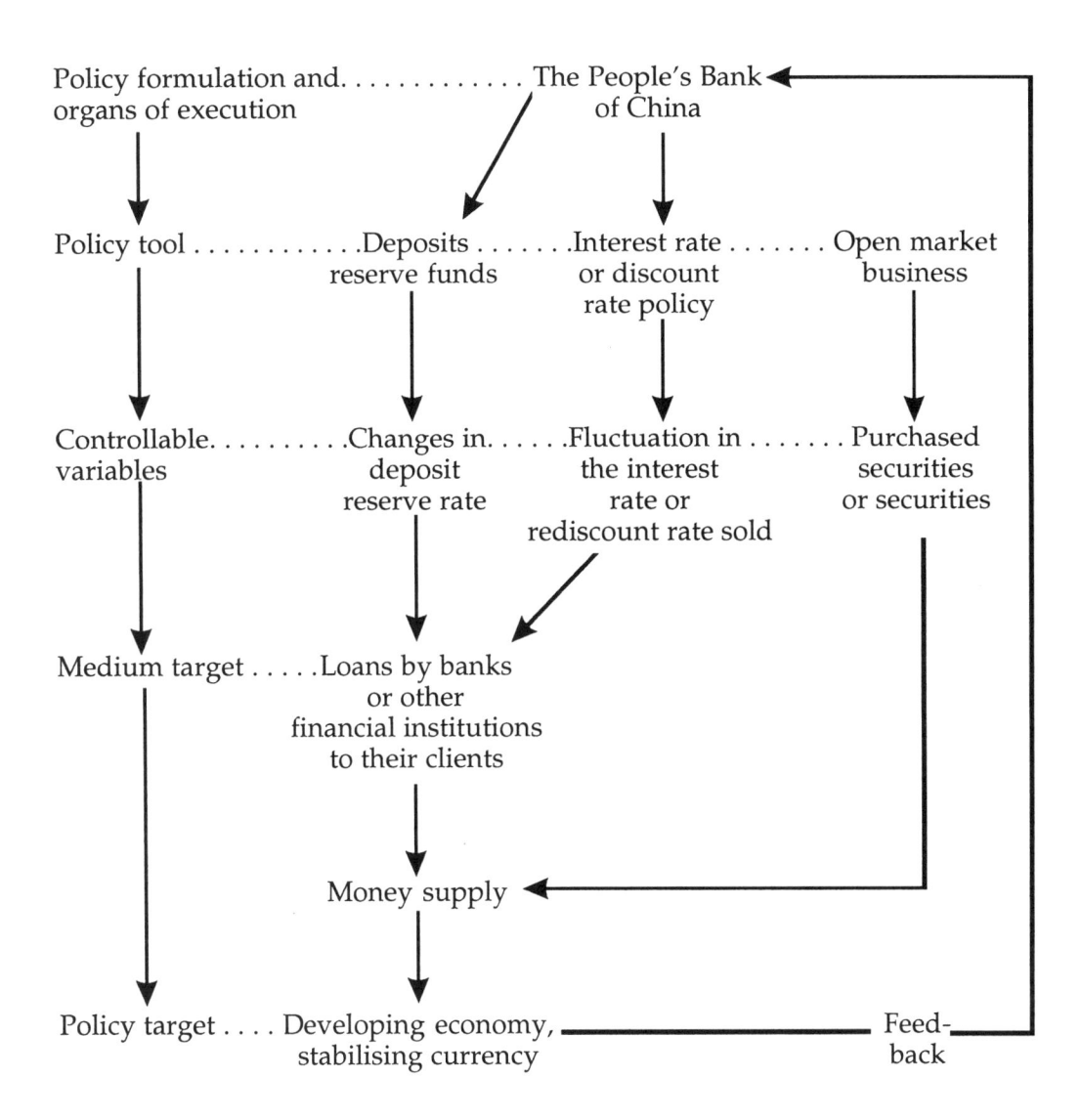

```
Policy formulation and............The People's Bank ◄─────────┐
organs of execution                 of China                  │
        │                  ╲          │                       │
        ▼                   ▼         ▼                       │
Policy tool............Deposits.......Interest rate.......Open market
                       reserve funds  or discount         business
                                      rate policy
        │                   │         │                       │
        ▼                   ▼         ▼                       ▼
Controllable..........Changes in......Fluctuation in.......Purchased
variables             deposit         the interest        securities
                      reserve rate    rate or             or securities
                                      rediscount rate sold
        │                   │       ╱                         │
        ▼                   ▼      ▼                          │
Medium target......Loans by banks                             │
                   or other                                   │
                   financial institutions                     │
                   to their clients                           │
                           │                                  │
                           ▼                                  │
                     Money supply ◄───────────────────────────┤
        │                  │                                  │
        ▼                  ▼                                  │
Policy target....Developing economy, ──────────────── Feed-───┘
                 stabilising currency                 back
```

II. RENMINBI CURRENCY

Renminbi is China's standard tender. It is the only tender to be legally used for quoting prices and for settling accounts. It is the tender that any unit or individual in China is not legally permitted to refuse to accept.

The basic unit of Renminbi currency is the yuan. (One yuan = 10 jiao = 10 fen). Renminbi denominations currently in circulation (1989) are: 12 paper notes with respective denominations of one hundred yuan, fifty yuan, ten yuan, five yuan, two yuan one yuan, five jiao, two jiao, one jiao, five fen, two fen and one fen. There are also seven Renminbi coins with denominations of one yuan, five jiao, two jiao, one jiao, five fen, two fen and one fen. Of these, the one yuan, five jiao, two jiao and one jiao coins were issued in April 1980, but only limited numbers were minted and they soon became collectors' items and so did not enter circulation.

1. THE SYSTEM FOR ISSUING RENMINBI

Issuing Renminbi is based either on a direct quota system (where the State sets the legal amount of issue and any extra issue must be supported by a similar amount of gold reserves) or on a reserve system where the amount of issue is kept at a proportion of national gold and foreign exchange reserves. The Renminbi issuing system is a commodity reserve system. It is a system of currency issue based on the supply of commodities. Each year the amount of currency issue is decided by the People's Bank of China based on economic growth (i.e., growth in the amount of commodities in circulation) and on consideration of other factors such as changes in the velocity of commodity circulation. After due consideration by the People's Bank of China, currency issue is approved by State Council.

When currency is subsequently taken into circulation the following channels are used. The People's Bank lends to the various special and commercial banks. This is a direct form of lending in the sense that the special or commercial banks immediately draw down ready funds and make them available to their customers. The other form is where, in a less direct manner, these banks withdraw their cash deposits (i.e., above-quota reserve funds) that have been lodged with the central People's Bank. At this point the special and commercial banks have no access to overdrafts. Overdrafts on banks' cash deposits are most definitely not allowed.

As these special and commercial bank deposits held by the central bank are usually considerably smaller than loans drawn down by the special and commercial banks, as a generalisation, it can be said that in China currency issue is realised through lending by the central bank.

In China gold is not used as the monetary standard and no quota is given in terms of gold parity to Renminbi.

2. MANAGEMENT OF CURRENCY ISSUE

Currency issue is a highly centralised process. Currency is issued exclusively by the People's Bank of China, that in turn, holds central place in a centralised and hierarchically ordered banking system.

Currency issue is managed and organised in the following manner:

(i) Establishment of a fund and establishment of fund vaults. The fund of issue is essentially a reserve fund. It is money in store which will be issued in time. The fund is composed of two parts (i) notes newly printed by the Printing House of

the People's Bank of China and (ii) money handed into the issuing bank's vaults by various local banks. The fund of issue is established by the People's Bank in line with plans approved by the State.

To ensure centralised storage and allocation of the fund of issue the People's Bank has established a system of vaults for funds to be issued. Vaults of the People's Bank, its provincial branches, second-class branches and sub-branches, are respectively referred to as the general vault, the branch vault, the central branch vault and sub-branch vault.

(ii) Allocation of fund of issue. Allocation of fund of issue between various vaults refers to the internal transfer of the fund of issue. This is a preparatory step for actual currency issue that is done in a level-by-level manner, i.e., the general vault is responsible for allocation between the general vault and branch vaults as well as among the branch vaults; branch vaults are then responsible for allocation between branch vaults and central branch vaults as well as central branch vaults under their jurisdiction; and the central branch vaults are responsible for allocation between central branch vaults and sub-branch vaults under their jurisdiction. It is this free transfer of funds between vaults that serves to facilitate fund use. The result is that customer demand for circulating currency is met and the fund of issue is not kept unused.

But before vaults of issue at various administrative levels can apply for allocation of the fund of issue, they must draft plans for allocation in line with consumer demand for currency. The plans must specify how much and when the money (including total amount and note denominations) is to be brought in or out. The actual transfer of the fund of issue can then only be carried out in accord with orders issued by the vault of issue at the higher level and only then with the seals of its director. Any other organisation or individual does not have any power to release currency to vaults.

3. FOREIGN EXCHANGE CERTIFICATES

Foreign exchange certificates (FECs) are used as a substitute for Renminbi but, unlike Renminbi, they have a foreign exchange value. When circulating in the Chinese market FECs serve to replace foreign currencies. They are mainly for use by foreigners, overseas Chinese and Hong Kong and Macao compatriots. In terms of their issue, circulation and withdrawal from circulation they are managed in a manner that parallels the management of Renminbi currency.

The State Council empowered the Bank of China to begin issuing FEC currency on 1 April 1980. Face value denominations of this currency are: one hundred yuan notes and fifty yuan, ten yuan, five yuan, one yuan, five jiao and one jiao notes. In formal terms they are Renminbi value equivalent.

Foreigners, overseas Chinese, and Hong Kong and Macao compatriots coming to China's mainland for short-term visits, and foreign diplomatic and non-governmental organisations and their personnel in China, are required to use FECs when buying goods or paying for services in the following designated areas:

(i) Travel agencies, friendship stores, foreign ship supply and replenishment companies, arts and crafts shops, antique shops, foreign trade centres and special imported goods counters that have been specially designated to serve foreigners, overseas Chinese and Hong Kong and Macao compatriots.

(ii) Hotels, restaurants and clubs specially designated to serve foreigners, overseas Chinese, and Hong Kong and Macao compatriots:

(iii) For payment of ship and train tickets to Hong Kong and Macao as well as consignment charges.

(iv) For payment of both domestic and international plane tickets and consignment charges.

(v) For payment of international post and telecommunications services:

(vi) For payment to units which have been approved by the State Administration of Exchange Control (SAEC) or its branches to accept FEC, or who should charge FEC when in accord with stipulations.

Foreigners, overseas Chinese and Hong Kong and Macao compatriots can freely exchange non-convertible foreign currencies, immediately payable foreign currency bills, foreign currency cheques and inward remittances for FECs at offices of the Bank of China or at exchange counters designated by the Bank of China. With FECs they can open special Renminbi accounts or foreign currency accounts at the Bank of China with the proviso applying to the latter that within six months FECs must be exchanged at equal value for Renminbi or exchanged at the current rate back to an exchangeable foreign currency or be remitted abroad.

Although the issue of FECs has played a positive role, it has also brought about a series of recognised problems. The biggest of these is that on the domestic market it has become another currency that is more valuable than Renminbi. Problems experienced due to the use of FECs have led to the suggestion that they should no longer be issued. But other difficult problems are associated with their abolition. These include the problem of satisfactorily calculating the proportion of foreign exchange earnings to be retained by and the distribution of foreign exchange income between various localities and departments. It has had to be concluded that current conditions do not yet allow for the abolition of FECs.

4. EXCHANGE RATES

(1) Non-Convertibility

Renminbi is a non-convertible currency. Without the approval of foreign exchange control authorities, Renminbi cannot be exchanged for foreign currencies, or vice versa. Except for cases which come under special stipulations, the foreign exchange incomes of all Chinese and foreign organisations or individuals must be sold to the Bank of China. The Bank then sells them for foreign exchange.

Using a formal decree, China bans the illegal purchase of foreign currencies in the following categories:

(i) Without first obtaining approval, paying Renminbi for import loans or other expenses which should be paid for in foreign exchange currency:

(ii) Chinese organisations paying Renminbi for various expenses on behalf of Chinese offices overseas, foreign organisations in China, overseas Chinese owned enterprises, foreign-funded enterprises, Sino-foreign joint ventures and foreigners coming to China for short-term visits when foreign exchange has been received from the visitors but not sold to the State:

(iii) Chinese residents and offices abroad using their Renminbi within the boundaries of China to pay for expenses on behalf of others who repay them in foreign currency:

(iv) Foreign resident offices located in China, overseas Chinese-invested enterprises, foreign-funded enterprises, and Sino-foreign joint ventures and their personnel, paying Renminbi for expenses on behalf of others who repay in foreign currencies or in other comparable ways.

All of the above constitute activities that amount to the fraudulent purchase of foreign exchange and they will be dealt with accordingly under the law.

Renminbi currency is also non-convertible abroad. The Provisions of the People's Republic of China on Banning State Currency From Leaving and Entering the Country stipulate that Renminbi currency taken or smuggled in or out of China (including that hidden in postal parcels) should be confiscated. The document titled Provisional Regulations of the People's Republic of China on Banning Bills and Securities in State Currency From Leaving and Entering the Country also stipulates that domestic money orders, cashiers' cheques, cheques, deposit receipts and bank-books should all be paid out in Renminbi currency. This latter regulation then also states that all securities issued in China, including government bonds, shares and company debentures, together with all other bills intended to be cashed in China, are not to be taken or posted in or out of the country.

(2) Principles Used for Adjustment of the Renminbi Exchange Rate

The principle for determining and adjusting the Renminbi exchange rate has gone through a complicated evolutionary process. In the early 1950s the exchange rate of Renminbi currency was set according to price parity between export commodities and overseas remittances. This was done in line with the principle of 'encouraging exports, while giving due consideration to imports and making allowances to overseas remittances'. From the mid-1950s to the early 1970s, the principle of stabilising the exchange rate was applied. This was related to both the highly centralised planned economic system and (especially) to the State monopoly of foreign trade. The latter being characterised by unified accounting for imports and exports and a policy of using imports to make-up for exports. Since 1972 the exchange rate of the Renminbi has been linked to a 'batch of currencies' of China's own choice. These have included the US dollar, Japanese yen, British sterling, Deutsche mark, French franc and the Hong Kong dollar—all frequently used in China's foreign trade and other economic exchanges.

China's pricing system has not been the same as that of other countries. The pricing system in China has not been reasonable and there has been hidden inflation. The result has been a too high Renminbi exchange rate, a situation that by 1980, had become increasingly evident.

For a few years the Renminbi exchange rate against the US dollar rose by 64.1%. This was a situation that had an extremely harmful effect on China's balance of foreign exchange revenue and expenditure. The result was that, from 1 January 1981, while not publicly announcing the official exchange rate, China adopted an internal account settlement price for foreign trade. This price was 86.7% lower than the official rate.

But the resultant dual exchange rates also caused considerable problems. Criticisms were raised. The result of this was that, from 1 January 1985 China unified the exchange rate with the internal accounting price and publicly announced an official exchange rate for Renminbi currency. This announcement marked the end of use of double exchange rates.

The principle now used for adjusting the Renminbi exchange rate is one based on purchasing power parity combined with consideration of foreign trade and balance of payments together with changes in exchange rates between foreign currencies. Given that China's balance of payments and its imports and exports are usually both counted and settled in US dollars, since July 1986 China has implemented what amounts to a system of fixing the Renminbi exchange rate on the basis of the US dollar. This has meant that the exchange rate of Renminbi currency against other foreign currencies is adjusted in accord with changes in the exchange rate between these currencies and the US dollar. No change is expected in this system for the foreseeable future.

(3)   Control of Foreign Exchange

For a long time China has exercised centralised control over foreign exchange. The aim has been to increase foreign exchange earnings and to economise on foreign exchange expenditure. This has been done in order to promote development of the national economy and to safeguard the interests of the State.

Control of foreign exchange is the responsibility of the State Administration of Exchange Control (SAEC) and its local branches under the People's Bank of China, but the major organisation for dealing with foreign exchange is the Bank of China. This is the State bank that specialises in foreign exchange and foreign trade. Over the past few years, with the approval of the SAEC, a small number of other banks and monetary institutions have also begun transacting foreign exchange business, but this business is usually transacted by the Bank of China.

Apart from general stipulations such as banning the circulation, use, mortgage, illegal buying and selling and the smuggling of foreign exchange within China, the content of domestic exchange control can be divided into the following aspects:

(i) Control over foreign exchange used or earned by State institutions and collectively owned economic organisations. Planned control is enforced over the foreign exchange income and spending of all Party and government organs, army units, organisations, schools, State enterprises and institutions, as well as domestic urban and rural collectively owned economic organisations. These entities must all sell their foreign exchange income to the Bank of China and must buy foreign exchange from the Bank in accord with plans approved by the State. However, in line with stipulations, they can retain a certain portion of their foreign exchange earnings. These retained earnings can then be sold to other units at foreign exchange regulation centres run by the People's Bank of China. (Currently foreign exchange is not allowed to be sold to individuals).

Domestic organisations are not permitted to deposit their foreign exchange outside China and they are not allowed to issue securities with a foreign exchange value without the approval of State Council. Loans that they receive from banks or other organisations in other countries and from banks in the Hong Kong and Macao area must be included in the annual plans drawn up by related departments under the State Council or by the governments of provinces, municipalities and autonomous regions. They must be subjected to approval of State Council via the SAEC and departments in charge of foreign investment control.

(ii) Control over foreign exchange owned by individuals. When Chinese or foreign nationals and stateless persons residing in China receive foreign exchange from other countries or from the Hong Kong and Macao area, they are allowed to retain 10-30%. The remainder must be sold to the Bank of China. If they then need to buy foreign exchange to remit or take out of China, they can apply to local branches of SAEC to buy it from the Bank of China. Individuals returning from work or study overseas or in Hong Kong and Macao are not permitted to deposit their foreign exchange abroad. They must remit it back to China.

If individuals want to sell their own foreign exchange they must sell it to the Bank of China or to foreign exchange regulation centres approved by the State. As for foreigners coming to China, overseas Chinese and Hong Kong and Macao compatriots on short-term visits, foreign experts, technical personnel and workers invited to work in China, as well as foreign students, they can keep the foreign exchange that they have brought in or they can sell it to or deposit it with the Bank of China. The same applies to foreign funds that may have been remitted to them from abroad. They can also remit or take foreign currencies out of the country with their entry declaration forms once they have presented the declaration forms to customs officials.

(iii) Control over foreign exchange held by foreign organisations and their personnel in China. Foreign diplomatic representative organisations, consular organisations, business offices, offices of international organisations and non-governmental organisations, diplomatic and consular personnel and resident staff of the above organisations can keep their foreign exchange or they can sell it to or deposit it with the Bank of China. They can also take their foreign currency out of the country or remit it overseas. If foreign diplomatic and consular organisations in China demand to convert their Renminbi earnings from their visa and attestation services for Chinese citizens into foreign exchange, they must obtain approval from SAEC or its local branches.

(iv) Control of foreign exchange in the case of enterprises funded by overseas Chinese, enterprises with foreign investment, and Sino-foreign joint ventures and their staff members. Enterprises in these three categories should open Renminbi and foreign exchange accounts at the Bank of China or at other Chinese banks authorised by SAEC. All foreign exchange income must be put into foreign exchange accounts from which foreign exchange to be used for normal business operations can be drawn.

Those who intend to open foreign exchange accounts in banks in foreign countries or in Hong Kong and Macao, must apply to SAEC for approval. Except those with SAEC approval, enterprises must deposit export earnings in foreign exchange currency in their bank accounts and go through the necessary procedures for having their export exchange verified. Their accounts with institutions, enterprises and individuals in China should all be settled in Renminbi currency. The only exception is where special prior approval has been granted.

Overseas Chinese investors and foreign investors may also apply to banks where they have established an account for approval to remit their after-tax profit and other legal earnings abroad. In cases where they feel that it is necessary to move their foreign exchange capital out of China, after ratification by SAEC, the required sum may be defrayed from the enterprise's foreign exchange accounts. These enterprises must file foreign exchange business report forms with SAEC on a regular basis. The SAEC has the power to demand that they supply information on foreign exchange business and to check foreign exchange receipts and expenditure.

Overseas enterprise staff or staff from Hong Kong and Macao employed in foreign funded enterprises, Sino-foreign joint ventures or enterprises with overseas Chinese investment, having paid Chinese taxes, may remit their foreign exchange earnings, including wages and other legal benefits overseas, but the remittance should be no more than 50% of net earnings. In the case where the remittance is more than this percentage, the remitter may apply for SAEC approval. The remitted sum must be defrayed from their foreign exchange accounts.

(v) Control of foreign exchange and of precious metals. Chinese customs officials will allow individuals to carry or re-carry foreign exchange out of China as long as they can produce certificates issued by the Bank of China or their entry declarations. Customs officials will also allow individuals to carry or re-carry precious metals (gold, platinum and silver) or precious metal products out of China in accord with State regulations or with their entry declarations. There is no limit to the amount of foreign exchange or quantity of precious metals and precious metal products brought into China, but the carrier must declare them when entering China.

5. CASH CONTROL

The current cash control system dates back to the Decision to Implement Cash Control in State Organs adopted by the Government Administration Council (the predecessor of the State Council) on 7 April 1950. At that time, the purpose was to regulate cash flow in a planned manner and to reduce cash expenditure and especially to fight the problem of serious inflation. Since then, the following reasons have meant that the system has continued:

(1) This system is conducive to cutting circulation costs. Cash control has limited the scope and amount of cash in circulation. Large numbers of transactions and other economic exchanges have been settled through the transfer of account funds in banks leading to a significant reduction in the use of cash. This economises on the costs involved in printing, transporting, storing and checking bank notes.

(2) This system is conducive to bank pooling of idle funds. Bank pooling of funds is made possible by the stipulation that any unit receiving cash must bank the funds. The result is much more efficient use of idle funds.

(3) The system allows bank supervision over economic activities. This allows the banks to play an inhibiting role over unlawful economic activities such as illegal transactions, tax evasion and the use of cash for bribes.

(4) The system promotes control of institutional spending and the inappropriate growth of individual consumption funds. This means that the system is effectively playing an auxiliary role in inhibiting inflation.

In the early 1980s the People's Bank of China relaxed cash control. This was done in order to better meet the needs of opening to the outside world and as a means of promoting the domestic economy. But there were problems. With use of the double-track pricing system combined with the relaxation of cash control there was opportunity for unlawful elements to speculate. These elements made use of price differences caused by the double-track pricing system to resell goods in short supply. They used cash transactions to engage in bribery and they evaded tax payments. Inflation occurred for several years running. The State Council then issued new regulations concerning cash control. These new regulations were stricter than the regulations for the previous period, but from a long-term point of view, China is bound to gradually relax or even abolish cash control in a manner that better suits the development of a commodity economy.

The new regulations were promulgated by the State Council on 8 September 1988. Called the Provisional Regulations Concerning Cash Control, the new regulations stipulated the following:

(i) That all government departments, organisations, army units, enterprises, institutions and other units (i.e., depositing units) that open accounts with banks or other monetary organisations must implement cash control.

(ii) That depositing units use cash within the following guidelines—for staff and worker wages and allowances, for reward to individuals for labour services; for bonuses issued to individuals for contributions in scientific and technological research, cultural and art work and sports; for labour protection and welfare allowances; for payment for the purchase of agricultural and sideline produce and other goods from individuals; for allowances for business trips; and for incidental expenses under Rmb 1,000.

(iii) That the practice of cash control will include three related aspects. First, the banks that have an account be responsible for checking and deciding the amount of cash reserves (i.e., provide an upper limit for cash reserves) to be kept by a depositing unit. These reserves are intended to offer readily available funds for 3-5 days' incidental expenses with the cash reserve limit being appropriately extended for units in remote landlocked areas, but never exceeding the estimated amount required for 15 days incidental expenditure.

Second, depositing units must remit their cash income to their bank on time, usually on the same day. Cash needed by depositing units must be drawn from their reserve or withdrawn from their bank account. They should never be allowed to immediately withdraw cash income deposited. Third, banks must conduct regular checks on cash income and on the use of cash reserves by depositing units. They then must report their findings to the central bank.

(iv) That when depositing units violate cash control stipulations, their banks can issue a warning to impose a fine or they can impose a fine. These fines are to be in line with stipulations set out by the People's Bank of China. In serious cases, banks are to stop loans or allowing withdrawals for a given period of time. If bank employees violate stipulations, administrative or economic measures are to be taken against them. If criminal offences are committed, judicial organisations are to take responsibility for investigating the crime.

III. THE CREDIT SYSTEM

1. *FINANCIAL CAPITAL*

Before the introduction of economic reform, joint-stock credit and commercial credit were banned. China did have bank credit, but bank deposits were small in sum and they were the only form of financial capital.

In the past there have been two factors contributing to scarcity of financial capital. First, the rural economy was not in a financial position to adopt the use of credit and in cities the bulk of industrial and commercial enterprises were State-owned and used the system of financial planning whereby income and expenditure was directly and centrally controlled by the State. Enterprises not only turned their profits over to the State, but also their depreciation funds. Their investment funds came from State financial allocation and they were not in a position to raise funds from society through the issue of stocks and bonds. In this situation, State-owned urban enterprises had only production and working capital and an insignificant amount of money in the bank.

Second, under State policy of low income, but universal employment and welfare, Chinese workers did not have very much money left once they had paid bills and met the cost of daily necessities. The result was that financial capital owned by Chinese residents was minimal. For example in 1978, financial capital for the whole society (excluding that held by banks) only accounted for 37.7% of national income.

After a decade of economic reform much has changed. First, financial capital is now diverse. Since 1981 the government has been issuing treasury bonds and since 1987 bonds have been issued for key construction projects and enterprises. Indeed, throughout the 1980s, many companies, enterprises and banks began to issue stocks, company debentures and financial bonds. The result has been that in the same period there has also been an impressive increase in financial capital owned by the whole society and by individual residents.

The 1980s also saw the commercialisation of the rural economy and an increase in farmers' income; the development of economies with different forms of ownership; increased autonomy of State-owned enterprises in terms of managing production and income; and a significant increase in the income of urban residents. By the end of 1987 social financial capital accounted for 78.9% of national income and stocks and bonds issued were valued at Rmb 64.6 billion.

It is clear that China has considerable future potential for increasing financial capital. It is also clear that bank deposits will increase in line with further economic development, that financial capital in the form of negotiable securities will increase and that stocks will increase at a fast rate. By 1987 China's negotiable securities capital accounted for a mere 6% of that year's GNP (stocks 0.1% and bonds 6.4%). This is a figure that is way below that of the economically developed countries and one that is even below that of some developing countries.

2. TYPES OF LOANS

(1) Producers' Loan

This type of loan is granted by banks and other financial institutions to economic entities engaged in industry, agriculture, internal trade, communications and transportation, the building industry, service trades and other production activities.

Prior to economic reform, banks only provided producers with short-term working capital loans. Now they provide both short-term (less than 1 year) loans and long-term (over 10 year) loans. These include working capital loans and fixed asset loans. Working capital loans are usually for a period of less than one year, with the shortest, such as overdraft loans and loans for the settlement of accounts, extending only a few days. Some however, may extend more than one year. For example, medium to long term loans granted by the Bank of China to aid the export of complete sets of equipment can extend for as long as 10 years. Fixed asset capital loans extended by the banks to producers usually fall into three categories:

... Loans to enterprises to aid technological renovation,

... Capital construction loans to either newly built enterprises or to older enterprises wishing to expand,

... Development loans to rural areas to aid the development of agriculture, forestry, animal husbandry and fishery production through reclaiming wasteland, barren hills, grassland and river and coastal beaches.

In addition, other types of loans, such as loans for the development of new technology and loans for scientific research, are extended to producers and scientific research institutes.

(2) Consumer Loans

This type of loan was non-existent in Chinese cities before the introduction of economic reform and in rural areas, prior to economic reform there were only loans to people in disaster-ridden areas and loans to people badly-off due to accident or illness. Consumer loans in their true sense did not exist until the early 1980s.

Today consumer loans are referred to as 'small-sum savings loans' and they are divided into two categories according to use: (i) loans for the purchase of durable consumer goods and (ii) loans for the purchase (construction) of houses. An applicant for a loan is required to first have a certain amount of savings deposited with the bank (or credit co-op). The sum should make up about half of the sum requested on loan and then the applicant must produce mortgages or a guarantee for securing the funds to be loaned. Once granted the loan, the applicant must deposit an agreed sum of money in the bank or co-op at agreed intervals as repayment for the loan until such time as the debt has been cleared.

Aside from consumer loans from banks (and co-ops), some commercial businesses (i.e., larger department stores) sell valuable durables that are in adequate supply on hire purchase. Money is repaid in instalments.

With further development of the economy and with progress in financial business, consumer loans will be gradually expanded in scope.

(3) Loans to Foreign-Funded Enterprises

The term foreign-funded enterprises refers to those enterprises that are funded exclusively by foreign investment, Sino-foreign joint ventures and Sino-foreign co-operative enterprises (including enterprises with investment from overseas Chinese). These enterprises are eligible for bank loans, usually loans from the Bank of China. These loans include fixed asset loans provided during the construction period and different forms of working capital loans provided during operation, such as revolving credit, temporary loans and overdraft facilities. These loans can be either in Renminbi or foreign currency. In addition, Chinese banks will also grant equity loans to Chinese partners in Sino-foreign joint ventures.

(4) Current Bank Loans

Currently China's banks are offering four different kinds of loans:
  (i) Loans on Credit—a non-secured loan depending on the trustworthiness of the borrower. No mortgage or guarantee is required.

  (ii) Mortgage Loan—a secured loan. The borrower has been required to use movable property (i.e., stocks, bonds, gold and silver and other negotiable securities) and/or real estate (housing or land) for mortgage purposes. The mortgaged sum is expected to be less than 70% of total value of the mortgaged property. Usually, movable property has been used as security.

  (iii) Loan on Guarantee— a secured loan. The borrower has been required to have a guarantor who is in a financial position to repay loaned capital with interest if the borrower is unable to meet his commitments. In the case of enterprise borrowing, another enterprise that has the status of an independent legal entity and with the ability to repay the loan is required.

(5) Bill Discount

The discount of bills demands that the bill should be based on the legal trade of commodities. This is done as a means of stopping dud cheques.

Although the above four types of loans do exist, over 95% of loans issued are loans on credit. The three loan types total less than 5% of total loans. It is recognised that the excessive amount of loans on credit has reduced the safe and floating nature of bank loans and it has reduced the effectiveness of central bank monetary policy. This has become an increasingly serious problem. China's banks have already begun to take measures to grant a lesser number of unsecured loans and a corresponding greater number of secured mortgage loans and bill discount based loans. It is anticipated that in future unsecured loans (loans on guarantee) will only be used for low-level development projects mainly in the countryside and in the private economic sector.

3. PRINCIPLES USED FOR THE ISSUE OF BANK LOANS

When granting loans Chinese banks have long followed these three principles:

(1) Planning Principle

This has meant that the banks, when issuing loans have been directed to strictly observe the dictates of central loan planning. It has also meant that enterprises which borrow must do so in accord with their plans.

(2) Principle of Material Guarantee

This has meant that a borrowing enterprise must have a certain amount of materials and it must have a ready market for its product. This requirement has acted as a guarantee.

(3) Compensatory Principle

This has meant that when borrowing, enterprises must set a repayment date and they must pledge to repay principal and interest when the loan is due.

During the period of economic re-adjustment—from the end of the 1970s and into the 1980s, the banks adopted two new credit principles. These are the principle of 'differentiating between enterprises with varying capabilities and providing support to units with better potential' and the principle of 'basing loans on sales prospects'. These principles are to ensure that financial support goes first to units which have done a good job in fulfilling their production plans and executing contracts using sound management principles. They are the units that enjoy high prestige. Loans to enterprises that are not in this category are to be tightly controlled. These controls are used to prompt enterprises to act in accord with the principle of basing output on sales and basing purchases on sales which means organising production and circulation in accord with market demand. Some banks have already been paying attention to enterprise profit when granting loans.

When applying for a bank loan, an enterprise must meet the following criteria:

(i) They must have the approval of departments in charge at or above county level and of the industrial and commercial administrative departments. The enterprise must have registered with the above administrative departments and it must have been issued with a business licence;

(ii) The enterprise must enjoy management autonomy in terms of independent economic accounting;

(iii) The enterprise must boast a certain proportion of capital; and

(iv) The enterprise must have established bank accounts.

The procedures necessary in order to acquire a bank loan are that:

... An enterprise must meet the requirements listed immediately above. The enterprise must then file an application offering explanation of the reasons for the loan, clearly stating the sum required and the intended repayment period.

... The bank must examine the application and the enterprise's standing as a legal entity and then investigate the feasibility of the intended project, including the likelihood of a good economic result. The bank must also investigate the reputation of the enterprise and its ability to repay principle and interest when due.

... The enterprise must sign a contract for the bank loan. Contracts for bank loans fall into two categories. First there are loans on credit. As already noted, these loans are increasingly being used for small sums over short repayment periods. They are the type of loan provided to prestigious enterprises who are not required to provide mortgage security or a financial guarantee. Second, there are loans borrowed for more complicated and longer term purposes or loans made to enterprises with a low credit rating.

... The loan must be issued in accord with the signed contract. If either party violates the contract, a penalty will be demanded by the injured party.

CHAPTER 3

Bonds, Stocks, Banks and Insurance

I. CENTRAL GOVERNMENT BONDS

Government bonds is the general term used to cover funds raised and borrowed both at home and abroad in the name of the government.

1. FOREIGN FUNDS

China's use of foreign funds has taken the following forms:
- ... accepting loans from international financial organisations,
- ... accepting loans from foreign governments, and
- ... issuing debentures in foreign countries.

When issuing debentures in foreign countries, exactly the same principles have been followed which pertain to the other two forms of foreign funds use. The primary principle has been that in the course of building socialism China must follow the principle of maintaining independence and retaining initiative. This has meant that when construction funds have been raised overseas, a policy of equality and mutual-benefit with absolutely no political conditions has been followed.

2. DOMESTIC FUNDS

Since 1950 the government has raised funds through authorising bond issues. To date this has been done on fourteen occasions. The first time was in 1950 with the issuing of the People's Victory Party Bonds. The reason given for issuing these bonds was to support the people's liberation war, to unite the whole country and to stabilise people's livelihood by promoting economic recovery and development. In order to guarantee bond subscribers' interest during the period when currency and price had still not stabilised, these bonds were issued using a standard based on calculation in kind. The unit of the bonds was the 'Feng' and the 'Feng' was calculated to total an average wholesale price of 3 kg of rice (millet in Tianjin), 0.75 kg of flour, four chi (=1/3 of a metre) of white fine cloth and 8 kg of coal. The price of these was taken from six cities—Shanghai, Tianjin, Hankou, Xian, Guangzhou and Chongqing. A total of 100 million 'Feng' was issued at an interest rate of 5% per annum. It was then refunded in instalments with principal and interest over a five year period.

Between 1954 and 1958 State Economic Construction Bonds were issued for five consecutive years. These bonds were, as their name suggests, to be used to boost State economic construction. The bonds were aimed at enterprises that were not State-owned and individuals with funds available.

3:1 STATE ECONOMIC CONSTRUCTION BONDS

	Issue (Rmb 100 million)	Interest rate (as a %)	Refund Period
1954	8.4	4	Began 1955 to be completed in eight instalments
1955	6.2	4	Began second year of issue to be completed in ten instalments
1956	6.0	4	Began second year of issue to be completed in ten instalments
1957	6.8	4	Began second year of issue to be completed in ten instalments
1958	8.0	4	Began second year of issue to be completed in ten instalments

From 1981 until the present the bonds that have been issued have been State Treasury Bonds. These have been issued eight times. They have been used to offset national financial deficits and to promote modernisation. These bonds were not aimed at individuals, but at State-owned enterprises, collective enterprises, enterprise departments responsible for their own accounting, local governments, institutions and organisations and the armed forces.

After the implementation of economic reform policy that allowed retention of profit at enterprise level, enterprise funds became available for investment in national construction and modernisation. Investment was facilitated through enterprise investment in State government bonds. Since the introduction of enterprise reforms the State can no longer legally mobilise enterprise funds without compensation and even the funds of government instrumentalities and departments cannot be legally procured by the State without compensation. This is because the system that is now in place is based on budget contract arrangements whereby surplus funds are to be used at the unit's discretion. It is this situation that has led to central government targeting of State enterprise, institution and organisation funds for government bond purchase.

3:2 STATE TREASURY BONDS

	Issue Rmb 100 million	Interest rate for (as %)	Interest rate in (as %)	Period years	Refund Period
1981	43	4		10	Began from 6th year to be redeemed at 20% per annum in five yearly instalments
1982	43	4	8	10	Began from 6th year to be redeemed at 20% per annum in five yearly instalments
1983	41	4	8	10	Began from 6th year to be redeemed at 20% per annum in five yearly instalments
1984	42	4	8	10	Began from 6th year to be redeemed at 20% per annum in five yearly instalments
1985	60	5	9	5	From sixth year - one lump sum
1986	60	6	10	5	From sixth year - one lump sum
1987	62	6	10	5	From sixth year - one lump sum
1988	90*	6	10	3	From sixth year - one lump sum

* *estimated*

In addition to the above, in recent years bonds have also been raised by local governments. Funds from these bond issues have usually been used for discrete construction projects, for example for the construction of small chemical fertilizer factories or small hydropower projects.

3.   OPERATION OF A DOMESTIC BOND MARKET

In the interest of strengthening the management and operation of government credit, the State Credit Management Bureau has been established. The role of this bureau is to oversee the reform of domestic bond issue.

Prior to 1985 all bonds issued in China were based on the issue and redemption of principal and interest with any further buying and selling, mortgaging and discounting of bonds being prohibited. But in 1985 a circulating market for State Treasury Bonds was partially opened. The banking service was allowed to discount and mortgage the 1985 State Treasury Bond issue. Then in 1988 a second level market for State Treasury Bonds was partially opened and during 1989 buying and selling of State Treasury Bonds issued to individuals in 1985 and 1986 was opened. Sixty large and medium-sized cities opened State bond markets.

In the past Chinese government bonds were only issued direct to the buyer. But since 1988 attempts to popularise the bond market have led to measures such as making State Treasury Bonds issued in a current year available for sale through post offices and construction banks. Subscribers can now buy these bonds at will. And at the same time, experiments are taking place in contract buying and marketing of bonds by banking institutions.

II.   DEVELOPMENT OF A STOCK MARKET

As noted above, State Treasury Bonds have been issued by the central government since 1981. Then in 1982, some localities were approved to issue a small number of enterprise bonds. They did this on a trial basis and then from 1984, enterprises were allowed to sell stocks and bonds. This was an important measure in terms of financial system reform. By the end of 1987 Rmb 64.6 billion worth of bonds and securities had been issued. They accounted for 5.8% of the period's GNP and by the end of August 1988 the figure had climbed to Rmb 90 billion. The result was that China's securities issuing markets became quite large, but the problem was that most of the Rmb 90 billion worth of securities were government bonds and so were only partially circulatable. The enterprise bonds that were transferable and circulatable accounted for only around Rmb 20 billion, or about 22% and of particular significance was the point that stocks accounted for only 2%.

The issuing of securities has adversely affected exchange of stock. In 1987 the total volume of stock exchange business came to about Rmb 100 million, or only 0.15% of total issue. Moreover, of the Rmb 100 million, most were bonds and almost no stocks were sold. An important reason for the under-development of the stock market is the situation where the handling of bonds and stocks runs no financial risk. Returns are fixed. The yearly rates of interest and dividends for stocks are more than 15% while the annual interest rate for bonds is over 9%. Both are significantly higher than the interest rate on bank savings and so when people need cash they usually prefer to draw bank savings rather than sell their stocks.

In spite of current problems, it is thought that the stock markets will make future progress. It is recognised that their development rests on enterprise joint-stock arrangements being further developed and on a future situation where companies and enterprises raise most of their funds directly on the market. It is also recognised that further development will depend on the standardisation of procedure for the issuing of stocks and bonds, the formulation of relevant laws and regulations and the 'normal' operation of interest rates.

III. FOREIGN CURRENCY EXCHANGE CENTRES

The Chinese government has long exercised strict control over foreign exchange. There has been no formal foreign exchange market in China, but since 1979 when China opened her doors to the outside world, an illegal trade in foreign currency has occurred. This has been partly due to the margin of benefit created by the inconsistency between domestic and international prices and partly because enterprises came to be allowed to retain part of their foreign currency earnings. Individuals were also allowed to keep foreign currency. It is this situation that has led to foreign currency exchange centres being established under the authority of the State Administration of Foreign Exchange Control. The aim of these centres is regulation of the supply and demand of foreign exchange, the promotion of the proper circulation of foreign exchange funds and eradication of black markets in foreign exchange.

The first foreign currency exchange centre was established in the Shenzhen Special Economic Zone in December 1985 and by the end of 1988 all provinces, municipalities and autonomous regions had their own foreign currency exchange centres. These centres are managed by their local foreign exchange administrations. They transact foreign exchange earnings or reserves that enterprises and individuals have retained under the Regulations Concerning the Control of Foreign Exchange. At the centres, enterprises are allowed to either sell or buy foreign exchange, but individuals are only allowed to sell foreign currencies. They are not permitted to buy.

Prices at the centres are allowed to fluctuate within a controlled range. The foreign exchange control administrations set the ceiling prices when they consider this to be necessary and it is within this range that both the seller and the buyer bargain.

China's foreign currency centres are quite different from foreign exchange markets in the true sense. It is intended that they will gradually develop into 'true' foreign exchange markets, but this will not happen until the scope for exchange has been expanded. For example, when individuals are permitted to buy and sell foreign currencies, when the restrictions on the purchase of foreign exchange have been relaxed, and when the selling and buying prices of foreign exchange are no longer subject to any government control.

IV. BANKING

Prior to 1979 China had one single bank—the People's Bank of China. Now after almost a decade of economic reform, well established specialised banks and a group of multifunction and multi-ownership banks are in operation.

The first step in establishing the new banks was the legislative empowering of the People's Bank of China to function as the country's central bank. Then the specialised banks were established. These banks are the Agricultural Bank of China, the Bank of China, the People's Construction Bank of China, the China Investment Bank and the Industrial and Commercial Bank of China. Then as a further step, the multifunction, multi-ownership banks were established. These are banks such as the Communication Bank, the Zhongxin Enterprise Bank, the Xiamen International Bank and co-operative banks and estate savings banks.

In addition to the above, various non-banking financial institutions have been developed. These have taken the form of trust and investment companies, stock and finance companies, insurance companies and rural and urban credit co-operatives.

1. THE PEOPLE'S BANK OF CHINA

The People's Bank of China is China's central bank. It is a State organ that controls and manages national financial matters. Throughout the period 1948 to 1983, the People's Bank was the only bank in China. It was responsible for the issue of currency, macro-financial management and for such matters as credits, savings deposits, account settlements and foreign currency transactions. But in time, this system no longer served to promote the further development of China's economy and so in September 1983 the State Council decided that as of January 1984 the People's Bank would cease to be China's only bank.

Now the main functions of the People's Bank of China are to research and formulate principles, policies, regulations and the basic financial system that will guide national level financial work. The bank then also takes responsibility for currency issue, the regulation and circulation of currency on the market and the maintenance of currency stability. The bank manages interest rates on deposits and loans and exchange rates. It formulates the State plan in relation to credits and loans and it manages foreign exchange business and gold and silver bullion exchange on behalf of the State. It also manages the State's reserves of foreign exchange and it examines and approves the establishment, closure and merger of banks and other financial institutions. It administers and regulates financial markets and it participates in international financial activities on behalf of the government.

The decision-making body of the People's Bank of China is its board of directors. The bank has established branches at provincial level and it has secondary branches at prefecture level and in medium-sized cities and sub-branches at county level.

In December 1985 the People's Bank of China was charged with the joint leadership of the newly formed China New Technology Pioneering Investment Corporation. The other partner with authority over the Corporation was the State Science and Technology Commission. The Corporation was formed for the express purpose of engaging in investment in research, development, adoption and production of new technology. This type of investment is recognised as relatively high risk investment.

The Investment Corporation offers research and development loans to medium, small and newly established enterprises and participates in their management. It handles Renminbi and foreign currency investment, including equity investment, trust investment, trust deposits, trust funds and loans and it provides consultancy services and financial guarantees for contract implementation, tendering and contracting. The Corporation also issues stocks, bonds and securities in foreign currencies.

2.   THE INDUSTRIAL AND COMMERCIAL BANK OF CHINA

The Industrial and Commercial Bank of China was opened for business on 1 January 1984 with a brief to handle industrial and commercial credits, loans and savings deposits. The bank operates in cities and towns where it serves urban residents and industrial and commercial enterprises. It provides loans for technical transformation and for some capital construction projects and it handles account settlements, trusts, financial leasing arrangements and foreign exchange business (especially in special economic zones and open coastal cities) and the issuing of bonds.

The head office of the Industrial and Commercial Bank is in Beijing. By the end of 1987, the bank had 26,564 branches and 450,000 employees. It is now the largest bank in China, with assets that represent more than 40% of total domestic bank assets.

3.   THE AGRICULTURAL BANK OF CHINA

This bank specialises in rural financial business. It is charged with handling deposits and settlement of accounts for rural enterprises and for rural public undertakings, government departments and army units. It handles rural residents' savings deposits, grants loans to rural agricultural, industrial and commercial enterprises and to farms and farming households (including contract-based farming households and other specialised farming households). The bank issues bonds and special loans, negotiates trusts and leasing and consultancy agreements and handles (on behalf of insurance companies) rural insurance business. It also transacts rural foreign-related financial matters and handles any foreign exchange business.

4.   THE BANK OF CHINA

The main brief of the Bank of China is settlement of international accounts, transacting foreign exchange business and handling foreign exchange-related Renminbi business. The bank has branches in big urban centres and in port cities.

The Bank of China was founded in February 1912. It was the bank of the Qing Dynasty. After the founding of New China in 1949 it was incorporated into the People's Bank of China.

The Bank of China accepts urban residents' foreign exchange deposits and their Renminbi deposits and it handles foreign trade credits, foreign exchange credits and Renminbi loans when they are relevant to foreign exchange transactions. It negotiates loans related to Sino-foreign joint ventures or international syndicates and it transacts international trust, investment, leasing and consultancy agreements and it buys and sells foreign exchange and gold bullion on international markets and issues bonds and other securities in foreign currencies. It also participates in international financial activities when authorised to do so by the government or when acting as an agent of the People's Bank of China.

The Bank of China is playing an increasingly important role in expanding China's financial relations and trade with other countries. It has established agency relations with more than 1,200 banks in overseas countries and has established branches in London, Singapore, Luxembourg, New York, Cairo, Sydney, Paris, Tokyo and in Hong Kong and Macao.

5. THE PEOPLE'S CONSTRUCTION BANK OF CHINA

Before the introduction of economic reform policy, the People's Construction Bank of China was an organisation concerned with State allocation of capital construction and administering financial affairs relative to capital construction. It operated under the leadership of the Ministry of Finance. After 1980 this administration was further developed to the point where it became a specialised bank.

The brief of the People's Construction Bank includes accepting deposits in the field of fixed asset investment (such as deposits from capital construction units), granting loans for capital construction and technical transformation, handling settlement of accounts between capital construction units, issuing stocks and bonds on behalf of regions, departments or enterprises and conducting trust and consultancy transactions.

The Bank is developing into an investment and long-term credit bank. Currently it has 6,176 branches and 95,000 employees.

6. THE INVESTMENT BANK OF CHINA

Established in December 1981, the Investment Bank of China is a specialised bank designated by the Chinese government to raise construction funds abroad and to handle investment credit. It has its head office in Beijing and branches in most of China's provinces, municipalities, autonomous regions, special economic zones and open cities. In regions where there are no branches of the Investment Bank, branches of the People's Construction Bank act on its behalf.

The main business transacted by the Investment Bank is first, raising medium and long-term foreign loan funds. It borrows funds from the World Bank and from other international financial institutions. These funds are usually borrowed at low interest rates and on preferential terms. Second, with government approval, the bank issues bonds in order to raise foreign funds from abroad. Third, the bank grants investment loans at home or participates in investment projects. These include medium-sized and small projects and particularly projects based on technical transformation. The bank provides loans in foreign currencies for the purpose of importing advanced foreign technology and equipment and it offers loans in Renminbi for the purchase of domestic auxiliary equipment and building construction projects, including granting loans to Sino-foreign joint ventures or participating in Chinese investment in such projects. Fourth, the bank offers guarantee and consultancy services.

7. THE COMMUNICATION BANK

This bank was originally established in 1908, but in 1954 it was suspended from trading. The State Council then decided that the bank should be re-established and it re-opened on 1 April 1987.

The re-established Communication Bank has become China's first bank to operate under a stock system. Of its Rmb 2 billion in working capital, Rmb 1 billion is in the form of shares held by the State and the remaining Rmb 1 billion is in the form of shares held by local governments, departments, enterprises and individuals.

The head office of the bank is in Shanghai and it has branches in major cities.

The bank is a commercial bank that casts a wide net in terms of the scope of the business that it transacts. It takes in deposits in both Renminbi and foreign currencies, handles loans for circulating funds in Renminbi and discount and fixed asset loans. It also offers foreign currency loans, discount loans and overdrafts. It negotiates domestic and foreign account settlements, issues bonds in both Renminbi and foreign currencies and handles deposits, loans, call money and discount business between international and domestic banks. The bank trades in foreign exchange and foreign currency stocks and organises and/or participates in syndicated loans. It establishes financial or non-financial subsidiaries, transacts trust, insurance, investment, leasing, consultancy and guarantee business and handles housing investment trade and the transfer of other valuable securities.

8. THE XIAMEN INTERNATIONAL BANK

The Xiamen International Bank is China's first joint-venture bank. It was established in Xiamen in June 1985 and has a registered capital of HK$800 million—60% contributed by a Hong Kong group, 15% by the Fujian branch of the Industrial and Commercial Bank of China, 15% by the Fujian Investment Enterprise Company and 10% by the Xiamen Special Economic Zone Construction Development Company. The bank has branches in Hong Kong and Macao.

The bank handles a wide range of business. It operates in the same manner as a foreign exchange bank. At present, it is focusing on establishing links with investment banks in the United States and Western Europe and on developing international consultancy services and attracting foreign fund deposits.

9. CHINA INTERNATIONAL TRUST AND INVESTMENT CORPORATION (HOLDINGS)

The China International Trust and Investment Corporation (CITIC) is under the direct leadership of the State Council. The Corporation was established in October 1979 and now has 21 subsidiaries and owns 90 Sino-foreign joint ventures, 149 domestic joint ventures and 13 enterprises where it is the sole investor. CITIC is a conglomerate that has diversified interests. It is engaged in production, promotion of technology, finance and trade. By the end of September 1988 the registered capital of CITIC was Rmb 20 billion.

The Corporation has actively sought business partners, both domestic and foreign. Its brief is to facilitate outbound and inbound investment, including organising Sino-foreign and domestic joint ventures and solely-owned enterprises. It is also charged with investing in small and medium-sized domestic enterprises, particularly if new technological development is involved. Promotion of venture capital investment to assist in technical upgrading of existing domestic enterprises is a priority. The Corporation floats various types of securities both at home and abroad, doing this on its own behalf or on a commission basis. It deals in international contracting and subcontracting, including labour service contracts. It provides insurance for foreign investors and international insurance and re-insurance. It undertakes leasing business both domestic and foreign and it engages in real estate transactions, economic consultancy services (including market surveys and feasibility studies) and provides legal, audit and accounting advice.

In addition to the brief outlined immediately above, CITIC has also been expanding its activities in the area of overseas investment. Since 1981 the Corporation has been engaged in overseas investment, particularly in areas where it has been able to use its investment to secure stable supplies of the raw materials that are most needed in China.

In 1984 CITIC purchased standing timber land in Washington State in the United States. It did this in order to obtain a constant supply centre for forestry products. Then in 1986, CITIC invested US$140 million in the Portland Aluminium Smelter in Australia. This is a US-Australian joint venture in which China has become a 10% shareholder. It is China's largest industrial investment abroad. Also in 1986, CITIC raised US$40 million for the purchase (with a Canadian partner) of the Celgar Pulp Mill in British Columbia, Canada. It has a 50% share in the mill.

In 1987 CITIC established the China International Trust and Investment Corporation Hong Kong (Holdings) Limited (CITIC HK Limited). It did this as a means of managing its interests in Hong Kong and Macao and in order to further develop its industrial, financial, trade, real estate, shipping and power station interests in the area. The Corporation has injected capital into the Ka Wah Bank, acquired 12.5% of the shares of Cathay Pacific Airways, participated in the construction of the second cross-harbour tunnel in Hong Kong, engaged in property development in the Lam Tim, Quarry Bay and Tseun Wan areas of Hong Kong and has investment in many other Hong Kong businesses.

In order to manage the above investment interests, the Corporation has established companies such as CITIFOR Inc. in Seattle, CITIC Australia Pty Ltd in Melbourne and CITIC Canada Inc. in Vancouver and in Hong Kong, CITIC (HK) Limited. In Hong Kong CITIC has also established specialised companies that include—Shortridge Ltd, Vitality Investment and Development Company, CITIC Shipping Agencies Ltd, and the Sunburst Investment Company. CITIC also has investments in Southeast Asia (development of timber resources), Thailand (automobile assembly using Chinese chassis for production for the local market), United States (establishing production of small power stations) and in Micronesia (fishing and textile production).

10. THE FINANCIAL MARKET BETWEEN BANKS

By 1985 Chinese banks had begun to borrow from each other. They were able to do this because a new system of credit fund management had been introduced.

Specialised banks were permitted to borrow from each other at the same time as the People's Bank of China implemented a credit retrenchment programme. This programme resulted in some specialised banks having an excess of credit funds while others were experiencing a funds shortage. In this context there was a rapid formation of a capital-lending market between the banks.

To date this capital-lending market has had the following three characteristics:

(1)   Use of a Tangible Market

Most of the capital lending markets are located in cities with the People's Bank of China having taken the lead in establishing a capital-lending centre or a specialised bank money-lending market. All the specialised banks (including those from other areas) come to the market to either lend or borrow with business being transacted through negotiation.

(2)   Use of Relatively Long Time Limits

Money-lending among the banks is done on a one month, and in some cases even a six month or yearly, lending basis. In the past any money-lending had been on a day-to-day basis. None of the banks now follow this day-to-day procedure.

(3)   Funds are Flowing from Backward Areas to the Developed Areas

This situation is because funds are now loaned and borrowed over a longer time period. In China's economically backward areas where agriculture predominates, funds are needed on a seasonal basis and yield low returns. This has meant that a natural flow of funds has occurred from these areas to those regions with developed industry and commerce where funds generate much higher returns. Funds have been flowing from northwest China to the coastal southeast.

11.   RURAL CREDIT CO-OPERATIVES

Aside from the banks that have been listed above, rural credit co-operatives have also taken their place in providing financial services available to enterprises, households and individuals. The rural credit co-operatives are financial organisations that have been established using shares contributed by farmers on a voluntary basis. Co-operative dividends are paid to share holders according to the performance of the co-operative.

Rural credit co-operatives have been established in villages below county level. By the end of 1987 China had more than 60,000 of these co-operatives employing 434,000 people (excluding part-time personnel).

The rural credit co-operatives play a vital part in promoting the development of the rural economy. They usually engage in small-scale credit activities. Their deposits and loan facilities are intended for use by rural households engaged in crop cultivation, aquatic farming and poultry raising, co-operative agricultural units, individual households engaged in light industrial production, commerce and service trades and township enterprises.

V.   INSURANCE

The People's Insurance Company of China was founded in October 1949. It is a State-owned enterprise that handles both insurance and re-insurance transactions. The People's Insurance Company is an economic entity situated directly under the State Council. It is now expanding rapidly and has 2,700 branches and a staff of 60,000, but in the period 1959-1979 China's domestic insurance industry was at a standstill. It is in the post reform 1980s that China's insurance business has experienced rapid development. In the 1980s the domestic insurance premium has increased at an average rate of 56.6% per annum and the foreign insurance premium (calculated in Renminbi currency) at an average of 32.2% and even when the exchange rate is factored in, foreign insurance still increased at an annual rate of 15%.

Insurance premium income for 1987 was Rmb 7.9 billion, with domestic insurance premium income accounting for Rmb 6.7 billion and foreign insurance premium income accounting for the remaining Rmb 1.2 billion/US$320 million. Money paid for domestic business compensation was Rmb 2.4 billion, of which property insurance (including agricultural insurance) amounted to Rmb 2.2 billion, personal insurance Rmb 210 million and compensation paid for foreign insurance business US$80 million.

1. DOMESTIC INSURANCE

Domestic insurance business is organised into three categories:
- ... property insurance,
- ... agricultural insurance and
- ... personal insurance.

Property Insurance—includes enterprise property insurance, family property insurance, freight transport insurance, motor vehicle insurance, shipping insurance, satellite launching insurance and motor vehicle third party liability insurance.

Agricultural Insurance—includes insurance of crop cultivation and aquatic farming and poultry raising. This form of insurance was offered on a trial basis in 1983 and now it has been expanded to cover all provinces, municipalities and autonomous regions with the exception of Tibet.

Personal Insurance—There have been over 30 types of personal insurance developed since this insurance category was established in 1982. It includes an individual's pension insurance, pension insurance for workers in urban collective enterprises, simple personal insurance, middle and primary school safety insurance, mother and baby health insurance and insurance against accidental personal injury. In 1982 personal insurance premium income was only Rmb 1.5 million. By 1987 the figure had increased to Rmb 2.5 billion.

By the end of 1987 there were 570,000 industrial and commercial enterprises involved in domestic insurance and the money involved in the business had exceeded Rmb 1.5 billion.

2. FOREIGN INSURANCE

The category foreign insurance refers to insurance business where account settlement is transacted in a foreign currency. This form of insurance includes property insurance, liability insurance and guarantee insurance. At present, there are more than 80 types of insurance provided under this category, including sea transport freight insurance, ocean-going shipping insurance, Chinese civil aviation insurance covering scheduled international flights, offshore oil prospecting insurance, nuclear power station insurance, satellite launching insurance, construction project insurance and installation project insurance, clients' comprehensive insurance, loss of profit insurance, machinery damage insurance, employers' liability insurance, employees' loyalty insurance, contract implementation guarantee insurance and investment (political risk) insurance.

Through re-insurance, the Chinese insurance business has developed close ties with the international insurance market. Chinese insurance enterprises have established re-insurance relations with over 100 overseas countries and have developed particularly close ties with the British insurance industry. Over half of outward re-insurance goes directly to the London insurance market and most inward re-insurance comes from the London market. In recent years the depression on the international insurance market has had an adverse effect on China's re-insurance business.

3. THE INSURANCE MARKET

In the period 1949-1979 the People's Insurance Company of China was the only insurer on the Chinese mainland. It handled all insurance business and there were no insurance brokers involved.

Now an insurance company in an urban area signs contracts with relevant State enterprises and institutions and then staff of the latter handle insurance business on its behalf. For example, residents' family property insurance is handled through the savings bank, railway freight transport insurance through the railway freight transport department and import and export goods transport insurance through the State's foreign trade companies. In rural areas, with the support of local government, insurance stations have been established at township level. They handle property insurance, agricultural insurance and personal insurance.

On 3 March 1985 the Provisional Regulations on the Management of Insurance Enterprises was promulgated by the State Council. According to this set of regulations, enterprises require a capital base of Rmb 30 million or more if they are to be granted a business licence that would entitle them to engage in personal and general insurance transactions. To date though, there have been no applications filed for the establishment of a new insurance company that have met this legal requirement. What has happened is that the State Council has authorised the Shanghai based Communications Bank to handle insurance transactions and it has approved the establishment of an insurance department in CITIC.

In the vast rural areas of China various forms of insurance experiments are being undertaken. In 1986 the Xinjiang Construction Corps Agricultural and Animal Husbandry Insurance Company was established in the Xinjiang Uygur Autonomous Region. This insurance company was established to handle crop cultivation insurance and aquatic farming and poultry raising insurance in the geographic area under its jurisdiction. Also in 1986, the State Council authorised the Ministry of Civil Affairs to experiment with rural relief co-operation insurance. In 1988 there were more than 100 counties experimenting with this type of insurance and, with the support of their local governments, some rural areas have established insurance co-operatives to handle property insurance in their own localities.

Some large companies are also planning to establish their own associated insurance companies and foreign insurance companies have just begun the process of establishing themselves in the Chinese insurance market. Eleven foreign insurance companies have established representative offices in Beijing, but to date, none of the foreign insurance companies have been permitted to begin transacting business.

In 1987 the People's Insurance Company of China established the Chinese People's Insurance Investment Company. It is an enterprise that has an independent legal status. The brief of the company is to re-invest insurance reserves with its annual investment amount being approved by the People's Bank of China. Some provincial level insurance companies have also established insurance investment companies.

CHAPTER 4

Price Reform

I. BACKGROUND TO PRICE REFORM

Prior to price reform in 1979, China's pricing system was irrational. Prices of agricultural, mining and raw materials used in industrial production were low relative to prices of products processed by industry. In terms of price parity, prices of industrial products were higher than those of agricultural products; those of grain lower than cash crops; and there was a wide gap between prices of mineral products, energy, raw and semi-finished materials on one hand and processed industrial products on the other.

In terms of price differences, products were not priced according to quality and prices for agricultural products did not change in the off seasons and in peak periods. Price differences for various kinds of consumer goods were too small and in some cases purchasing prices were even higher than selling prices.

The irrational situation with regard to charges made by service trades and urban public utilities, including rent, was also striking. The seriously irrational price structure had affected industrial and agricultural production as well as development of tertiary industries and it had caused chronic shortages of many important commodities. Many commodities were poor in quality, high in price and overstocked.

The problem with past price policy was over-centralised administrative power and over-pricing. Central authorities exercised too much control and local authorities had little say. Enterprises had practically no price fixing power at all. They had no price flexibility and so were unable to readjust prices in accord with market supply and demand. It was against this background that price reform was undertaken.

II. THE DEVELOPMENT OF PRICE REFORM

For the past ten years, price reform has accorded with a policy of 'combining readjustment with decontrol'.

1. PRICE REFORM 1979 TO 1984

During this period major efforts were made to readjust prices in a planned manner. This readjustment involved the following four aspects:

(1) Raising the Purchasing Price for Agricultural and Sideline Products

This was done to promote rapid development of agricultural production and to form a support network for the contracted responsibility system that linked remuneration to output.

In 1979 the purchasing price for grain, oil-bearing crops, castor oil, cotton, pigs, cattle, sheep, eggs, aquatic products, beet, sugar-cane, ramie, oxen hides, silk-worm cocoons, timber and bamboos in south China, was substantially increased. The purchasing price of eighteen major agricultural products was raised by an average of 25.7%, while the purchasing price of grain rose by 30.5%, fat and edible oils 38.7%, and cotton 25%.

Above quota purchases of grain and edible oil at higher prices was expanded by 30-50% and a policy of a 30% increase in the purchasing price of above-quota cotton was implemented.

In 1980 the purchasing price for cotton was increased once again, this time by an average of 10%, and in 1981 the purchasing price for soybean was increased by 50%.

Between 1979 and 1981 the purchasing price for agricultural and sideline products rose by 38.5%. Coupled with the expansion of the scope of purchases at negotiated prices, farmers received an additional income of Rmb 20.4 billion.

Between 1982 and 1984 some minor readjustments were made to the prices of a few agricultural products.

(2)   *Raising the Selling Price of Eight Major Types of Non-Staple Food*

In order to change the situation where the increased purchasing price of farm and sideline products stood much higher than their selling price, the State increased the selling price of eight major types of non-staple food. These were pork, beef, mutton, poultry, eggs, aquatic products, vegetables, and milk, together with their processed products. There was an average 30% increase in selling price.

(3)   *Increased Producer Price of Means of Production, Transport and Communication*

From 1979 the State raised the producer price of coal by 30%, pig iron by 33%, and steels by 20%. Correspondingly, the producer price of iron ore, coke, non-ferrous metals, cement and plate glass was increased. This upward adjustment of price was then coupled with an effort to reduce the price of some processed products, i.e., automobiles, general machinery and parts, instruments and meters, measuring and cutting tools. This policy reduced the price ratios between mining industry products and other raw materials and processed industrial products.

Then in August 1982 the State increased short-haul railway freight and adjusted water transport charges, improving the irrational price structure of freight.

(4)   *Price adjustment for textiles and other light industrial products*

In order to solve the problem of the rapid increase in output of trueran cloth and its high price, the latter serving to restrict mass consumption, from November 1981 the price of trueran cloth was reduced. The retail price of trueran khaki, fine trueran cloth, and other kinds of trueran cloth materials was reduced by an average of 13%. However, the ratio between the reduced price of trueran cloth and cotton was then irrational. Therefore in January 1983 the price of cotton textiles was also reduced. The State then reduced the price of some other industrial goods, i.e., wrist watches, alarm clocks, cloth shoes with rubber soles, electric fans and colour television sets.

In the period 1981-1983 the State increased the price of some brands of cigarettes and liquor, but the price was then considered to be too high and so a downward price adjustment was made.

It was during the 1979-1984 period that traditional price management began to change. Prices began to be set jointly by industrial and commercial sectors of the economy through negotiation. The price of small commodities was released in 1982 and in 1983. At the beginning of 1979 floating prices had been introduced on a trial basis for the electronics and machinery trades and departments. Some electronic and machinery products began to follow, (i) State guidance price under administrative regulation and (ii) market price subject to market regulation.

By 1984 the proportion of State guidance price and market regulated price for the purchase of farm and sideline products respectively rose from 1.8% and 5.6% in 1978 to 14.6% and 18.1% in 1984. Their proportion in terms of social retail sales of consumer goods rose from 0.5% and 2.5% in 1978 to 10.5% and 16% in 1984.

A decision made by the Party Central Committee on Economic Structural Reform in October 1984 re-affirmed that the over-centralised price management system must be reformed in order to gradually narrow the scope of State unified pricing. In that month the price for all small goods was released and early in 1985 the price for industrial means of production additionally produced and marketed by producers themselves was released. This policy promoted the 'double-track' pricing system.

2. PRICE REFORM FROM THE END OF 1984 TO 1986

As noted above, during this period price reform focused on freeing the price of a greater number of products to allow adjustment in accord with market price.

(1) *Pricing of farm and sideline products*

From 1985 to 1986 special attention was paid to decontrolling prices. The 'double-track pricing system' served to significantly relax control over prices of agricultural and sideline products and over the prices of several industrial consumer goods.

In 1985 the State unified purchase of grain was changed to contract purchase. Grain subject to contract purchase attracted a price equivalent to 70% of the former additional price for above-quota purchase. The selling price in rural areas was made equivalent to the purchasing price. This was a change from past practice where purchasing price had exceeded selling price.

In 1986 the State quota for contract purchase grain was cut by 22% and subsequently more grain was marketed at negotiated prices. The purchase price of cotton in the north was lowered by Rmb 4.4 per 100 kg; the price of timber in the north was raised by an average of 44%; the price of jute and bluish dogbane was reduced 10-15%; the price of maize in northeast China and Inner Mongolia was raised by Rmb 2.7 per 100 kg and the price of soybean and sunflower-seeds in the same region was raised by Rmb 0.09 per 100 kg and Rmb 0.04 per 100 kg respectively. In major pastoral areas sheep wool followed the State guidance price and was allowed to rise within the State-stipulated ceiling price band. In the meantime, guidance or negotiated prices were introduced for major Chinese medicinal herbs.

(2) *Price of some light industrial products*

In 1985 the State readjusted the price of some Western and traditional Chinese medicines and in 1986 the price of newsprint and relief printing paper was raised by 18% and 7% respectively and the price difference for salt between urban and rural areas was increased.

(3) Price of heavy industrial products

In 1985 the price ratio between various types of State-allocated coal was adjusted. This included coke, rich coal and lean coal as well as the price ratio between 17 types of coal such as jet, lump coal and coal dust. The regional price difference was widened. The price of electricity generated with fuel purchased at an additional or negotiated price was then increased. Different rates were also worked out for electricity used during peak and off-peak periods and between high and low water periods, the latter accommodating hydro-electric production.

In 1986 the price of important non-ferrous metals was raised. These metals included aluminium, zinc, tin, antimony and tungsten ore as well as industrial silicon and aluminium oxide. The increased price rate reached an average of 37%. The price of some ferrous metals, including manganese ore, ferromanganese, ferrosilicon and carbon products, was raised by 31-100%, averaging 58%. There was also a rise in the price of petrochemical products, some types of building materials, and machinery products.

(4) An Agency Price Instituted for the Bulk of Import Commodities

Agency price for imported commodities was implemented together with readjustment of the domestic selling price for a large number of imported goods.

3. PRICE REFORM 1987-1988

This period marked the third stage of price reform. During this stage there was no major reform of the pricing system. Since 1987 a policy of stabilising the economy and prices has been implemented. Attention has been focused on summing up the experience of price reform, perfecting and consolidating price reform measures already adopted, strengthening control over total price level and preparing for further price reform.

During 1987-1988 an effort was made to continue to readjust prices listed for adjustment and to ease the impact of released prices on State controlled prices. Important measures taken in line with this policy were:

(1) In January 1988 the central government set a ceiling for major means of production prices not subject to State allocation and reaffirmed the price of ten major categories of products. These categories included energy, industrial raw materials, agricultural means of production and transport and communications.

(2) Between April and July 1988 various localities raised the price of four rationed non-staple food products: meat, eggs, vegetables and sugar; and they began to give financial subsidies to urban residents to offset the increased purchasing price of these items. This is a change from past practice of raising the purchasing price and then selling at list price.

(3) In July 1988 the State relaxed control over the price of thirteen name-brands of cigarettes and liquor and at the same time readjusted the price of other cigarettes and liquor. Also the airfare for 56 air routes, involving eighteen airports, was raised during the tourist season (from April to November).

Aside from unified price readjustment made by various State departments, there was also a major improvement in the price ratios and price differences between comparable products. The price of farm and sideline products was raised and the price ratio between industrial and agricultural products was improved. Compared with 1978 the purchasing price of farm produce had risen by around 99% by 1987, including a 140% increase for grain; a 62% increase for cotton and oil-bearing crops; a 33% increase for tobacco; and a 65% increase for sugar crops. The farmers had earned several hundred million Renminbi from selling their produce and in doing so had created conditions that promoted their own development. The price ratio between industrial products also saw much improvement. With the readjustment of price for industrial means of production and the institution of the 'double-track' pricing system, there was a large-scale increase in the price of energy, raw materials and other primary industrial products whose price was formerly relatively low. Comparing 1987 with 1978, the price for raw materials had risen by 55%, for mining industry products it had increased by 77% and for the processing industry it had increased by 21%. This had improved the formerly irrational price structure.

The table shows products which were priced jointly by the State Pricing Administration Bureau and central departments concerned, or which followed the State guidance price in 1988.

4:1   PRODUCT PRICING

Form of Price Management	No. of products	Product Categories
1. Farm produce Purchase price		
State-set price	17	Grain, oil-bearing cotton, cured tobacco, sugar crops and silk-worm cocoons
Guidance price	11	Pigs, sheep wool, jute, resin and Chinese herbal medicines
2. Farm Produce selling price		
State-set price	14	Grain, oils, cotton for wadding, timber and bean cake
Guidance price	4	Pork, tea, timber owned by collectives in south China and musk
3. Light industrial and textile products		
State-set price	50	Including light industrial products (sugar, salt, cigarettes, liquor, newsprint,

PRODUCT PRICING (cont'd)

Form of Price Management	No. of products	Product Categories
		pulp, benzene alkalis and pencils), textiles (cotton yarn, cotton cloth, woollen fabrics, knitting wools and cotton blend cloth, silk, silks and satins and chemical fibres), medicines and medical apparatus and synthetic materials (polyester fibre chips, polyethylene, polypropylene and acrylonitrile)
Guidance price	8	Including enamelware for daily use, carpentry nails, cotton jersey, undershirts, cotton trousers and bed sheets
4. Producer price for heavy industrial and chemical products		
State-set price	314	With varieties divided into the following 21 categories: electric heating products, coal, coke, petroleum, mineral ores, chemical fertiliser, pesticides, organic chemical products, synthetic materials, dyestuffs, rubber and rubber products, film, tape, construction materials, iron and steel, ferrous and non-ferrous metal ores and intermediaries, non-ferrous metal products, refractory materials, electroplating equipment, locomotives, freight and postage
Guidance price	431	With varieties divided into 27 categories including: mining equipment, smelting equipment, petroleum equipment, chemical equipment, cement equipment, cranes, pumping and general engineering machinery, compressors, air-blowers, machine tools, automobiles,

PRODUCT PRICING (cont'd)

Form of Price Management	No. of products	Product Categories
		television sets, electrical appliances, electric wires, cables, electric materials, instruments and meters, power driven vessels used for agriculture, electronics and civilian aircraft
5. Selling price for heavy industrial and chemical products		
State-set price	13	Including coal, gasoline, kerosene, diesel oil, lubricant, chemical fertiliser and pesticide

* Note: because this table only applies to goods purchased or produced in accord with the State plan, the table does not imply that all products on the list follow either State-set or guidance prices.

During 1987-1988, in overall terms, the price of consumer goods and small merchandise was released. This resulted in the price difference between items beginning to widen and a consequence of this situation was that some places then made appropriate readjustment to the rate paid for housing, water, electricity, gas, medical care and other public utilities. Also the price for the bulk of services and repairs was released. This price release served to improve the position of low-income service trade workers. In addition, during the first half of 1988, ceiling prices were implemented for steel.

III. CURRENT PRICE CATEGORIES AND SYSTEMS

1. PRICE CATEGORIES

China's current pricing system can now be divided into several sub-systems composed of different classifications of prices. The main pricing categories are:

(1) Prices Fixed by the State

These are fixed by pricing departments and other related government departments functioning at and above county level.

(2) Guidance Prices

These are also State set prices. Government departments above county level give guidance to enterprises for fixing commodity prices and charges. They determine a basic price, a floating scope for price, a discriminating rate, a profit rate, ceilings and a minimum protected price. In short, guidance prices are prices that function within a government set pricing band.

(3) Market Prices

These are prices regulated by changes in supply and demand. They are prices arrived at through consultation between industrial and commercial enterprises. They are formally negotiated prices for buying and selling products and they include free market prices.

2. THE SYSTEM OF PRICES FIXED IN ACCORDANCE WITH PRODUCTS AND LABOUR SERVICE DEPARTMENTS

These fixed prices include:

(1) Agricultural Product Prices

These prices refer to prices fixed for farm, forestry, animal husbandry, sideline and fishery products produced by agricultural departments. These products are divided into twelve categories, i.e., grain, cotton, oil, hemp, silk, tea, sugar, vegetables, tobacco, fruit, medicinal herbs and sundry goods.

(2) Prices of light industrial products or industrial consumer goods

These refer to prices of consumer goods produced by various industrial departments for the daily life of the people, i.e., foodstuffs, textiles, sewing machines, leather goods, paper products, stationery articles and wooden products.

(3) Prices of Heavy Industrial Products or Capital Goods

These refer to prices of capital goods manufactured by industrial departments. These goods are the means of production. They include items such as metallurgical products, power, coal, oil, chemical, machine-building, building materials and the forestry industry products.

(4) Prices of Communications and Transport

These refer to charges for use of railway, highway, water, air and pipeline transport services.

(5) Prices of Construction Services

These are also known as construction and installation engineering costs. They refer to all expenses collected from the unit for which the project is being built by a construction and installation enterprise. They are the expenses collected by a construction and installation enterprise for completion of a contracted project.

(6) Catering Trade Prices

These are prices of foodstuffs and drinks manufactured and sold by the catering industry.

(7) Charges for Labour Services

These are charges collected by trades and professions who have offered various types of labour services, but who have not offered specific products for sale. These prices include the charges levied for hotel accommodation, hairdressing, public baths, picture taking, washing and dyeing and repair, garment processing, medical, cultural and recreational services.

3. CIRCULATION PRICES

These are prices fixed in line with different stages of circulation. They include:

(1) Ex-factory Prices of Industrial Products

These are prices adopted by factories and mining enterprises for their products. If the products are sold to commercial departments, the ex-factory prices will become purchasing prices paid by commercial departments. If they are directly purchased by other factories and mining enterprises as means of production, the ex-factory price will be the purchase price paid by the buyer.

(2) Purchasing Prices of Agricultural Products

These are prices paid to agricultural producers by commercial departments or sideline products processing enterprises when they purchase agricultural products and sideline products. As far as agricultural producers are concerned, these are the sale price for their agricultural and sideline products.

(3) Allocated Prices

These are account settling prices between commercial and capital goods supply departments. They operate when these departments allocate commodities and goods between themselves using wholesale prices or supply prices. These prices contain preferential terms for units trading within the same department.

(4) Wholesale Prices or Supply Prices

Wholesale prices are the price that wholesale commercial departments use when supplying commodities to retail businesses. Supply prices are prices that are used when capital goods are supplied to enterprises and they are the prices that wholesale commercial departments use when supplying means of production to factories and mining enterprises.

(5) Retail Prices

These are the prices used when retail shops or marketing organisations run by industrial enterprises sell commodities to individual consumers or to social groups.

4. FORMULATING PRICE INDICES

Price indices are formulated by the State Statistical Bureau. Price indices officially set include the purchasing price index of agricultural and sideline products, the State-run commercial retail price index, the market fair price index, a general retail price index of commodities, a price index of living expenses of urban employees, and overall parity indices of industrial and agricultural products.

When formulating price indices, the number and type of indices is set in terms of their intended useful purpose. When it comes to the commodity index, it is divided into a single-commodity price index, a group price index and a general price index. Further divisions are then made in the comparative base used. For example, a division is drawn between fixed-base period price index, chain index, and chronological chain index. When it comes to commodity circulation, a division is drawn between wholesale price index and retail price index. In terms of both planning and circulation, a division is made between State fixed price index and negotiated price index.

When formulating price indices 'representative standard products' are selected. Rather than using a mechanical sampling method, products are chosen according to the following:

(1) Selection on the basis of classification. For example, agriculture is divided into agriculture, forestry, animal husbandry, sideline occupations and fishery production. Industry is divided into twelve departments and each major category is divided into a number of smaller categories. It is on this basis that 'representative standard products' are chosen for each category of commodities.
(2) In each category of commodities, standard products will be chosen as being representative.
(3) Commodities which are representative in terms of changes in prices will be chosen and commodities with special change trends will be chosen.
(4) The category of commodities and the representative standard products will remain relatively stable over time. This is to allow a comparative aspect to price indices.
(5) Typical places for price sampling will be selected. Representative markets will be chosen.
(6) A base period is selected. When formulating fixed-base period a period of comparatively stable commodity prices is chosen. The base periods most frequently used have been 1950, 1952, 1957, 1962, 1965, 1970, 1975, 1978, 1980 and 1987.

4:2   MAJOR PRICE INDICES 1987

Base period	General retail price index	Index for urban citizens' living costs	Purchasing price index for agricultural sideline products	Retail price index for industrial products in rural areas
1930-36*	462.2		815.4	334.6
1950	198.0	226.3	432.4	132.2
1952	177.2	195.8	355.6	120.3
1957	163.2	178.5	295.9	117.9
1962	129.7	145.7	216.2	104.4
1965	146.8	162.8	230.2	111.6
1970	150.4	164.2	221.6	118.1
1975	150.1	162.0	207.3	120.5
1978	145.7	156.2	198.8	120.2
1980	134.8	142.7	152.1	119.2
1985	113.7	116.4	119.2	108.2

* with average price as 100

4:3   MAJOR PRICE INDICES TAKING 1950 AS 100

	General retail price index	Index for for urban citizens' living costs in rural areas	Purchasing price index for agricultural and sideline products	Retail price index of industrial products
1951	112.2	112.5	119.6	110.2
1952	111.8	115.5	121.6	109.7
1957	121.3	126.6	146.2	112.1
1962	152.6	155.3	200.1	126.6
1965	134.6	139.0	187.9	118.4
1970	131.5	137.8	195.1	111.9
1975	131.9	139.5	208.7	109.6
1978	135.9	144.7	217.4	109.8
1979	138.6	147.4	265.5	109.9
1980	146.9	158.5	284.4	110.8
1981	150.4	162.5	301.2	111.9
1982	153.3	165.8	307.8	113.7
1983	155.6	169.1	321.3	114.8
1984	160.0	173.7	334.2	118.4
1985	174.1	194.4	362.9	214.2
1986	184.5	208.0	386.1	126.1
1987	198.0	226.3	432.4	132.2

5.   THE SYSTEM OF COMMODITY PRICE PARITY

The commodity price parity system refers to the price differential between one commodity and another at the same time and on the same market.

Important price parities include those between industrial and agricultural products, those between agricultural products and those between industrial products.

(1)   Price Parity between Industrial and Agricultural Products

Price parity between industrial and agricultural products is also recognised as price parity in the exchange of industrial and agricultural products. It refers to the gap between retail prices of industrial products and purchasing prices of agricultural products (the 'price-scissors').

(2)   Single Item Price Parity between Industrial and Agricultural Products

This refers to the ratio between the purchasing price of an agricultural product and the retail price of an industrial product at the same time and on the same market. This single item price parity between important industrial and agricultural products includes the price parity between the means of agricultural production and major agricultural products; price parity between industrial products that are made with agricultural products as raw materials and agricultural raw materials; and price parity between industrial daily necessities required by farmers and major agricultural products.

4:4 CHANGES IN THE PRICE PARITY OF MAJOR AGRICULTURAL AND INDUSTRIAL PRODUCTS

Agricultural products (100 kg)	Industrial products	1952	1957	1978	1985	1987
Wheat and rice	Salt (kg)	43	40	79	118	134
	Sugar (kg)	8	9	14	22	26
	Cloth (metre)	13	14	25	28	31
	Matches (100 boxes)	6	7	11	12	13
	Kerosene (kg)	9	12	32	47	55
Maize	Salt (kg)	38	39	66	99	121
	Sugar (kg)	6	7	12	18	23
	Cloth (metre)	10	12	21	24	28
	Matches (100 boxes)	5	6	9	10	12
	Kerosene (kg)	8	11	27	40	50
Soybean	Salt (kg)	63	61	141	221	273
	Sugar (kg)	9	10	26	41	52
	Cloth (metre)	13	18	45	53	64
	Matches (100 boxes)	6	8	20	23	27
	Kerosene (kg)	13	17	57	89	112
Rapeseed	Salt (kg)	64	93	189	318	326
	Sugar (kg)	13	21	35	58	62
	Cloth (metre)	19	35	61	76	76
	Matches (100 boxes)	10	18	28	33	32
	Kerosene (kg)	16	28	77	128	133
Sugar-cane	Salt (kg)	7	7	12	21	24
	Sugar (kg)	2	2	3	4	5
	Cloth (metre)	2	3	4	5	6
	Matches (100 boxes)	1	1	2	2	2
	Kerosene (kg)	2	2	5	8	10

CHANGES IN THE PRICE PARITY OF MAJOR AGRICULTURAL AND INDUSTRIAL PRODUCTS (cont'd)

Agricultural products (100 kg)	Industrial products	1952	1957	1978	1985	1987
Flue-cured tobacco	Salt (kg)	353	319	482	515	649
	Sugar (kg)	67	68	91	95	125
	Cloth (metre)	103	110	153	124	152
	Matches (100 boxes)	54	56	69	53	64
	Kerosene (kg)	70	89	192	208	265
Ginned cotton	Salt (kg)	638	545	796	1184	1173
	Sugar (kg)	117	112	147	217	225
	Cloth (metre)	185	189	258	284	274
	Matches (100 boxes)	93	99	116	123	116
	Kerosene (kg)	159	165	325	477	479
Silk cocoons	Salt (kg)	607	555	836	1237	1631
	Sugar (kg)	116	119	164	227	309
	Cloth (metre)	143	186	274	296	377
	Matches (100 boxes)	87	100	123	128	159
	Kerosene (kg)	104	161	341	498	658
Sheep wool	Salt (kg)	932	839	1133	1771	2147
	Sugar (kg)	203	122	183	325	412
	Cloth (metre)	571	215	361	425	502
	Matches (100 boxes)	82	112	161	183	212
	Kerosene (kg)	161	200	458	713	876
Fattened pigs	Salt (kg)	190	226	361	593	728
	Sugar (kg)	34	48	65	109	140
	Cloth (metre)	59	78	113	142	170
	Matches (100 boxes)	25	40	50	61	72
	Kerosene (kg)	43	67	144	239	297

Before 1984 the exchange price parity listed in the above table was counted according to the purchasing price of agricultural products and the retail price of industrial products listed. Since 1984 calculation has been based on average purchasing price of agricultural products and retail price of industrial products adopted by State-owned commercial departments.

(3) *Comprehensive Price Parity between Industrial and Agricultural Products*

This refers to the ratio between the general purchasing price index for agricultural products and the general retail price index for industrial products sold in rural areas.

(4) Price Parity between Different Agricultural Products

This refers to the differences in the prices of various agricultural products at the same time and on the same market, particularly purchasing price parity.

This price parity refers to price differences for products turned out by farming, forestry, animal husbandry, sideline occupations and fisheries. Farm produce covers grain, cotton, oil, hemp, silk, tea, sugar, tobacco, fruit, medicinal herbs and sundry goods, all having different prices.

Calculation of price parity of agricultural products is also divided into single-item and comprehensive price parities.

(5) Price of Industrial Products

This refers to parity between prices of different industrial products during the same period on the same market. It includes the parity of ex-factory prices and parity of sales prices of industrial products.

Ex-factory price parity is also divided into price parities for raw and semi-finished materials, fuels and processing of industrial products; price parities for different designs, specifications and series of the same types of products; price parities between new and old products; price parities between standardised and non-standardised products; price parities between products in large batches and single commodities in small batches; and price parities between machine-made and handicraft products.

Sales price parity of industrial products refers to price parity for products which can be substituted in terms of use value. It includes price parity for various types of energy; price parity for various kinds of textiles and knitwear made with different raw materials; price parity between soap and washing powder; price parity between imported goods and domestically made products; price parity between ordinary consumer goods and high-grade consumer goods; and price parity between whole machines and parts and components of durable consumer goods.

6. THE PRICE DIFFERENCE SYSTEM

Commodity price differences are when price gaps exist between the same kind of commodities that are sold in different circulation links, different places, different seasons, different specifications and quality, and in different amounts. They include:

(1) Purchase and Marketing Price Difference

This is the balance between purchasing and sale price of commercial units for the same kind of product at the same time and in the same producing area and market.

(2) Regional Price Difference

This denotes a price gap between the same kind of products at the same time and in different regions.

(3) Wholesale and retail price difference

This refers to the gap between wholesale and retail prices for the same kind of product on the same market at the same time.

(4)   Price Differences for Different Amounts of Goods Purchased or Sold

This is the price balance formed when the same sales enterprise sells the same kind of product in different sizes and batches at the same time.

(5)   Seasonal Price Difference

This refers to differences in purchasing or marketing price for the same kind of product in different seasons on the same market.

(6)   Price Differences Denoting Different Specifications and Quality

This refers to price balance between the same kind of products (i.e., same category of product) on the same market and at the same time due to different specifications and quality. It takes the form of different prices for differing quality, grades, design and colour and for new and old products.

IV.   THE CONTINUING PROGRAMME FOR PRICE REFORM

1.   *PRICE CONTROL AND MANAGEMENT*

Since the introduction of price reform several attempts have been made to make price control and management work more indirectly. Now a goal has been fixed for changes in the general index of retail prices and the various levels of government administration have been asked to adopt economic and administrative measures to control price hikes in the marketplace.

Price control measures have become more diversified and comprehensive and different places have invented new methods for indirect price control, such as the price-raising report system, the price adjustment fund, price compensation, etc. At the same time the State Price Information Centre has been established, price supervisory and checking organisations in various places have been strengthened and legislation concerning prices has been improved.

But the task of price reform still requires a great deal of work if it is to be accomplished. While problems in the old price system are yet to be solved, some new ones have cropped up in the process of reform.

The major problems are: continuing price irrationality in terms of price parity between important products; profit rate for some industries that is excessively high while profit rate is too low for other industries; the scope covered by the double-track pricing system for capital goods is too large and the gap between State-set prices and prices in the marketplace is unduly wide; the prices of major agricultural products and energy and charges for transport need to be appropriately increased in a planned manner; measures have to be found and improved for adjusting commodity prices upon which the control over commodity prices has been lifted. The most serious problems are excessive inflation and price hikes. The latter have caused wide-spread concern.

It is intended that in the period 1988-1990, attention will be focused on improving the economic environment and rectifying the economic order. Under the prerequisite of strictly controlling the general level of price hikes, it is intended that there will be a steady rationalisation of market prices and a gradual improvement in the mechanism for price formation and price control.

Reform of the price structure is a long-term task. The final target of price reform cannot be a short-term goal. The short-term goal should be rectification of the economic environment and consolidation of the market, while the long-term goal (i.e., the goal for the next five years), should be to have achieved basic rationalisation of commodity prices and to have tackled the most outstanding irrationalities in prices (i.e., those that seriously effect economic development and the growth of a market system).

2. MEASURES TO BE ADOPTED

In order to achieve the longer term pricing goal of achieving basic rationalisation of commodity prices, the following measures must be undertaken:

(1)   Relaxing Control Over Prices

Control over prices is to be relaxed in a planned way and gradually the role performed by the 'double-track pricing system' is to be reduced. Commodity price differences that currently exist under the 'double-track' system would then be narrowed. In the case of some commodities, the 'double-track' pricing system would be removed.

In the case of capital goods, where prices can easily be released, conditions are to be created whereby State-set prices can be abolished and market prices adopted. For capital goods that remain State-priced, the State-set prices are to be gradually adjusted to the point where they are close to market-set prices.

(2)   Raising the Price of Energy, Transport and Communications

The price of energy, transport and telecommunications, as well as other basic industries and public utilities, is to be raised. This action is intended to change the situation where prices for infrastructural and public utility facilities are relatively low.

(3)   Narrowing the 'Price Scissors' through Raising the Purchasing Price of Farm Staples

The present pricing of industrial and agricultural products better reflects the principle of exchange of equal values. But the 'price scissors' continues to exist. ('Price scissors' refers to the unreasonable price ratio between industrial and agricultural products that favours the industrial sector of the economy). Step by step the price of farm staples purchased by the State is to be raised. At the same time, the excessively high prices of agricultural products over which price control has been lifted are to be reduced.

4:5 CHANGES IN PRICE RATIOS BETWEEN INDUSTRIAL AND AGRICULTURAL PRODUCTS*

	Procurement price index of farm and sideline products	Retail price index of industrial products sold in rural areas	Overall parity indices of industrial and agricultural commodities
1952	101.7	99.5	97.8
1953	109.0	98.6	90.5
1954	103.2	101.9	98.7
1955	93.8	101.5	102.7
1956	103.0	99.0	96.1
1957	105.0	101.2	96.4
1958	102.2	99.4	97.3
1959	101.8	100.9	99.1
1960	103.5	102.8	99.3
1961	128.0	104.9	82.0
1962	99.4	104.5	105.1
1963	97.2	99.0	101.9
1964	97.5	98.1	100.6
1965	99.2	96.3	97.1
1966	104.2	97.1	93.2
1967	99.9	99.2	99.3
1968	99.8	99.7	99.9
1969	99.8	98.5	98.7
1970	100.1	99.8	99.7
1971	101.6	98.5	96.9
1972	101.4	99.5	98.1
1973	100.8	100.0	99.2
1974	100.8	100.0	99.2
1975	102.1	100.0	97.9
1976	100.5	100.1	99.6
1977	99.8	100.1	100.3
1978	103.9	100.0	96.2
1979	122.1	100.1	82.0
1980	107.1	100.8	94.1
1981	105.9	101.0	95.4
1982	102.2	101.6	99.4
1983	104.4	101.0	96.7
1984	104.0	103.1	99.1
1985	108.6	103.2	95.0
1986	106.4	103.2	97.0
1987	112.0	104.8	93.6

* The price of the previous year has been counted as 100.

According to available statistics, compared with 1952 the purchasing price of agricultural products rose by 122.3% in 1979, while the selling price of capital goods for agricultural production fell by 7.3%. With the introduction of price reform the 'price scissors' has gradually narrowed. In the past decade the purchasing price of farm products has risen 2.3 fold (the 2.5 fold rise for cereals being the highest).

Since the introduction of price reform, the price ratio between industrial and agricultural products has been cut by almost 50%. In other words, the same amount of agricultural product today can trade for almost twice the amount of industrial goods that it could trade for ten years ago. But closing the 'price scissors' must still remain an important aspect of continued price reform. The rise in the price of farm produce will drive up the price of foodstuffs and so to make sure that the real income of urban residents does not come down, measures will have to be taken to *gradually* narrow the 'scissors' within a given period of time. Meanwhile popularisation of agricultural science and technology should be used to promote rural reform through raising agricultural productivity and through reducing agricultural production cost.

(4)   *Reducing the Number of Old State-Priced Goods*

In terms of consumer goods prices, the number of State-priced goods will be gradually reduced and in terms of price formation, the market mechanism will be strengthened.

In order to give guidance to production and to consumption, different pricing policies will be adopted for consumer goods. A high-price and high-taxation policy will be applied to high-grade consumer goods. This is a policy that will aim to increase price parities between the high-grade consumer goods and commonplace consumer goods. For ordinary consumer-goods, price hikes will be brought under control and enterprises will be encouraged to sell more at a low rate of profit. The price of foodstuffs for urban consumption will be reformed in line with the principle of providing a reasonable diet structure for urban workers while gradually reducing current State food subsidies.

(5)   *Matching International Market Prices*

The domestic price of goods that are imported and exported in large quantities is to be altered to match international market prices.

V.   PRICE POLICY AND ADJUSTING THE OPERATION OF THE NATIONAL ECONOMY

1.   BASIC STABILITY AND MARKET PRICES

Basic stability of prices does not mean that the general price level and the price of special commodities will remain unchanged for a long time. What it does mean is that the general price level will not fluctuate violently. It means that the price of important commodities and labour services, which have a vital bearing on the national economy and on people's livelihood, will not be allowed to fluctuate violently just because the relations between supply and demand become strained in a given place or at a given time.

This is a policy that is to be recognised as being in the interests of the people and one that is conducive to economic development. If prices fluctuate up and down by wide margins, people will not feel secure, the social order will fall into confusion and orderly production and construction will be out of the question. Violent price fluctuations will also lead to speculation.

2.   THE INFLUENCE AND IMPACT OF INFLATION

Since 1985 China's general price level has risen rapidly. The general retail price index rose 8.8% nationwide in 1985 6% in 1986, and 7.3% in 1987 with an annual average of 7.4%. It is also estimated that the rate of inflation reached 17-18% in 1988.

In comparative terms the influence of inflation on the life of urban people is more serious than on rural people. This is clearly manifest in the following examples:
(1)   In the countryside the general retail price index is lower than in the cities and towns. For example in 1987 the general retail price index nationwide was 107.3, but for cities and towns it was 109.1. For the countryside it was 106.3.
(2)   The price index of living expenses is lower for farmers than for workers. Again using 1987 figures, the national general price index for living expenses was 107.3 (in 1986 it was 100), for workers it was 108.8 and for farmers it was 106.2.
(3)   The price index for consumer spending by workers and other employees in thirty two big and medium-sized cities was higher than the general price index of retail prices nationwide. For example the nationwide general index of retail prices from January to September 1988 (that in the same period of the previous year was taken as 100) was 109.5, 111.2, 111.6, 112.6, 114.7, 116.5, 119.3, 123.2 and 125.4 respectively, while the price index of consumer spending for workers in these cities stood at 112.2, 113.6, 114.6, 114.3, 116.5, 120.0, 123.7, 128.8 and 130.7.

The main reason for the different influences produced by inflation is that rural and urban areas have different consumption patterns. This means that consumption statistics that are collected are based on different commodities and labour services. For instance in the cities, vegetable price increases account for a large part of the rise in the general price index of consumer spending (especially as price control over vegetables has been lifted in most cities and towns). But when statistics are collected for calculating the price index in rural areas, vegetables are not included in farmers' consumption expenditure. Also the much sought after consumer goods that have been subject to very large price increases are far less popular in the countryside than in the cities.

3.   CAUSES OF INFLATION

In theoretical circles there are different views on the causes of inflation. The view most often subscribed to is the monetarist view that economic growth in the past few years has been overheated. Both investment in fixed assets and funds for consumption have increased significantly and the growth of capital construction and consumption has exceeded growth expectations. This situation has made it impossible for State finances to cope. The result has been an ever-increasing financial deficit and this has been a problem solved by overdrafts from the banks. This situation inevitably led to the excessive issue of currency.

At the same time the reform of the management of enterprises fell behind. This caused slow growth of labour productivity and poor economic returns which, coupled with the lack of resources, has resulted in a large gap between purchasing power and the supply of commodities. According to statistics, by the end of 1986 surplus purchasing power reached Rmb 420 billion. In 1987 the gap widened further. Under these conditions inflation is inevitable.

4. MEASURES TO TACKLE INFLATION

First, efforts are to be made to achieve a general balance between supply and demand. This is to be done by significantly raising economic returns, curtailing the scale of capital construction, drastically readjusting the structure of investment, and by firmly preventing an excessively rapid growth in consumption.

Second, strict methods are to be adopted in order to control currency issue and credits. The growth rate of money supply is to be kept within the economic growth rate.

Third, the pace of price reform is to be slowed appropriately. Factors that might fuel price increases are to be kept under control. There is to be a strengthened control of commodity prices and wilful price rises and unreasonable charges will be stopped.

5. PROTECTIVE PRICE POLICY

Protective price is a policy that is to be used to safeguard the interests of both producers and consumers. Divided into ceiling prices and floor prices, it is an indispensable means for State regulation and control of the market. It is argued that this type of regulation and control is necessary at the current stage of economic reform.

An example of protective price policy is when government departments establish a grain reserve regulating fund. These funds also have corresponding government regulatory organisations at central and provincial level. These organisations regularly study the ceiling and the floor prices acceptable to both producers and consumers. When the price is lower than the acceptable floor price, the State will make purchases using a protected price. These purchases protect the interests of the producers. And in the case of a price staying higher than the ceiling, the State will sell the product at ceiling price in order to protect the interests of consumers. It is intended that this form of price regulation will gradually expand through the wholesale market.

It is now argued that past economic reform price policy has overstressed ceiling prices of agricultural products while neglecting the floor prices of these products. As a result, even when products are in ample supply, panic purchasing at inflated prices has occurred or there has been a situation where no purchases at all have been made. It is this situation that has led some cities to establish price regulating funds that are intended to prevent either skyrocketing or plummeting prices.

6. USE OF PRICE SUBSIDIES

It is now argued that price subsidies are an important guarantee for the implementation of the protective price policy.

4:6 STATE SUBSIDIES FOR COMMODITY PRICES
Unit: Rmb 1 billion

	Total	Subsidies to offset differences between buying and selling price of goods used in daily life	Subsidies for purchase of means of agricultural production	Subsidies to offset losses incurred in selling imported grain, cotton, fertiliser, etc.
1978	93.9	55.6	23.9	14.4
1979	180.7	136.0	21.8	22.9
1980	242.1	178.6	20.4	43.1
1981	327.7	217.7	21.7	88.3
1982	318.4	240.2	21.4	56.8
1983	341.7	269.5	13.5	58.7
1984	370.0	320.9	8.2	41.0
1985	299.5	274.9	7.0	17.6
1986	257.5	243.9	6.2	13.3

Between 1979 and 1986 subsidies offered for stabilising people's living standards (people's real wage) made up 80.5% of total subsidies provided by the State. Most of this subsidy was used to subsidise the price of farm and sideline produce.

In the case of subsidies to agricultural and sideline production, the main portion has been used to subsidise the commodity price of cereals and oils. In order to promote farmers' incentive to grow grain and oil-bearing crops and in order to narrow the price difference between industrial and agricultural products, the State has found it necessary to repeatedly adjust the purchasing price of grain and oil while at the same time stabilising the selling price of grain. The result has been an inverted price difference between the purchase and selling price of cereals. The losses incurred have been drawn from the State treasury. In 1986, for every half kilogram of grain purchased by the State, a subsidy of Rmb 0.14 was paid.

At the present stage of China's economic development price subsidies cannot be completely abandoned. Price subsidies yield positive results in terms of ensuring the living standards of the people, political stability and the steady development of the economy. But there are also some negative aspects of price subsidisation. These are: upsetting price relations and so effecting the readjustment of the price system, placing a heavy burden on the State treasury, and producing new factors that may result in instability in commodity prices.

In the longer term the relations between price subsidies on one hand and financial expenditure and wage compensation on the other, must be correctly handled. No excessive reliance should be placed on the economic lever of price subsidies. In future the government will readjust the amount, form, variety and links of subsidies in an effort to promote advantages and to overcome disadvantages.

7. PRICING POLICY FOR NEW PRODUCTS

Prior to the introduction of economic reform, attempts were made to price according to product quality, but two main problems continued in relation to quality and price of product. These were; first, price difference based on quality was not widened resulting in good and poor quality products carrying the same price, and second, the method used for setting prices was irrational. The latter led to the price of all new products and products of new design and specifications being set according to the standard price used for both old and new products. This was a situation that failed to provide incentive for enterprise upgrading of products.

In an attempt to encourage new highly technical civil industrial products, the government now formulates a plan for trial production and has adopted a series of preferential policies to promote the manufacture of important new products. Policies that relate to prices are:

(1) New products in the category of means of production can be marketed on a trial basis by the producer for three years. New products in the category of civil consumer goods can be marketed on a trial basis for two years. During the period of this trial marketing the prices of these goods can be set by the producers without either State guidance or control.

(2) An extension to the trial marketing period may be granted after application has been made to and by the relevant administrative department that functions under the State Council and after approval by the State Price Administration, following assessment of overall economic balance by the State Planning Commission. Such approval would be relevant to important new products that involved difficult techniques and had comparatively long production lead times.

(3) After the trial marketing period has expired and in line with level-to-level price management, the department in charge, in accord with government stipulations, will make suggestions on price to be set. The price will then be formally set.

CHAPTER 5

Taxation Policy

After the establishment of New China, the Government Administration Council issued the Implementation Procedures Concerning the National Taxation Policy. These procedures stipulated that, except for agricultural (animal husbandry) tax, fourteen types of tax were to be levied. These were a commodity tax, an industrial and commercial tax (including business tax and resident and itinerant trader income tax), a salt tax, customs tariffs, income tax on salaries and remunerations, income tax on deposit interest, stamp duty, inheritance tax, trading tax, a slaughtering tax, house property tax, real estate tax, tax on some consumer items, i.e., luxury foods, recreation, cold drinks and hotels. And it was suggested that a licence tax should be levied on the use of vehicles and vessels.

The collection of income tax on salaries and other remuneration and an inheritance tax was not considered for implementation, but tax laws pertaining to all other taxes were published one after the other and tax collection was instituted.

I. THE TAXATION SYSTEM

1. THE TRANSFER FROM A DOUBLE TAX SYSTEM TO A SINGLE TAX SYSTEM

In the past it was mistakenly argued that after effecting national ownership of the means of production, there was no longer a need to use taxation as a regulatory instrument. It was also argued that multi-tax categories and multiple collection of taxes was too complicated and so must be simplified. This was the reason why the first taxation simplification programme was undertaken in 1958.

Simplification consisted of merging tax categories i.e., commodity circulating tax, merchandise tax, business tax and stamp-duty were merged into an industrial and commercial consolidated tax. At this time too, tax payment procedures were also simplified. Multi-tax collection was reduced to a double tax collection. Tax was to be collected once at the point of production and once at the point of commercial consumption.

In 1973 further taxation simplification was undertaken. This simplification programme was undertaken on the basis of 'merging four taxes into one'. The industrial and commercial consolidated tax and its surcharge, the urban house and real estate tax, the licence tax for vehicle and vessel use and the slaughtering tax were merged into one tax that was called the industrial and commercial tax. Then the number of taxed items was reduced and tax rate categories were further simplified. Tax items were reduced from 108 to 44 and tax rate categories were reduced from 141 to 82. Of these 82 tax rate categories, only 16 were actually different tax rates.

After the 1973 simplification of the taxation system, only one type of tax was to be collected at state-owned enterprise level—the industrial and commercial tax, while only two kinds of tax, the industrial and commercial tax and the industrial and commercial income tax, were to be collected from collective enterprises.

From 1973 to 1980, except for small local taxes (i.e., slaughtering tax, urban house and real estate tax, licence tax for vehicle and vessel use, animal trading tax, fair trade tax and the contract tax), there have only been five types of large taxes: the industrial and commercial tax, customs tariffs, salt tax, industrial and commercial income tax and agricultural (animal husbandry) tax.

2. REFORM OF THE TAXATION SYSTEM

Reform of the taxation system began in 1980. Taxation is to be seen as both a means of providing financial revenue for the State and as a means of regulating the economy. It should also be recognised as a system that can adapt to China's post reform open-door policy. It is a system well adapted to the requirements of China's planned commodity economy.

To date the 1980 programme for substantial reform of the taxation system has been only partially implemented. Reform that has been implemented is in two important areas. One is the area of recovering tax categories and establishing new tax categories and the other is the policy of substituting tax for enterprise repatriated profit. The main component of the latter substitution of tax for repatriated profit is the collection of income tax on State-owned enterprise profits and at the same time regulating the industrial and commercial tax collected from State-owned enterprises.

The Ministry of Finance issued an instruction titled Provisional Regulations Concerning the Collection of Income Tax from the State-Owned Enterprises on 29 April 1983. This regulation was implemented from 1 June of that year, completing the first step in substituting tax for enterprise repatriated profit. In September 1984 the State Council passed the Ministry of Finance's Report Concerning the Second Step to Carry Out Substituting Tax for Surrendered Profit in the State-Owned Enterprises. Six (draft) taxation regulations were then issued. They covered product tax, value-added tax, salt tax, business tax and resources tax and the Measures to Collect Regulating Tax on the State-Owned Enterprises. It was stipulated that the Measures to Collect Regulating Tax on the State-Owned Enterprises would be implemented almost immediately: from 1 October 1984.

In the period up to October 1988 five major tax categories (that included 34 different types of tax) were implemented. The five categories are exchange tax, returns tax, behaviour tax, property tax and objective tax.

The exchange tax category consists of a products tax, value-added tax, business tax, customs tariffs, salt tax, animal trade tax, fair trade tax and an industrial and commercial consolidated tax. The latter is a tax that is only applicable to Sino-foreign joint ventures, cooperatives and sole-foreign investment enterprises.

The returns tax category consists of income tax levied on State-owned enterprises, regulation tax levied on State-owned enterprises, income tax on collective enterprises, income tax on town and village self-employed industrial and commercial households, income tax on Sino-foreign joint venture enterprises, individual income tax, agricultural tax and a resources tax.

The behaviour tax category consists of a slaughtering tax, stamp duty, a feast (luxury) tax, contract tax, a land use tax, the vehicle and vessel use tax, and tax for possession and use of farmland. Property tax consists of such taxes as house property tax. Objective tax, consists of an urban construction maintenance tax, architectural tax, bonus tax levied on State-owned enterprises, bonus tax on collective enterprises, bonus tax on units engaged in entrepreneurial productive and service activities, wage regulation tax, individual income regulation tax, a special tax on burning oil, and an energy tax levied on major State construction projects.

In future, following the development of the reform of the financial management system, the new taxation system that is already taking shape will be further improved and reformed, with the present single track taxation system becoming a dual track system based on a division between central tax and local tax.

II. PRESENT TAXATION POLICY

The target of present taxation policy is to regulate macro-economic management, to promote the balanced development of the economy, to coordinate economic interests, to promote economic development, to promote the open-door policy, to promote fair social distribution, and to promote improved economic efficiency.

Under the present taxation system individual taxation is composed of three levels. The first level is to effect regulation of income through use of individual income tax. The second level is to regulate individual property accumulation through use of a house and a real estate tax and a soon-to-be implemented inheritance tax. The last and third taxation level is intended to regulate consumption through use of a luxury tax. The former two taxation levels are aimed at promotion of social fairness in the realm of income distribution and the latter tax is intended to guide social consumption and so promote fairness in terms of consumption.

The system of enterprise taxation consists of four levels. The first level is intended to regulate production and circulation through use of a products tax, value-added tax, business tax and customs tariffs. The second level is to be used to regulate enterprise returns through use of an enterprise income tax, agricultural (animal husbandry) tax and through use of a regulation tax on State-owned enterprises. The third level of taxation is to be used to regulate the distribution of enterprise profits through use of an enterprise bonus tax and a wage regulation tax. The fourth level is to regulate enterprise consumption through a special tax levy on burning oil and through a tax on land use.

Aside from the general regulatory function of taxation, the collection of differing types of taxes also has particular policy targets. In short, taxation is being used as an economic lever.

1. PRODUCTS TAX

Apart from regulating production and circulation, collection of the products tax specifically targets safeguarding financial revenues. It is intended to restrict enterprise focus on quantitative output value at the expense of production efficiency. This tax is then also intended to ameliorate inequality of benefits between enterprises that can result from unreasonable prices.

The products tax is included in the calculation of prices, in other words, it becomes a component part of product price. Consequently, under present economic conditions where price cannot be regulated smoothly, tax is a useful means for the amelioration of inequality of benefits between enterprises. But as reform of the Chinese economy continues and the pricing mechanism matures, this products tax will be replaced by a value added tax.

2. BUSINESS TAX

The collection of business tax is intended to dredge commodity circulation channels. It is also intended to develop the market and to effect the regulation of commercial business income, communications and transport income and income from the service trades.

3. RESOURCES TAX

There are two objectives in collecting a resources tax. One is to protect reasonable utilisation of State resources and the other is to regulate the great disparity in level of profits between enterprises. The latter is due to the wide gap in resources and conditions and in the level of resource utilisation.

4. STATE-OWNED ENTERPRISE INCOME TAX AND REGULATION TAX ON PROFITS OF STATE-OWNED ENTERPRISES

These two taxes operate simultaneously on the State-owned enterprise. Use of these two taxes is an attempt to use a part of profits earned by the enterprise to ensure necessary revenue for finance; to regulate the level of enterprise retained profits (in a bid to make the level of various enterprise retained profits remain similar); and to promote enterprise striving for increased profits.

It is intended that in future, two aspects of the present tax system will be replaced simultaneously. The dual tax regulation of enterprises will be replaced and the present proportional tax rate will be changed to a progressive income tax to be levied when income is in excess of specified amounts.

5. LAND USE TAX

This tax is collected in fixed amounts from units and individuals in return for use of State-owned lands. Tax is calculated in accord with area of land used. The object of this tax is to promote the reasonable and economic use of land.

6. ARCHITECTURAL TAX

This is a tax levied on construction investment activities that are funded from extra-budgetary enterprise funds and by various types of self-raised funds. The object of collecting this tax is to control the scale of capital construction, to prevent blind construction, and at the same time, to regulate funds available for construction in a bid to centralise extra-budgetary funds by directing these funds into the State budget. The centralisation of funds would serve to boost the State's key construction objectives.

7. STATE-OWNED ENTERPRISE BONUS TAX

This is a tax levied on bonuses granted to workers by State-owned enterprises. The tax is collected within a year of enterprises providing bonus payments in excess of centrally set quotas. Collection of this tax is intended to promote two policy targets. One is the restriction of excessive bonus payments; an objective that in turn, is intended to promote the control of consumption and the inflation of consumption funds. The second is regulation of enterprise bonus levels in order to restrict undue disparity between income levels.

8. INCOME TAX ON SINO-FOREIGN JOINT VENTURE ENTERPRISES AND INCOME TAX ON FOREIGN ENTERPRISES

The policy intention behind collecting these two taxes is the promotion of open-door policy, encouraging foreign investment, strengthening international economic and technological cooperation and the protection of State sovereignty. Foreign taxation laws and regulations are based on a light tax burden, lenient and preferential treatment and simplified administration for joint and foreign investment enterprises.

III. TAXATION MANAGEMENT

1. ORGANISATION OF TAX COLLECTION

In China there are three administrative systems in charge of taxation management. The first is responsible for the collection of agricultural tax and enterprise profit tax. The second is the customs system that is responsible for the collection of customs tariffs and the third is the General Administration of Taxation system. It is responsible for the collection of the various industrial and commercial taxes.

The General Administration of Taxation is the central authority. Taxation bureaus directly under its control have been established in provinces, autonomous regions and municipalities. Taxation offices staffed by specialists operate under these bureaus.

Management of taxation is based on a centralised and unified administrative system. Local authorities operate under a central authority. This means that local taxation offices are under the combined leadership of their local government at the first level and of the central government's taxation department at the second and upper level.

It is the upper level of administration that is organisationally dominant. The central taxation administration has control over the following: all powers related to changes in State taxation policy, the regulation and implementation of tax laws, the establishment and suspension of taxation categories, and the increase or reduction in the number of tax items and the adjustment of tax rates. With regard to all powers concerned with tax reduction or exemption, local tax departments have no right to act on their own. When the need for reduction or exemption arises it is presented to the Ministry of Finance for approval. Provincial governments and autonomous regions and municipalities directly under central authority can control tax reductions or exemptions only if their right in this instance is clearly and definitely stipulated by the State Council and the Ministry of Finance.

In order to implement the central consolidated tax law, specific taxation measures can be formulated by the provinces and autonomous regions and municipalities directly under central authority, but this specific measure must not be in conflict with the consolidated taxation law.

2. THE TAXATION REGISTRATION SYSTEM

All units and individuals engaging in industry and commerce should be listed on the taxation register. All tax-payers who have been approved by the industrial and commercial administrative departments to open businesses should apply and report to local taxation offices for registration. This must be done within thirty days from the time that they were granted a business licence.

Taxation registration consists of listing the tax-payer's name, address, form of business ownership, staff and lines of command, type of business, and other relevant matters. When applying for taxation registration, the tax-payer should include application for business registration and for relevant documents granting registration approval. A certificate of taxation registration will then be issued. This certificate is only for the use of the tax-payer. It is not transferable. Branches and subsidiary organisations that have a non-independent accounting system should also apply for registration with their local tax office within thirty days from the date of their founding, unless included in taxation registration by their respective head offices.

When there is a need to change taxation registration, such as the geographic transfer of a business, business reorganisation, the establishment of branches, merger, joint-operations, suspended business operations, close down, or bankruptcy, a declaration must be submitted to the responsible tax office for changed registration, re-registration or cancellation. This must be done within thirty days from the date of administrative approval of changed business conditions. When a tax-payer leaves China, all taxes due should be paid to the local taxation office seven days prior to departure. It is only then that exit registration procedures can be processed.

3. TAX DECLARATION

Tax declaration is a legal procedure performed by the tax-payer in order to determine tax rate. The tax-payer must prepare a tax declaration. This must accord with administrative stipulations and must be sent, together with financial and accounting reports and tables and relevant taxation materials, to the responsible taxation institution. The declaration should be in duplicate, one copy is to be kept by the tax-payer and the other is to be sent to the tax office. The responsible taxation institution has the power to fix the tax amount to be paid and the time limit for payment if a period of longer than thirty days (or in excess of fifteen days of the time limit for payment) is required.

4. THE FORM OF TAX COLLECTION

This process includes two aspects of taxation policy. One is the form and the other is the management of tax collection. The main forms of tax collection are: cheque account, collection from those assessed, collection of a fixed amount at a fixed time, and deduction of tax from consignment.

The management of tax collection consists of stipulating the different collection forms in accordance with the different situations of tax-payers.

5. TAX INSPECTION

The tax-payer and the agent collector are required to accept the supervision and inspection of the tax office and to provide relevant materials for inspection. Concealment and obstruction will not be tolerated. When undertaking a tax inspection, personnel should produce a certificate of tax inspection. Inspection is undertaken to prevent tax evasion and to ensure that tax payments and collection accord with the taxation decree.

6. TAXATION PENALTIES

A fine will be imposed on those violating tax laws and tax-paying procedures. The following measures can be adopted at the discretion of the responsible taxation office, for example, in the case of a tax-payer being in arrears with tax payment, formal written information can be solicited from the tax-payer's bank in order to deduct and pay tax from the tax-payer's funds to the treasury. Also the taxation registration certificate can be cancelled and the tax office can ask the industrial and commercial administrative department to cancel the tax-payer's business licence and so stop him legally transacting business. When the above measures are of no avail, then the taxation office can refer the matter to the People's Court.

7. TAXATION INVOICING

The taxation invoice system is an important means for the control of tax resources. Taxation invoices must be authorised by a taxation institute at county level and above. Except for special bills acknowledged by a relevant taxation institute, invoices must be printed with a seal that shows taxation institute responsibility at county level or above. Tax-payers or tax agents collecting taxes must only use these invoices in accord with taxation institute Regulations.

SECTION II

ECONOMIC LAW AND THE ADMINISTRATION OF INDUSTRY

CHAPTER 6

The Economic Legal System

I. ECONOMIC LEGISLATION

Economic laws and regulations are effective tools through which the State protects and improves the socialist relations of production, manages the national economy and promotes the development of the productive forces.

Economic legislation is the general term used to cover economic laws, administrative rules and regulations and local laws and regulations. These have been enacted by the State's legislative organ, the State's administrative institutions and local legislative bodies.

When economic reform was introduced in 1978, the subsequent reform and development of the national economy made it necessary to set in place legal forms based on the principle of guiding an increasing number of economic ties and activities. Past development of the Chinese legal structure had not been consistent. By 1953, when the First Five Year Plan was launched, the State had already promulgated the Law on Agrarian Reform, the Interim Regulations on Foreign Trade Management, Provisional Regulations on Budget and Final Accounts and other economic laws and regulations. With the introduction of the First Five Year Plan, the State formulated further laws and regulations: the Interim Regulations on Joint-State-Private Industrial Enterprises, Statutes on the Development of Agricultural Co-operatives, Statutes on the Development of Advanced Agricultural Co-operatives and others. From 1957, legislative work was some-what weakened until the early 1960s when, in the course of implementing the policy of readjustment, consolidation and raising standards for the national economy, economic legislative work was again promoted. At this time the State drew up Regulations on the Work of Rural People's Communes, Regulations on the Work of State-Owned Industrial Enterprises and other laws and regulations. However, the Cultural Revolution then effectively stopped any further economic legislative work.

Since 1978, in order to meet the needs of the planned commodity economy, the National People's Congress (NPC) and its Standing Committee have formulated the General Rules on Civil Law, the Law Governing Civil Procedures (for trial implementation), the Law Governing Economic Contracts, the Law on Technological Contracts, the Patent Law, the Trademark Law, the Law on State-Owned Industrial Enterprises, the Bankruptcy Law Concerning State-Owned Industrial Enterprises (for trial implementation) and other important civil laws in the economic field.

In order to implement the State policy of opening to the outside world, the NPC and its Standing Committee have also drawn up the Law on Joint Ventures Using Chinese and Foreign Investment, the Law on Sino-Foreign Co-operative Enterprises, the Law on Foreign Enterprises, the Income Tax Law on Joint Ventures, the Income Tax Law Concerning Foreign Enterprises, the Economic Law Concerning Overseas Interests, the Customs Law and other laws.

The NPC and its Standing Committee have also enacted such laws as the Law on Accounting, the Statistical Law, the Measuring Law and they have formulated laws for the protection of natural resources. These later laws are: the Law on Land Control, the Law on Mineral Resources, the Forestry Law, the Grassland Law, the Fisheries Industry Law, the Water Law and the Law on the Protection of Wild Animals. Laws aimed at protecting health have been the Law Governing Sanitary Production and Handling of Food (for trial implementation) and the Law on Medicine Management. Currently legislative bodies are formulating Maritime Law (in draft form) and the Law on the Prevention and Control of Air Pollution (in draft form).

As a means of managing the State's economic work, the State Council has formulated a large number of economic and administrative laws and regulations. These include: Certain Regulations on Granting Greater Decision-Making Powers to State-Owned Industrial Enterprises in Their Operation and Management, the Provisional Regulations on Promoting Economic Association, the Interim Provisions on Price Control, the Interim Regulations on Banking Management, the Provisions for Encouraging Foreign Investment, and Regulations for the Implementation of the Law on Joint Ventures Using Chinese and Foreign Investment.

In line with the Party Central Committee's decision on reform of the economic structure, the People's Congresses and their Standing Committees in provinces, autonomous regions and municipalities have enacted local laws and regulations. These laws and regulations have sought to promote technological development, the import of foreign capital and advanced technology, Sino-foreign joint ventures, urban management, control of rural fairs, environmental protection and price and land control. In addition, the people's governments of provinces, autonomous regions and municipalities and of various ministries and commissions under the State Council have also enacted a large number of economic rules and regulations.

Since 1979 the NPC and its Standing Committee have formulated more than thirty economic laws; the State Council, more than 300 administrative laws and regulations on the economy; and provincial, autonomous region and municipal People's Congresses and their Standing Committees, more than 400 local economic laws and regulations.

II. ECONOMIC LEGISLATIVE BODIES AND PROCEDURES

In China there is not much difference between economic regulatory bodies and the enactment of economic laws and regulatory bodies and the enactment of laws concerned with other matters.

China's economic laws are of three types:
- ... economic law,
- ... economic administrative laws and regulations, and

... local economic laws and regulations.

These laws are formulated respectively by the State's legislative bodies, administrative organisations and local legislative bodies.

1. ORGANISATIONS AND PROCEDURES FOR FORMULATING ECONOMIC LAWS

The National People's Congress (the NPC) is the supreme organ of State power. Its role is stipulated in the Constitution and it is the NPC that has the power to amend the Constitution and it is the NPC that has the power to enact and amend basic laws governing criminal offences and civil affairs. The Economic Contract Law, the Law on Joint Ventures Using Chinese and Foreign Investment, the Law on Foreign Enterprises, and the General Rules on Civil Law, were all enacted by the NPC.

The NPC Standing Committee is elected by the NPC. A session of this Committee is usually held once every other month. The Constitution stipulates that the NPC Standing Committee has the power to 'enact and amend laws with the exception of those which should be enacted by the NPC' and that it has the power to 'partially supplement and amend laws enacted by the NPC when the NPC is not in session'. The latter with the proviso that the basic principles of these laws is not contravened.

There are seven special committees of the NPC. These are the committees on nationality, law, finance and economics, education, science, culture and health, foreign affairs, overseas Chinese and internal affairs and a judicial committee. A law in draft form that has been submitted to the NPC, or to its Standing Committee, is to be subjected to examination and discussion by the law committee with other special committees putting their relevant opinions before the law committee.

Under the NPC Standing Committee there is a Legal System Working Committee. The tasks of this committee are to assist the NPC Standing Committee and the NPC's law committee to study and revise law drafts.

Procedure for enacting a law are divided into three stages, i.e.,

... putting forward legislative motions,

... examining, discussing and adopting motions, and

... promulgating laws.

Those entitled to submit law drafts to the NPC are:
    the Presidium of the NPC session,
    the NPC Standing Committee,
    the State Council,
    the Central Military Commission,
    the Supreme People's Court,
    the Supreme People's Procuratorate,
    the various special committees of the NPC, and
    a NPC delegation or group of more than 30 deputies.

The procedure for examination and discussion of a law in draft form are: submission of a draft law to the NPC Standing Committee for examination and discussion and then referral to the NPC for examination and approval.

When the NPC is examining and discussing a draft law the plenary session and delegation meeting are conducted alternately. At the plenary session the sponsor of the draft law explains the draft and then discussion of the draft is conducted by various delegations and the law committee then discusses and revises the draft law on the basis of opinions advanced. A report on the results of the discussion and a revised draft are then submitted to the presidium of the NPC Session.

After the report and the revised draft have been examined and discussed by the presidium, the law committee decides whether they should put the draft law to the vote at the plenary session. If the draft law is passed with more than half affirmative votes from all NPC deputies, the law is enacted and adopted by the NPC. It is promulgated by the President of the State in the form of an 'Order of the President of the People's Republic of China'.

2. ORGANISATIONS AND PROCEDURES FOR ENACTING ECONOMIC AND ADMINISTRATIVE REGULATIONS

'Administrative regulations' is the general term used for the rules and regulations formulated by the State Council. It is the State Council that governs the State's administrative work. Its rules and regulations are second only to the Constitution and to NPC enacted laws. Its rules and regulations take priority over local laws and regulations. It is the State Council that has been empowered by the Constitution to enact administrative regulations.

It is the legal institutional bureau established under the State Council that assumes full responsibility for the State Council's legal and administrative work and it is the ministries and commissions directly under the State Council through their law and regulation bureaus or divisions who are responsible for the legal work of their relevant departments. The State Council's legal institutional bureau is then responsible for organising, co-ordinating and guiding the legal work of the ministries and commissions.

The procedures for the State Council to enact and promulgate administrative regulations are as follows:

(1) To present a draft of administrative regulations to the State Council. The Council draws up a five-year plan for guiding the formulation of draft administrative regulations.

(2) To examine the draft of administrative regulations. Drafts sent to the State Council (excluding those directly drafted by the legal institutional bureau) are examined by the legal institutional bureau. This examination determines whether drafts accord with the requirements for formulating administrative regulations. An examination report is then written and sent to the higher authorities together with the draft administrative regulation.

(3) Examination and approval of the draft administrative regulation. The proposed administrative regulation, examined and/or revised by the legal institutional bureau is, depending on the degree of its importance, referred to the State Council or to the State Council Standing Committee for discussion and for a decision on whether or not it will be adopted.

(4) Promulgation of the administrative regulation. There are two methods for the promulgation of administrative regulations, i.e., promulgation by the State Council or, with approval of State Council, promulgation by the State Council department in charge. The former is signed by the Premier and the latter by the head of the department in charge.

3. ORGANISATIONS AND PROCEDURES FOR THE ENACTMENT OF LOCAL ECONOMIC LAWS AND REGULATIONS

China's local legislative bodies are the provincial, autonomous region and municipal People's Congresses and their Standing Committees.

In accord with the provisions of the Constitution and with the Organic Law of the Local People's Congresses and People's Governments at different levels, the People's Congresses and their Standing Committees may enact and promulgate local laws and regulations. They are empowered to do this on the premise that these local laws and regulations do not contravene the Constitution, the law or administrative regulations. Also, for recording purposes, they are obliged to report their local laws and regulations to the NPC Standing Committee.

The enactment of local laws and regulations requires three stages:

... putting forward a motion,
... examining, discussing and adopting the motion, and
... promulgating local laws and regulations.

In order to gradually standardise and institutionalise the work of formulating local laws and regulations, the Standing Committees of the People's Congresses have each adopted the above procedures when enacting laws and regulations and they have also set out specific stipulations with regard to the scope of these laws and regulations, the drawing up of the draft laws and regulations, and the examination, discussion, adoption, promulgation and abolition of their laws and regulations.

Local laws and regulations are legally binding within the administrative regions that they concern. When the State promulgates a new law and a new administrative regulation, the People's Congresses and their Standing Committees are encouraged to check their local laws and regulations to ensure that they do not contravene State law and administrative regulation. If local laws do contravene State law or State regulations they must be either abolished or revised.

Apart from the above legislative conditions, China's Constitution and the Organic Law of Local People's Congresses and People's Governments at Various Levels, stipulates that, with the approval of State Council, People's Congresses and their Standing Committees in cities where provincial and autonomous region People's Governments are seated and in larger cities, have the power to formulate local laws and regulations; the People's Governments of these cities have the right to formulate administrative rules and regulations; and the ministries and commissions under the State Council also have this right. But the effective province of these laws and regulations and rules and regulations has not always been explicit. It was not until July 1988 that the Supreme People's Court formally decided that these laws and regulations and rules and regulations can be taken as the basis for the trial of cases. This was done on the premise that they do not conflict with State law and the laws and regulations of higher authorities.

III. THE ECONOMIC JUDICATURE

1. THE JUDICATURE

Economic 'cases' are tried in accord with legal procedure by State judicial organisations, the People's procuratorates and the People's courts.

Economic cases include economic criminal cases and economic disputes. The prosecution of economic cases by the State's judicial bodies cracks down on criminal economic activities and solves economic disputes between legal entities or between a legal entity and a citizen. It adjusts social economic relations, maintains economic order and guarantees the smooth development of socialist economic construction.

Shortly after liberation an economic judicial system was established. The Interim Organic Regulations of the People's Court and the Provisional Organic Regulation of the People's Procuratorates (promulgated in September 1951), as well as the Organic Law of the People's Court and the Organic Law of the People's Procuratorates (promulgated in September 1954), all contained stipulations with regard to economic matters. But in the period from liberation to the introduction of economic reform, due attention was not paid to the establishment of the socialist legal system.

After 1978 with the focus on economic construction, law was regarded as an important means for effecting economic adjustment. The new Organic Law of the People's Courts and the Organic Law of the People's Procuratorates were adopted at the Second Session of the Fifth NPC held in July 1979.

The Organic Law of the People's Courts stipulates that economic judicial courts be established in the Supreme People's Court, that the higher People's Court and the intermediate People's Courts in provinces, municipalities and in cities under the jurisdiction of municipalities and provinces hear cases of economic dispute between socialist economic organisations, foreign-related economic disputes and three types of criminal economic cases i.e., smuggling, speculation and graft. In early 1982 (at the Second Session of the Fifth NPC Standing Committee held in March 1982) the Law Governing Criminal Procedures was adopted and the Supreme People's Court placed the responsibility for the trial of the above three criminal economic charges on the criminal judicial court. The Law Governing Civil Procedures (trial implementation) was also adopted, in principle, by the Second Session of the Fifth NPC Standing Committee.

In 1983 the NPC Standing Committee revised the Organic Law of the People's Courts and expanded the scope of the economic judicial court to cover over 2,000 grass-roots courts.

At the Eighth Session of the Sixth NPC Standing Committee, held in November 1984, it was decided that maritime courts would be established in some port cities. The cities concerned would be those responsible for handling domestic and foreign-related marine and maritime cases.

Since the 1983 establishment of courts at various levels, the number of economic disputes handled has doubled and redoubled. In 1983 courts at various levels handled more than 44,000 cases. In 1984 the figure jumped to more than 85,700 (almost double the 1983 figure) and by 1985 the figure had reached over 226,500 cases (a 60% increase over the previous year). In 1986 the courts handled 78,133 economic criminal cases and 322,000 economic disputes.

China's economic judicial work is recognised as having played a positive role in guaranteeing the smooth development of economic reform.

2. ECONOMIC JUDICIAL ORGANISATIONS AND PROCEDURES

(1) The Chinese People's Courts

The organisational system of the Chinese People's Courts is based on:
- The Supreme People's Court,
- Local People's Courts at various levels, and
- Special People's Courts.

The Supreme People's Court is the highest judicial organ of the People's Republic of China. The Local People's Courts at various levels include:
- Higher People's Courts established in provinces, autonomous regions and municipalities;
- Intermediate People's Courts established in municipalities and in cities under the jurisdiction of provinces and autonomous prefectures;
- Grass-roots People's Courts established in counties, autonomous counties and districts under the jurisdiction of cities; and
- Special People's Courts established in designated regions, including military tribunals, maritime courts, forestry courts and railway transport courts.

The People's Courts are a State judicial organ. They consist of criminal, civil, economic and administrative judicial courts. The Criminal Judicial Court is responsible for the trial of criminal cases, including economic crimes. The Economic Judicial Court is responsible for handling economic disputes.

Cases handled by the Economic Judicial Court include:
- disputes over economic contracts; economic disputes concerning overseas interests and interests based in Hong Kong and Macao;
- cases concerned with rural contract transactions;
- disputes between legal entities or between a legal entity and an individual or individuals (the latter recognised as legal entities) over compensation for loss or damage caused by infringement of rights in the areas of production and distribution; and
- other economic disputes between legal entities or between legal entities and individuals where a case, as stipulated in the law or regulations, can be filed with the People's Courts.

The Civil Court handles civil disputes between citizens over marriage, inheritance, debts and infringements of rights.

The Administrative Judicial Court is responsible for handling cases in which the litigant refuses to comply with an administrative disciplinary decision that has been taken by an administrative organ and the administrative organ has then filed a suit with the People's Court.

The establishment of Administrative Judicial Courts began in 1986. By June 1988 these courts had been established in almost half of the nation's People's Courts and by September 1988 the Administrative Judicial Court had been established in the Supreme People's Court. Prior to this, administrative lawsuits of an economic nature had been handled by the Economic Judicial Court of the People's Court.

(2) The People's Procuratorates

The People's Procuratorates consist of :
- ... The Supreme People's Procuratorate,
- ... Local People's Procuratorates at various levels, and
- ... Special People's Procuratorates.

Local People's Procuratorates then also consist of three levels:
- ... People's Procuratorates of provinces, autonomous regions and municipalities,
- ... People's Procuratorates of autonomous prefectures and of cities under the jurisdiction of a province, and
- ... People's Procuratorates of counties, autonomous counties and city districts.

The People's Procuratorate is a legal supervisory body of the State. With the exception of cases of statutory private prosecution, the People's Procuratorates are responsible for the work of prosecuting criminal cases. They have the right to investigate economic criminal cases including those of graft, bribery, evasion of and refusal to pay taxes. Economic procuratorial departments, divisions and sections which handle economic criminal cases are established in procuratorates and see themselves as being responsible for putting economic criminal cases on record for the purpose of public prosecution.

(3) Economic Judicial Procedures

The proceedings against economic crimes should be conducted according to the Law Governing Criminal Procedures. After the People's Procuratorates have begun proceedings, the criminal judicial court of the People's Courts should form a collegiate bench and send a duplicate copy of the indictment to the defendant. This is to be done seven months prior to the opening of a court session. The defendant then has the right to defend himself, either by himself or by using someone he trusts with a defence on his behalf.

With the exception of criminal cases involving State secrets, personal privacy and minors, in the first instance cases should be tried openly. Within ten months after a legal decision has been made by the People's Courts, the defendant may lodge an appeal, but if the defendant has refused to accept the court's decision, the People's Procuratorates have the right to refuse the appeal. Cases regarding appeal or refusal of appeal should be referred to the higher level People's Courts for a second hearing. The court of the second hearing shall not increase the defendant's punishment because of his appeal.

The procedures for economic disputes come under the Law Governing Civil Proceedings (for trial implementation). Parties involved in these lawsuits have equal rights and they have the right to debate controversial questions. The Economic Judicial Court of the People's Court stresses mediation when handling economic disputes. On the basis of finding out the truth and distinguishing right from wrong, it urges the parties involved to reach a mutual understanding. If the mediation is successful, the court then works out a mediation document and sends it to the litigant. The document then becomes legally effective and the parties involved are not at liberty to go back on their agreement. In a situation where mediation has failed, a timely judgement is made. If the litigant refuses to accept the Court's judgement, within 15 days after the judgement the litigant may lodge an appeal. The second hearing is to be conducted by a higher level People's Court.

For economic disputes involving overseas interests, the first hearing should be handled by the Intermediate People's Court. A foreign party who needs a lawyer to provide legal assistance in a suit in a Chinese law court can only engage a Chinese lawyer. The lawsuit procedures for economic cases concerning overseas interests, aside from some special stipulations, are basically the same as those for domestic economic disputes.

China has introduced a system of second hearing and final hearing procedures. Verdicts made after the second court hearing (and those made by the Supreme People's Court) have legal force. According to the Provisions of China's Criminal Law and the Provisions of the Civil Law (for trial implementation), the litigant of economic disputes and offenders involved in economic criminal cases, may appeal against the legal decision already in force and may request that the People's Court re-examine the case. However, we should not cease implementing the legal decision during the period of the appeal.

IV.   THE LAWYER SYSTEM

The use of lawyers was first instituted in China in the mid 1950s. In 1954 when the first Constitution was promulgated together with the Organic Law of the People's Courts, it was clearly stipulated that the accused has the right to a defence. It was in accordance with this stipulation that the Ministry of Justice began to establish a system of lawyers on a trial basis in cities such as Beijing, Shanghai and Tianjin. This system of using lawyers was subsequently officially adopted in July 1956 when the State Council approved a report to that effect from the Ministry of Justice.

By 1957, 817 legal advisory offices or lawyers' offices staffed with more than 2,800 lawyers had been established. But in the second half of 1957, magnification of the anti-rightist struggle which had launched a fierce onslaught on the ranks of lawyers, resulted in a general lack of a correct understanding of the role of lawyers in defending the accused. Much criticism was piled on the work of lawyers and consequently the newly established lawyer system came to a premature end.

In the late 1970s China began to re-establish a system of lawyers. The Law Governing Criminal Procedures and the Organic Law of the People's Courts that had been promulgated by the Chinese legislature in 1979, together with the 1982 Law Governing Civil Procedures (for trial implementation), justified the use of lawyers and the system of attorney on behalf of the accused.

The Provisional Regulations of the People's Republic of China Concerning Lawyers (passed at the 15th session of the Standing Committee of the 5th National People's Congress held in August 1980—becoming effective 1 January, 1982) specified lawyers' tasks, principles governing their activities, qualifications and organisational structure.

In September 1979 the Standing Committee of the 5th NPC passed a motion to restore the Ministry of Justice. As noted previously in this chapter, this re-establishment of the Ministry was then followed by the establishment of judicial departments (bureaus) within local governments. It is under the leadership of these judicial organs that the work of lawyers has developed. Statistics show that by July 1987 there were more than 3,100 legal advisory offices manned by more than 20,000 lawyers. The Ministry of Justice now predicts that the number of lawyers will top 100,000 by the end of the century.

Since 1979 lawyers have acted on laws, offered legal services and defended the legitimate rights and interests of the accused. Even so, generally speaking, China's system of lawyers is still in its infancy, with many practical problems still to be solved.

1. LAWYERS' QUALIFICATIONS

Lawyers are required to carry out their work in accord with the law and they are protected by the law. No organisation or individual is permitted to interfere with a lawyer's work. When involved in a lawsuit, lawyers have the right to consult case materials and they have the right to investigate relevant organisations and individuals. When defending criminal cases, lawyers can meet and correspond with the accused while he is under detention. When lawyers touch on matters of State secrecy and personal privacy in their professional activities, they are charged with the responsibility of respecting secrecy.

Chinese lawyers can be divided into three categories:

- ... full-time lawyers,
- ... part-time lawyers, and
- ... guest lawyers.

These divisions vary according to the organisations that the lawyers work for.

Full-time lawyers are the main force among Chinese lawyers. They are the State's specialised legal workers. They belong to the State's judicial organs. Part-time lawyers are lawyers who are employees of government departments, enterprises and public undertakings and are invited by legal advisory offices to work as part-time lawyers with the consent of their employing units. Part-time lawyers should work no fewer than 60 working days a year on legal affairs. Guest lawyers are lawyers who have retired from their legal jobs and are then invited by legal advisory offices to work as lawyers. Part-time and guest lawyers have the same duties as full-time lawyers.

All three types of lawyers must acquire the same qualifications. Before 1985 all those who had received legal education and training and then worked for legal advisory offices for one year qualified as lawyers. In 1985 qualification by examination was instituted. This meant that Chinese citizens who have the right to elect and the right to be elected, and who have received higher education, can apply to take the examination for qualification as a judicial sponsored lawyer. Those who subsequently pass this examination will be qualified once they have received approval from the judicial departments (bureaus) of provinces, autonomous regions and centrally administered municipalities.

2. MANAGEMENT OF LAWYERS' WORK

The legal advisory offices where lawyers work are under the leadership and supervision of the judicial organs of the places where they are located. These offices have established the director responsibility system. According to the Provisional Regulations Concerning Lawyers, the director of a legal advisory office should be elected by all the office's lawyers and approved by the judicial organs of the province, autonomous region or municipality. As things stand now, however, most directors of legal advisory offices are appointed by judicial organs.

To date the lawyer system in China has effectively been a State 'monopoly' system. The problem with this system is that it lacks competition and lawyers working under the system get equal pay whether they work hard or not. The result has been that lawyers' enthusiasm has been dampened and parties to a case have lacked confidence in lawyers. In addition, this system has been restricted by financial allocations and by a limited number of available lawyers. The Ministry of Justice adopted the method of using part-time and guest lawyers in an attempt to address this latter problem.

From early 1988 the Ministry of Justice has set out to reform the State 'monopoly' lawyer system. While recognising the continued need for State control over the work of lawyers, the Ministry introduced a new system of State-paid lawyers, lawyers working in co-operation and private lawyers. Of these, co-operative lawyers are intended to be the main group. Co-operative lawyers work in a legal advisory office composed of no fewer than three lawyers. These lawyers come together on a voluntary basis and they choose their director by election. They are paid on the basis of their economic returns.

Private lawyers and lawyers of the co-operative legal advisory offices are not included in the staff of the State judicial administrative organs and they do not receive financial allocations from the State. They are responsible for their own profit and loss. Co-operative legal advisory offices have begun to be established and in future private legal advisory offices will be allowed to operate.

In line with the new lawyer system, use of part-time and guest lawyers will be gradually phased out and the majority of full-time lawyers will become co-operative or private lawyers. Indeed the Ministry of Justice is now beginning to curb the role of part-time and guest lawyers. In future the only citizens legally eligible to be lawyers will be those who have acquired lawyers' qualifications, those who work in the State's judicial administration as lawyers and those who work for co-operative legal advisory offices or who are awarded qualifications to open a private legal advisory office.

3. LAWYERS' WORK

The Provisional Regulations of the People's Republic of China Concerning Lawyers stipulate that the task of lawyers is to offer legal help to government offices, enterprises, public undertakings, social organisations and individuals. A lawyer must guarantee the correct implementation of laws, protect the interest of the State and the collective, and the legitimate rights and interests of citizens and must act on the basis of facts.

In practice a lawyer's work usually consists of the following:

(1) Being engaged by the parties to a case and acting on their behalf. When engaged, the lawyer's responsibility is to defend the party's legitimate rights and interests. The lawyer's action in litigation and in other legal proceedings is as legally effective as that of the engaging party.

A lawyer may choose whether or not to conduct litigation on behalf of an engaging party. A lawyer who litigates on behalf of a party is referred to as the agent *ad litem* while a lawyer who is engaged to participate in all matters without going through legal proceedings (such as mediation, arbitration, the handling of credit and trust, transfer, compensation, trade and commercial registration) is called an agent without litigation.

(2) Offering legal consultancy services and preparing documents on behalf of an engaging party. Offering legal consultancy services means that a lawyer explains and interprets questions about legal affairs and offers suggestions and solutions. Preparing documents on behalf of a party means that, on the basis of facts and laws, a lawyer prepares legal documents in the name of a party for expression of that party's legitimate intent.

(3) Working as a legal adviser at the invitation of legal entities, citizens and social organisations. As a legal adviser a lawyer has responsibility for offering legal opinions on the affairs of the party seeking representation, drawing up and examining legal documents, and participating in litigation, mediation and arbitration activities on behalf of the engaging party.

Lawyers are usually invited as legal advisers on a yearly basis. Once a lawyer finished his work for a particular party, his formal relations with this party come to a close. As a legal adviser a lawyer usually establishes long-term stable ties with a party and so can offer timely and comprehensive legal assistance to that party.

(4) Being engaged by an accused, or appointed by the People's Court, to act as the defender of the accused.

As a criminal defender a lawyer's responsibility is to protect the legitimate rights and interests of the accused on the basis of facts and laws. In criminal lawsuits the lawyer is independent and not influenced by the opinions of the accused. And if they do not think the accused has given a true picture of the case, lawyers have the right to refuse to act as the defender of the accused.

Since legal problems concerning lawyers are different in nature, lawyers are usually divided into three categories—criminal, civil and economic. In the period after the lawyer system had been restored, most lawyers handled cases of all descriptions. Now, as their role has increased, there appears to be a trend toward specialisation. Accordingly, many legal advisory offices have divided their lawyers into groups responsible for one of the three categories of cases.

In some big cities lawyers have broken away from comprehensive legal advisory offices to establish civil lawyers' offices, economic lawyers' offices and foreign affairs lawyers' offices. To date the State judicial administration has not developed any official regulations concerning lawyer specialisation.

Those who engage lawyers to act as their agents, defenders, or legal advisers should sign contracts with the legal advisory office or with the private legal advisory office. Lawyers are not allowed to conduct legal activities and receive fees as private individuals. When lawyers offer legal consultancy services or prepare legal documents, it is usually not necessary for contracts to be signed. Most legal advisory offices rotate their lawyers in order to be in a position to offer services at any time.

Lawyers' services should be paid for. Fees are usually relatively low for activities such as offering legal consultancy services and preparing legal documents, but they are relatively high for services such as defence in a criminal case. In economic and civil cases, apart from attorney fees, the legal advisory office usually requires the winning party to pay a certain percentage of the sum involved in the case to the office. Usually fees are determined by the economic circumstances of the parties and by the amount of work undertaken.

V. ECONOMIC ARBITRATION

Arbitration is a method used for solving disputes. After the 1983 establishment of economic judicial courts, numerous economic disputes were resolved through judicial means. Now, while strengthening economic judicial work and while paying attention to the work of lawyers, the State is also paying attention to improving the economic arbitration system.

The Regulations on the Arbitration of Disputes Over Economic Contracts, promulgated by the State Council in August 1983, is a document that sets out explicit provisions for the composition, function, power and working procedures of the arbitration organisation. The Regulations on the Arbitration of Disputes Over Economic Contracts stipulates that domestic organs of arbitration should be established within the State Administration for Industry and Commerce and within local administrations for Industry and Commerce. It is these organs of arbitration that are to handle cases of dispute over economic contracts between Chinese legal entities or between Chinese legal entities and individual citizens. Their jurisdiction over a case is to be determined by the location of the case, the amount involved in the case, and the impact of the case on society.

It is usual for cases of dispute over economic contracts to be handled by an organ of arbitration in the place where the contracts were signed or implemented or in places where the accused is resident. Cases involving an amount of less than Rmb 500,000 are handled by arbitration organs in counties (or cities) and in city districts. Disputes that involve an amount of more than Rmb 500,000 are to be handled by an organ of arbitration at prefecture level (or at the level of autonomous region or city directly under the administration of a province), provincial (or autonomous region or municipal level when the municipality is directly under the administration of the central government), or by the Arbitration Commission of the State Administration for Industry and Commerce.

At all levels Economic Contract Arbitration Commissions are to be composed of one chairman, one (or possibly two) vice-chairmen, plus a number of members and arbitrators. When handling cases arbitration organs are to form arbitration tribunals each composed of three arbitrators and with the chief arbitrator appointed by an Arbitration Commission. The Arbitration Tribunal is to follow the principle of the minority being subordinate to the majority and its judgements are to accord with the State's laws, administrative regulations and policies. Difficult cases can be submitted to an Arbitration Commission for discussion and decision with the subsequent Arbitration Commission decision being executed by the Tribunal.

In terms of arbitration procedure, the litigant shall file an application and its duplicate copies. If, after examination, the organ of arbitration accepts the case, it will deliver a duplicate of the application to the accused within five days after receipt of the application. The accused shall, within 15 days of receipt of the duplicate of the application, present a letter of reply.

When handling a case the organ of arbitration will first mediate. When an agreement has been reached through mediation, a letter of mediation is written by the Arbitration Tribunal and when this mediation letter has been delivered, disputing parties must automatically observe it. If no agreement has been able to be reached through mediation, the Arbitration Tribunal conducts arbitration. This is the arbitration award. If one of the disputing parties (or indeed both parties) refuse to accept the arbitration award, within 15 days from receipt of the arbitration award, they can bring the case before the People's Court. If no action has been taken within the prescribed time limit, the arbitration award becomes legally binding. If one party involved in the dispute refuses to implement the arbitration award, the other party may apply to the People's Court for enforcement of the arbitration award. One year is allowed for disputing parties to apply for arbitration and organs of arbitration will not accept a case in which one disputing party has applied for arbitration while the other has brought the contested matter before the People's Court.

The Chinese court will not accept cases of foreign economic and trade and maritime dispute if the disputing parties have already had agreement based on arbitration.

When making an application for arbitration the names and addresses of the disputing parties, the history of the case, claims and evidence of the case, must all be submitted to the Arbitration Commission.

As noted earlier in this chapter, cases are heard by an arbitration tribunal composed of three members. Two of the members are respectively chosen by the two parties in the dispute or they are authorised by the chairman of the Arbitration Commission. The third member of the Arbitration Tribunal is chosen by the chairman of the Arbitration Commission to act as presiding arbitrator. All the members of the Tribunal are chosen from among members of the Arbitration Commission.

As an alternative arrangement to the above Tribunal, disputing parties can jointly choose or authorise the chairman of the Arbitration Commission to appoint for them a sole arbitrator from among members of the Commission. Arbitrators are to hear cases in open session, but they may, upon the request of both or either of the parties, decide to hold hearings in closed session or arbitrate on the basis of written documents alone.

Usually the Arbitration Tribunal hears cases in closed session. But if the disputing parties ask for hearings to be conducted in open session, the Arbitration Tribunal decides whether a session will be open or closed.

Disputing parties may appoint Chinese citizens or foreign citizens as their attorneys who, with authorisation, may appear in the Arbitration Tribunal on behalf of the disputing parties.

The arbitration award is to be made within 45 days from the date of the reading of the conclusion of the hearings. The award of a three-member Arbitration Tribunal is decided by majority vote. The minority opinion can be noted in the case file. The ruling is final and legally binding.

In recent years economic contract arbitration organs have handled a large number of disputes involving economic contracts. Statistics show that in three years, from 1984-1986, there were over 66,000 cases. Approximately 58,000 of these were solved through mediation. The remaining 7,900 cases were settled through arbitration. The settlement of these disputes is recognised as having effectively protected the legitimate rights and interests of disputing parties and to have maintained socio-economic order.

VI. FOREIGN-RELATED ARBITRATION

In 1987 China joined the United Nation's 1958 Convention for Recognizing and Implementing Foreign Arbitration Awards. Most countries in the world are members of this convention. It means that if one party refuses to implement an award passed in China, the other party may apply to the Chinese court for enforcement of the award.

China's foreign arbitration organs arbitrate cases on the basis of Chinese laws. They adhere to the principle of 'maintaining independence and keeping the initiative in one's own hands, upholding equality and mutual benefit and acting with reference to international practice'.

The main characteristic of China's foreign arbitration work is the combination of arbitration and mediation. The greatest possible effort is made to settle disputes through mediation. In recent years China's two arbitration commissions concerned with foreign disputes—the China International Trade Arbitration Commission and the China Maritime Arbitration Commission—have settled cases of dispute in combination with foreign arbitration organs using 'joint mediation'. For example, when a dispute arises between a Chinese party and a foreign party, the two disputing parties apply for mediation in their respective countries. Then the two country's organs for arbitration each send an equal number of arbitrators to mediate between the two disputing parties.

In 1978 China's Maritime Arbitration Commission reached a protocol agreement with its Japanese counterpart. This agreement is for settling Sino-Japanese maritime disputes. The agreement stipulates that when it is difficult to decide which of the two countries' maritime arbitration commissions should settle a Sino-Japanese maritime dispute, the case must be handled jointly by the maritime arbitration organs of the two countries.

In March 1980 the State Council decided to rename the Foreign Trade Arbitration Commission the Foreign Economic and Trade Arbitration Commission. At this time too, the Commission's terms of reference were expanded to include disputes arising in relation to Sino-foreign joint ventures, co-operative management, co-operative production, co-operative development, technology transfer, financial loans, foreign investment in China, and leasing arrangements. The Commission is also authorised to handle disputes arising in the course of foreign trade agreements, trade on commission basis and disputes arising in the course of transportation, insurance and maintenance.

In 1982 the Maritime Arbitration Commission also had its terms of reference expanded. Since 1959 the Commission has had clear procedural rules for handling maritime disputes and was responsible for disputes regarding remuneration for salvage services, disputes arising from collisions between sea-going vessels and disputes arising from chartering sea-going vessels, agency services, and maritime transportation and insurance. Since 1982 the Commission's responsibilities have included the handling of maritime disputes when two disputing parties agree to undergo arbitration. The Maritime Arbitration Commission now has 67 arbitrators.

In 1983 the Foreign Economic and Trade Arbitration Commission established a representative office in the Shenzhen Special Economic Zone. This office handles disputes arising in the course of the local foreign economic relations and trade. This Commission now has 71 arbitrators who are highly experienced in the fields of foreign economic relations, foreign trade, industry, agriculture, finance, monetary affairs, transportation, insurance and legal affairs. In addition the Commission has invited eight well-known public figures from Hong Kong and Macao legal, industrial and commercial circles and seven from the Shenzhen Special Economic Zone to act as arbitrators for the Shenzhen Special Economic Zone.

In disputes over foreign economic relations and trade, disputing parties in Shenzhen may choose as their arbitrator, an arbitrator from among the 71 members of the Foreign Economic and Trade Arbitration Commission or from among the 15 members of the Shenzhen Special Economic Zone Arbitration Commission.

In August 1988 the two arbitration commissions concerned with foreign related disputes were, with the approval of the State Council, separated from the China Council for the Promotion of International Trade. At this point they were renamed the China International Trade Arbitration Commission and the China Maritime Arbitration Commission. The two re-named commissions then released their arbitration rules which became effective from 1 January 1989.

CHAPTER 7

Economic Planning

China is a socialist country with a planned commodity economy. Since the introduction of economic reform policy a system has been introduced whereby 'the State regulates the market and the market guides the enterprise'. This is a system that combines planned economic regulation with market regulation.

I.   PLANNING

Since economic reform the planning system has been undergoing considerable improvement and further reform of the system is expected.

The planning system is composed of several parts with each of these parts operating as a clearly defined system.

1.   THE SYSTEM OF LONG, MEDIUM AND SHORT-TERM PLANS

(1)   Long-term Plans

These are the comprehensive plans that are used for plotting economic and social development. They are also plans that are used for solving key problems. Long-term plans cover a period of over ten years. They set strategic targets and priorities and they are the basis of industrial policy and of distribution of the productive forces. They are also vital for the direction to be taken by science and technology and for the planned use of natural resources.

Special long-term plans that have been formulated are: the Agricultural Development Plan (1956-1967), the 12-Year Long-Range Plan for Scientific and Technological Development (1956-1967), the outline of the 10-Year Plan for the Development of the National Economy (1976-1985), the outline of the Long-Term Plan for the Development of Science and Technology up to the Year 2000, and the outline of the Plan for the Rehabilitation and Development of the Country's Land.

(2)   Medium-term Plans

These are plans with a duration period of 5 years. It is medium-term plans that are instrumental in setting the speed of growth, regulating proportions within the national economy, specifying demand for improved economic returns, arranging key fixed asset construction projects, promoting the tackling of key scientific and technical problems and the application of scientific and technical results, and for stipulating the growth rate for people's living standards.

Since the founding of New China eight Five-Year Plans have been formulated. The First Five-Year Plan (1953-1957), the Second Five-Year Plan (1958-1962), the Third Five-Year Plan (1966-1970), the Fourth Five-Year Plan (1971-1975), the Fifth Five-Year Plan (1976-1980), the Sixth Five-Year Plan (1981-1985), the Seventh Five-Year Plan (1986-1990) and now the Eighth Five Year-Plan (1991-1995).

(3)   Short-term Plans

These are one year plans. They are more specific than medium-term plans. They set the output of principal industrial and agricultural production for the year, stipulate measures for increasing economic returns and they seek a balance between finance, credit, foreign exchange, materials, markets and available labour. With the exception of the year 1967-1968, a short-term plan has been formulated and transmitted to lower levels every year since 1953.

2.   THE SYSTEM OF STATE, LOCAL AND GRASS-ROOT PLANS

(1)   State Plans

These are formulated by the State and transmitted to lower levels. They include plans formulated by the State Planning Commission, the State Council and other departments. They are the plans that lay down the guiding ideas for national economic development. They set the direction and they set the targets and tasks for economic, scientific, technological and social development.

(2)   Local Plans

These are plans formulated by each locality within the limit of the locality's power and within the frame of both the State Plan and local conditions. These plans include plans formulated by provincial, autonomous region and municipal planning commissions and by other departments.

(3)   Grass-root Plans

These are the plans used by independently accounting enterprises and independently managed institutions. On the premise that they fulfil the tasks stipulated by State and local plans, enterprises have the right to arrange their own production, supply and marketing activities. They also have the right to adopt flexible and varied management methods and to accumulate and distribute profit.

3.   THE SYSTEM OF ECONOMIC, SCIENTIFIC, TECHNOLOGICAL, AND SOCIAL PLANS, INCLUDING MANDATORY AND GUIDANCE PLANS

(1)   Economic Plans

These are the plans that guide production. They include plans for gross social output value, national income and gross national product, agricultural production plans, industrial production plans, plans for transport and for post and telecommunications, fixed asset investment plans, economic efficiency plans, financial income and expenditure plans, plans for income and payment in the case of operations based on credit, plans for balanced distribution of important materials, plans for the purchase and allocation of principal commodities, import and export trade plans, foreign exchange revenue and expenditure plans, plans for use of foreign funds, and technology import plans.

(2) *Scientific and Technological Plans*

These include plans for tackling key scientific and technological problems, plans for popularising scientific and technological results, and plans for importing science and technology.

(3) *Social Plans*

These are plans that guide the continued improvement in people's living standards. They include plans for education, population, labour and wage issues, environmental protection, culture, public health, physical culture and tourism.

(4) *Mandatory and Guidance Plans*

In terms of macro-economic management, planning for economic and social development can be further divided into two categories of plan. These are mandatory and guidance plans.

Mandatory Plans are formulated by the State and transmitted to lower levels. They are compulsory plans and must be carried out. Units or individuals who fail to fulfil these plans due to subjective reasons, will be held responsible for the failure. During the course of implementing these plans, if the plans are found not to be practical in terms of existing conditions, reports can be submitted to responsible departments for readjustment of the plan.

It is only in relation to important products that the State practises mandatory planning. It is in cases where production and/or allocation and distribution concern overall economic management that direct management by the State, through mandatory planning, is deemed to be necessary. At the same time, it is recognised that interests of various parties have to be accounted for and in this respect attention has been paid to improving direct planning methods.

Guidance Plans are indirect plans formulated and transmitted to lower levels by the State. These plans have some flexibility, they are not to be carried out compulsorily. The State applies economic means to rationally readjusting interest relations and to guide enterprises in the fulfilment of their planned tasks. In terms of production, a large number of ordinary products and ordinary economic activities are managed by the State using guidance plans.

II. PLAN FORMULATION

1. PROCEDURES FOR FORMULATING PLANS

In China the procedures for plan formulation can be roughly divided into four stages. These stages are effective first from bottom to top and then second from top to bottom. This is a method that combines the decision of higher administrative authorities with suggestions from lower levels.

The first stage consists of submitting suggestions to higher authorities. All departments under the State Council and all provinces, autonomous regions and cities directly under the central government submit their planning suggestions to the State Planning Commission.

The second stage is that of transmitting controlled figures to lower levels. Based on the plans of various departments, provinces, autonomous regions and cities, the State Planning Commission investigates and studies, collects information and solicits expert opinion and on the basis of this work makes predictions and attempts to attain an overall balance between economic, scientific, technological and social development. It then presents these predictions in the form of the controlled figures.

After examination and approval by State Council, these figures are transmitted to all departments under the State Council and to each province, autonomous region and city directly under the central government. The figures then allow them to formulate their plans. Controlled figures contain two parts (i) literal directives and (ii) controlled targets. These two directives contain such important information as analyses of the national economic situation, tasks for economic, scientific and technological and social development, major economic and technical policies and measures to be adopted and important planned targets.

The third stage in formulating a draft plan is when, in line with the controlled figures that have been transmitted down, each department under the State Council and each province, autonomous region and city under the central government, organises subordinate enterprises and institutions to formulate their draft plans. They must do this in accord with the conditions of their own departments and localities. After collecting these plans each department and locality will formulate a balanced draft plan and submit this plan level-by-level up to the State Planning Commission. Based on the information it receives, the State Planning Commission then unifies the plans seeking overall balance and formulates a draft plan for the nation's economic and social development. After being examined by the State Council, the draft plan is submitted to the National People's Congress for examination and discussion.

The fourth stage again consists of transmitting formal plans downward. After approval of the National People's Congress, the draft plan is transmitted as a formal national economic and social development plan to each department, province, autonomous region and city and then it is transmitted to grass-roots enterprises and institutions for implementation.

2. CONCERNS WHEN FORMULATING PLANS

The following concerns are primary when the State undertakes plan formulation.

(1)   To Achieve a Basic Balance between Overall Supply and Demand

Overall supply represents gross national product and overall demand is demand for gross national product. A balanced economy must dovetail and unify the two. This will provide for the proportionate development of the national economy.

When drafting its economic and social development plan, the State must set an appropriate economic growth rate and must strive to increase supply. At the same time the State seeks to strictly control the scale of investment in fixed assets and to control the growth rate of consumption funds and so prevent excessive growth in demand.

(2)   When Formulating Plans, the State Strives to Keep Expenditure within the Limit of Income

The State strives to keep a balance between budgetary revenue and expenditure; to rationally set the amount of money and credit to be issued; to strictly control the issuing of credit; to rationally arrange production and supply of the means of production and means of livelihood according to demand and the condition of material supply; and it strives to arrange the use of foreign exchange and import based on foreign exchange earning ability. The State recognises the need to ensure a balance between national foreign exchange earnings and outlay.

The method used to approach overall balance in the national economy is to establish a balance table system for the economy and to establish mathematical economic models.

(i) The national economic balance table system. This system uses a series of tables that reflect various proportionate relations that exist in the course of production. The system serves to balance, co-ordinate and formulate plans.

The system of economic balance tables includes tables concerning population and labour force; a balance table of national property; a balance table of production, consumption and accumulation of social products; a balance table of production, distribution, redistribution and individual consumption; and a balance table of relations between production and distribution.

The main function of this system is to analyse and set the plan's proportionate relations and basic targets. Indeed the formulation of the national economic balance table permeates the whole process by which the plan is drafted.

(ii) Mathematical economic models. Mathematical economic models used in the course of plan formulation include the model of expansion of reproduction, the inter-departmental balance model and the optimal model. Used correctly mathematical economic models can provide a scientific basis for plan formulation.

3. PLANNING INDICES AND TARGETS

Plan formulation is based on basic and guiding principles, but if effective economic and technical policies are to be adopted, then plan formulation must be made concrete. This is done through a series of planning indices.

Each planning index is made up of two parts: (i) title of index and (ii) planned numerical value. For instance, in revenue 'Rmb 100 million', 'revenue' is the title of the index while 'Rmb 100 million' is the planned numerical value.

China's planning indices can be divided into the following types:

(1) Quantitative and Qualitative Indices

Quantitative indices are targets that reflect scale of national economic development. They cover gross industrial and agricultural output value, national income, GNP, output of industrial and agricultural production and investment in fixed assets.

Qualitative indices are targets that reflect production and management levels and economic return. They cover productivity, rate of cost reduction, utilisation rate of equipment, utilisation rate of fixed assets, duration of construction and investment in terms of recouping cycles.

(2) Material Products Index

The material products index uses measurement units such as weight, capacity, length and number of units. For example, 10,000 metric tons of steel, 10,000 metres of cotton cloth, 10,000 cubic metres of timber and 10,000 bales of cotton yarn. And the index includes measurement units in kind and they in turn include compound measurement units and standard measurement units. For instance, goods handling capacity is indicated by ton kilometre--a compound measurement unit. Every 7,000 kilocalories of calorific capacity of raw coal is the equivalent of 1 kilogram of standard coal--a standard measurement unit.

(3)   Value Index

Value indices include wage bill, profit, financial revenue and expenditure, income and credit payments. A value index can be calculated according to constant prices (as a means of overcoming the influence of price changes) used for comparison information and for analysing different periods, and it can be calculated according to current prices. The latter is used when seeking information on changes in the magnitude of value of commodities and for comparison during the same period.

(4)   Assessment Index

Assessment indices are targets transmitted level by level down to grass-root units. They are the basis for assessing a grass-root unit's plan implementation. Assessment indices are set in accord with the principle that grass-root enthusiasm, initiative and creativity are to be mobilised while ensuring that plan implementation is in line with State plans.

Aside from the indices listed immediately above, plan formulation also includes macro-targets, micro-targets, overall targets and special targets.

Macro-targets are overall aggregate indices. They cover gross industrial and agricultural output value, national income and gross national product. Micro-targets are partial and individual indices that reflect production and management activities at the level of grass-root enterprises and institutions. They include enterprise output value, profits, sales volume and wage bill.

Overall targets seek to reflect economic or social development in a specific field. They are derived from multiplying several special targets by weight. For example, ten special targets are chosen (gross national income, per capita average national income, national income added by every Rmb 100 of productive accumulation, per capita average annual energy consumption, average per capita calorie consumption for each day, urban employment rate, adult literacy rate, number of professionals per 10,000 of population, average life expectancy, and retail price index) and then a weight is set for each of these according to target importance. The 10 targets are then multiplied by their respective weights and after adding these figures an overall target is obtained.

III.   PLAN IMPLEMENTATION

The State uses administrative, economic and legislative means to organise implementation of its plans. The following measures are among its means.

1.   ECONOMIC CONTRACTS

After the State plan has been broken down and transmitted to lower levels, State and related local departments organise plan implementing units for signing of economic contracts. Economic contracts are used to regularise economic exchange between production, supply and marketing; between production and construction; between production and transportation; between the State and the enterprise; and between different enterprises. Planned tasks of the national economy are fulfilled using signed economic contracts. It is through contracts that tasks are linked and co-ordinated and a reliable guarantee is provided.

2. ECONOMIC MEANS

Having set planned targets and tasks, the State then must draw up corresponding economic policies and measures and through such regulatory means as pricing, taxation and interest rates, must regulate the relationship between supply and demand. The State uses economic means to guide the plan implementing units to make correct decisions on issues of production, construction and management and to make their activities meet the requirements of the State plan.

In terms of practical plan management, the State adopts means such as raising prices, cutting tax rates and reducing the interest rate to encourage production of undersupplied products. Then for oversupplied products, the State adopts methods such as lowering prices and raising taxes and interest rates to discourage and so restrict production and reduce supply.

The State Planning Commission is requested to study the use of the various economic means for regulating economic decision-making (means such as price, taxation and interest rates), because each of these regulatory means play their role in a different manner. This means that in order to ensure that the various economic means are co-ordinated and work jointly for the implementation of State planned targets and tasks, the State Planning Commission must study the means and its effect.

3. STRENGTHENING ECONOMIC INFORMATION MANAGEMENT

In the course of plan implementation, the State relies on economic information. It must rely on this information in order to be able to exercise frequent supervision, control and regulation of economic decisions. In line with the State's need for economic information, the State Planning Commission and other relevant departments have established economic information centres which use economic mathematical methods and computer technology to collect, process, analyse, store and pass on economic information. These centres also offer different forms of consulting services and they guide plan implementing units in such matters as production, construction, management, technology import and the use of foreign capital.

4. IMPROVING ECONOMIC LEGISLATION AND ECONOMIC JUDICIAL WORK

In order to ensure the smooth fulfilment of the State plan, it is necessary to bring planned management work into line with the law. As noted in the previous chapter, China is currently striving to establish a complete economic legislative system; to strengthen economic judicial work; to exercise supervision and management of enterprises and markets in line with the law; and to safeguard the overall interest of the State plan.

5. EXAMINATION OF THE PLAN

For effective planning it is necessary to chart the progress of plan implementation and to identify problems encountered in the course of implementation. In order to do this various investigations must be undertaken.

(1) Statistical Investigation

This involves the State statistical department undertaking statistical surveys and analyses in order to produce data that reflects State plan implementation. The data provide new information concerning development of the national economy.

(2) Bank Supervision

The People's Construction Bank of China, the Industrial and Commercial Bank of China, the Agricultural Bank of China and the Bank of China are responsible for issuing loans for fixed assets, circulation funds, for the purchase of agricultural and sideline products, payment of wage-funds and for issuing foreign exchange for imports. This role played by the banks is one that provides the State, through the banks, with access to improved regulation of the economy.

(3) Tax Management

Income distribution between the State and enterprises is regulated through taxes. Tax must be paid in accord with regulations and rules and through tax collection the State is in a position to pool necessary funds to ensure implementation of planned targets and tasks.

(4) Supervision Through Audit

All plan implementing units are audited by the State. Auditing includes examination of financial income and payments and it includes checking financial source documents, statements and reports, account books, property, stocks, cash and contracts. It is a process that serves to exercise frequent and overall examination and supervision of plan implementation by enterprises.

(5) Plan Readjustment

If in the course of plan implementation, State plans do not conform to reality, or if changes take place that are due to such matters as natural disaster or unforeseen changes in supply and demand in the domestic or international market, then readjustment of plans will be necessary. This is done by submitting a report to the higher authority that had formerly approved the plan. But in order to protect the State plan, it is not permissible to readjust the plan if it has not been fulfilled due to poor management.

IV. ADMINISTRATIVE PLANNING ORGANISATIONS

1. THE STATE PLANNING COMMISSION

The State Planning Commission is the largest planning department under the State Council. Its brief is to manage the national economy and to oversee social development. It is a high level organisation in charge of macro economic management.

The main functions of this organisation are:

(1) To set out strategic targets for national economic and social development; to draw up long-term, medium-term and annual plans; and to ensure a balance between overall demand and supply, including a balance between finance, credit, materials, foreign exchange, market and labour force.

(2) To study and analyse major macro-economic management problems such as problems of imbalance between national distribution, accumulation and consumption.

(3) To use economic levers--price, tax, credit, interest rates, exchange rates and wages for regulation of the national economy.

(4) Guiding the planning work undertaken by departments and localities and overseeing inspection and supervision and enforcement of plans and inspecting production and key construction projects.

(5) Analysing economic returns.

(6) Compiling relevant policies and measures for the medium- and long-term development of science and technology, including promotion of technological progress through assimilation of imported technologies and through production of Chinese-made parts and spare parts.

(7) Analysing problems associated with policy concerning social development in areas such as population, labour, culture, education, public health and social security and insurance.

(8) Promoting conservation through rational utilisation of natural resources.

(9) Promoting economic reform policy, including promotion of the fund system for capital construction, overseeing the work of special investment companies, and supervising and inspecting bidding activity and the submission of tenders for major fixed asset construction projects.

(10) Promotion of economic and technical legislation. The State Planning Commission uses a committee system. Its organisations include the long-term planning department, the national economic department, the production despatching bureau, the industrial policy department, the structural reform and legislation bureau, the scientific and technological department, the fixed asset investment department, the technical renovation department, the co-ordination and supervision department for key construction projects, the No 1 industrial department, the No 2 industrial department, the rural economic department, the department for conservation and utilisation of natural resources, the consumption market department, the foreign economic relations and trade department, the department for utilising foreign capital, the financial and monetary department, the social undertakings department, the planning department for the exploitation of land, and the regional economic department. In addition it has institutions such as the economic research centre, the economic information centre and the training centre for planning cadres.

2. PROVINCIAL PLANNING DEPARTMENTS

Aside from the State Planning Commission, planning departments have been established in various ministries, commissions and bureaus that are under the State Council.

In conjunction with planning offices, these have been established in various departments/bureaus of the People's Governments of provinces, autonomous regions and municipalities directly under the central authorities.

The major functions of the planning departments are:

... to study development and important and economic and technological policies for departments under their jurisdiction;

- ... on the basis of investigations and studies carried out and on the premise of overall economic balance, work out draft plans for departments under their jurisdiction;
- ... to examine the implementation of department plans;
- ... to study and improve their own planning work; and
- ... to train planners for their own departments.

3. LOCAL PLANNING ORGANISATIONS

The main function of local planning organisations is to investigate and study the economic and social development of their own localities and to make suggestions for making full use of local advantages. They are required to work out the draft plan for economic and social development for each locality; to inspect the implementation of the plan and to promote co-operation between departments with regard to solving problems incurred during plan implementation; to study and improve planning work; and to train local planning cadres.

V. THE SYSTEM FOR STATISTICAL INVESTIGATION

The basic task of the statistical investigation system is to analyse national economic and social development, to offer accurate statistical data and to exercise statistical supervision. It is statistical investigation that provides the major basis for plan and policy formulation and it is an important means for the exercising of scientific management.

1. METHODS OF STATISTICAL INVESTIGATION

The State has adopted a number of methods of statistical investigation. These are in line with the different objectives of investigation. They include:

(1) A System of Fixed-term Statistical Statements and Reports

This is a method used for the periodic gathering of statistics. The State Statistical Bureau, or the responsible department under the State Council, stipulate the form of various statistical statements and reports, quota explanations and the time and procedures for the delivery of statements and reports. They then transmit this information, level-by-level, down to grass-roots enterprises and institutions. The grass-roots institutions then fill in relevant forms and lodge them with the statistical organisation under the local government or the relevant department in charge.

After the itemised statements and reports collected have been sorted by the statistical organisations of local government or departments in charge, they are reported grade-by-grade to the State Statistical Bureau or responsible department at the same level. Then they are divided into daily, ten-day, monthly, quarterly, six-month and annual categories.

(2) General Surveys

These are specially organised overall and systematic investigations. The aim of these surveys is to investigate data that are impossible to investigate through the fixed-term statistical statement and report system.

These surveys are undertaken in two ways. The first is by using specially established survey organisations that send their staff to directly investigate the units to be surveyed. The second is by using a survey unit's own statements and reports compiled on the basis of their internal records and available data. Data can either be gathered grade by grade or by skipping over the immediate leadership.

General surveys include the first, second and third national census, the survey of scientists and technicians, the survey of capital construction and technical revamping projects, the industry survey and the survey of the stock of goods and materials.

(3) Key Surveys

These surveys concentrate on key units. The distinctive feature of these surveys is their ability to grasp the basic situation in terms of problems and to do this in plenty of time.

In accord with the stipulated tasks of the survey and the nature of the problem, key units to be surveyed can either be key enterprises, trades, cities or regions. Two methods are used:

... undertaking a special survey, and

... requesting key units to complete fixed-term statistical report forms.

(4) Sample Surveys

These surveys use some units from among the total number of units to be surveyed. Based on information from these selected units, analysis is provided and used for predicting an overall situation.

All statistical surveys should include detailed investigation plans and should clearly define the intention and method of the survey, the statistical scope, the database used for categorisation, quota explanations, and the calculating method. They should also identify the unit compiling the report, the time-frame for completion and the organisations that will be in receipt of the report. This is information that will help units at grass-roots level to fill out the statement and report.

The State Statistical Bureau publishes information both domestically and abroad. It uses the following publication methods:

... A yearly communique on the implementation of the previous year's plan for the national economy and social development. To this end the State Statistical Bureau publishes the *China Statistical Yearbook* and *China Statistical Excerpts*.

... Publication of the monthly *China Statistical Monthly Report*.

... Publication of the results of each national and large-scale survey.

... Publication of systematic statistical data on agriculture, industry, investment in fixed assets, the building industry, and other fields of the national economy.

... The release of statistical data by spokesmen at press conferences.

China's statistical system includes the government statistical department, statistical systems and the statistical organisations (consisting of statistical personnel) of enterprises and institutions.

The government statistical system is composed of statistical personnel from the State Statistical Bureau, statistical bureaus of all levels of local government and township statisticians. It is the State Statistical Bureau that is responsible for leading and co-ordinating national statistical work and it is local statistical bureaus at all levels and township statisticians that are responsible for leading and co-ordinating statistical work in their own administrative regions.

Statistical bureaus of all levels of local governments are under the dual leadership of same level governments and the statistical bureaus of a higher level. In their statistical work they are led by the statistical bureaus of the higher level, while the statistical personnel of township governments are led by statistical bureaus of county governments.

The department statistical system consists of the statistical organisations of various ministries and commissions under the State Council and of various local government departments. It is the department statistical system that is responsible for organising and co-ordinating the statistical work of various functional organisations, enterprises and institutions. Department statistical organisations receive guidance from the State Statistical Bureau or same level local government statistical bureaus.

According to need, statistical organisations are established in enterprises and institutions. These organisations co-ordinate the statistical work of their own units, undertake set statistical tasks and receive guidance from local government statistical bureaus.

VI. IMPROVED PLANNING METHODS

Efforts have been made to improve the method of planning and to gradually perfect the planning system. Priority has been given to the following major tasks.

(1) Paying Attention to Economic Returns and Striving to achieve Both Speed and Beneficial Results

In 1983 the State Planning Commission decided that while assigning the planned control figures to lower levels, demand would be put forward for major economic return targets. The result was a plan drawn up on an experimental basis in 1983 and formerly worked out in 1984.

(2) Laying Stress on Combining Economic, Scientific and Technological Plans and the Plan for Social Development

Since 1982 the national economic plan has been changed into the plan for economic and social development. Population, people's living standards, housing construction, environmental protection, tackling key scientific and technological problems and popularisation of scientific and technical results, have all been added to the plan. This has been done in order to promote scientific and technological progress, to improve the quality of the workforce and to give impetus to better overall national economic development.

(3) Paying Close Attention to Medium-term and Long-term Plans and Gradually Perfecting the Planning System

During the life of an existing Five Year Plan, the State Planning Commission collects the information that provides the basis for formulation of the next Five

Year Plan. After two years of work and after examination and approval by the National People's Congress, the draft plan is transmitted down to lower administrative levels for implementation. Meanwhile people from related departments are mobilised to study and draw up a long-term plan for the development of science and technology and for the use and protection of land resources.

A planning system that combines long-term planning with medium-term and short-term planning is one that is being perfected through practice.

(4) Supplementing the Planning System

After localities, departments and enterprises have been given more decision-making power, a considerable part of economic activity will no longer be directly controlled by the State. In order to bring all economic activity into line with the State's strategy for economic growth, the State will supplement its planning system with the social plan for investment in fixed assets, the overall financial and credit plan, and the comprehensive material plan for major products.

Supplementing the planning system in this way will provide an overall national economic balance.

(5) Perfecting Overall Planned Targets in such a way that they will Accurately Reflect the Size and Speed of National Economic Development

For a long period in the past, 'gross industrial and agricultural output value' was used as the overall planned target that reflected size and speed of national economic development. In 1983 it was decided that 'total social product' and 'national income' should be included as planning targets. Later, 'gross national product' was also included in the plan.

(6) Expediting Modernisation of Planning Measures, further improving Statistical Investigation and Improving National Economic Forecasting

In recent years construction of a nationwide economic information network has been stepped up. This information network has adopted the analytical method of economic quantity analysis and the use of popularised computer techniques.

Aside from the six tasks listed immediately above, other measures that have been most effective in streamlining planning have included:

(i) Approval simplification for large and medium-sized projects. In the past large and medium-sized projects examined and approved by the State Planning Commission required project suggestion documents, feasibility study reports, planned task documents and preliminary design and construction reports. Now only project suggestion documents and planned task documents (and for large projects, preliminary design reports) are required for examination and approval by the State Planning Commission.

(ii) Use of the planned contract responsibility system. The planned contract responsibility system has been introduced in industrial production and transport and communications. Since 1981 the Ministry of Petroleum Industry, the Ministry of Coal Industry, the Ministry of Metallurgical Industry, the Nonferrous Corporation, the Petrochemical Corporation and the Ministry of Railways have introduced the planned contract responsibility system. Implementation of this system has meant that the State and various departments have defined each other's rights and responsibilities and have gradually unified their functions, powers and interests.

In capital construction and in the construction industry a system of overall investment responsibility has been instituted. The main content of this system is that each project contracting unit will contract for investment, construction period, quality, quantity of main materials required and comprehensive production capacity. Then the department in charge of the construction project is made responsible for 'five guarantees'. These are to guarantee availability of construction funds, equipment and materials; outside auxiliary projects; personnel required for construction; and the raw materials, fuel and power supply needed for a trial run of the industrial project.

(iii) Empowering some large conglomerates and capital construction groups to independently work out their own plans. Together with the growth of horizontal economic ties, conglomerates and capital construction groups have taken shape in China. In March 1987 the State Council approved the Provisional Stipulations on Large Associated Industrial Enterprises Which Are Empowered to Draw Up Plans Independently. Up to January 1988 eleven conglomerates had been empowered to independently formulate their plans. These are the Jiefang Motor Vehicle Industrial Associated Corporation, the Dongfang Motor Vehicle Industrial Associated Corporation, the Heavy-Duty Motor Vehicle Industrial Associated Corporation, the Harbin Power Station Complete Set of Equipment Corporation, the Shanghai Electrical Integrated Corporation, the Dongfang Power Station Complete Set of Equipment Corporation, the Xian Power Machinery Manufacturing Corporation, the China new-Type Construction Materials Corporation, the China Nonmetal Ore Industrial Corporation, the Great Wall Computer Group Corporation, the Changjiang Computer (Group) Integrated Corporation and the Shenfu Dongsheng Coalfield under the Huaneng Float Corporation.

Contents of the independent plans of these conglomerates vary from group to group. They usually include output of major products, allocation of major products, investment in capital construction and re-equipment and key projects, distribution of unified allocated materials, import and export trade, finance, labour and wages, and the assignment of university graduates. At the same time, in terms of examination and approval of investment in fixed assets and in terms of the utilisation of foreign capital and the import of technology with their own foreign exchange, they enjoy powers similar to those afforded a ministry.

The draft plans of these conglomerates are submitted directly to the State Planning Commission. After being related to planned targets, they are transmitted directly to related business groups by the State Planning Commission.

Empowering some conglomerates and large construction groups to work out their own plans is a measure that helps break administrative barriers between different departments and regions, helps to reduce managerial levels and creates favourable external conditions for strengthening the vitality of enterprises.

(iv) Empowering some cities directly under provinces to work out their own plans. This is a policy intended to allow some cities to act as economic centres. Between February 1983 and October 1988, the State Council approved Chongqing, Wuhan, Shenyang, Dalian, Harbin, Guangzhou, Xian, Qingdao, Ningbo, Shenzhen and Xiamen as cities with authority to independently draw up their own economic plans. These cities are to enjoy the same economic management powers as provincial authorities.

Management of enterprises formerly under various ministries and provinces has been transferred to these cities and pilot projects of overall economic structural reform have been launched in these cities. It is a reform policy that has enhanced the ability of some cities to organise economic activity.

Since economic reform importance has been attached to employing economic policies and methods of economic regulation for the realisation of planned targets. In the course of determining planned targets and tasks, the State studies and maps out major economic and technological policies and measures and pays close attention to integrating planned targets with measures necessary for their realisation. For instance, through the adjustment of the price of some commodities, the State can guide enterprise decision-making in a way that develops production in accordance with the State plan. And through the collection of construction tax and through different interest rates on bank loans, the State can control the size of investment in fixed assets and so adjust investment structure. Also by adjusting tariff and exchange rates, the State can encourage or restrict exports and imports.

Over a fairly long period in the past, 'gross industrial and agricultural output value' was used as the overall planning target that served to reflect size and speed of economic development. This form of organisation and plan implementation is now considered to be quite inadequate. Now direct control over enterprises by the State has been replaced by indirect control. The scope of mandatory planning has been significantly reduced. Today the State regulates and influences relations between supply and demand and guides enterprise decision-making through economic, legal and necessary administrative means. This means that the State requires a great deal from its statistical system. With the deepening of reform, further reform of both the planning and statistical systems is expected.

CHAPTER 8

Administration of Industry and Commerce

I. STATE ADMINISTRATION OF INDUSTRY AND COMMERCE

Special government organs have been established for the supervision and administration of industrial and commercial enterprises. The legal operation of enterprises and trade is to be protected, social economic order is to be protected and the development of a socialist commodity economy is to be promoted. To this end administration of industry and commerce manages matters such as registration of enterprises, economic contracts, the individual and the private economy, and patents and advertising.

The State Administration of Industry and Commerce is directly under the State Council. It is the administrative entity that is not only responsible for industrial and commercial administrative policy, but also for formulating and implementing relevant laws, regulations and systems, stopping and dealing with any illegal operations by enterprises, and protecting the legal rights and interests of enterprises.

Industry and commerce administrative bureaus have been established in all provinces, autonomous regions and municipalities directly under the central government. These bureaus operate under dual leadership. They operate under the administrative bureau for industry and commerce at a higher level and under their local government. The bureaus are in charge of administration of industry and commerce within their localities.

Grass-roots units for administration of industry and commerce are offices that have been established under the direct leadership of the county (prefecture) administrative bureaus for industry and commerce. There are now more than 25,000 of these offices.

Both the State Administration for Industry and Commerce and local administrative bureaus for industry and commerce are organs of economic administrative supervision and of law enforcement. This has meant that, particularly since 1979, these organs have undertaken the enactment of laws concerned with administration of industry and commerce. These laws now include the Trademark Law, the Economic Contract Law, the Interim Provisions on Corporation Registration, the Interim Regulations on the Administration of Urban and Rural Individual Labourers and Businessmen, Regulations on the Registration and Administration of Legal Entities, and the Interim Regulations on Private Enterprises.

1. ENTERPRISE REGISTRATION

All types of enterprises, institutions which engage in production, and scientific and technological organisations must apply for registration. Registration with the administration for industry and commerce or its bureaus provides legal recognition for production, research and commercial entities and it provides administrative organs with a tool for the exercise of supervision and control. For example, as a means of strengthening the supervision and control of enterprises, an annual examination system has been adopted. This has meant that within a prescribed time an enterprise must submit to examination by registering organs. The enterprise must provide an annual statement and a balance sheet of funds or a statement of assets and liabilities.

Enterprises engaged in all trades and of all sizes and in all sectors of the national economy, including Sino-foreign joint ventures, Sino-foreign cooperative enterprises and solely foreign-funded enterprises established on Chinese territory, must obtain approval for registration from the administrative organs for industry and commerce. National corporations established with the approval of State Council or departments authorised by it, large enterprise groups, and companies engaged in import and export, must secure approval of registration from the State Administration for Industry and Commerce. Sino-foreign joint ventures, cooperative enterprises and solely foreign-funded enterprises must also obtain approval for registration from the State Administration for Industry and Commerce, but in the interest of convenience, the Administration has authorised a number of provincial and municipal administrative bureaus for industry and commerce to handle registration for these enterprises when resident in their localities.

Companies that are affiliated or branch companies of national corporations and enterprises and enterprise groups that have been established with the approval of a provincial government or the government of an autonomous region or municipality directly under the central authorities and companies engaged in import and export, should seek registration from their local provincial, autonomous region or municipal administrative bureaus for industry and commerce. Other enterprises must register with administrative bureaus for industry and commerce in the cities and counties where they are located.

According to statistics compiled at the end of 1987, there were 4.828 million enterprises registered with the administrative organs for industry and commerce. These enterprises employed 169.2 million people and had a total registered capital of Rmb 1.6 billion. There were 8,546 enterprises with foreign investment, including 4,405 joint ventures, 3,940 cooperative enterprises and 201 wholly foreign funded enterprises.

2. ENTERPRISE REGISTRATION: EXAMINATION AND APPROVAL

The procedure for examination and approval for enterprise registration is divided into three stages—application, examination and approval, and business licence issue.

(1) Application

Within 30 days of the date of approval by the department in charge or an approving authority, an industrial or commercial enterprise applying for registration should file an application with the administrative bureau for industry and commerce in the city or county where it is located. The enterprise should meet the following conditions:

- ... it must have a name, organisational frame-work and regulations—each enterprise can only use one name;
- ... it must have a fixed place of operation and necessary operating facilities;
- ... it must have funds and employees in line with its intended scale of operation;
- ... it must be able independently to assume civil duties; and
- ... the scope of its operation must be in keeping with national legal provisions.

(2) Examination

After accepting an application from an enterprise, the administrative bureau for industry and commerce must make a decision within 30 days. In the case of enterprises whose application does not conform to regulations or whose papers are incomplete, the bureau must ask them to supply necessary documentation and certificates. In the case of enterprises that are not qualified for registration, the bureau will reject the application. When an enterprise application meets application conditions the bureau will approve registration. Items that must be included in an application for registration are: name of enterprise, place of residence, place of operation, legal representation, economic nature, scope of operation, mode of operation, registered capital, number of employees, term of operation and branch offices.

(3) Issuing a Business Licence

Once an enterprise application for registration has been approved, the enterprise will be issued with a business licence. It will be issued by the administrative organ for industry and commerce.

A business licence is a certificate that confirms that the enterprise is a legal entity and that it has the right to engage in production. There are four types of business licence:

- ... A Legal Person (Entity) Enterprise Business Licence. This is a business licence issued to State-owned enterprises, collective enterprises, private enterprises, joint-venture enterprises, and associated enterprises and enterprise groups which are economic entities and independently assume civil responsibilities.
- ... A business licence issued to private enterprises, individual producers and dealers, individual partnerships and joint ventures, associated enterprises and enterprise groups which are not economic entities.

- ... A Business Licence for Legal Person Enterprises of the People's Republic of China. This is a business licence that is issued to Sino-foreign joint ventures, Sino-foreign cooperative enterprises and solely foreign-funded enterprises which have qualified as a legal person (entity) of China.
- ... An interim business licence. This is business licence that is issued to enterprises engaged in seasonal production (for a period of less than six months) and individually owned industrial and commercial enterprises.

All four types of business licence have legal force. Any enterprise which has been issued with a business licence has a legal status and its legal operation is protected by the laws of the State.

When an enterprise alters the items listed in its registration it must apply for alteration of registration and when an enterprise terminates its business it must register for cancellation of its licence.

(4) The Procedure for Examination and Approval for Registration of Resident Representative Offices of Foreign Enterprises

Foreign enterprises and other economic organisations which need to establish resident representative offices in China must file an application for registration with the relevant authority of the State Council. Then within 30 days of approval of their application, they must apply for registration by the administrative bureaus for industry and commerce of provinces, autonomous regions or municipalities where they are located. After initial examination of their application, those considered to be qualified are issued with further application forms that must be completed in both Chinese and English. These latter forms are then forwarded to the State Administration for Industry and Commerce. After formal approval by the Administration, applicants are issued with 'registration certificates for resident representative offices of foreign enterprises'. This registration is valid for one year. Those representative offices who wish to continue their stay must, within 15 days of the date of expiry of their registration, take their registration certificate to their original registration authority for renewal of registration and a new registration certificate.

II. MARKET ADMINISTRATION

1. MARKET ADMINISTRATION TASKS

In terms of commodities, market administration includes agricultural and sideline products and manufactured goods, means of livelihood and means of production. In terms of sectors of the economy and channels of circulation, it includes purchasing and marketing activities of State, collective and private enterprises, individual producers and dealers, government organs, mass organisations, army units and schools. It also includes urban and rural fairs and markets.

In accordance with State laws, regulations and policies concerning market administration, the administrative organs for industry and commerce exercise supervision and control of all kinds of market business activities, protect legal trade and curb illegal trade in order to preserve market order, and they promote brisk market activity and the development of production.

The main tasks of market administration and of administrative organs for industry and commerce include:

- studying market administration policy and formulating relevant rules and regulations;
- invigorating the market, unclogging circulation channels and protecting legal purchasing, marketing and transportation of goods for sale;
- controlling urban and rural trade fairs and participating in the administration of the marketing of key elements of production in co-ordination with departments concerned;
- supervising the quality of manufactured goods and safeguarding the interests of consumers;
- stopping illegal operations, investigating and dealing with violations of laws and regulations and cracking down on speculation and profiteering; and
- exchanging market information and providing consultancy services.

(1) *Administration of Urban and Rural Trade Fairs*

In China the trade fair is a traditional form of commodity exchange. However, for a considerable period in the past, the development of trade fairs was significantly restricted. Since 1979, with the promotion of economic reform and the development of the commodity economy, trade fairs have quickly expanded and become increasingly prosperous.

In 1978 there were only 33,302 trade fairs with an annual business volume of Rmb 12.5 billion. By 1987 the number of trade fairs had increased to 69,683 with an annual business volume of Rmb 115.8 billion. Of these, 10,908 were urban trade fairs with a business volume of Rmb 34.7 billion and 58,775 were rural trade fairs with a business volume of Rmb 81.1 billion.

Trade fairs have played an increasingly important role in people's life. For example, most vegetables and non-staple food required by urban residents were supplied by State stores but they are now supplied by trade fairs. In 1987 vegetable transactions at urban fairs came to 116.1% of the amount of retail sales at State stores, pork amounted to 48.1%, beef and mutton 103.8%, eggs 90.7%, chicken, duck and goose 270.7% and aquatic products 135.6%.

Commodities transacted at trade fairs are usually agricultural and sideline products. Except for those commodities which are banned by State provisions (such as cotton) all other agricultural and sideline products can be sold on the market once peasants have fulfilled State quotas and contract production for State purchase.

With the expansion of trade fairs, an increasing number of garments and manufactured goods for daily use have been offered for sale. At fairs there is direct exchange between producer and consumer as well as transactions between dealers. Prices of commodities sold at fairs are not fixed by the State. They are free prices negotiated between buyer and seller.

The administration of trade fairs by industrial and commercial administrative bureaus is aimed at maintaining market order, investigating and dealing with violations of laws and regulations, supervising public hygiene, curbing such illegal business activities as giving short weight, passing off inferior quality goods for high quality goods and selling adulterated commodities.

Business at most trade fairs is done in the open air, but in the past few years administrative organs for industry and commerce have stepped up the construction of facilities for fairs and conditions have gradually improved. Fairs in a number of cities have become large scale markets equipped with good service facilities and supplying all kinds of commodities.

(2) Investigating and Handling Law and Regulation Violations

An important aspect of market administration is the maintenance of economic order. In the past few years, together with enlivening the economy, cases of violating economic laws and regulations have occurred repeatedly. In 1987 fines imposed by the administrative organs for industry and commerce for violation of laws and regulations came to Rmb 386 million.

Speculative activities that breach economic laws and regulations have included: illegally selling materials and articles which the State has banned from free sale; illegally buying up commodities in short supply from State retail shops or other channels and selling them for increased prices; illegally selling coupons for materials to be supplied under the State plan, illegal sale of vouchers, permits, licences, bills of lading and securities; illegally selling cultural relics, gold, silver and foreign exchange; illegally selling economic contracts and using economic contracts or other means to practise deception when buying and selling; manufacturing or selling imitation brand-name products, forgeries or shoddy goods at the expense of consumers or doing inferior work and using inferior materials resulting in serious consequences; printing, selling and publicising illegal publications for profit; providing sources of goods, cheques, cash, bank accounts and other facilities for speculative activities or furnishing certificates and vouchers for speculators or signing contracts on their behalf; monopolising commodity sources, bullying other businessmen, jacking up commodity prices in order to disturb the market and other speculative activities that serve to disrupt economic order.

III. ECONOMIC CONTRACTS

1. ECONOMIC CONTRACT ADMINISTRATION

Economic contracts are signed in order to protect the legal rights and interests of contracting parties, to safeguard economic order, to urge contracting parties to abide by State laws and policies, and to meet State plan requirements. The administrative organs for industry and commerce are the organs in charge of the administration of economic contracts.

Administration of economic contracts involves the following tasks:
- ... supervision and checking of signing and fulfilment of economic contracts;
- ... mediating or arbitrating disputes arising from economic contracts;
- ... confirming invalid economic contracts; and
- ... investigating and handling cases of use of economic contracts in acts that breach the law.

(1) Guaranteeing Economic Contracts

The administrative organs for industry and commerce offer consultancy services to contract signing parties so that contracts conform to legal and policy requirements and contain and clearly state all relevant details. And in addition to this service, the State Administration for Industry and Commerce will stand guarantee for economic contracts. This guarantee is not compulsory, but is sought with the agreement of and on the request of contracting parties. It is an administrative guarantee that serves to increase the weight of the contract. It is only given after administrative organs for industry and commerce have thoroughly checked an economic contract. This examination includes inquiry into whether parties to the contract have necessary legal qualifications; whether the aims of the contract conform to requirements of State law and policy; whether the contract is in keeping with the principle of equality and mutual benefit and whether terms have been reached through consultation; whether all necessary articles and clauses have been included in the contract; and whether the language used is clear and formalities have been completed.

In 1987 there were more than 1.9 million guaranteed contracts, involving a total sum of Rmb 45.5 billion.

Once an economic contract has been signed, it is the responsibility of the administrative organs for industry and commerce to constantly supervise and check contract fulfilment. As these economic contracts are numerous, administrative organs can only undertake spot checks on key contracts or organise the department in charge to make joint checks on contracts relevant to that department.

(2) Arbitrating Economic Contract Disputes

When disputes arise in the course of fulfilling contract requirements and when the parties concerned cannot solve the dispute through consultation, they can seek legally binding arbitration through the Economic Contract Arbitration Authority.

The Economic Contract Arbitration Authority is a committee set up by the State Administration for Industry and Commerce and local administrative bureaus for industry and commerce. Economic Contract Arbitration Committees have a chairman, one or two vice-chairmen and a number of members. A tribunal of the Committee consists of two arbitrators and a chief arbitrator designated by the Committee. They deal with disputes, with the most difficult cases being submitted to the Committee itself for discussion and decision. Provision exists for cases involving uncomplicated economic contract disputes to be arbitrated by a single designated arbitrator.

When handling economic contract disputes, the Arbitration Authority adheres to the following principles:

- ... it insists on investigating and studying the facts and in view of the facts taking law as its criterion;
- ... it ensures that the concerned parties exercise their powers on an equal footing in line with their equality before the law;
- ... it mediates first and tries, as far as possible, to resolve disputes through mediation; and
- ... it implements a single instance adjudication system when handling disputes.

In 1987 administrative organs for industry and commerce handled 28,104 cased of economic contract dispute, mediated 19,998 cases and arbitrated 2,642 cases.

(3)   Violations of Economic Contract Law

Most economic contracts are signed in accordance with the law and thus are protected by State laws. But there are some contracts which are found to be outside economic contract law and so are void. The following contracts would be considered void:

- ... contracts that violate the law or State policy;
- ... contracts that are signed through the use of fraud, duress or similar means;
- ... contracts signed by an agent who exceeds the scope of his power of agency; and
- ... contracts that violate the interests of the State or public interest.

According to China's Economic Contract Law, the power to confirm that an economic contract is void is vested in the administrative authorities for industry and commerce and the people's courts. In 1987 the administrative organs for industry and commerce confirmed that 10,110 economic contracts were void.

Some people have used economic contracts to commit law-breaching acts. These have included forging economic contracts, selling economic contracts for profit, illegally transferring economic contracts and using economic contracts to engage in speculation, offering or taking bribes. Where criminal responsibility has been involved cases of wrongful use of economic contracts are dealt with by judicial organs. Otherwise, they are dealt with by the administrative organs for industry and commerce. In 1987 the administrative organs for industry and commerce exposed and dealt with 4,906 cases of contract violation.

IV.   ADMINISTRATION OF INDIVIDUAL INDUSTRY AND COMMERCE AND OF PRIVATE ENTERPRISES

1.   INDIVIDUAL INDUSTRY AND COMMERCE

In the past decade rehabilitation and development of individual industry and commerce has been one of the most remarkable results of ownership adjustment in the context of restructuring the national economy. After 1979 individual industry and commerce, which had almost disappeared in the period of the 'cultural revolution', grew quickly. In 1976 there were only 180,000 people engaged in private industry and commerce. By the end of 1987 there were 13.7 million individual producers and businesses employing 21.56 million people. Their investment totalled Rmb 23.6 billion. Of these, 3.4 million were in cities and towns, employing 4.9 million people and with Rmb 5.6 billion of investment and 10.4 million were in rural areas employing 1.1 million people, with Rmb 18.02 billion of investment.

By 1987 annual business volume of urban and rural individual industry and commerce came to Rmb 103.8 billion. With retail sales amounting to Rmb 74.4 billion these enterprises accounted for 12.8% of national retail sales.

Rehabilitation and development of individual industry and commerce has first, promoted commodity production and circulation and enlivened the market. It has done much to satisfy people's needs. Second, it has supplemented the State and collective economies, in particular, the supply of agricultural and sideline products, aquatic products, and the supply of small commodities used for daily life. It has also provided repair and general services. Third, it has created jobs for large numbers of unemployed people in both town and country. It has been particularly useful in offering employment for the surplus labour force in rural areas. Fourth, it has added to State revenue. In 1987 alone, people engaged in individual industry and commerce paid more than Rmb 7 billion in taxes to the State. Fifth, a large number of people with experience in the operation and management of equipment and with professional skills have emerged among individual labourers and dealers. These people have promoted the growth of the commodity economy.

2. ADMINISTRATION OF INDIVIDUAL INDUSTRY AND COMMERCE

Administration of individual industry and commerce includes the following:

(1) Perfecting Laws and Regulations

Since 1981 the State Council has promulgated a number of policy provisions concerning the individual economy. It was on the basis of such policy provisions that, in August 1987, it made public the Interim Regulations on Administration of Urban and Rural Individual Industry and Commerce.

(2) Legal Protection for the Interests of Individuals Engaged in Industry and Commerce

In the past few years the administrative organs for industry and commerce have actively assisted individual businessmen in solving their production difficulties. They have especially assisted in problems associated with commodity sources and in correcting instances where individual businessmen have been wilfully evicted or had unjustified fees imposed.

(3) Strengthening the Education of Individual Labourers

Most individual labourers and businessmen abide by the law, but there are a small number of individual labourers and businessmen who have engaged in illegal operations such as giving short weight, bullying fellow dealers and evading taxes. While protecting their legal interests, the administrative organs for industry and commerce have strengthened education and control over these types, instilling professional ethics in them. Those who engaged in illegal activities are dealt with by law.

In the past few years individual labourers' associations have been established. The tasks of these mass organisations of individual labourers has been to educate individual labourers, safeguard their legal interests, convey their views and demands to relevant authorities, assist in solving problems of production and operation and assisting the government to administer individual labourers and attend to their welfare.

Education of individual labourers in political thinking, the legal system and professional ethics has achieved remarkable success. Large numbers of advanced people have emerged in their ranks. Altogether 4,083 people drawn from the ranks of individual labourers have been elected to People's Congresses above county level and 3,271 people to the people's political consultative conferences.

3. ADMINISTRATION OF PRIVATE ENTERPRISES

In the course of developing individual industry and commerce, some individual businesses employed more labourers than the norm set by the State. The result has been that a number of private enterprises have emerged.

(State Council has stipulated that individual businesses cannot employ more than 7 helpers or disciples.)

Private enterprises are obliged to abide by the law, regulations and policies of the State. They are obliged to establish sound finance and accounting procedures, to pay taxes and to accept supervision, inspection and administration by relevant State organs.

Initial statistics compiled at the end of 1987, showed that there were roughly 225,000 private enterprises employing 3.6 million people. Most of these enterprises are concentrated in productive trades which require a labour force of more than seven employees. Private enterprises in industry, handicrafts, communications and transport and the building industry account for 81.8% of the total number of private enterprises, their employees 87% and their funds 83.4%.

At present China's private enterprises are still in the early stage of their development. They are usually small scale and have poor conditions. The average number of hired labourers for each enterprise is 16. Less than 1% of private enterprises hire more than 100 people, but just a few enterprises hire several hundred labourers and there are unusual individual cases where the number comes to 1,000. The average capital of private enterprises is Rmb 50,000 with some enterprises having a capital of Rmb several hundred thousand and a small number having capital that exceeds Rmb 1 million.

Current policy seeks to encourage the development of private enterprises. The First Session of the Seventh National People's Congress held in April 1988 adopted an amendment to China's Constitution. Article 11 of the Constitution now has the added provision that:

> *The state allows [the] private economy to exist and develop within the scope prescribed by law. [The] Private economy is a compliment to the socialist economy of public ownership. The state protects the legal rights and interests of [the] private economy and gives it guidance, supervision and control...*

In order to encourage and guide private enterprises, to protect their legal rights and interests, and to strengthen the administrative work, on 25 June 1988 the State Council promulgated a further regulation governing private enterprises. This regulation—the Interim Regulation of the People's Republic of China on Private Enterprises, contained the following main points :

(1)   A Standard for Private Enterprises

The term 'private enterprise' refers to profit-making organisations using privately owned enterprise funding and hiring more than eight labourers. The enterprise must have funds, place for operating and equipment commensurate with the scale of its operation.

(2)   Eligibility for Establishing a Private Enterprise

Villagers in rural areas, unemployed in cities and towns, individual labourers and businessmen, people who have resigned from office or who have retired and other people permitted by State law can apply to establish a private enterprise. Those who apply to establish a private enterprise must carry relevant papers in order to register at the administrative organ for industry and commerce where the enterprise is located. They can start operation only when their application has been approved and a business licence has been issued.

(3)   The Business Scope of Private Enterprises

Within the scope permitted by State law, regulations and policies, private enterprises may engage in production and operation in industry, the building industry, communication and transport, commerce, catering and service trades, repairs, scientific and technological consultancies, and profit-making cultural and educational undertakings, technical training, recreation, planting and aquatics. There are three categories of commodities which private enterprises are not allowed to produce or market. First, there are the commodities which no enterprise or individual is allowed to produce or market. These include superstitious articles and medicines which are no longer used. Second, commodities which the State has designated for unified production by State enterprises such as jewellery and military industrial products. Third, commodities which are banned from private production, for example, motor cars and explosives.

(4)   Qualifications Required for the Purpose of Legal Identity

At present there are three types of private enterprise. These are personally funded enterprises, partnership enterprises and limited liability companies. China's General Rules of Civil Law link an enterprise's legal entity (its legal person status) with its limited liability. Personally funded and partnership enterprises bear unlimited liability or joint liability for debts and therefore cannot obtain the status of a legal person (entity). Limited liability companies can obtain legal person status because their shareholders are responsible to the company for the amount of their shares and the company assumes responsibility to its debtors through its property.

(5) Rights and Duties of Private Enterprises

Private enterprise investors have ownership over their property and their property can be inherited according to law. A private enterprise enjoys the right to exclusive use of the name that it has registered and had approved. Within the scope of approved registration, it has full authority of management and it enjoys the right to decide on organisational matters, to recruit and dismiss workers and staff, to decide on the enterprise's wage system and on the manner of profit distribution, to fix prices and to set the standard of its commodities, to sign contracts and apply for registration of trademark and patents. In accordance with the provisions of the law and regulations, private enterprises can establish Sino-foreign joint ventures or cooperative enterprises in conjunction with foreign economic interests or individuals and they can undertake processing with supplied materials or samples and engage in compensation trade.

V. TRADEMARKS

After the founding of the People's Republic of China, the government promulgated the Interim Regulations on Trademark Registration. This was done in 1950 and was one of the earliest economic laws enacted after the founding of New China. Then, in March 1983 a new Trademark law was enacted and both the Criminal Law and the General Rules of the Civil Law had special articles and clauses included for the protection of the right of exclusive use of registered trademarks and for the prevention illegal use of another's trademark.

The following points are characteristic of the administration of China's trademark system.

1. POINTS CHARACTERISTIC OF TRADEMARK ADMINISTRATION

(1) Registration is centralised. While administration is carried out at various administrative levels, all matters concerning registration of trademarks (both domestic and foreign) are handled by the Trademark Office under the State Administration for Industry and Commerce.

A Trademark Review and Adjudication Board has been established under the State Administration for Industry and Commerce. This Board handles trademark disputes. But while trademark registration is centralised, trademark sections that have been established under provincial or municipal administrative bureaus for industry and commerce undertake a large amount of trademark administrative work. (County administrative bureaus have also assigned people to take charge of trademark work.) This work involves curbing infringement, stopping the fraudulent use of trademarks or the practice of passing off unregistered trademarks as registered ones, and overseeing the printing of trademarks.

(2) Administration that covers the printing of trademarks. The State Administration for Industry and Commerce has published Interim Measures on the Administration of Trademark Printing. These measures provide that enterprises must have a trademark approved by the administrative organs for industry and commerce and that when printing registered or unregistered trademarks, they should take a trademark registration certificate or a business licence to the administrative organ for industry and commerce in order to get a necessary certificate of approval.

(3) When a trademark right has been infringed. When this has happened the party whose right has been infringed may file a lawsuit at a court in order to settle the matter through judicial procedure, or may ask the administrative organ for industry and commerce to handle it through administrative procedure. The latter is a simpler procedure and leads to the matter being settled in a shorter time.

In some cases a party whose right has been infringed has not discovered the infringement. In these cases the administrative organ for industry and commerce discovers the infringement and steps in to prevent it. In the 30 year period from 1949-1979 there were approximately 30,000 registered trademarks in China. By the end of 1987 the total was 187,626. This is a figure that in the space of nine years was six times greater than the figure for the previous 30 years.

VI. ADVERTISING

Advertising has a long history in China, but in New China it is a newly emerging business. For a long time after the founding of the People's Republic, advertising disappeared from the scene. It was not until after 1979 that the country's advertising business was restored and developed. By the end of 1987 there were 8,225 advertising enterprises employing 92,279 people with an annual business turnover of Rmb 1.1 billion. Meanwhile Sino-foreign joint advertising enterprises have also been established. There are now six Sino-foreign joint ventures engaged in the advertising business.

1. THE RESTORATION AND DEVELOPMENT OF ADVERTISING

Today restoration and development of advertising still has a long way to go. The number of advertising enterprises is still small, the level of advertisement design and quality is low and there are problems in terms of the management of advertising. This situation is one that has made it necessary to tighten control of the advertising industry.

On 6 February 1982 the State Council promulgated the Interim Regulations on the Supervision of Advertising. This was the first ever Chinese statute on the administration of advertising. Then on the basis of reviewing advertising in the period since 1982, the State Council promulgated the more recent (26 October, 1987) Regulations on the Supervision of Advertising. And in addition the State Administration for Industry and Commerce made public a number of regulations on the administration of advertising together with the departments concerned. The latter included the Methods on the Administration of Advertising of Pharmaceuticals and the Circular on Strengthening the Administration of Advertising for Lottery Tickets.

It is the State Administration for Industry and Commerce and its local administrative bureaus that are the management authorities for advertising. In accord with the Regulations on the Supervision of Advertising, the administration of advertising is conducted in the following manner:
(1) Enterprises and individual businesses engaged in advertising business must apply to the administrative organs for industry and commerce for registration.

(2) Advertisements are examined and if they contain the following they will be prohibited from publication or from broadcast, i.e.., those that go against Chinese law and decrees; those injurious to the dignity of the Chinese nation; those bearing marks of the Chinese national flag, national emblem and national anthem and the music of the Chinese national anthem; those that are reactionary, obscene, superstitious or preposterous; those that are falsified; and those that are uncomplimentary to other products of the same kind.

(3) Advertisers applying for publication or broadcast of advertisements for certain commodities must submit relevant certificates. For advertising that indicates the high quality of a product, certification of the high quality of the product must be submitted. For advertising commodities with registered trademarks, trademark registration certificates must be produced. For advertising commodities with patent rights, the patent right certificate must be presented.

(4) Publication or broadcasting of advertisements by news departments in the form of news reports and for remuneration is forbidden. Soliciting advertisements by news reporters in the name of reporting is also forbidden.

(5) Plans for advertisements that are to be posted outdoors must be mapped out by a competent department, organised by the local government and be implemented by the administrative organs for industry and commerce.

(6) Standard rates must be fixed for advertising. These fees are to be fixed by the advertising units and then reported to the local administrative organs for industry and commerce and presented to the price control department for their records.

(7) Administrative organs for industry and commerce are empowered to mete out punishment to advertisers or advertising units who violate the regulations and in serious cases of crime, those who violate laws and regulations will be dealt with by the judicial authorities.

CHAPTER 9

Enterprise Classification and Management

I. ENTERPRISE CLASSIFICATION

Chinese enterprises fall into three categories. First there are administrative units. These are usually government economic management organisations. The cost of these units is accounted as administrative expenses disbursed from State revenue. Second there are institutions such as scientific research organisations and prospecting and design organisations. Third there are enterprises that operate using independent accounting procedures. The latter two categories of institutions and enterprises meet expenditure from income drawn from production or other operating activities and they remit profit and tax to the State. They are institutions and enterprises that are afforded the status of a legal person (that of a legal entity).

1. CLASSIFICATION BASED ON TRADE

When classified according to trade, China's enterprises are divided into seven categories—industrial, agricultural, building and construction, commercial, transport, post and telecommunications, and financial enterprises.

(1) Industrial Enterprises

These enterprises can in turn be divided into those that engage in mining and processing and those engaged in heavy and light industrial production. By the end of 1987 China had 7,474 million industrial enterprises (including 494,000 industrial enterprises at township level and above), 5,249 million of these were engaged in light industrial production and 2,225 million were engaged in heavy industry.

(2) Agricultural Enterprises

These enterprises are divided into two groups: those engaged in cultivation and those engaged in raising animals. Enterprises in these two categories are engaged in crop planting, forestry, livestock raising, aquatic farming and various sideline occupations. By the end of 1987 there were 2,124 State farms and pasturelands and 484,100 rural economic associations.

(3) Building and Construction Enterprises

These are independent construction units that engage in productive activities—they build structures (including houses) and they install machinery and equipment. They are divided into two groups: construction and installation enterprises and units in charge of construction. The former are construction, installation and engineering companies and the latter are construction enterprises affiliated to existing production enterprises or administrative organisations. They account independently and are engaged in building or repairing their own fixed assets.

(4) Commercial Enterprises

These enterprises specialise in commodity circulation and exchange. They are divided into enterprises dealing in the means of production and those dealing directly in goods and services for consumption (means of livelihood). The category of commercial enterprise includes service enterprises such as those engaged in catering, hairdressing, washing and dyeing, photography and operating public bathhouses. By the end of 1987 there were 8,814 million retail commercial enterprises, 1,551 million catering enterprises and 1,694 million service enterprises.

(5) Transport Enterprises

These are enterprises concerned with commodity and passenger transport. They are divided into railway, highway, water, air, and pipe transport enterprises. The enterprises are often large with numerous departments and a large number of personnel. Enterprises in each of the transport groups have their own rules, regulations, laws and decrees and they have their own independent communication systems. At the end of 1987 there were 25 railway enterprises, 5,344 highway enterprises, 1,411 water transport enterprises and 11 aviation enterprises. All were accounting independently.

(6) Post and Telecommunications Enterprises

Post and telecommunications enterprises are divided into enterprises engaged in postal and telecommunication services and enterprises engaged in postal transport and maintenance of telecommunication lines and equipment. Enterprises engaged in postal and telecommunication services are established on the same lines as government administration. For example, post offices and telecommunication bureaus are established in provincial cities, capitals of autonomous regions and municipalities directly under the central government. These bureaus then have branch bureaus and offices operating under them. Enterprises engaged in postal transport and the maintenance of telecommunication lines and equipment include mail car general stations, circuit general stations, microwave general stations, and stations and substations under the jurisdiction of the general stations. Also, aside from the two types of post and telecommunications enterprise cited above, there are some enterprises that produce communication equipment for communications departments. At the end of 1987 there were 2,548 post and telecommunications enterprises.

(7)   Financial Enterprises

These are enterprises dealing with currency and credit. They receive deposits, issue loans and negotiable securities, handle payments and transfers and settlement of accounts. They also handle Chinese and foreign currency remittances, gold, silver and foreign exchange. They are involved in investment, trust and insurance and they offer financial advice and other financial services. Financial organisations and businesses directly operated and managed by the State include the People's Bank of China, the Industrial and Commercial Bank of China, the Agricultural Bank of China, the People's Construction Bank of China, the Bank of China and the Rural Credit Co-operative.

2.   CLASSIFICATION BASED ON OWNERSHIP

When classified according to ownership, China's enterprises fall into three groups—State-owned enterprises, collectively owned enterprises and individually owned enterprises. Though it should also be noted that there are enterprises that have mixed ownership.

(1)   State-Owned Enterprises

Prior to the 1979 introduction of economic reform policies, these enterprises were directly managed and administered by the State. But since 1979 government departments at all levels have, in principle, ceased to directly manage and administer these enterprises. The enterprises have become relatively independent entities with enterprise management assuming sole responsibility for profit and loss. At the time that economic reform was introduced (at the end of 1978) there were 97,600 State-owned industrial enterprises. They amounted to 19.8% of China's industrial enterprises with an output value of Rmb 825 billion or 69.7% of total industrial output value.

(2)   Collectively Owned Enterprises

These are enterprises that are collectively owned by the labouring masses. There are city, town and rural collectively owned enterprises with some city and town collectively owned enterprises having grown out of the individually operated economy. Other city and town collective enterprises were established by residents on the basis of voluntary participation and mutual benefit and others were established with investment made available by city and town government departments. Rural collective enterprises were nurtured by the agricultural co-operative movement. They were originally established in 1958 and after several periods of readjustment and consolidation they are now making rapid progress under economic reform.

The production and operating of collectively owned enterprises must be guided by the State plan. Compared with State-owned enterprises these enterprises have greater decision-making power. As long as these enterprises abide by the laws, decrees and policies of the State they are free to conduct capital construction, formulate their own production plans, recruit workers and staff and to independently handle their financial relations.

Collectively owned enterprises are economic organisations engaged in independent accounting and assuming sole responsibility for profit and loss. After paying tax to the State, the net income of these enterprises can be used as accumulation funds, welfare funds and for worker payment. No limit, neither maximum or minimum, is set for payment of workers and staff. Payment depends entirely on enterprise performance and management decision-making.

(3)   *Individually Owned Enterprises*

Usually individually owned enterprises are enterprises established and operated by households. They are private enterprises. Though they are permitted to employ a restricted number of wage workers, in most cases the owners, managers and labourers are individual workers and their families. Individually owned enterprises enjoy full autonomy in decision-making. They can make production choices in accord with market indicators and as long as they observe policies and laws and pay taxes on time, nobody is allowed to interfere with their operation.

(4)   *Enterprises with Mixed Ownership*

These are enterprises whose means of production are owned by different economic sectors. They are enterprises jointly owned by the State (the whole people) and collectives, by the State and individuals and by collectives and an individual. They must abide by government policies, laws and decrees and they must pay tax and profit to the State in accord with State stipulations. Their income must be shared in proportion to profits and in an agreed manner. Agreement must have been made through consultation at the time when the joint venture was established. Parties to a joint venture buy shares with their funds or properties and then use and allocate raw and semi-finished materials and machines and equipment in a unified way. In accord with government stipulations, they distribute profit only after they have remitted required profit and tax to relevant government authorities.

Sino-foreign joint ventures and co-operative enterprises are also enterprises with mixed ownership.

3.   *CLASSIFICATION BASED ON SIZE*

Enterprises are divided into large, medium-sized and small-sized with production capacity being used as the main criterion of enterprise size, but with some industries using original value of enterprise fixed assets, installed capacity or amount of equipment. Prior to the 1970s, many textile and light industrial enterprises determined their size category according to the number of workers and staff members employed. Now with improved enterprise mechanisation and automation, this method is no longer used.

9:1 ENTERPRISE TYPE DETERMINED ACCORDING TO PRODUCTION CAPACITY

Type of enterprise	Unit	Large	Medium	Small
Iron and steel complexes	Annual output of steel (10,000 metric tons)	Over 100	10-100	Under 10
Coal mining enterprises	Annual output of raw coal (10,000 metric tons)	Over 500	200-500	Under 200
Oil refineries	Annual processing capacity (10,000 metric tons)	Over 250	20-250	Under 50
Auto manufacturing plants	Annual production capacity (10,000)	Over 5	0.5-5	Under 20
Cement works	Annual production capacity (10,000)	Over 100	20-100	Under 20
Wrist-watch plants	Annual production capacity (10,000)	Over 100	40-100	Under 40
Bicycle plants	Annual production capacity (10,000)	Over 100	30-100	Under 30

When enterprise size has been determined by installed capacity or amount of equipment, a power plant with an installed capacity of more than 250,000 kW is categorised as a large enterprise, if it has an installed capacity of 25,000 kW to 250,000 kW it is categorised as medium-sized and with an installed capacity of less than 25,000 kW it is rated as a small enterprise. Taking another example, a cotton mill with more than 100,000 spindles is a large enterprise, with 50,000 to 100,000 spindles it is a medium-sized enterprise and with less than 50,000 spindles it is categorised as a small enterprise.

When an enterprise has its size category determined according to original value of fixed assets, it would be the case that a universal equipment producing factory with more than Rmb 30 million worth of original value fixed assets would be considered to be a large enterprise. An enterprise with between Rmb 8-30 million would be considered medium-sized and an enterprise with less than Rmb 8 million in original value fixed assets would be rated as a small enterprise.

9:2 NUMBER AND OUTPUT OF LARGE, MEDIUM AND SMALL INDUSTRIAL ENTERPRISES

	Number of enterprises		Gross industrial output value of enterprises	
Type of enterprise	Absolute number	% of total number of enterprises	Absolute output (Rmb100 million)	% of industrial output
Large	2,908	0.6	3,532	29.9
Medium	6,957	1.4	2,243	19.0
Small	483,708	98.0	6,054	51.2

Usually large and medium-sized enterprises are key enterprises which occupy an important position in the national economy. With advanced science and technology these enterprises have seen fairly good economic returns, but this has not meant that all large and medium-sized enterprises are advanced and it does not mean that larger enterprises are better. There are a large number of small enterprises in China's industrial sector that perform well. With a relatively small amount of investment, short construction periods, quick economic returns, flexible production and considerable ability to adapt, these enterprises play an important role in fully utilising local resources. But there have also been problems. There has been the problem of overlapping construction, waste of energy and poor quality but high-priced products and this situation has led to recent policy aimed at dealing with those small enterprises which consume high rates of energy, produce poor-quality goods, run at great losses and have no market for their products. These enterprises have been closed down or merged with other enterprises or they have been required to switch their manufacture to other more suitable products. For example, measures have been adopted to restrict the establishment of small inefficient cigarette factories which compete for scarce raw materials with large enterprises. Overall though, the State has followed the principle of promoting the simultaneous development of large, medium-sized and small-sized enterprises.

II. ENTERPRISE MANAGEMENT

1. *RELATIONS BETWEEN ENTERPRISE AND STATE*

Enterprises under the authority of the ministries of the State Council are called central enterprises and are directly managed by the ministry that they have been allocated to. Enterprises under the authority of provinces or local governments below provincial level are called local enterprises. They are managed by local industrial departments or bureaus. And there are enterprises which are subject to dual leadership. They are managed by both ministries of the State council and by local government departments. In these cases one administrative organ will be the principal managing department taking primary responsibility for the enterprise and the other will have secondary responsibility.

The department in charge of an enterprise is responsible for determining production scale, for relying planning targets, assessing fulfilment of production plan and for ensuring supply of funds, raw materials and services necessary for production. The department is also charged with arranging sale of product and with solving enterprise problems arising from management and production procedure.

During the process of economic reform, administrative structures have been streamlined and administrative power has been delegated to localities and enterprise relations or subordination have been changed, but the basic pattern whereby enterprises are subordinate to various administrative departments of government has remained unchanged. In future government departments will, in principle, no longer take direct charge of enterprises. But at present, when reform of the entire economic structure is still incomplete and the market has not yet fully developed, mandatory planning is still in use and enterprises continue to need to be guaranteed by a higher administrative authority. To date it is only a handful of large enterprise groups that have rid themselves of the restriction of the original relations of subordination. For example some enterprise groups have separate plans and are no longer subject to their original administrative arrangements.

In the past, distributed, profit and depreciation charges incurred by State enterprise were all handed over to the State with fixed capital and circulation funds needed for the enterprise production being supplied by the State. Enterprise losses, if any, were then also subsidised by the State. Staff were assigned to enterprises by government departments of labour and personnel and enterprises had no right to employ workers on their own or to recruit the best qualified. The wage system and workers' wage scales were determined exclusively by government departments and though bonus funds were drawn, they were drawn in proportion to total enterprise wages and directly included in production costs. They had nothing to do with enterprise profit and loss figures. Even enterprises running at a loss drew bonuses. Through planning and technical and economic indicators the State guided enterprise production and management and appraised enterprise performance. Indicators for assessing enterprise performance went through many changes. During the First Five-Year Plan period (1952-1957) there were 12 mandatory indicators. They included total output value, the output of major products, the trial manufacture of new category products, and in April 1975 one more indicator (use of circulating funds) was added. In April 1978 the 30 Points on Industry, The CPC Central Committee's Decision (Draft) on a Number of Questions Concerning Speeding Up Industrial Development was published. It set out the following eight technical and economic indicators for enterprise assessment: output, variety, quality, consumption of energy and materials, labour productivity, costs, profits and use of circulating funds. Then in 1979 it was stated that pilot enterprises that were enjoying significantly greater decision-making powers would be subject to assessment based on only four indicators—output, quality, profit and contract implementation. When it came to export-oriented enterprises, success in implementing contracts and amount of foreign exchange earned was also examined.

Policy during the decade of the 1980s was concentrated on economic reform that explored ways of readjusting and changing the limits of authority and the interest relationship between the enterprise and the State. A basic policy of simplifying administration, delegating power, reducing taxes and ceding interests from the State to the enterprise was followed. By and large changes were effected in the following four stages:

(1) 1979-1980—the Experimental Period

During this period efforts were concentrated on experiments in granting greater decision-making powers to enterprises. In October 1978 Sichuan Province began experimenting by granting greater power to the Chongqing Iron and Steel Company and to five other enterprises. By April 1979 the province had extended this experiment to 100 other selected enterprises. Yunnan Province had also begun similar experiments with 50 enterprises and in July 1979, after the State Council had issued its Regulations Concerning the Extension of Decision-Making Power in the Operation and Management of State-Owned Enterprises, together with four other documents concerned with reform of enterprise management, other provinces, autonomous regions and municipalities conducted similar experiments. By the end of 1980 more than 6,000 enterprises were enjoying greater decision-making power. These represented 16% of industrial enterprises under the State budget, but they were enterprises that were responsible for 60% of total output value and 70% of industrial enterprise profit.

Enterprises enjoying greater decision-making power began to have some autonomy over planning, over purchase of production materials, marketing of products and over wage determination. The system of comprehensive State control over income and expenditure was replaced with a system that allowed partial retention of profit which in turn allowed enterprise funds to be used for production development, workers' welfare and profit based bonus payments to workers.

(2) 1981-1982—the Economic Responsibility System

The introduction of the system of allowing enterprises to retain a portion of their profits gave rise to a difficult problem. Due to the price situation (the irrational pricing structure) in relation to industrial products, enterprise profit could not accurately reflect the level of enterprise operation and management. This meant that it was necessary to define percentage of profit to be retained in accord with the production and marketing conditions of each enterprise. By 1981 this situation had led to various localities introducing various forms of economic responsibility systems on a trial basis. These systems held enterprises responsible for a quota of profits, for a quota of deficits, a progressive profit growth rate and some allowed enterprises to pay tax rather than deliver profit to the State. The aim was to experiment widely in order to find the best available form of standard enterprise management.

(3) 1983-1984—the First Phase of Replacing Profit Repatriation with Tax Payment

The results from trials with various forms of economic responsibility systems proved that it was much better to introduce tax payment rather than adopt a system based on enterprise profit repatriation. At first enterprises were required to pay tax and to deliver profit payments. They were required to pay income tax according to a tax rate set by law and then they were required to deliver a set percentage of profit to the State. Profit repatriation was based on the relevant government department assessing the conditions of production faced by the enterprise. For example, when there was a difference in prices and conditions for acquiring raw materials, even when enterprises were producing the same type of product, percentage of profit repatriated would be adjusted in order to provide enterprises with similar profit margins.

(4)   The Last Quarter of 1984 to 1986—the Second Tax-Replacing-Profit Stage

This stage resulted in enterprises paying only tax to the State. This stage required that tax rates be adjusted to accord with the actual economic conditions encountered by each trade and by each enterprise. The solution adopted was that each enterprise would pay a resource tax and an income regulation tax paid after income tax. Enterprises were then free to retain their after-tax profit.

In the last decade, since the introduction of economic reform policy, the State Council has released a dozen or so documents and some 100 regulations concerned with expanding enterprise decision-making powers. The most important of these have been The Provisional Regulations for Further Expanding the Decision-Making Powers of State-Owned Industrial Enterprises released by the State Council in May 1984 and The Law Concerning Industrial Enterprises Owned by the Whole People released in August 1988. These regulations and law specify enterprise decision-making arrangements in the following ways:

(i)   Production management and planning. Under the guidance of the State plan enterprises are given the right to arrange production. Enterprises charged with the task of fulfilling State mandatory plans have the right to require the State to adjust its mandatory plan when supply of materials or sale of products is not guaranteed by the State.

(ii)   Enterprises are given the right to sell their products through their own channels. Only products under State regulation are exempt. Enterprises charged with the task of filling State mandatory plans have the right to sell above-quota production together with that portion of product allowed to be retained within the State-set quota.

(iii)   Except in the case where prices are subject to the management of State Council-authorised pricing departments, enterprises are afforded the right to set the price for their products and for labour services.

(iv)   When purchasing materials, enterprises are free to select their own suppliers.

(v)   In terms of funding, enterprises have the right, in accord with different percentages set by the relevant superior government departments, to allocate funds to production development, new product experimentation, reserve funds, employees' welfare funds and bonus funds. They also have the right to use funds independently.

From 1985 enterprises were allowed to retain 70% of depreciation charges and in 1987 all depreciation charges were allowed to be retained by the enterprise.

Enterprises then had the right to invest in existing fixed assets, working funds and property rights of other enterprises and public undertakings. They were free to hold the stocks of other enterprises and they had the right to issue bonds in accord with State Council regulations.

(vi)   In terms of asset disposal, enterprises have the right to lease or transfer, with compensation, any fixed assets deemed to be surplus.

(vii)   In organisational terms, enterprises have the right to determine both enterprise size and organisational structure.

(viii) In terms of personnel and labour management, enterprise directors are either appointed and invited by a government authorised department to take their position or they are elected by congresses of workers and staff of the enterprise and then approved by the relevant government-authorised department. Deputy directors are approved by government-authorised departments. Administrative cadres at the level of middle management are appointed and dismissed by enterprise directors. Enterprise directors have the power to reward or punish staff and workers, to promote, dismiss and to select staff and workers according to their qualifications.

(ix) While implementing State-set wage rates and recognising regional wage differentials and financial subsidies, enterprises have the power to determine wage patterns and to reward in accord with profit earned. Enterprise directors have the power to promote as many as 3% of their workers and staff each year.

(x) Enterprises are in a position to organise and/or participate in trade with other enterprises, including those in other regions, and they are free to organise trans-regional co-operative management and to select partners for co-operative production as long as no change in ownership takes place.

2. THE SEPARATION OF OWNERSHIP FROM RIGHT OF MANAGEMENT

Granting enterprises greater decision-making power and allowing the retention of a larger portion of profit played an important role in invigorating enterprise behaviour, but this policy made it important that a solution be found to the problem of separating ownership from the right of management. This problem has resulted in government departments at various levels interfering in enterprise affairs and decision-making. Profits supposed to be retained by the enterprise were not guaranteed. The result was that at the beginning of 1987 a thorough reform of the nexus between government administration and enterprise management was put in place.

Enterprise management must enable enterprises to make decisions independent of external interference. Enterprises must be guaranteed their due interest and they must be allowed to benefit from improved management decision-making. It is only when this has been achieved that the enterprise will have an internal driving force.

Three management patterns for realising the separation of ownership from the right of management were adopted. These were a leasing system, a joint-stock system and a contract-based management responsibility system. The leasing system is usually applied only to small enterprises. By the end of June 1988 53.3% of small State-owned enterprises had been leased to be managed by collectives or individuals. The joint-stock system has been used in a few pilot enterprises with the State holding proprietary shares and with other departments and individuals holding the remaining shares. This system is applied to enterprise groups and enterprises formed through horizontal economic co-operation. It is a system that is likely to form a new pattern of management, but to date, it is still a controversial system that has many problems that are yet to be clarified. It is the third innovation, the contract-based management responsibility system, that is the system that has been most widely implemented. It is now used by almost all enterprises.

By June 1988 90% of large and medium-sized State-owned enterprises were using some form of contract-based management responsibility system. This is a policy that has proved to be most effective in promoting the separation of ownership from the right of management. Once a contract has been signed, the relationship between the enterprise and its administrative government department changes from one of administrative superiority of the government department over the enterprise to a legally protected contract relationship between partners. A contract is signed that specifies economic responsibility and the economic powers and benefits of both government and enterprise in relation to enterprise production, operation and income distribution. This system has been most effective in promoting enterprise management responsibility for self-growth and for self-restraint. It would not have been sufficient to have simply allowed enterprises more decision-making power and retention of a greater proportion of profit.

The contract responsibility system has taken various forms, but the most important are the following:

(1) *The 'Double-guarantee, One-link' Contract Management Responsibility System*

The term 'double-guarantee' refers to the enterprise guaranteeing to fulfil government-designated quotas for tax and profit repatriation and guaranteeing to fulfil technical transformation tasks set by the State. The term 'one-link' refers to linking the total wage bill of an enterprise with economic performance. An example of the 'double guarantee, one-link' contract management responsibility system in practice is the Beijing No 1 Machine Tool Plant and seven other factories who, operating as a single accounting entity, were, during the Seventh Five-Year Plan (1986-1990), required to remit to the State a total of Rmb 387 million in tax and profit (an increase of 74.8% over the previous planning period). After payment of tax and profit to the State they were then required to accumulate a total of Rmb 285 million to use for technical transformation. In addition, every time their tax and profit increased by 1% their total wage bill was to be increased by 0.8%. After meeting this requirement they were then free to determine the form and method of their wage distribution.

(2) *Contracts Covering Delivery of Progressively Growing Profits to the State*

These contracts were adopted during the change-over period between enterprise payment of profit to the State to enterprise payment of tax to the State. In the case of some large enterprises, after remitting product tax to the State, they are also required to continue to remit a base amount of profit (decided during the first year of a contract) plus a portion of their progressively increasing enterprise profit to the State. For example the Capital Iron and Steel Company has an agreed contract with the State to deliver funds from profit (base amount plus agreed proportion of profit increase) that increases annually at the rate of 7.2%. The enterprise then retains the remaining profit that is in turn allocated to production development funds, collective welfare funds and wage and bonus funds. This allocation is on the ratio of 6:2:2.

Enterprises that have only a small margin of profit increase or that return a deficit, are required to pay a base amount of profit to the State or they receive an agreed subsidy from the State. These enterprises are not required to remit a profit share subsidy to the State.

(3)   The Input and Output Contract

By 1987 eight sectors of the economy—petroleum, coal, petrochemical, non-ferrous, railway, post and telecommunications and civil aviation, had instituted this type of contract. In practice it is a form of contract that has been effective in promoting enterprise productivity. In 1987 total tax and profit remitted from enterprises using the input and output contract system increased by Rmb 11.8 billion, a 9.9% increase over the previous year.

3.   REFORM OF ENTERPRISE LEADERSHIP AND THE ROLE OF THE ENTERPRISE DIRECTOR

The key to reform of enterprise leadership has been the introduction of the 'factory director responsibility system'. After extensive pilot reform of enterprise leadership, it was decide that a change must be instituted.

In September 1984, on the basis of experience gained through pilot reform, the CPC Central Committee and the State Council promulgated the Regulation on the Work of Directors of Industrial Enterprises Owned by the Whole People, The Regulations on the Work of the Grass-Roots Organizations of the Communist Party of China in Industrial Enterprises Owned by the Whole People, and The Regulations on the Work of the Workers' Congresses in Industrial Enterprises Owned by the Whole People. These three regulations promoted enterprise leadership reform. After the Enterprise Law went into effect in 1988, most State enterprises adopted the system of the factory director assuming full responsibility.

In terms of content, factory director responsibility means that the factory director of a State industrial enterprise is seen as the legal representative of the enterprise. It is the director who assumes full responsibility for the enterprise.

The factory director is invested with power to do the following:
- ... to direct the production and ideological work of his or her unit;
- ... to decide on plans for the factory and submit them to the relevant administrative department of government for examination and approval in accord with State law and State Council Regulations;
- ... to appoint or dismiss administrative medium level factor cadres and to seek (from the department authorised by government) the appointment or dismissal of cadres at the level of deputy factory director;
- ... to establish schemes for the adjustment of wages and salaries, schemes for distribution of bonus payments, for the utilisation of welfare funds and the establishment of proposals concerned with worker and staff welfare and submit same to the workers' congress for examination; and
- ... to give awards or to mete out punishment for workers.

When it comes to selection of a factory manager, this is done either through the relevant government department appointing the manager or through the workers' congress establishment and any re-adjustment of enterprise administrative organisations.

The factory director has the power to decide on the business management and operation of the enterprise and the power to direct production. When the factory manager does not agree with the majority of management committee members over an issue of enterprise management, it is the factory director who has the power to make the final decision.

4. REFORM OF ENTERPRISE LEADERSHIP AND THE WORK OF THE ENTERPRISE PARTY COMMITTEE

In the past it has been the enterprise Party committee that has exercised leadership over the work of the enterprise. But with the introduction of the system whereby the factory manager assumes full responsibility for the enterprise, the function of the Party Committee has had to change. In line with the principle of separating Party from economic administration, the enterprise Party Committee no longer exercises leadership authority over enterprise decision-making. Major tasks now to be undertaken by the Party Committee are:

- ... supervising implementation of Party principles and policies;
- ... undertaking enterprise ideological work, including ideological and political education of workers and staff;
- ... providing support for the enterprise director in the exercise of leadership and in fulfilling his or her production responsibility target within the period of holding office;
- ... ensuring the socialist orientation of enterprise production and management;
- ... ensuring that the democratic rights and interests of workers and staff are protected;
- ... ensuring that the enterprise observes State law;
- ... ensuring that the relationship between interests of the State, the enterprise and the workers and staff is correctly handled by the enterprise; and
- ... ensuring that the enterprise director correctly implements the policies and principles of the Party.

The ideological and political work of the enterprise must serve the general task and the general goal of the Party and it must be carried out in close co-ordination with the enterprise's economic work. When undertaking economic work enterprise management must adhere to the 'four cardinal principles' [to keep China to the socialist road, to uphold the people's democratic dictatorship, to uphold the leadership of the CCP and to support Marxism-Leninism-Mao Zedong Thought] and the general principle of reform and opening to the outside world. And enterprise management policy must also ensure that workers and staff meet the needs of the Party's modernisation drive.

5. THE ROLE OF THE WORKERS' CONGRESS

The role of the workers' congress is to provide democratic management at enterprise level. In the interest of advancing this role the workers' congress undertakes the following:

(1) Discussion of the factory director's report including the long-term plan, the fiscal plan, any schemes for enterprise expansion or renovation, schemes for enterprise expansion or renovation, plans for technical training of workers and staff, plans for the distribution and use of enterprise capital for any leasing arrangements. Members of the workers' congress then express their opinions of the report.

(2) Review of schemes proposed by the enterprise director for implementation of the enterprise economic responsibility system, for re-adjustment of wages and salaries, for distribution of bonuses, labour protection measures and methods to be adopted with regard to worker and staff reward and punishment.

(3) Discussing and deciding on proposals concerning use of workers' welfare funds, the allotment of housing and other important matters concerning the welfare of workers and staff;

(4) Discussing and supervising the performance of leading enterprise cadres; and

(5) Electing the enterprise director.

The trade union is the working organ of the congress of workers and staff. It is the trade union that does the routine work of the congress. The enterprise trade union serves as the important representative of workers and staff. It represents the interests of the workers and staff, voices their opinion and acts on their behalf.

6. ENTERPRISE PLANNING OFFICES

In addition to the leadership role of the factory director, the role of the Party committee and the role of workers' congresses, a large portion of factory management is undertaken by what are referred to as the 'functional offices'. These offices consist of the general office, the technology office (the technical and design office in some enterprises), the production co-ordination office, equipment and power office, materials supply office, marketing office, finance office, labour and wages office, workers' education office, personnel office and security office. Each of these offices has an office director and one or two deputy directors who take care of the day-to-day running of the enterprise. The offices administer the implementation of the enterprise director's instructions and they provide information that enables the enterprise director to exercise leadership over the enterprise, but these offices do not have the power to directly interfere in the organisation of workshop production. It is the workshop director and below him or her the workshop group who organise the individual worker in the production process.

7. THE ROLE OF THE FACTORY WORKSHOP

The workshop is the basic production unit within an enterprise. The workshop director is responsible for production and for administration of the workshop. The director works under the leadership of the enterprise director organising production, including planning, quality control, labour discipline, making necessary technical preparations for production, guaranteeing production safety and accounting at workshop level in order to reduce production cost. Larger enterprise workshops are usually complete functioning groups who are in charge of planning, quality control, production co-ordination and economic accounting.

Within the workshop, workshop groups are formed by the workers themselves. It is these groups that organise the work of individual workers on a per day per machine basis. The workshop groups have leaders who, in turn, are responsible for organising the group's production while acting in a productive capacity themselves

9:3 THE POSITION OF FACTORY AND WORKSHOP DIRECTORS, ADVISORS AND GROUPS

Factory director
↓
Deputy factory directors
↓
Chief engineer, general financier,
chief accountant, and legal advisers,
↓
Functional offices
↓
Workshop directors
↓
Workshop groups

8. PLANNING AT ENTERPRISE LEVEL

Enterprise planning involves putting forward feasible enterprise targets and organising the implementation of these targets. Enterprise planning is divided into three sections long-term plans, annual plans and production and operation plans.

(1) Long-term Plans

These plans usually cover the period of five, ten or even fifteen years. They are constructed in line with the long-term plan of the State. They include:
- ... enterprise development plans which involve production magnitude, technological advances and the development of enterprise products:
- ... overall ideas and a general outline for the raising of funds, capital construction, key projects of technical renovation and guidelines for the development of new products and for monitoring quality of enterprise product:
- ... plans for profit-making, for raising production efficiency, reducing cost and for improving the efficient use of enterprise funds:
- ... plans for specialised co-operation and plans for marketing of both products and technical services:

... plans for worker welfare including worker and staff training plans and plans for meeting the day to day living needs of staff and workers.

(2) Annual plans

These are plans formulated for a specific year or covering a specific portion of a year. They are more detailed and more specific than long-term plans. Annual plans are usually composed of two parts: (i) fixed assets and circulating funds and (ii) funds for production development and welfare funds. Fixed asset and circulating funds serve to co-ordinate production and management activities within the enterprise and development and welfare funds allow arrangements to be made for new production capacity and for improving the well-being, welfare and production conditions of workers and staff. The former includes enterprise operating and comprehensive plans, plans for technological development and for improving quality of goods, sale of product, supply of materials and labour and wages. The latter includes enterprise plans for overall development, capital construction, updating and upgrading and the supply of equipment and funds.

(3) Production and operation plans

These are more specific than annual plans. They are formulated monthly for a period of ten days, weekly or daily. They are used for arranging production tasks, for charting workshop progress and for organising sectors of construction projects.

9. MANAGEMENT OF ENTERPRISE FUNDS

Enterprise level financial management is charged with organising the supply of funds to the enterprise, the proper use of fixed capital, provision of circulating capital and special funds, control of enterprise costs, reduction of production cost and increase of profit, distribution of enterprise income and the remittance of tax and profit to the State.

Funds used by an enterprise include those drawn from fixed capital, circulating capital and from special funds. Since the implementation of economic reform policy, enterprises have usually raised their own capital. They have received State appropriations, but they have then had to raise bank loans and to have received funds from accounts settled. In addition many enterprises have undertaken various other fund operating activities. These have included activities such as selling shares to workers and staff, issuing bonds and inter-enterprise investment.

9:4 SIX CHANNELS FOR FUNDING STATE ENTERPRISES

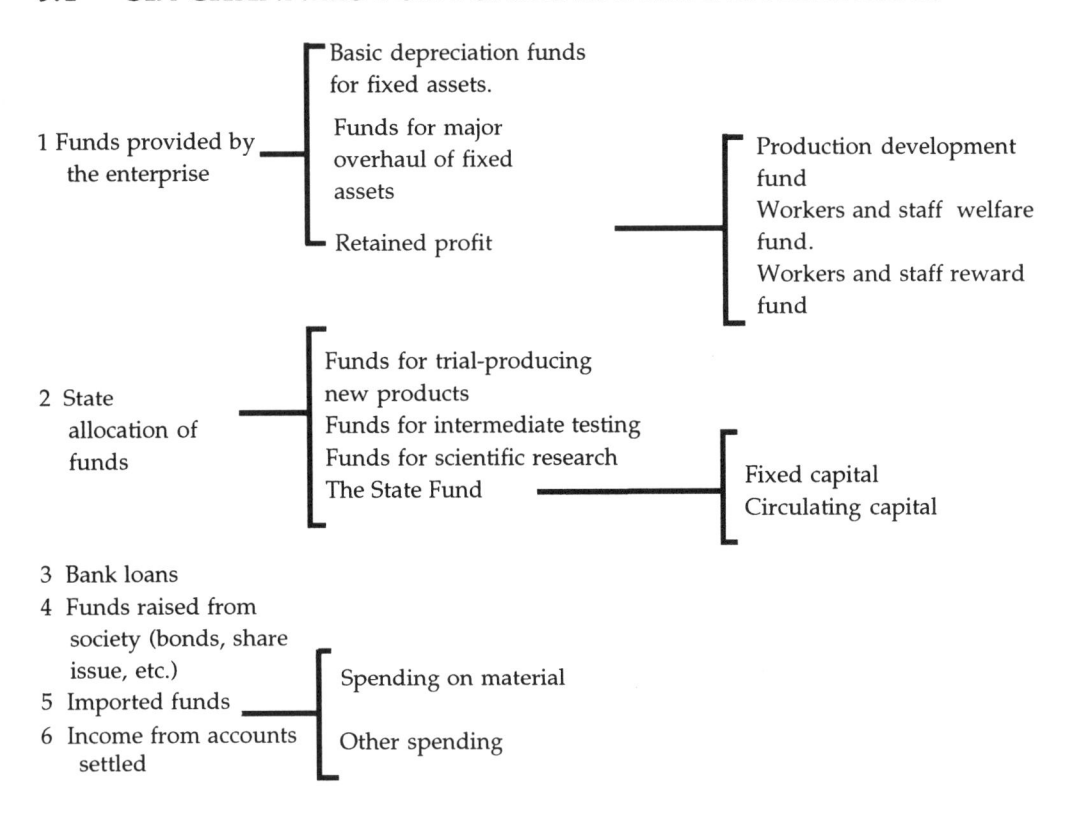

1. Funds provided by the enterprise
   - Basic depreciation funds for fixed assets.
   - Funds for major overhaul of fixed assets
   - Retained profit
     - Production development fund
     - Workers and staff welfare fund.
     - Workers and staff reward fund

2. State allocation of funds
   - Funds for trial-producing new products
   - Funds for intermediate testing
   - Funds for scientific research
   - The State Fund
     - Fixed capital
     - Circulating capital

3. Bank loans
4. Funds raised from society (bonds, share issue, etc.)
5. Imported funds
6. Income from accounts settled
   - Spending on material
   - Other spending

(1) Enterprise Fixed Capital

This is the monetary form of the various types of fixed asset belonging to the enterprises. Fixed assets are usually means of production and other material goods which can be used by the enterprise. Fixed assets include factory buildings and land, machinery and equipment and productive tools and instruments. Non-productive fixed assets include workers' dormitories and hostels, canteens, hospitals, clubs, child-care centres, bath houses and schools.

For a long time China practised a system based on the free use of fixed assets. For a new enterprise, capital for fixed assets came from State financial departments in the form of capital construction investments. For existing enterprises, capital required for renovation and expansion projects also came from State financial allocation. Enterprises then used the fixed assets without shouldering any economic responsibility. In order to change this situation, in 1980 a compensatory system was introduced. Under this system enterprises were required to pay for the use of fixed assets on a monthly basis. Then in 1985, the State began to budget investment from enterprise bank loans rather than from financial allocation.

(2) Circulation Capital

Funds in this category are the funds required by the enterprise to pay for raw materials, wages and other costs of production. It is the enterprise working capital. It is divided into monetary capital, reserve funds, funds for production, finished product funds and account settlement funds. In a process that extends from buying raw materials through organising production to the finished product and sales, circulation capital changes from reserve funds to funds for production and then to funds for finished products and finally to account settlement and monetary funds.

Circulation capital is divided into fixed-quota circulation capital and non fixed-quota capital. Fixed-quota capital usually consists of three sections—reserve funds, funds for production and funds for finished products. Non fixed-quota circulation capital refers to account settlement funds and monetary funds used in the process of circulation. It is provided by banks in the form of enterprise loans and it is often referred to as credit funds. Since July 1983 the system whereby the banks take overall responsibility for the management of circulation capital has been in operation. A new system was then added to this system. This new system allows enterprises to replenish their own circulating capital. With the expansion of production and circulation, enterprises can fund a part of additional circulating capital and then they can use a bank loan to cover the remaining portion.

(3) Special Funds

The Fixed Asset Depreciation Fund. At present the depreciation rate for enterprises is calculated monthly in line with the ascertained monthly comprehensive depreciation rate. Annual depreciation rate is calculated according to the following—original value of fixed assets less estimated income from the scrap value of fixed assets and the costs of their disposal divided by years of use.

The fixed assets depreciation fund is a source of capital for an enterprise intending to invest in equipment renewal and technological updating. Methods used to facilitate distribution of monies from the fixed asset depreciation fund have varied considerably over time. In the past the fund was handed over to the State treasury for concentrated use. Usually the funds were pumped into new projects rather being made available for equipment renewal and the technological upgrading of enterprises. Local government and central government departments shared the fund using the ratio 3:3:4. Then a change was instituted. This change led to the enterprises being free to retain 70% of the fund, the remaining 30% being remitted to higher government departments. Then there was another change. This change was a change to the present system where the total fund is left for use by the enterprise. The enterprise is free to use the fund in conjunction with other funds such as the enterprise production development fund. According to the State stipulations the fund can be used to:

... renew machinery and equipment and to rebuild factory buildings;
... to carry out technological upgrading of existing enterprise fixed assets;
... to develop new products;
... to make better use of raw materials and for use in such matters as the disposal of waste gas, waste water and industrial residue;

... to improve worker safety; and

... to buy small fixed assets or small lots of (fragmentary) fixed assets.

Aside from the basic fixed assets depreciation fund outlined immediately above, enterprises can also establish a fund referred to as the Major Overhaul Depreciation Fund. This fund is used, as its title suggests, for the major overhaul of enterprise fixed assets. It is calculated in accord with the number of years of use and the total amount of funds spent on overhaul during the period of use. In order to keep pace with scientific and technological developments, a major overhaul of enterprise fixed assets usually takes place when technological upgrading projects are in process. All of the overhaul depreciation fund is left to be invested at the discretion of the enterprise.

10. BANKRUPTCY OF ENTERPRISES

Under the old economic system the debts incurred by an enterprise were not paid through improved management and increased income or by sale of fixed assets. They were paid by State financial subsidy. Today, when an enterprise is deep in the red because of poor management and it is unable to pay its debts in time, it is considered to be on the brink of bankruptcy.

In 1984, with the introduction of a bankruptcy system under discussion, some enterprises were selected as testing grounds for a bankruptcy system. Shenyang city in Liaoning Province was the first to experiment. The city first tried the bankruptcy system on a few enterprises and then in February 1985 the city's government promulgated the Provisional Regulations Concerning the Bankruptcy of Collective-Owned Industrial Enterprise for trial implementation. This document clearly stipulated that when an enterprise cannot produce enough to offset its debts (that is, when its debts are as much as, or more than its total fixed assets) or when it has run in deficit for two consecutive years and the deficits have already accounted for more than 80% of net value of total fixed assets, it must be considered to be on the brink of bankruptcy. The enterprise is then given one year to overcome its problems and if there is no sign that the enterprise can trade its way out of its problems, at the end of the one-year period of grace, it will be declared bankrupt.

The city of Wuhan in Hubei Province was the first to experiment with bankruptcy in State-owned enterprises. In May 1985 the city government declared that the State-owned No 3 Radio Factory was 'at the brink of bankruptcy and needed to be consolidated'. After nine months of restructuring this factory began to make a profit.

In the two years that followed the Shenyang promulgated provisional bankruptcy regulations, six cities and regions in China selected enterprises (both collectively owned and State-owned) for experimentation with the bankruptcy system. Most of these enterprises (13 collective and 15 State) were able to trade out of their financial problems. There were just two exceptions, the Shenyang Anti-Explosion Appliances Factory and a department store in Nanchang, Jiangxi Province.

On the basis of experiences gained while piloting the bankruptcy law, the 18th Plenary Session of the Standing Committee of the Sixth National People's Congress approved the Law of the People's Republic of China About Enterprise Bankruptcy for trial implementation. This was on 2 December 1986. This law was to be applicable to all State-owned enterprises with the legal interests of creditors and debtors of enterprises of other ownership types coming under the protection of other laws. For example, the General Principles of the People's Republic of China includes clear stipulations with regard to the responsibility of debtors and the scope of their assets. It states that 'an enterprise under collective ownership, as a legal person [entity], shall bear civil equity joint venture, a Chinese-foreign contractual joint venture or a foreign-capital enterprise as a legal person [entity] shall bear civil liability with the property it owns...' It also states that 'the debts of an individual business or a lease-holding farm household shall be secured with the individual's property if the business is operated by an individual and with the family's property if the business is operated by a family...'

The enterprise bankruptcy law stipulated that the law was to be implemented three full months after the Law on Industrial Enterprises with Ownership by the Whole People came into effect. It came into effect in August 1988.

Use of the bankruptcy law was, at this time, considered to be a preferable system to the provision of direct State subsidies to ailing enterprises and it was seen as being preferable to simply allowing enterprises to remain in arrears in payment of debt over a long period of time. After the introduction of economic reform policy the situation had arisen where enterprises in arrears with debts owed to other enterprises and even in arrears with bank loans, were granted new loans even though their old debts remained unpaid. This resulted in relations between creditors and debtors becoming increasingly abnormal. The bankruptcy law was also, at the time of its adoption, seen as a preferable method of dealing with failing enterprises to the often used method of forcing these enterprises to produce other products or merging them with other enterprises. These administrative measures had often led to the continued use of technically outdated enterprises that consumed too much raw material. They often had costs that were high while the quality of their products was poor. In the end these enterprises were sometimes forced to close down, but even when they did close down, they did so without having borne any liability for their inefficiency. What happened was that their debts to banks or other enterprises were written off as 'losses'. The creditor enterprises had not been able to recall their debts while the workers and staff of the failed enterprise had received their pay.

The most striking problem arising from the introduction of bankruptcy law was the question of how to re-employ the workers and staff of bankrupt enterprises. It was recognised that if no solution was found to this problem social stability would be endangered. This is why the bankruptcy law stipulates that 'the State through various means shall arrange for the appropriate re-employment of the staff and workers of bankrupt enterprises and shall guarantee their basic living needs prior to re-employment...' To this end, on 12 July 1986 the State Council promulgated the Provisional Regulations Concerning the Insurance of Staff and Workers of State-Owned Enterprises Waiting for Re-employment. These regulations were applicable to staff and workers of those enterprises declared bankrupt and staff and workers made redundant by enterprises declared to be at the brink of bankruptcy. They were also extended to be made applicable to staff and workers whose contracts with their employers expired and were not renewed.

The three sources for insurance funds for staff and workers waiting for re-employment are as follows:
- ... enterprise contribution of the equivalent of 1% of total standard wage bill to an insurance fund;
- ... bank interest on these insurance funds; and
- ... local financial subsidies contributed to insurance funds.

The insurance funds are administered by the government of provinces, autonomous regions and centrally administered municipalities with these administrations granting subsidies if the insurance funds cannot cover expenditure.

The maximum time that unemployment relief is given is 24 months. For the first twelve months relief is given at a rate of between 60% and 75% of average monthly wages calculated on the basis of the last two years employment. If payment is given for the second twelve months, it is at the rate of 50% of average monthly wages and it is only given for a second year if the worker or staff member has spent five years or more in the workforce.

CHAPTER 10

Employment, Wages and Welfare

I. EMPLOYMENT

1. LABOUR RESOURCES

China is rich in labour resources and there is a large population that is still growing. By the end of 1987 mainland China had a population of 1.08 billion. A total of 527.8 million of the population were participating in the labour force and in cities and towns and an estimated 2.8 million were waited for employment.

Future growth of labour resources is reflected in the number of students attending both school and pre-school. By 1987 there were 237.6 million school students and more than 100 million pre-school children.

In terms of present composition of the labour force, the proportion of labourers engaged in production in the agricultural sector is very large, while the proportion engaged in the industrial sector continues to increase and the proportion employed in transport and communications, commerce and in service industries is relatively small.

Since the introduction of the contract responsibility system in rural areas, the composition of the agricultural labour force has undergone remarkable change. It was with the introduction of this system that considerable numbers of labourers freed themselves from grain production in order to engage in various types of special undertakings, usually industrial or sideline occupations, or employment and business in cities and towns.

2. THE 'THREE-INTEGRATION' EMPLOYMENT SYSTEM

In 1980 a 'three-integration' employment system was introduced. This system consisted of:

... employing through the use of labour departments,
... voluntarily organised employment, and
... looking for job openings oneself.

The first aspect of the system, i.e., 'employing through introduction', refers to labour management departments assigning people to work for government institutions in accord with State planned job quotas. The second, 'voluntary organised employment', refers to people who organise themselves to run various types of collective economic units and who in the process create more job opportunities. And the third aspect of the system, 'looking for job openings oneself' refers to the situation where labourers are allowed to run various types of self-operated industrial workshops or to engage in various types of commercial and service businesses.

In order to guarantee the implementation of the 'three-integration' employment system, the State reformed the labour system. Gradually workers were selectively recruited and a flexible recruiting system was instituted. The latter enables enterprises to either increase or decrease their labour force in light of their production requirements.

Reform of the labour system also meant that by integrating their own speciality and aspirations with the needs of the State, workers could choose their own job. And at the same time, the government did its best to create job openings through improving the industrial structure and the structure of ownership. Efforts were also made to improve the running of the urban collective economy and to encourage young people waiting for employment to organise themselves into these collectively owned economic units. The urban individual economy was also encouraged and private industrial and commercial households were allowed to have helpers or apprentices.

The 'three-integration' policy will continue to be implemented in the future and the following reforms will also be introduced:

... farmers will be allowed to work in the small and medium-sized cities and in particular in small cities and towns;

... the employee examination system will be strengthened whereby all government jobs are open to those who do best in a pre-employment examinations; and

... an unemployment management institution will be established. It will carry out employment training, issue unemployment relief funds and introduce jobs to job-hunters.

The problem of workers waiting for employment is mainly a problem that is confined to cities and towns. Those able and wishing to work, but who cannot find a job, need to register themselves at local employment offices. The employment waiting group is most often composed of middle and high school graduates aged between 16 and 25 years who have failed to pass examinations for higher education or who have not joined the army, although the group does also include other types of people who are aged between 25 and 50 years.

3. THE CONTRACT WORKER SYSTEM

As a means of providing State-owned enterprises with flexibility in terms of their workforce, on 1 October 1986 the State Council promulgated the Provisional Regulations concerning the Implementation of the Contract Labour System in State-Owned Enterprises. These regulations state that from 1 October 1986: the contract worker system applies to the workers holding perennial jobs, employed by various enterprises in accordance with the job quotas including the state plan on labour and wages, not including those of enterprises implementing state special policies.

Under this system the relationship between the employing enterprise and the worker is set out in the form of a contract which specifies the rights, interests and obligations of both the enterprise and the worker.

When the contract is due or is terminated, either side is free to make a decision about its renewal or otherwise.

While contract workers enjoy the same rights, interests and treatment as permanent workers in the same units, they differ from permanent workers in that, as long as they make no serious mistakes and no matter how they perform, permanent workers are employed until their retirement. Contract workers are employed only until the end of their contract period. All those employed in accord with State-issued job quotas before 1 October 1986 are permanent workers. Those employed by State enterprises since that date are contract workers.

The contract work system should not be confused with the temporary worker system or with the seasonal worker system. The temporary worker system refers to the system where a given number of temporary workers are employed to cope with irregular work. These workers are not a part of the permanent workforce. (Permanent workers and contract workers are a part of China's permanent workforce.) The seasonal worker system refers to enterprises whose production is of a seasonal nature, employing a back-bone of permanent workers and then adding seasonal workers in accord with seasonal needs. Unlike contract workers, seasonal workers are dismissed once the seasonal period in which production was called for is ended.

4. WORKER RECRUITMENT AND THE DEPLOYMENT OF WORKERS

(1) Worker Recruitment

State enterprises work out their own plan for labour force use and proceed to recruit workers within the scope and areas designated by labour administrative departments. Unlike State enterprises, collectively owned units don't have to win approval for recruiting workers, but they must file a report with the relevant labour management department on the workers that they have recruited. Workers are generally recruited from cities and towns. If workers are recruited from among the farmers, approval of the provincial, municipal or autonomous region government must be sought and given.

Under normal conditions workers are recruited in the following manner:

(i) Workers are publicly recruited on a voluntary basis. The enterprise involved makes public a written requirement for workers. The requirement must detail type of work, technical requirements and remuneration. Workers then apply for the position on the basis of their respective skills and interests.

(ii) The recruiting unit gives an all-round examination to the workers. This examination includes moral, intellectual and physical aspects. Only the best are then recruited.

(iii) With respect to those that they have chosen to recruit, the recruiting unit goes through all necessary procedures at the local labour management department.

A labour contract is then signed.

(iv) Newly recruited workers are put on probation for a certain period of time. During this period they are to both work in production and to receive education in production, technology and labour security. Anyone who, during the probation period, is found to be unqualified will be discharged. And similarly, if those who have been recruited are dissatisfied, they are free to resign and seek another opening.

Training for recruited workers includes both pre-employment training and on-the-job training. The former is provided for young people awaiting employment and the latter is offered by recruiting units to their new employees. And in addition to the above, enterprises conduct on-the job training for workers with a view to improving their existing workforce.

(2) Worker Deployment

Deployment of workers takes place both inside and outside enterprises. External deployment takes place among enterprises owned by the whole people. External deployment can take place either outside or within the locality in which the worker is originally employed. It is done in accord with changes in production and tasks. Internal deployment takes place when enterprises seek to redeploy their labour force within the same factory or work-place.

5. WORKER REWARD AND PUNISHMENT

When rewarding workers, China adheres to the principle of integrating ideological with material encouragement. When a worker violates labour discipline, the principle of ideological education is adhered to and if thought necessary, it is coupled with a form of punishment.

Ideological encouragement can include awarding a citation for merit, citation for merit first grade, a promotion, issuing an order of commendation and awarding the title of advanced worker or the honour of the title of model worker. When giving the above awards, bonus payments may be given in a lump sum or a wage scale may be upgraded. On the other hand, punishment includes a warning, recording a demerit, recording a serious demerit, demotion on the wage scale, dismissal from office, being kept for examination and being laid off. When any of the above disciplinary sanctions are imposed, a fine may also be imposed either in the form of a lump sum or in the form of a demotion down the wage scale. 'Being kept for examination' usually lasts for one to two years. During this period, living expenses lower than one's original wage are given. After this period, those who behave well will be restored as regular workers and will receive a re-graded wage and those who fail to turn over a new leaf will be laid off.

6. LABOUR SERVICE COMPANIES

The labour service company is a new form of social labour organisation which has come into existence in recent years. It has been established as a means of solving the labour employment problem. It plays an important role in developing the collective economy and in supporting self-employment among individual labourers.

The labour service companies have expanded their business scope by cashing in on the reform of the labour system.

By the end of 1986, various forms of such companies numbered 46,000. One-third were established by labour administrative departments at various levels of government and the remainder by enterprises and by government institutions. To date the labour service companies have organised 230,000 collective enterprises, employing around 7 million workers. This, plus the 1.1 million temporary workers and the 1.7 million people who took part in pre-employment training conducted by the companies, brings the total number of labour force personnel organised by labour service companies to more than 9 million.

Enterprises under the labour service companies earnt Rmb 40 billion from production, business operations and labour services and they have paid Rmb 2 billion in tax to the State. In return they receive many forms of assistance from the State.

Aside from organising young people waiting for employment into collective undertakings and aside from providing the pre-employment training (both services already noted as being provided by the labour service companies), the following services are also part of the work undertaken by the companies:

- ... co-operating with farmers or farms by integrating industry with agriculture and town with country in a manner that develops agricultural-industrial-commercial joint enterprises;

- ... developing commercial retail sales networks and developing catering and service trades (including household run services and such services as go-it alone repair services); and

- ... providing a labour service for those enterprise and government institutions that need temporary and seasonal workers.

In some cases enterprises and government institutions and schools (in the process of consolidating management, raising work efficiency and implementing the responsibility system), have found that they have a considerable number of surplus employees. When they have found themselves in this position, some of these enterprises and institutions have established their own labour service companies. They have done this especially for the purpose of transferring their surplus labour force to other positions or for the purpose of finding new work for them.

7. THE LABOUR MARKET

China's socialist labour market functions by applying market mechanisms under the guidance of the State plan.

It does not follow the past practice of administratively deploying workers. In practice it acts in the following manner:

- ... work units and labourers register separately at the labour market, each declaring their requests;

- ... meetings are then arranged for both sides by the labour market; and

- ... when agreement has been reached, the employer and employee go through the necessary formalities and then sign a labour contract.

Aside from the practice listed immediately above, the labour market will also help employees to change jobs by negotiating with their current work units.

In addition to the formally established labour markets, spontaneous labour markets have emerged in many cities and towns. Most of the people who deal with the spontaneous labour markets are rural job-seekers, while most of the employers are urban individual households. Agreements are made between the people involved. This type of labour market makes it possible for the urban private economy and specialised households to solve their labour shortage problems and it makes it possible for rural surplus workers to find employment. The only drawback with this type of spontaneous and unplanned labour market is that it is difficult to guarantee and supervise agreements and transactions as such transactions are rarely legally documented.

II. WAGES

1. WAGE POLICY

Employees' salaries are controlled in many different ways by different departments and enterprises. Rises in wage scales and in labouring time for wage payments for employees of government institutions and State-owned enterprises are directly controlled by the government. But wages for employees of collectively owned enterprises and institutions are decided by the units themselves with the approval of government departments in charge. Salaries of employees of individual businesses, Sino-foreign joint ventures and exclusively foreign-funded enterprises are also decided by the enterprise concerned.

The basic principle informing Chinese wage policy is that of 'from each according to his ability and to each according to his work'. This means that distribution is based on the quantity and the quality of labour contributed by labourers. A further principle then is to consider the interests of the State, the collective and the individual and to handle proportionate relations in terms of distribution of national income between the State, the collective and the individual in an appropriate manner. And at the same time, attention should be paid to preventing a wide gap from developing between high and low incomes and between the incomes of urban and rural producers.

2. WAGE FUNDS

Wage funds include time wages, piece rate wages, various types of bonuses and subsidies and overtime pay. These funds come from two sources:

... State financial allocation to State organisations and institutions, and

... management incomes generated by the enterprise concerned.

Management of wage funds is based on 24 February 1985 State Council promulgated Provisional Measures for the Management of the Wage Fund. This document stipulates that the management of wage funds will cover remuneration allowances and subsidies that State-owned enterprises, government institutions, and people's organisations pay to their employees. The stipulations apply irrespective of the source of the funds. Furthermore, any enterprise payment from the gross pay-roll must be drawn from a special account of the wage fund through the bank.

On the condition that the yearly gross pay-roll established by the State has not been exceeded, surplus monthly or quarterly wage funds can be used in the next month or quarter of the same year, but no funds are allowed to be used in advance.

In the case of collectively owned enterprises it is the provincial, autonomous region or municipal government that formulates methods for the management of their wage funds.

3. WAGE LEVELS

Since the founding of New China the principle that has been adhered to is that of 'low wages and more employment'.

Wage levels are set by the State and the index reflecting wage level is the average annual wage calculated as yearly gross pay-roll divided by number of employees for the year in question.

With development of the economy, wage level has risen constantly. The only two exceptions have been two periods prior to the introduction of economic reform policy. These periods were during the Second Five-Year Plan when there was an average annual reduction of 1.5% and during the decade of the 'Cultural Revolution' when there was a fall of 0.5%. Since the introduction of economic reform the rise in wage level has been rapid.

10:1 CHANGES IN MONEY WAGE OF STATE ENTERPRISE WORKERS

	Per capita average money wage (Rmb per annum)
1952	446
1957	637
1965	652
1978	664
1980	803
1985	1213
1986	1414
1987	1548

4. REFORM OF THE WAGE SYSTEM

Since the 1950s China's basic wage system has been a graded system. It is a system that divides work into several categories with each category being called a 'branch of work' in the case of workers and a 'post' in the case of office workers. Then each branch or post is further divided into several job grades. These grades accord with the complexity, intensity and responsibility that the job carries.

Under the graded wage system most trades practise an eight-grade wage scale (though a few trades do use other scales, i.e., the building industry uses a seven grade scale), while administrative workers (a grouping that includes engineering, technical and managerial personnel) have over time, been subject to reform aimed at a significant reduction in the difference between the wage of those who are members of the highest and lowest grades.

In 1955 a post-rank salary system was introduced for administrative workers. At that time this system had 30 grades with the highest salary being 31.1 times more than the lowest one. Over time this system was subject to several reforms. Salaries for leaders were scaled down and the lowest wage rates were scaled up. The result was a significant reduction in the wage differential.

On 1 July 1985 a structural salary system was introduced for employees of government organisations and institutions. This is a system that is composed of three parts.

(1)   The Introduction of a Structured Salary System

Under this system administrative workers received a salary consisting of:
- ... a basic salary that provides employee subsistence,
- ... a subsidy for years worked, and
- ... a post-rank (professional title) salary.

Basic salary is paid irrespective of difference in post filled and the provision of a service subsidy provides a fixed pay rise for administrative employees regardless of whether or not a promotion has been gained. The post-rank salary that is then awarded to administrative workers represents the principal portion of the wage and it is the portion of the wage that reflects the principle of to each according to his work.

(2)   A Trial Wage System that Seeks to Link Wages to Economic Return

This system applies to enterprises that seek to link enterprise gross pay-roll to enterprise economic returns. The wage system is one that focuses on enterprise State relations. The calculation is one where different trades choose targets that they consider best represent their economic returns. It is done in several different ways:

(i) By calculating wage content in every Rmb 100 of output value. Gross pay-roll is determined by total output value fulfilled during a fixed period (usually one year) and while wage content for every Rmb 100 of output value is being calculated, other indices such as quality of product and product cost, are also considered.

(ii) By calculating wage content per metric ton of coal. Some coal mines are practising this system on a trial basis. Reward for every metric ton of coal produced is calculated in accord with a standard production quota. This system then also takes into account safety and the index of consumption.

(iii) By using a contract wage system. Under this system, during the course of implementing the contract responsibility system in enterprise management, the department in charge will check the base figure for contracted gross pay-roll of each enterprise and will decide the relation between its production plan, growth rate of profit and tax payment and then the growth rate of its gross pay-roll. If any enterprise overfulfils its plans for production and profit and tax payments to the State, its gross pay-roll will float upward. Otherwise it will float downward. The contracted base figure will remain unchanged irrespective of changes in number of employees.

(iv) Floating enterprise gross pay-roll in line with output value. Under this system the enterprise will draw its gross pay-roll for distribution among its employees according to net output value that it has fulfilled each year. The system requires that the department in charge set a standard production quota

for an enterprise and that it sets the proportion for increase or decrease of gross pay-roll if the enterprise overfulfils or fails to fulfil its standard production quota.
(v) Floating gross pay-roll in accord with profit and taxes paid to the State. When total amount of profit and tax paid by an enterprise to the State rises 1%, gross pay-roll may rise 0.3% to 0.7% and the increase of the gross pay-roll of enterprises in special trades or in special areas may rise up to 1%.

(3) Diversified Forms of Wage Payment Within Enterprises

Now the unified wage pattern practised in enterprises has been broken down and a more diversified wage form has been introduced. This includes:
(i) A Floating Wage. This wage consists of part or all of the employee's standard wage plus bonuses awarded in line with enterprise performance and with the production contribution of the employee.

The wage has different forms, i.e., combining the entire standard wage with bonus payment so as to float all the wage; combining part of the standard wage with the bonus so as to achieve partial floating of the wage; and the original standard wage remaining unchanged with only the bonus being floated.
(ii) Wage Rises Within Enterprises. Unlike the fixed wage rise that is stipulated by the State, under usual circumstances a floating wage rise will be decided by the enterprise. It is based on the contribution made by its employees during a given period of time. When an employee transfers to another unit the floating component of his or her wage is not transferred to the new unit as though it was the standard wage.

This type of wage rise usually lasts for three years. During this period, those who fail to fulfil their tasks or who have violated discipline and rules will be deprived of the increased portion of their wage. The wage rise can only be awarded when an employee has fulfilled his or her tasks for three successive years.
(iii) Wages Based on Retained Business Volume or Profits. In some commercial and service businesses under contract system management, a certain proportion of turnover or net profit is used as wages for employees.

III. SUBSIDIES

In China's enterprises, institutions and government organisations, subsidies are an important component of the money income of employees. The subsidies are wide ranging.

1. TYPES OF SUBSIDIES

Subsidies are divided into either salary subsidies or non-salary subsidies. Salary subsidies are a supplement added to the graded wage system and non-wage subsidies are usually welfare benefits.

Some subsidies are drawn from wage funds and some from welfare funds and some are drawn from special State financial allocations. Some subsidies are only for specific types of work or for a small number of employees and some are available to all employees and are even available to retirees.

The following are the principal subsidies currently in operation:

(1) Subsidies as benefits to employees working in special environments or who work at special tasks. These include subsidies paid to miners, those working forest areas, those engaged in geological field prospecting and those who work in high temperatures. Subsidies are also given to those who are employed constructing water and electricity supply systems and new railway systems.

(2) Subsidies paid to compensate for extra labour contributed by employees. These include the subsidy to primary and secondary school teachers in charge of classes.

(3) Subsidies paid to encourage employees to make a special contribution. These include technical and post-rank subsidies.

(4) Subsidies in the form of welfare benefits that serve to cut employees' cost of living. These include subsidies for winter coal and subsidies that serve to offset increased non-staple food prices and a commuter subsidy.

2. SUBSIDY MANAGEMENT

(1) Examination and Approval of Subsidies

Examination and approval of subsidies is conducted level by level. Each new subsidy system must be approved by the responsible labour administration department at the central level, while subsidies to be introduced in localities must be approved by responsible labour administration departments in the locality concerned. Enterprises, institutions and government organisations must have the approval of responsible labour administration departments and higher authorities before introducing subsidies.

(2) Management of Subsidy Funds

Enterprise subsidy funds are managed by different departments. Those outlayed from enterprise wage funds are managed by the labour administration department, those outlayed from enterprise management expense are managed by the security management department and those paid by enterprise welfare funds are managed by the welfare management department. Subsidies are paid to employees monthly.

IV. BONUS PAYMENTS

1. REWARD

As noted, bonus payments are a supplementary form of wage payment. They are a supplement to standard wages and they are an important part of employee's money income. Bonus payments serve to reflect the difference between actual work results of labourers of similar technical levels. Payments are closely tied to practical economic results. They increase or decrease in response to the rise or fall in production. Basically they are a reward system seen as a means of further arousing employees' enthusiasm for labour.

China's reward system adheres to the principle of combining spiritual reward with material incentives. Egalitarianism is opposed.

When deciding on level of bonus payments the interests of the State, collectives and individuals all have to be considered. On condition that the State has provided necessary construction funds and that collectives have sufficient funds to expand production and to satisfy the need for collective welfare facilities, employees' money income can be constantly increased as production is developed. But at the same time, rewards should be suited to each unit's level of production, management and administration.

2. FORMS OF BONUS PAYMENT

There are numerous reward systems for workers and staff, but they really boil down to two forms—bonuses on separate items and comprehensive bonuses.

(1) Bonuses on Separate Items

This is a reward form based on fulfilment of conditions for a certain item of production which has requests attached for guaranteeing certain conditions. For instance, the reward system is used to encourage employees to increase output on the premise that quality of product is guaranteed and that the quota for raw and semi-finished materials and for energy consumption is adhered to.

(2) Comprehensive Bonuses

Comprehensive bonuses are a form of reward that is based on conditions for fulfilling several major production targets. Point recording is often used when this form of reward is applied. That is to say, performance in fulfilling various targets is converted into points which are then converted into an amount of money that accords with unit price of product.

Aside from bonuses for separate items and comprehensive bonuses that have been outlined immediately above, temporary and lump-sum rewards are also practised. The requirements for these latter rewards are stipulated in accordance with specific conditions.

3. SIZE OF BONUS PAYMENTS

In April 1984 the State Council promulgated the Circular on Issuing Bonuses by State-Owned Enterprises. This Circular stipulates that 'no ceiling or bottom guarantee' for bonuses will be practised. That is to say, when an enterprise has fulfilled State plans and has provided more profit and taxes to the State than it did in the previous year, the bonus payments that it makes to its workers and staff can be appropriately increased. And conversely, bonuses will be reduced or suspended if less profit and tax has been forwarded to the State.

The circular also states that enterprises will be exempt from bonus tax if the total amount of bonus that they issue is less than two and a half months of employees' standard wage. Tax will be paid at 30% if bonus payment is equivalent to two and a half months to four months of standard wage and it will be paid at the rate of 100% if bonus payment is equivalent to four to six months of standard wage. If bonus payment exceeds more than six months' standard wage, a very high tax rate of 300% will be levied by the State. Bonus payments made to miners, dockers and construction workers are exempt from bonus tax.

Enterprises have the decision-making power over use of their reward funds. They are free to adopt different forms of reward such as issuing bonuses by recording points, paying floating wages and by using above-norm piece-work wages. Enterprises are also free to reduce their bonus payments to workers and staff and divert funds saved to a fund to be used for payment of floating wages to selected workers and staff or for meeting collective welfare costs.

V. LABOUR INSURANCE

1. *THE LABOUR INSURANCE SYSTEM*

The main purpose of the labour insurance system is to give a material guarantee to workers that they will receive help during difficult times.

Labour insurance funds are covered by the State and the enterprise. The employee does not pay any fee. Remuneration under labour insurance is based on the receiver's standard wage and on length of service.

Not all labour insurance systems are identical. Different labour insurance systems have been implemented by State-owned enterprises, government organisations and institutions and in the case of collectively owned enterprises in cities and towns, contracts covering labour insurance are agreed upon and signed. Currently a social insurance system for individual businesses is being trialed.

In practice most labour insurance systems include the following:

(1) Child-birth Provisions. Women workers are given 56 days maternity leave with full pay and 14 additional days if they have given birth to twins. When a worker has undergone a sterilisation operation, he or she can also have time off work on full pay.

(2) Provision for Medical Treatment. During illness, injury and hospitalisation, a worker's expenses for treatment, operations, hospitalisation and general medical-care are all covered by their enterprise while the employee's directly-related family receives 50% off the cost of any medical care that they receive. Those whose sick leave is for a period under six months will receive 60-100% of their standard wage. Those who have sick leave that exceeds six months will receive 40-80% of their standard wage.

(3) Provision for Injury and Disability. Employees who are wounded or crippled either at work or while not on duty, will receive relief funds in accord with the extent of their injury or disability.

(4) Retirement, Resignation or Release from Work Provisions. When an employee has lost the ability to work and has not yet reached the usual retirement age, he or she may, having produced hospital certificates confirmed by the labour appraisal committee, retire early.

After working for more than ten consecutive years, the usual age for retirement for men workers and staff members is 60 years while for women workers it is 50 and for women staff members it is 55. Those who work underground, in high temperatures, who engage in strenuous physical labour or other types of work deemed to be harmful to health, can retire five years earlier.

Pensions range from 60% to 90% of standard wage. It is a percentage that is decided in terms of length of service with the added condition that if the monthly pension then works out to be less than Rmb 40, the retiree will receive a minimum payment of Rmb 40 per month. All retirees receive free medical care.

Veteran cadres are released from work when they become too old and their health is too poor to enable them to work regularly and when they step down and retire they receive full pay and free medical care.

(5) Funeral Expenses and Pensions for the Family of the Deceased. The family of the deceased will be given funeral expenses equivalent to two to three months enterprise average wage. The directly related family of employees who have died on duty will be receive a monthly pension ranging from 25% to 50% of the

deceased's monthly wage and directly related family of employees who died while not on duty will receive a lump sum relief payment that is equivalent to 2 to 12 months of the deceased's monthly wage.

2. REFORM OF THE LABOUR INSURANCE SYSTEM

(1) The Establishment of a Job-Waiting Insurance System

In order to meet needs created by reform of the labour system and in order to promote a rational flow of labour, there is now a need to guarantee the basic needs of employees of State-owned enterprises during any period when they are waiting for a job. In light of this situation, in July 1986 the State Council promulgated the Interim Provisions on Job-Waiting Insurance for Employees of State-Owned Enterprises. These provisions stipulate that from 1 October 1986 employees who have been laid off in the course of re-organisation of their enterprise (usually when their enterprise is on the brink of bankruptcy), workers whose labour contracts have expired and have not been reinstated or whose contracts have been terminated, and employees who have been discharged by an enterprise, can receive relief funds that are equivalent to 50-75% of their former monthly wage.

The maximum period to be in receipt of this type of job-waiting relief is two years for those who have been in the work force for five years and one year for those who have worked for less than five years. Job-waiting insurance funds paid by each enterprise are equivalent to 1% of standard gross pay-roll and the fund is administered by a labour service company that is under the control of the local labour administration department.

(2) Reform of Contracted Workers' Insurance

Since the October 1986 introduction of labour insurance, State-enterprise contracted workers have been assured of relief payments if they become unemployed or retire. In the case of contract workers, funds are paid into an enterprise insurance fund by both the enterprise and the contracted worker and if these funds prove insufficient to cover need, the State will undertake appropriate subsidisation.

The amount paid by contracted workers into the insurance fund is set at no more than 3% of standard wage and the amount paid by the enterprise is 15% of total wages paid to the enterprise's contracted workers. The fund is administered by a labour service company that is under the control of the local labour administration department.

VI. THE WELFARE SYSTEM

The welfare system that has been instituted in China's enterprises, institutions and government organisations is intended to lighten the burden of workers' daily life.

Since 1979 the source of enterprise welfare funds has been in accord with State policy of replacing enterprise profit delivery to the State with enterprise retained profit and enterprise tax payments to the State. In line with this policy enterprises draw 20% of net funds for retention as welfare funds.

The enterprise welfare system includes individual and collective welfare facilities for workers and staff. Individual welfare provided for workers and staff is intended to alleviate the expenses otherwise borne by workers and staff under given conditions. It can include such items as a heating allowance paid to workers and staff in winter, travelling expenses for home leave, traffic allowances and allowances for life difficulties.

Facilities funded by collective welfare funds include the construction of worker residential quarters, public utilities and cultural and recreational facilities built either with investment provided by the State or with investment drawn from the enterprise collective welfare fund.

Collective cultural and recreational facilities for workers and staff include workers' cultural palaces, libraries (or reading-rooms), clubs, sports-grounds and spare-time schools run by enterprises. Almost all large and medium-sized enterprises have their own cultural palaces, clubs, libraries and film projection teams and some large enterprises have their own gymnasiums and their own sports-grounds and sports-teams.

Collective welfare facilities for the daily life of workers and staff include workers' dormitories, canteens, nursing rooms, creches, kindergartens, barber-shops and bathrooms. Charges for these enterprise run welfare facilities are low with any short fall in funds being made up from the enterprise welfare fund. Units which have difficulties in establishing collective welfare facilities usually issue allowances to their workers and staff, such as subsidies for child-care or bathing.

VII. LABOUR PROTECTION

Labour protection involves a series of organisational and technical measures taken to improve working conditions and to prevent accidents, injuries and occupational diseases.

1. BASIC LABOUR PROTECTION POLICY

Safety in production is the core of labour protection policy. As early as the first years of new China, the State promulgated Regulations on Production Safety for Factories, Safety and Technical Regulations for Construction and Installation Workers and Regulations on Accident Reports of Injuries and Deaths of Workers and Clerks. These regulations have played a positive role in protecting workers.

Alternating work periods with rest and recreation is vital for worker safety. To this end the eight-hour-work system had been implemented for workers and staff and in the case of workers engaged in strenuous work or working in a hazardous environment, a shorter work week is presently being trialed.

2. LABOUR PROTECTION MEASURES

Those who are newly employed by factories must receive safety education. Before operating machines they must pass examinations that test their knowledge of safety and technical regulations and related rules. New workers engaged in special types of work should receive special safety and technical training and must not be allowed to operate machines until their knowledge has been rigidly tested.

Since the 1963 State Council promulgation of Some Stipulations on Strengthening Enterprises' Safety Work in Production, safety stipulations have defined the responsibility of leaders at all levels. If accidents do occur, leaders are held responsible.

While working out production and financial plans, enterprises must also draw up safety measures. These should include improvement of working conditions, prevention of accidents, injuries and occupational diseases, and publicity and education. Funds needed for improving safety are drawn from funds for technical renovation and transformation of enterprises.

CHAPTER 11

Housing, Land Use and Environmental Protection

I. HOUSING AND REAL ESTATE MANAGEMENT

In China land in cities belongs to the whole people. All institutions and individuals have a right to land use, but they do *not* have a right to ownership of land. Currently urban land accounts for approximately 9% of total land area. The remainder is rural land occupied and used by the 80% of the Chinese population who live in the countryside.

Housing and real estate management has predominantly been an urban concern. Rural concern has focused on rural land management that in turn has focused on protection of cultivated land against encroachment from rural industry or housing, with serious cases of farmland destruction constituting a crime. To date the main work of rural land management has been:

- approving the use of land for building township enterprises, rural public facilities, construction of public welfare undertakings and for building peasant houses:
- registering land ownership and land use rights; in the case of collectively-owned land, the county people's government registers land ownership and land use rights, issues certificates and confirms ownership; when collective or State-owned land is required for use, the government will issue a user certificate that provides for the legal use of the land: and
- mediating land disputes and preventing illegal seizure of land for housing construction.

In the interest of clarity, in this chapter China's housing and real estate management policies, achievements and intentions will be divided into discussions that list urban housing stock, outline housing reform and real estate administration and note the main features of an increasing number of real estate business transactions.

1. URBAN HOUSING

During the year 1985-1986 China carried out its first nationwide general survey of urban housing stock. The results were as follows:

- total floor space of urban housing was 4.7 billion square metres;
- one-storey houses and buildings of two or more stories accounted for 50% of housing stock; and

... property right divisions showed that public houses managed by institutions accounted for 3.5 billion square metres or 75% of housing stock, that public houses under the unified control of housing management departments cover 421 million square metres or 9% of housing stock, and that private houses accounted for 738 million square metres or 16%.

This first survey is categorised as a nationwide general survey of urban housing, but for the purposes of this survey *the term 'housing' has been used in the widest sense possible*. It is a break-down of the survey that makes this obvious, i.e., the survey estimates that houses used for commercial purposes account for over 388 million square metres of stock (9% of housing stock), houses used for educational, medical and scientific research purposes cover 338 million square metres (7%), houses used for culture and sports—50 million square metres (1%), houses used for offices—196 million square metres (4%), and houses used for other purposes—60 million square metres (1%).

The survey has also shown that the average floor space *used* by each household of urban residents is 37.9 square metres—10 square metres per person, but the average *living* floor space for each household is 24 square metres—6.4 square metres per person.

It only remains to add that, together with the considerable increase in urban housing stock, there has been an accompanying substantial increase in rural housing stock and that during the same period the quality of rural housing has been significantly improved. (Of the new houses built in the countryside in 1985, 61.2% were of brick and wood construction, 28.7% brick and cement and 26% were houses of two or more storeys.) Aside from urban construction, in the nine years from 1979-1987, 5.4 billion square metres of new housing was constructed in rural areas. This is a figure that represents 66% of the 8.2 billion square metres of housing constructed in the period 1949-1987.

In terms of the future, the target fixed for urban housing is that by the year 2000 each urban household should have a flat to live in with an average living floor space of eight square metres per person.

To date, urban housing has consisted of the following:

(1)   Housing Construction Facilitated Solely by State Investment

For a long period prior to 1979 houses in cities and towns were built only with State investment. But since 1979, in order to speed up housing construction and so alleviate the acute shortage of urban housing, enterprises have been encouraged to, and have, invested heavily in housing construction using their own funds and in small cities and towns house building by individuals has developed. However in big and medium-sized cities, State investment has remained the main facilitator of housing construction.

(2)   Administrative Distribution of Housing

Once housing had been built with State investment, it was not sold or rented to workers and staff members, but distributed by the organisation where people work. It was distributed using administrative means. Under normal conditions housing applicants would be on a waiting list organised in the order of years worked, office held, and urgency of housing need.

2. LOW RENTS

China has for a long time enforced a policy of low wages and low consumption. To make it possible for low wage-earning workers and staff to bear the burden, rent collected was nominal. Today national average monthly rent for each square metre of floor space is merely 1/10 of cost. It hardly covers repair expenses. Rent accounts for only a little over 1% of family expenditure and residents living in public houses actually receive a monthly rent subsidy from the State or from the organisation where they work.

The main defects of such a housing system are:

- ... It seriously dampens the enthusiasm of the people to build or buy houses. The result is that their living conditions are hard to improve.
- ... It increases the financial burden of the State and at the same time, housing stock is badly in need of repair.
- ... It stimulates the demand for housing and aids and abets bureaucratic, rather than market distribution of housing.
- ... It leads to an irrational consumption pattern.
- ... It saps the vitality of the building industry and makes it impossible for the real estate business to develop.

3. REFORM OF THE HOUSING SYSTEM

The target of housing reform is commercialisation of housing in accord with the requirements of a socialist planned commodity economy. This reform should begin by changing the low rent charged for public housing. Residents should obtain the right to own houses or to live in houses by paying a reasonable amount of rent. Houses will then have entered the consumer goods market. This will be helpful in solving the urban housing problem and it will stimulate the development of the real estate business and the house building and building materials industries.

To achieve this target, housing reform based on the following must be instituted:

(1) A change in the system of fund distribution and a gradual normalisation of housing consumption funds. The latter should be done in such a manner that the huge subsidies for construction and repair of housing should be paid for from worker and staff wages.

(2) A change from the existing planning and management system that views housing as fixed asset investment to a planning and management system that views housing as a commodity.

(3) The establishment of a housing fund on the basis of reform of finance, taxation, wages, money, price and real estate management in such a way that a sound housing fund circulation system is established.

(4) Readjustment of the industrial structure in such a way that the real estate market is opened up and real estate business, finance and construction are developed.

In light of these tasks, a main focus of the next three to five years (from 1988) will be the readjustment of public housing rent. Rent should be calculated in such a way that factors such as depreciation, maintenance expenses, management fees, interest on investment and housing tax are accounted for. It is this type of measure that will serve to curb unreasonable housing demand and to encourage workers and staff to buy houses and so lay the foundation for the commercialisation of housing.

4. MAKING HOUSES PRIVATE PROPERTY

According to statistics compiled by the Ministry of Construction, by the end of 1987 public housing had a total floor space of 2.4 billion square metres. Some of this housing has been included in the plan for rebuilding old city stock and some is located by the side of streets and is suitable for transforming into shops. Some housing is involved in ownership dispute and some has historical significance. But leaving aside these types of housing, there is about 1.2 billion square metres of housing that can be sold. This is 50% of total housing stock. The newly built houses are to be sold first.

Data from 212 cities and 430 counties show that in 1987, 4.6 million square metres of public housing was sold. It recovered Rmb 1.3 billion. Some county towns have even managed to sell 90% of public housing stock to individuals.

To speed up the process of privatising housing, the State has decided that in county towns the reform of raising rents and increasing housing coupon issue will stop. Instead, public houses will be sold directly to residents and measures will be taken to encourage resident purchase of houses. But in big and medium-sized cities, the reform of raising rent and increasing housing coupon issue will continue.

5. REAL ESTATE ADMINISTRATION AND MANAGEMENT

At the level of central government, the administration of real estate is the responsibility of the Ministry of Construction and the State Bureau of Land Administration.

The Department of Real Estate and the Department of Urban Planning are under the Ministry of Construction. They are directly in charge of the administration of real estate. The main function and duties of the Department of Real Estate are:

- ... to study and formulate the principles, policies and administrative regulations with regard to real estate management and oversee their implementation;
- ... to participate in drawing up strategy and long and mid-term plans for the development of real estate and urban housing and ensure implementation of same;
- ... to take charge of guiding and coordinating reform of the system of urban housing;
- ... to guide and promote urban construction and the building of urban housing and the replacement of old city housing stock;
- ... to take responsibility for the management of the urban real estate market and for price control and to provide guidance for reform of urban real estate management;
- ... to take responsibility for setting and checking grading standards with respect to enterprises engaged in urban construction, house repair, or other real estate business;

- ... to take charge of the use and management of urban land and to ensure implementation of policy promoting privatisation of housing stock;
- ... to participate in mapping out long and mid-term plans for the development of real estate related science and technology and to appropriately train personnel;
- ... to take charge of working out annual plans and to oversee fulfilment of same; and
- ... to ensure a technical approach to real estate business transactions and to increase the ranks of real estate workers.

The main functions and duties of the Department of Urban Planning are:
- ... to guide and promote the drawing up and implementation of urban plans, including urban land management and urban housing construction; and
- ... to participate in both choice of site and feasibility studies undertaken in the case of large construction projects that will have an important impact on urban development.

The State Bureau of Land Administration is situated directly under the State Council. It is in charge of land management throughout the country and of urban and rural land administration. Its main functions and duties are:
- ... to administer State law, statutes and policies concerning land;
- ... to take charge of investigation, registration and compilation of statistics with regard to land;
- ... to organise relevant departments to draw up overall plans for land use;
- ... to take charge of requisition and allocation of land and where State Council approval is required, to take charge of the examination and approval of land requisition;
- ... to investigate, study and solve major problems with regard to land management;
- ... to supervise land use undertaken by localities and departments and to coordinate same; and
- ... to work with departments concerned in solving land disputes and to investigate and deal with cases of land seizure in violation of the law.

The State Bureau of Land Administration has six departments under its direction. They are the Department of Land Registration, the Department of Land Use Planning, the Department of Land for Construction Use, the Department of Supervision and Inspection, the Department of Scientific and Technological Publicity and Education and the Department of Policies and Statutes.

Real estate administration at the level of local government consists of provinces, municipalities directly under the central government and autonomous regions having real estate management departments. These departments are under their construction commissions (or under their urban and rural construction commissions or departments) and their land administration departments. The functions and duties of these departments correspond with those of the Ministry of Construction and the State Bureau of Land Administration. In short, they are in charge of real estate management within their administrative areas.

In cities the administration of real estate management is carried out by urban and rural construction commissions, real estate administrative bureaus, planning bureaus and land administrative bureaus. But in a number of open coastal cities such as Guangzhou, Dalian, Tianjin and Ningbo, the Development District Administrative Committee is vested with the power to manage land, including the power to manage the use of land.

County people's governments have also set up land administrative bureaus and urban and rural construction administrative bodies. These handle the work of real estate management. County people's governments assign land management personnel and urban and rural construction management personnel to towns to take charge of land management work.

Aside from the above government administrative organs, there are many government and non-government real estate management organisations and research bodies at both central and local levels. These include the China Real Estate Association, the China Land Society, the China Housing Problem Research Society, and the Real Estate Economics Research Association.

6. LAWS AND REGULATIONS GOVERNING REAL ESTATE

Chinese laws and regulations governing real estate consist of laws, administrative statutes, departmental regulations, local statutes, local regulations and administrative decisions and decrees.

The basis of the real estate system stems from relevant provisions of the Constitution and Constitutional Amendments and Provisions such as the provision that the State protects citizens' legal ownership of houses and that land use right can be transferred according to legal provision. Statutes concerning real estate management include: The Land Administration Law, Amendment to the Land Administration Law, Regulations on City Planning, Regulations on the Management of Urban Private Houses, Measures on Management of Housing Construction by Urban Individuals, Interim Provisions of the State Council on the Use of Land for Construction by Chinese-Foreign Joint Ventures, and Provisions of the Ministry of Urban and Rural Construction and Environmental Protection on the Management of Private Houses of Foreigners.

Laws and regulations on real estate tax include the Interim Regulations on Housing Tax, Interim Regulations on Urban Land Use Tax, Interim Regulations on the Use of Cultivated Land Tax, and Notice of the Ministry of Finance on the Levying and Exemption of Taxes on Houses and Residences Owned by Chinese-Foreign Joint Ventures, Overseas Chinese and Their Relatives and on their Use of State Land.

In terms of the management of real estate transactions, in 1988 the Ministry of Construction, the State Bureau of Commodity Prices and the State Administration for Industry and Commerce, jointly issued a notice on Strengthening Management of the Real Estate Transactions Market. And with regard to the selling and transfer of land use rights, there are now the Interim Regulations on the Selling and Transfer of the Use Right of Urban State-Owned Land.

7. REAL ESTATE BUSINESS

For a long period real estate business was almost non-existent in China. This was because land and housing were not regarded as commodities. In more recent times, with reform of land use rights, including payment of compensation for land use, and with commercialisation of housing, real estate business has been developing at a rapid rate.

By 1988 the number of enterprises involved in real estate development had exceeded 2,500 with a business volume exceeding Rmb 15 billion. And if operation, maintenance and repair service enterprises are included, the number of enterprises engaged in real estate business exceeds 7,000. These enterprises are employing over 2.4 million workers and staff.

More than 200 cities have now established real estate dealing organisations. Their real estate business includes transfer of land with compensation, real estate development, selling new houses, buying and selling and renting old houses, house decoration and repair, real estate appraisal and consultancy work and serving as real estate agents. The following are examples of such real estate dealing organisations and the scope of their operations.

(1) The China Real Estate Development Corporation

This corporation was established in 1981. It was originally the China Housing Development Corporation, but in January 1988 it changed to its present name. During the seven years that it has operated the scope of its business has expanded rapidly. It has established 145 branches in 135 cities and its annual turnover in terms of commodity housing development accounts for a quarter of the national total. The corporation is also actively developing business abroad.

(2) The Beijing House Swapping Meeting

Having begun in 1982, by 1988 this meeting had held eight sessions. To begin with it helped workers and employees to swap houses so that they can live nearer to their work. But today, in addition to helping workers swap houses, the meeting has developed 20 additional services. These include buying and selling old houses, renting houses, appraising house safety and repair, estimating house prices, calculating rent, rebuilding one-storey houses and training housing management personnel.

(3) The Shenyang Real Estate Market

This is a market engaged in house and land transactions. The market conducts real estate dealings, sells houses, deals in securities, real estate mortgages, house swapping, transfer of State-owned land use rights, housing decoration and maintenance. And in addition to its daily business, it holds a fair on the fifth day of each month. The market's real estate dealings and auctions are held on the thirtieth day of January, April, July and October with house swapping meetings held twice a year, one in spring and the other in autumn.

II. LAND USE COMPENSATION

1. COLLECTION OF AN URBAN LAND USE TAX

For a long time urban land has been allocated to users without payment of compensation. This practice was one that had many defects.

On 27 September 1988 the State Council promulgated the Interim Regulations on Urban Land Use Tax. The Regulation came into force on 1 November 1988. It required that land use tax be calculated on the basis of area of land actually used. The amount of land use tax to be paid per square metre used per annum being as follows: Rmb 0.5-10 in big cities, Rmb 0.4-8 in medium-sized cities, Rmb 0.3-6 in small cities, and Rmb 0.2-4 in county towns, towns and industrial and mining areas. There is also allowance for land use tax in economically backward areas to be appropriately reduced (but the reduced payment must not exceed 30% of the minimum tax stipulated above) and there is provision for the amount of land use tax in economically developed areas to be appropriately increased.

The following land is exempt from land use tax: land used by government organs, people's organisations and the army; land used by units which have been allocated operating expenses by State financial departments; land used for religious temples, parks, scenic spots and historical sites; land for public use such as streets, squares and forested areas; land used directly in agricultural production, forestry, animal husbandry and fishery production; and officially approved created land from filling the sea, improving waste land or opening mountainous regions. This 'new' land will be exempt from land use tax for five to ten years beginning from the first month of its use. Also land used for energy production, communications and water conservancy will be exempt as will any other land granted exemption by the Ministry of Finance.

2. TRANSFER OF RIGHT OF LAND USE

Land use right is transferred by means of an agreement, open bidding or auction. Transfer of land use rights through agreement involves the government and the interested party seeking land use rights to negotiate price and terms for the use of the land and then to reach an agreement and sign a relevant contract. Transfer of land use rights by way of public bidding means that in an appointed period interested parties submit tenders for the right to land use and then the successful tender is decided by the sponsors of the public bid. Auctioning land use right means that at a given time the auction sponsor offers the land use right to the highest bidder.

The period of time covered by the transferred land use right is fixed according to the needs of different trades, business operations and individuals. At present most areas provide for a maximum period of 50 years, but some have overstepped this limit. On Hainan Island for instance, the longest period is 70 years and in some places even a period of 90 years has been provided for. With the approval of the department concerned, at the expiration of the stated period of land use, the term can be extended and the price for continued use of the land will be set at the market price that prevails at that time.

All enterprises, other economic institutions or individuals of countries and regions that have established diplomatic relations with China, or who have established commercial representative offices in China, can hold land use rights.

Transfer of land use right often involves compensation payment. This is the case when the government allows a party who has already legally obtained the right to use a designated land site to receive payment from another party for the right to use of the land. Underground natural resources, ores, etc., are exempt from transfer of land use right with compensation.

Institutions and individuals who have obtained land use rights can transfer their land use right by either sale, exchange or mortgage. Obviously the period of transfer and mortgage must not exceed the affirmed term of the land use contract and, in the course of the transfer of land use rights, the government usually collects taxes such as a value added tax.

3. RECOVERY OF LAND USE RIGHT

Land use right is recovered under the following conditions:

(1) When the term of use of the land that has been provided for in the contract expires and when the extended period of use expires, the right to use of a given piece of land will be recovered by the government without compensation. When the land use right is recovered, the buildings and other appendages on the land will be simultaneously recovered and this will be without compensation being paid for same.

(2) Generally speaking, when a contract term has not yet expired, land use right cannot be withdrawn. However, now and again special circumstances do arise. In such circumstances the government can recover the right to land use and appropriate compensation will be paid or the right to use an alternative piece of land will be given.

(3) In case of failure to meet contract requirements with regard to transfer of land use right, the government will recover the right without compensation being paid.

4. LAND USE BY FOREIGN-FUNDED ENTERPRISES

The term 'foreign-funded enterprises' refers to enterprises that are solely foreign funded, Chinese-foreign joint venture enterprises and Chinese-foreign cooperative enterprises. When a cooperative enterprise or joint venture has been established with compatriots from Taiwan, Hong Kong, Macao, or with other overseas Chinese, or when enterprises or engineering projects have been undertaken with investment entirely drawn from overseas Chinese, use of land is handled in accord with provisions governing foreign-funded enterprises.

(1) Laws and Regulations on Land Use by Foreign-Funded Enterprises

The government has attached great importance to land use by foreign-funded enterprises. The Law on Chinese-Foreign Joint Ventures (promulgated in 1979) has explicit provisions on the right to the use of land sites by foreign-funded enterprises. It is on the basis of this law that the State Council promulgated the 1980 Interim Provisions on the Use of Land for Construction by Chinese-Foreign Joint Ventures. And in addition to these provisions, in 1985 the Regulations for the Implementation of the Law on Chinese-Foreign Joint Ventures were promulgated. These regulations have a special chapter on the right to the use of land sites and land site fees.

By October 1986 still further Provisions had been made public. These were the Provisions of the State Council on Encouraging Foreign Investment. They include special preferential stipulations on site use fees for enterprises whose product is mainly exported and for those enterprises that adopt advanced technology.

Currently the State Council is drawing up Measures on the Management of Land Used by Foreign-Funded Enterprises.

In addition to the central government laws noted, local government laws, regulations and policies have also been established by a number of provinces, municipalities directly under the central government and autonomous regions. These have included laws, regulations and policies relative to land management in special economic zones and economic and technological development areas.

(2) Obtaining Land Use Rights

All foreign businessmen who qualify as a legal person (entity) in countries or regions that have established diplomatic relations with China, or have commercial representative offices in China, can obtain land use rights.

China is now in a period in which a new land use system is replacing the old. This means that at the moment foreign-funded enterprises have two avenues for obtaining land use rights. They are the following:

... in areas where the new system is already implemented, they can participate directly in concluding a land use agreement, submit tenders and take part in an auction to obtain right of land use; and

... in areas where the old system is still in force, they can obtain right to land use by going through relevant administrative approval procedures.

(3) Procedures for Administrative Approval of Land Use by Foreign-Funded Enterprises

At present the procedures for approval of land use by foreign-funded enterprises are not identical in each place. The State Bureau of Land Administration and concerned departments have studied this problem and have decided that, for the time being, foreign-funded enterprises should go through the following procedures when applying for land use rights:

(i) Land Use Rights Application. When applying for approval for land use, foreign-funded enterprises must lodge a project proposal or relevant papers at the land administration department of the local people's government at, or above, county level. After examination the land administration department will give priority to their approval.

(ii) Site Selection. On the basis of the lodged application for land use, the land administration department will work together with the planning, environmental protection, construction, public security, fire fighting and other concerned departments to choose a site that accords with urban and rural planning. The application is then approved by the next level of government. Then the party that has lodged the application is issued with an interim land use certificate which is valid for one year as of the date of issue.

(iii) Filing a Formal Application. Within the period of the validity of the interim land use certificate, the foreign-funded enterprise should take the approved

design papers and other legally valid papers to the department where it initially filed its application for land use. The foreign-funded enterprise should then affirm the land area requested and in the case of requisitions of collective land, the land administration department should consult with the unit concerned in order to work out a compensation proposal and then report on this proposal to the people's government at, or above, county level.

(iv) Allocation of Land. After approval by the people's government at county level or above, the land administration department issues a land use certificate. The certificate lists the amount of land for use, the location, time covered by the land use provision, terms of use and site use fees and other relevant matters. Or alternatively, the land administration department and the foreign-funded enterprise can sign a land use contract containing the above-mentioned terms.

The land use certificate or the land use contract is the legal evidence of the right to land use awarded to a foreign-funded enterprise.

If the foreign-funded enterprise is a joint venture or a cooperative enterprise and intends to use the original site of its Chinese partner, a formal application for land use can be filed directly. However the application still has to be examined by the land administration department and the departments concerned with urban and rural construction planning and a report must be made to, and approval gained from, the people's government at county level or above.

The term for the right of land use that has been granted to the foreign-funded enterprise should be identical with the approved term of its operation in China. At the expiration of the land use term, or in cases where business has been suspended or the foreign-funded enterprise dissolved before expiration of the term, the land must be returned by the enterprise. If for justifiable reasons, the enterprise changes the purposes it puts the land to, or changes the boundaries of the land or the type of production or operation, or if the enterprise needs to continue to use the land after expiration of the given term, it should apply to the original approving department three months before any change is made and six months before expiration of term of use. The enterprise must then again follow the formalities for approval of land use.

(4) Site Use Fees for Foreign-Funded Enterprises

Policy with regard to site use fees levied on foreign-funded enterprises is that, except where land has been obtained through transfer of a land use right involving payment, land use fees are to be collected both on newly requisitioned land and on the site of existing enterprises. These site use fees should include site development charges and land use fees.

The land development charges should include compensation fees for land requisition, charges for dismantling any original buildings and funds for resettlement of any people living in original buildings. Land use fees, on the other hand, are fixed according to locality and the purpose that the land will be used for. This means that in principle, land use fees for coastal areas will be higher than they are for inland areas; sites in large and medium-sized cities dearer than sites in small towns; downtown areas dearer than other areas of a city and the suburbs; existing industrial areas higher than newly opened industrial areas; and use of existing enterprises through updating higher than building new factories.

With economic development, land use fees will be gradually readjusted.

In the case of Chinese-foreign joint ventures and Chinese-foreign cooperative enterprises, site use fees can be regarded as shares of investment contributed by the Chinese partner or they can be paid annually by the joint venture to the local government.

III. CITY PLANNING

1. CHINA'S CITIES

The size of Chinese cities (excluding counties under a city's jurisdiction) is calculated on the basis of the number of non-agricultural residents. A city with a population exceeding half a million people is categorised as a big city, a city with a population of 200,000 to 500,000 is a medium-sized city and a city with a population of less than 200,000 is a small city.

The government has established a policy of controlling the size of big cities, of rationally developing medium-sized cities and of vigorously developing small cities. In addition, since the beginning of the 1980s, importance has been attached to establishing and promoting city-country networks and to promoting the role of key cities.

The tasks of city planning were clearly defined in the January 1984 State Council promulgation the Regulations Regarding City Planning. This document listed the tasks of city planning as: setting planning period targets for a city's economic and social, cultural development; fixing the size and layout of a city and working out a unified plan for the rational use of city land; drawing up a comprehensive plan for the orderly and coordinated development of urban infrastructure; and ensuring the rational distribution of cities and towns within a given area.

Since the introduction of China's First Five Year Plan, government policy had been based on turning consumer cities into productive industrialising cities, but this policy, while promoting the development of China's economic construction and city building, has neglected the comprehensive functions of cities; the building of urban infrastructure; and the improvement of the urban environment. Since 1979 government policy has clearly stipulated that city planning should be based on use of the existing resources of cities; that it should account for a city's historical and cultural features; that it should promote the development of urban infrastructure and that it should protect a city's ecological environment.

In 1981, in order to protect the historical and cultural features of China's cities, the State Council announced a list of 24 cities renowned for their historical and cultural features. It was decreed that planning in these cities must include the protection of famous historical and cultural features. Then in 1986 a second list of 38 historically and culturally important cities was announced. (The two lists include cities such as Beijing, Shanghai, Nanjing, Tianjin, Wuhan, Suzhou and Hangzhou.)

When planning the open coastal cities construction of urban infrastructure has been given priority. This investment is now recognised as an important element in China's general investment climate. Environmental protection has been incorporated into the regional economic and social development plans of these cities. This has been done in order to provide a favourable climate for investment and in order to ensure the good health of urban residents.

The Bureau of Urban Planning under the dual leadership of the Ministry of Construction and the State Planning Commission is in charge of city planning work. The Bureau is responsible for formulating the principles and policies for urban development and for formulating the laws and regulations that govern urban development; organising and giving guidance to the drawing up of overall plans and detailed plans for all cities in the country; carrying out the task of examining overall development plans assigned to the Bureau by the State Council; land planning and management of city district development; participating in regional planning; and the selection of sites for key projects. The bureau is also responsible for the provision of feasibility studies for key projects.

Under the construction departments or construction commissions of various provinces, municipalities directly under the central government and autonomous regions there are urban planning departments (or urban construction departments). These departments are in charge of city planning and administrative work within their respective provinces, municipalities or autonomous regions.

A plan for the development of a city is drawn up by planning and designing institutions. These institutions are under the leadership of the Municipal People's Government. Once a plan has been drawn up it is examined and approved. For municipalities that are directly under the central government, capitals of provinces and autonomous regions, cities with a population of over one million and cities designated by the State, this means examination and approval by the State Council. For other cities and county seats it means examination and approval by the People's Government of provinces, municipalities under the central government and autonomous regions and for county towns under the administration of cities it means examination and approval by the City People's Government.

Planning at city level is divided into two planning categories: overall planning and detailed planning.

2. OVERALL PLANNING

This is comprehensive planning that is designed to control the city's use of land and to guide the rational development of the city. This plan usually covers a 20 year period and consideration of the city's long-term development dictates that the main contents of such a plan are:

- ... determining the distribution of towns in the area under the administration of the city;
- ... defining the nature of the city and its scale of development;
- ... marking out land for development purposes and fixing city layout;
- ... planning of the city communication system;
- ... planning communication facilities to link the city to the outside and planning the road network;
- ... mapping the system of pipes and lines for municipal engineering projects;
- ... fixing standards for major engineering facilities;

- ... mapping river systems, lakes and green-covered land within city limits;
- ... planning environmental protection and prevention of natural disasters; and
- ... drawing-up short-term five year construction plans.

3. DETAILED PLANNING

This is planning that covers the construction plan for city districts. It is drawn up on the basis of the overall plan. The main contents of detailed plans are:
- ... marking out the limit of land to be used for construction;
- ... planning the road system and the system of engineering pipes and lines in districts to be developed;
- ... fixing the density and height of buildings;
- ... determining the layout of newly constructed or reconstructed projects;
- ... working out plans and designs for building groups and for all types of engineering projects; and
- ... estimating total building prices.

A detailed plan has to be worked out for a section of city to be built under a short-term development plan and it must accord with the principles of the overall plan.

The overall plans for the development of most Chinese cities have been completed and in recent years cities in various regions have done a great deal of detailed planning work. They have planned and designed residential areas, production areas, scientific research areas and city living areas, city (district) centres, main street areas, tourist areas and gardens and the afforestation of land. These planning and design efforts have promoted good economic results and considerable social and environmental benefit.

4. URBAN INFRASTRUCTURE

China's urban public utilities have achieved tremendous advances since the founding of the People's Republic, particularly in the decade since the introduction of economic reform. In the Sixth Five-Year Plan period (1981-1986) alone, urban gas production capacity increased 46%, the length of roads by 30%, the number of public transport vehicles by 40%, the capacity of waterworks by 35% and sewage disposal capacity by 120%.

(1) Water Supply

The Yangshupu Waterworks in Shanghai was built in 1893 and was the earliest urban water supply installation in China. On the eve of the Communist Party coming to government, there were only 58 cities and 14 towns with water supply facilities. With the subsequent expansion of cities and the development of urban industry, large manpower and material resources were required for building water supply facilities.

By the end of 1987 facilities had been installed in 371 cities with 951 waterworks supplying 14.3 billion cubic metres of water annually. An urban population of 126.8 million has been supplied with tap water. Today approximately 87% of urban residents are supplied with running water and in many big cities the rate is 100%. In addition, 2,556 country towns have water supply facilities with a daily capacity of 8.5 million cubic metres giving 36 million people access to tap water.

The most usual source for tap water in cities is surface water drawn from rivers, lakes and reservoirs. Surface water accounts for 70% and ground water for only 30% of water sources used. In cities water for industrial use accounts for 70-80% of water consumed, water for people's daily life, mainly drinking water, 5-12%, and the remainder is water for indirect use, such as washing, cooling and fire fighting.

At present only about 30% of water is re-cycled. Many cities, particularly big cities in the north, are acutely short of water. Investigations at the end of 1987 showed that about 200 cities were short of water with the daily shortfall in supply exceeding 10 million cubic metres.

In order to alleviate the shortfall in water supply in cities, a variety of measures have been taken to increase water supply and save on the use of water. Projects designed to alleviate urban water shortage include: diverting the Launhe river water to Tianjin, Bihe river water to Dalian and Liaohe river water to Tianjin— all completed in 1984. In 1987 construction began on the projects that will divert Yellow River water to Qingdao and the water in the upper reaches of the Huangpu to Shanghai. While opening new sources of water supply, all cities have taken measures to save on water use. At present more than 160 cities have established water saving bureaus. These administrative offices have strictly controlled the use of ground water, rewarding those who save water and penalising those who use water in excess of plan. They have also sought to increase the rate of water recycling.

(2) Gas Supply

From 1864 when the first gas company was established in Shanghai, to 1949, only nine cities had small-scale gas supply facilities. These had an annual capacity of 39 million cubic metres and supplied gas to 270,000 people. The gasification rate was only 0.7%. By the end of 1987, after more than 30 years of hard work, total annual gas supply to cities was: artificial gas, 6.9 billion cubic metres, including 1.7 billion cubic metres for use in daily life; liquefied petroleum gas, 1.3 million metric tons, including 955,000 metric tons for use in daily life; and natural gas 5 billion cubic metres. The number of people using gas is estimated to be 42 million, with gas reaching 32.6% of the population. By 1990 the estimated population that has access to gas will be 50 million, a rate exceeding 40-60% of the population, with the rate in Beijing, Tianjin and Shanghai reaching 70%.

(3) Heating

The supply of heating comes from three sources. First, is the concentrated heat supplied by thermo power plants and regional heat supply facilities. Second, there is a decentralised heat supply drawn from boiler rooms of various government organisations, enterprises and institutions and third, there is scattered heat supply situated in households.

By the end of 1987 many cities had installed central heating facilities supplying heat to residential areas and public buildings covering an area of 152.8 million square metres. At the same time they also supply a part of the heat required for production. Heat supply pipes total 1,739 kilometres. They supply a total amount of 66.7 million metric tons of steam and 63,495.9 billion kilocalories of hot water annually. More than a dozen cities have now established computerised heat network monitoring systems.

(4) City Roads

In 1949 city roads extended for only 17,600 km, but by 1987 they had increased to extend 78,500 km and since China's first subway was built in Beijing in 1970, urban subways have been extended to 47 km.

In 1949 there were only 2,292 buses and trolley buses, but by the end of 1987 this number had increased to 52,504. In the 1949-1987 period passenger transport capacity increased from a mere 3 million persons to 27 billion persons. And as well, there were 61,525 taxi cabs in operation by 1987. But there is a problem. The growth of the number of urban vehicles has been much faster than the increase in roads. City road construction has not met demand. In 1987 there were only an average of 4.6 buses or trolley buses for every 10,000 urban residents. This meant that each bus carried around 700,000 passengers per year and in some very large cities each bus had to carry more than 900,000 passengers annually.

Bicycles are the main means of transport for individuals. The number of bicycles in cities has increased sharply. The annual growth rate is around 10% and in some cities it is more than 20%. China tops the world in terms of number of bicycles and in terms of bicycle output. In 1987 there were 176.5 bicycles for every 100 urban households.

(5) Sewerage, Sanitation and Pollution

In 1949 China's cities had 6,000 kilometres of sewers and 4 sewerage treatment plants with a daily capacity of 16,000 metric tons. After liberation large numbers of drainage projects were undertaken and many open sewers were filled. By the end of 1987 sewers extended to 47,107 kilometres and there were 73 sewerage treatment plants with a daily capacity of 2 million metric tons. And in addition to the urban sewage plants, in many cities large and medium-sized enterprises established industrial waste water treatment plants.

Aside from increased sewerage services, by the end of 1987 cities had 21,418 environmental sanitation vehicles. It is estimated that about 90% of night soil is now cleared away by sanitation workers and peasants in the suburbs and that the remaining part is disposed of through the sewerage system.

Garbage disposal is another area of sanitation and pollution that is receiving attention in cities. In 1987, 54 million metric tons of garbage was removed.

In order to solve its urban garbage problem, Shenzhen has invested Rmb 33 million in importing garbage incineration equipment from Japan. Guangzhou has imported equipment from Denmark and Shanghai has built an experimental garbage treatment plant.

(6) Greening of Cities

Before liberation a small number of cities had classical gardens left from the past, but they were in disrepair. Since liberation large-scale campaigns have been carried out to plant trees and grass in cities—to green the cities.

In September 1979 the Environment Protection Law was promulgated. This law clearly stipulates that efforts must be made to plant trees in cities, towns and industrial and mining areas. Scattered empty ground in and around factories, mines, schools and government offices and by the side of rural roads, waterways and houses is to be used for tree and grass planting. Large and medium-sized cities, particularly those with famous historical and cultural sites and those that are key tourist spots, have been directed to put extra effort into planting trees and grass so that the cities will have a new look.

By the end of 1987 the country's cities had a total of 378,000 hectares of forested land, 1,399 parks and 49 zoos. In terms of greening of the urban area, Nanjing and Zhengzhou are ahead of other cities. In Nanjing city, 6,700 hectares of land have been covered with trees and grass and 30% of the city has been greened. In Zhengzhou, where prior to liberation, there was not a single piece of green land, no parks and no tree-lined streets, there are now 4 parks and 13 gardens covering 200 hectares of land, 170 hectares of public land with trees and grass, and 200 kilometres of city roads lined with 116,000 trees. The city now has 1.6 million trees of all species. It has a total green area of 2,270 hectares covering 33% of the city.

(7) Future Development of Urban Public Utilities

Even though tremendous advances have been achieved in the development of urban infrastructure, particularly since 1979, China is a developing country with an extremely weak economic foundation and for this reason, together with the shackles of old city administration systems, the pace of urban construction has been rather slow.

In order to hasten urban development and in order to provide a good urban environment for both economic development and for people's life-style, the Chinese government will adopt the following principles and policies:

(i) Promoting an understanding of the importance of developing urban infrastructure. This will involve changing long established ideas about stressing production while relatively under-investing in urban infrastructure and neglecting the environment. Municipal governments and economic departments must now take development of public utilities as a key link in the promotion of economic and social development. The stress of People's Municipal Government work will gradually be switched from simply paying attention to industrial production to paying attention to balanced urban planning, construction and management.

(ii) While readjusting production structure and conducting technical transformation, arrangements are to be made for saving energy, improving communication facilities, water supply and drainage, environmental protection and beautifying the environment.

(iii) Business operations should be encouraged to undertake urban construction through the promotion of the sound circulation of construction funds. To this end appropriate commodity prices and service charges should be fixed for urban infrastructure undertakings that are suitable for business investment.

(iv) A substantial increase in funding for urban infrastructure should be promoted through securing stable sources of funds. Aside from increasing the proportion of government investment, more funds should be made available through diverse channels. These channels include making land an important source of income for municipal governments by collecting land use fees, collecting necessary taxes and charges to compensate for the use of public utilities and collecting development funds. With the full-scale reconstruction that is currently

under way, it is extremely difficult to rely only on State appropriations for urban development. The post-reform scale of urban reconstruction has made it necessary to raise funds by every means and through a number of channels.

IV. ENVIRONMENTAL PROTECTION

1. INDUSTRIAL POLLUTION

In China the main source of pollution is industrial pollution. It accounts for over 70% of general pollution.

At present China's drainage volume of industrial waste water stands at approximately 26 billion metric tons annually. The main pollutant materials contained in this industrial waste water are organic substances and heavy metals. The drainage volume of waste water for every Rmb 10,000 of industrial output value has reached a figure of over 393 metric tons, while the drainage volume of industrial waste water that has not been treated has reached 19.5-20 billion metric tons.

Monitoring of the 1985 figures for discharged industrial waste showed that it consisted of 36 metric tons of mercury, 1,600 metric tons of chromium, 1,188 metric tons of arsonium, 1,865 metric tons of lead, 1,477 metric tons of phenol, 6,450 metric tons of cyanide and 65,931 metric tons of petroleum products. These pollutants enter China's seven large river systems (that include the Changjiang, Huanghe, Zhujiang, Songhuajiang, Liahe, Haihe and Huaihe) and with 47,000 km of river being polluted the pollutants also enter the seas (the Bohai, Huanghai, Donghai and Nanhai).

In terms of waste gas exhaust entering the air, it is estimated that the annual level has reached more than 7,000 billion cubic metres that includes 10 million metric tons of sulphur dioxide and more than 4 million metric tons of nitrogen oxide. In addition the monitoring of sixty cities for general suspended air particles showed that all exceeded the standard stipulated by the State. Cities in the north showed a substantially higher reading than cities in the south.

The discharged volume of industrial solid waste exceeds 80 million metric tons annually. Fifteen million tons is discharged into waterways—rivers, lakes and seas and the remainder is stockpiled on land. The latter is estimated to total six billion metric tons and to cover over 500 million square metres of land. Farm land accounts for over 40 million square metres of this alienated land.

Noise is another aspect of environmental pollution. In Chinese cities and towns noise level can be more than 80 decibels. The source of this noise pollution is twofold. First, noise from communication and transport vehicles. And second, according to incomplete statistics, there are over 530,000 industrial sources of noise pollution and it is estimated that of these, 280,000 emit noise that exceeds the standard set by the State.

2. ENVIRONMENTAL PROTECTION POLICY

Environmental protection has become a basic State policy. At the same time as economic construction is being promoted it is being stipulated that natural resources must be protected and that considerable effort should be given to overcoming environmental pollution. The aim is to achieve balanced economic planning that promotes both economic development and the protection of the environment. This must be done in order to maximise economic benefit and to maximise the social benefit that is provided by a healthy environment.

A series of policies and principles concerning environmental protection have been formed. These are as follows:
- ... Bringing environmental protection into national economic and social development plans. When implementing overall planning, pollution prevention is to be put first and is then to be followed by the integration of pollution prevention with pollution treatment.
- ... The integration of pollution prevention and treatment with industrial structure, product mix, adjustment of energy structure and the technical updating of enterprises.
- ... Integrating pollution prevention and treatment with improvement in the rate of resource utilisation.
- ... Practising the principle of those who pollute being responsible for solving the pollution problem that they have created.
- ... Comprehensive regional prevention based on treatment at pollution source.
- ... Promoting environmental education in order to raise the consciousness of the people and so strengthen environmental supervision and management.
- ... The use of law in administering and supervising environmental management.

3. ENVIRONMENTAL PROTECTION ACHIEVEMENTS

Since the introduction of economic reform policy in 1979, four aspects of environmental protection have been stressed.

(1) The establishment of legislation for environmental protection. In September 1979 the Standing Committee of the National People's Congress promulgated and adopted the Environmental Protection Law of the People's Republic of China (for trial implementation). This legislation was then followed by further laws that were adopted one after the other. They were the Prevention and Treatment Law for Water Pollution, the Prevention and Treatment Law for Air Pollution, the Urban Noise Control Law, the Wild Animals Protection Law, and the Ocean Environmental Protection Law of the People's Republic of China.

(2) Since China's first environmental protection meeting was held in August 1983, administrative means of implementing environmental protection have been gradually established. In 1984 the Environmental Protection Committee of the State Council was established. This committee took charge of studying, examining, organising and implementing principles and policies relevant to environmental protection.

The executive organisation for environmental protection is the State Environmental Protection Bureau. It is directly subordinate to the State Council. Environmental protection organisations have also been established at three levels of administration, province, city and county and some provinces and cities have established their own environmental protection committees and some towns and counties have provided personnel for the management of environmental protection. Including all levels of administration, there are now an estimated almost

50,000 people working in the area of environmental protection and when those engaged in environmental works in other fields are included, the estimated figure is almost 100,000 people.

In order to promote environmental protection and to enforce environmental law, China's environmental management department has formulated over seventy standards and regulations. These include the Trial Implementing Standard for Discharging the 'Three Wastes' of Industry; Prevention Stipulations Concerning Radioactivity; The Quality Standard for Sea-water; The Quality Standard for Atmospheric Environment; The Noise Standard for Urban Regional Environment; and The Quality Standard of Water Environment over the Earth's Surface.

In order to carry out environmental monitoring, China's General Station of Environmental Monitoring and 1,277 local monitoring stations have been established. China now has an atmospheric monitoring network focusing on the large metropolitan centres and a water quality monitoring network focusing on river water systems and sea area.

In order to control new polluting sources, the Management Measures for Environmental Protection on Capital Construction Projects was issued as an edict in 1981. It stipulates that the design and construction of all newly built projects, rebuilt or extended projects, can only proceed after environmental impact examination and approval has been granted by a relevant environmental management department. When construction includes measures to prevent and tackle pollution these must go into operation at the same time as the main body of the project. If they are not implemented the project will not be allowed to operate.

In 1982 the Provisional Measures to Collect Waste-Discharging Fees was formulated. This was done in order to reduce pollution and in order to explore sources of funds for pollution projects. Waste-discharging fees are collected from those enterprises that exceed the standards stipulated by the State and those who are responsible for polluting accidents are penalised.

In the past, construction of China's industrial factories has lacked planned pollution management. Factories with enormous waste discharge have even been built in urban upwind positions, in the upper reaches of water catchment areas, in scenic tourist areas and in densely populated areas. This has meant that harm from pollution has been even greater than it might otherwise have been.

During the Sixth Five-Year Plan period (1981-1985), measures were taken to redress the problem of unsuitably sited enterprises. Factories were shut down, had their operations suspended, were amalgamated with other factories, switched manufacture to other products and were relocated.

(3) A basic reason for the enormous volume of waste discharged by China's industrial enterprises is the use of obsolete equipment. Backward technology and operating methods and a low rate of energy and raw material utilisation are a serious problem.

Calculated according to per Rmb 10,000 of industrial output value, the discharge volume of waste water dropped from 477 metric tons in 1980 to 310 metric tons by 1985 and the discharge volume of waste residue was reduced from 9.8 metric tons in 1980 to 5.8 metric tons in 1985. The State encourages the recovery and use of waste water, waste gas and waste residue and implements tax reductions and exemptions for their comprehensive utilisation.

During the period 1981-1987 funds invested in environmental protection reached Rmb 23.5 billion and there were 188,000 projects involved in pollution prevention. There were also 145,000 projects completed in the same period that had improved industrial waste water discharge. The result was that the percentage of industrial waste water that reached the government's discharge standard rose from 26% to 46%.

During the period 1981-1987 China's national output value increased by 85.7%, but energy consumption volume grew by only 44.5% and discharged volume of waste did not increase proportionally. This has meant that the environmental quality of the majority of cities was kept at the 1980 level, though the environmental quality in some areas did show some improvement.

4. ENVIRONMENTAL PROTECTION TARGETS

In the period between now and the end of the century the target of China's environmental protection policy will be:

... to bring environmental pollution under control;

... to improve the environmental quality of major cities;

... to halt further deterioration in the ecological environment; and

... to provide the foundation needed for the realisation of a clean, beautiful and tranquil environment in cities and towns.

In order to achieve these results environmental principle and policy will concentrate on furthering the coordinated development of economic construction and environmental protection. Attention will be paid to unified planning and there will be a particular emphasis on environmental protection in heavily industrialised areas and cities that are seriously polluted.

The policies that are to be followed are:

(1) Within the limits of State financial capability, the share of funds to be used for environmental protection will be gradually increased.

(2) A push for technical improvement and so a reduction in the consumption of energy, raw and semi-finished materials and a considerable reduction in the discharge coefficient of industrial wastes.

(3) Within the confines of the energy production mix, the supply of energy will be adjusted. Availability of gas for use by urban consumers (civilian burning of fuels is second only to industrial pollution) should be improved step by step and supply of heating needs should be centralised. Coal washing will be promoted and coal of low sulphur content and volatility, but with high heat value, will be supplied for civilian use.

(4) Purifying installations must be constructed. They will be used for purifying waste water, waste gas and waste residue. The problem of making various types of polluting substances non-harmful is to be addressed and technological answers will be sought for preventing water pollution and for turning polluted urban water into a resource.

(5) Trees and grasses will be planted. Efforts will be made to contract peasants to plant waste hills and slopes and urban afforestation will be promoted. It is intended that in the near future the area of per capita greenland in cities will be more than doubled.

(6) Popularisation of ecologically sympathetic agriculture is also a policy that is to be pursued.

Effort will be made to perfect the system of environmental protection decrees, to standardise and strictly enforce environmental law and to improve environmental monitoring. There is also to be an improvement in the collection of waste discharge fees and an increase in the scope of fee collection. This latter policy will strengthen the economic means for environmental management. In addition special funds are to be established by drawing 20-30% from the waste discharge fees collected. These funds are to be used to tackle pollution.

In future environmental protection quotas are to be brought into enterprise contracts and they are to be included in the system of registration application. They are also to be included in the system of licence issue.

From January 1989 the results of environmental examinations have been reported to the government at the upper level and then published. The latter is a means of promoting public supervision of pollution.

SECTION III

INDUSTRIAL PRODUCTION AND INFRASTRUCTURE

CHAPTER 12

The Structure of Industry

I. CHANGES IN THE STRUCTURE OF CHINESE INDUSTRY

Since the founding of New China the structure of national production has changed. This change has corresponded with the development of the Chinese economy.

1. CHANGES IN THE RELATIONS BETWEEN PRIMARY, SECONDARY AND TERTIARY INDUSTRIES

Old China was an extremely poor agricultural country. Its primary, secondary and tertiary industries were very backward. Primary industry accounted for more than half of the total industry, but was relatively unproductive while secondary industry was fragmented and lacked an adequate industrial infrastructure. In terms of China as a whole, tertiary industry was undeveloped even though some lop-sided development had taken place in some eastern sea-board cities.

Immediately after the Chinese Communist Party took power, in three-year rehabilitation period and in the First Five-Year Plan period, the growth of the primary, secondary and tertiary industries gained momentum. It is estimated that in 1952 primary industry accounted for 50.5% of Gross National Product, secondary industry 20.8%, and tertiary industry 28.7%. In 1957 the figures were 40.6%, 29.2% and 30.2% respectively. In terms of the distribution of workers, in 1952 primary industry employed 83.5% of the workforce, secondary industry 7.4% and tertiary industry 9.1%. By 1957 the figures were 81.2% and 9.0% and 9.8% respectively.

In the period 1958 to 1978 internal ties between the primary, secondary and tertiary industries were neglected. As a result primary industry grew slowly and the proportion of the secondary industry in the GNP increased too fast relative to the tertiary sector of the economy. It is estimated that in 1978 primary industry accounted for 29.1%, 11.5 percentage points less than 1957; secondary industry 47.9%, an increase of 18.7 percentage points over 1957; tertiary industry 23%, a decrease of 7.2 percentage points.

With the 1979 introduction of economic reform both urban and rural reform was undertaken. It resulted in substantial development of agriculture, light industry and tertiary industry and in improved coordination between the urban and rural sectors of the economy.

Prior to the introduction of economic reform, there had been inadequate investment in the tertiary sector of the economy. Areas such as transport and communication services, financial and insurance services and science and education were promoted and developed under economic reform policy and new industries were established and advanced. But during the period of the Seventh Five-Year Plan there was a slowing in the extraordinary growth of the agricultural sector. In both 1986 and 1987 the agricultural growth rate was much slower than the average rate of growth during the period of the Sixth Five-Year Plan. Secondary industry maintained a high growth rate and the growth rate of tertiary industry was slightly higher than the GNP, but slower than the secondary industry growth rate. The result was that there was again a gap in the growth of primary, secondary and tertiary industries. The 1987 GNP was Rmb 1,104.9 billion. The percentages of the primary, secondary and tertiary industries were 28.8%, 45.7% and 25.5% respectively.

2. CHANGES IN THE RELATIONS BETWEEN AGRICULTURE AND INDUSTRY

Since the Chinese Communist Party came to power both agriculture and industry have developed and the relations between them have undergone considerable change.

During the period of the national economic rehabilitation and the First Five-Year Plan (1949-1957) agriculture and industry grew rapidly. They promoted the development of each other and there was a balanced relationship between them. But from 1958 industry, particularly heavy industry, was one-sidedly promoted. This situation deprived the agricultural sector of investment funding. The result was a decline in agricultural production that in turn starved industry of raw materials and of accumulated investment funds. Then after three years of readjustment from 1963-1965, the relations between industry and agriculture gradually returned to normal. In 1965 agriculture made up 37.3% of the total industrial and agricultural output value and industry made up 62.7%.

In 1966 the Cultural Revolution began. It resulted in the slowing of both the industrial and the agricultural growth rate. Gross industrial and agricultural output value for 1975 is estimated to have consisted of 28.2% agricultural production and 71.8% industrial production.

The 1979 introduction of economic reform policy meant that the one-sided stress that had been placed on the development of heavy industry, at the expense of light industry and the tertiary and agricultural sectors of the economy, was to be addressed. Reform policy began a process of altering the proportions of industrial and agricultural production in the national economy. The proportion of agriculture in terms of gross industrial and agricultural output value rose from 24.8% in 1978 to 25.3% in 1987, while that of industry dropped from 75.2% to 74.7%.

12:1 OUTPUT VALUE OF INDUSTRY AND AGRICULTURE

	Total output value of industry and agriculture (Rmb 100 mill)	Total output of industry (as a %)	Total output of agriculture (as a %)
1952	810	43.1	56.9
1957	1241	56.7	43.3
1965	2235	62.7	37.3
1978	5634	75.2	24.8
1980	7078	72.8	27.2
1985	13337	72.9	27.1
1987	18489	74.7	25.3

Note: The output value in the above table is calculated in terms of the current year price. The total output value of industry includes the output value of industrial enterprises run by villages and below.

3. CHANGES IN RELATIONS BETWEEN LIGHT AND HEAVY INDUSTRY

In Old China light industry was very backward and heavy industry was fragmented. With the exception of a small number of mining, power generation, iron and steel, building material and machine-building enterprises, there were no other branches of heavy industry to speak of. During the First Five-Year Plan period the State formulated the policy of giving priority to heavy industry. During this period heavy industry grew by an average of 25.4% annually and light industry grew by an average of 12.9%. New industries were established and the capacity of industrial production was significantly increased.

With the introduction of Great Leap Forward policy in 1958 a one-sided policy of giving priority to the development of heavy industry and 'taking steel as the key link' was implemented. This policy is now seen as having been detrimental to agriculture and to light industry. During this Second Five-Year Plan period the total output value of light industry grew by an average of only 1.1% annually and in 1960, 1961, and 1962, it fell continuously. This led to a serious disproportion between light and heavy industry. After three years of readjustment (from 1963 to 1965) the proportion between light and heavy industry became more balanced. In the total 1965 output value of industry, light industry made up 51.7 and heavy industry 48.4%. After the beginning of the Cultural Revolution in 1966 policy again favoured the development of heavy industry and again there was an imbalance between the light and heavy industrial sectors of the economy. By 1978 light industry accounted for 43.1% and heavy industry 56.9% of the total output value of industry.

While the relations between industry and agriculture were readjusted with the 1979 introduction of economic reform policy, measures were also being taken to readjust the relationship between light and heavy industry. The development of light industry was promoted. The result was an average annual growth rate of light industry in the period between 1979 and 1987 of 14.1%. The average annual growth rate of heavy industry during this period was 12.8%. In terms of the total industrial output value in 1987 light industry accounted for 48.2% and heavy industry 51.8%.

(1)   Structure of Light Industry

In the early stage of New China most light industrial production used agricultural products as raw materials. With the development of industry the proportion of light industry using manufactured goods as raw materials gradually increased. In 1952, in terms of the total output value of light industry, the proportion of light industry using agricultural products as raw materials was 87.5% . By 1957 this figure had been reduced to 81.6%. In terms of light industry using manufactured products as raw materials, the increase was from 12.5% to 18.4%.

During the Second Five-Year Plan period light industry using manufactured goods as raw materials grew very slowly. Affected by continuous reductions in agricultural output, light industry using agricultural products as raw materials registered negative growth. By 1965 its output value had dropped to 71.7%. During the Third Five-Year Plan and the Fourth Five-Year Plan periods, agricultural production fluctuated, which affected the growth of light industry using agricultural products as raw materials. Output value hovered around 70%.

Since 1979 both the growth rate of light industry using agricultural products as raw materials and the growth rate of manufactured products used as materials for further production, has grown very quickly, the latter growing even faster than the former.

In world terms the Chinese people's standard of living continues to be relatively low. Most people have only recently solved the problem of being adequately fed and clothed. Their demand for food and clothing is constantly increasing. This situation means that the textile and food industries which use agricultural products as raw materials have considerable scope for further development. The result of this situation is that the present proportion of light industry that uses agricultural products as raw materials can only be reduced slowly.

12:2 OUTPUT VALUE OF LIGHT INDUSTRY USING AGRICULTURAL MATERIALS AS RAW MATERIALS AND USING MANUFACTURED GOODS FOR PRODUCTION

	Light industry using agricultural goods as raw materials		Light industry using manufactured goods as raw materials	
	Growth rate (as a %)	Proportion of output value (total output value of light industry =100)	Growth rate (as a %)	Proportion of output value (total output value of light industry =100)
1952	87.5			12.5
1957	11.2*	81.6	21.9*	18.4
2nd 5-year plan	-1.5	76.5	11.0	23.5
1963-1965	20.3	73.3	23.3	26.7
3rd 5-year plan	7.9	68.7	9.6	31.3
4th 5-year plan	7.5	70.9	8.2	29.1
5th 5-year plan	10.5	68.8	12.1	31.2
6th 5-year plan	10.7	68.7	14.9	31.3
1986	8.3	67.7	14.6	32.3
1987	14.2	70.1	16.9	29.9

* denotes the period 1953-1957

Under the item of proportion of output value in the above table, the 1952 and 1957 figures are calculated in terms of the constant price of 1952; the figures for the Second and Third Five-Year Plan periods are calculated in terms of the constant price of 1970. Figures for the Sixth Five-Year Plan period and 1986 are calculated in terms of the constant price of 1980; the figures for 1986 and 1987 are calculated in terms of the current year price. If the 1987 figures were calculated in terms of the constant price of 1980, the proportion of the output value of light industry using agricultural products as raw materials would be below 69%.

(2) Structure of Heavy Industry

Since the Communist Party came to power the manufacturing sector of the economy has developed fastest. The second fastest areas of growth have been the raw material and mining sectors. During the First Five-Year Plan period the growth rates of these three heavy industrial sectors of the economy were similar, but over time a gap between growth rates has continued to widen. During the first Five-Year Plan the average annual growth rate of the manufacturing sector was 28.6%, the growth rate of the raw materials sector was 23.4% and the mining sector's growth rate was 21.5%. In the two decades between 1958 and 1979 the average annual growth rate of the manufacturing sector was 12.4%, raw materials 10% and the mining sector 8.3%. From 1979 to 1985 the average annual growth rate of the manufacturing sector was 9.9%, raw materials 7.7% and mining 3.5%. This situation led to the steady decline of the proportion of raw material and particularly mining sector production in the total output value of heavy industry.

12:3 OUTPUT VALUE OF THE MANUFACTURING, RAW MATERIALS AND MINING INDUSTRIES

	Manufacturing		Raw materials		Mining	
	Growth rate	Proportion of output value (as a %)	Growth rate	Proportion of output value (as a %)	Growth Rate	Proportion of output value (as a %)
1952		41.9		42.8		15.3
1957	28.6*	45.7	23.4*	39.7	21.5*	14.6
2nd 5-year plan	6.1	49.9	7.5	36.6	6.0	13.5
1963-1965	18.8	47.9	13.5	40.3	6.2	11.8
3rd 5-year plan	16.6	52.3	13.7	37.2	8.7	10.5
4th 5-year plan	12.7	51.2	6.6	36.9	10.5	11.9
5th 5-year plan	6.9	52.1	9.4	36.1	6.3	11.8
6th 5-year plan	12.8	49.2	7.6	37.7	4.5	13.1
1986	6.5	53.5	9.6	35.1	5.8	11.4
1987	17.5	48.8	13.1	38.9	5.0	12.3

* denotes the period 1953-1957.

If the figures of 1987 were calculated in terms of the constant price of 1980, the proportion of output value of the mining industries would be below 11.3% and would continue to fall.

In centralised economies there is a tendency for the growth rate of the output value of manufacturing within the heavy industrial sector of the economy to be increasingly higher than that of either the raw material or mining industries. Under present conditions the differences in this growth rate must be balanced. It is clear that excessively rapid development of the manufacturing sector will stress the mining industry and branches of the raw materials industry and that this is a problem that has not yet been solved.

4. CHANGES IN THE RELATIONS BETWEEN BRANCHES OF INDUSTRY

China's industry is divided into eleven major industries, 44 divisions and 155 subdivisions. An analysis of the eleven major industries shows that in 1952 the textile industry made up the largest proportion of the total output value of industry. It accounted for 27.5% of industrial output. Second place went to the food industry which accounted for 24.1% of total output value. The two sectors combined made up more than half of total industrial output value.

From 1953 to 1985 the total output value of industry grew at an average annual rate of 11%. Of these the petroleum, chemical and machine-building industries registered the fastest development. They had an average annual growth rate of 17.3%, 16.4% and 15.2% respectively. Next came the electricity, metallurgical and building materials industries with an average annual growth rate of 13.1%, 11.6% and 11.7% respectively. The growth rate of the forest, food, textile, paper making and coal industries was in each case less than the average 11% annual rate of growth in industrial output value. The lowest growth rate was experienced by the forest and food industries. Their respective growth rates were 4.6% and 6.9%.

As the growth rate of various industries differed, marked changes took place in the proportions of output value in industry. By 1987 the proportion of output value contributed by the textile and food industries dropped to 13.0% and 12.4% respectively while that of the machine-building, chemical and petroleum industries rose from 1.4%, 4.8% and 0.5% to 25.2%, 12.1% and 5.4% respectively.

12:4 CHANGES IN PROPORTION OF OUTPUT VALUE OF A NUMBER OF IMPORTANT INDUSTRIES

Industry*	1952	1957	1965	1978	1980	1985	1987
Metallurgy	5.9	9.3	10.7	8.7	8.6	8.0	9.5
Power industry	1.3	1.4	3.1	3.8	3.8	3.3	3.1
Coal industry	2.4	2.3	2.6	2.8	2.3	2.3	2.2
Petroleum industry	0.5	0.9	3.2	5.5	5.1	4.5	5.4
Chemical industry	4.8	8.2	12.9	12.4	12.5	11.2	12.1
Machine-building	11.4	18.2	22.3	27.3	25.5	26.9	25.2
Building materials	3.0	3.3	2.8	3.6	3.6	4.2	5.8
Forest industry	6.5	5.4	2.9	1.8	1.7	1.6	2.2
Food industry	24.1	19.6	12.6	11.1	11.4	11.5	12.4
Textile industry	27.5	18.2	15.8	12.6	14.7	15.3	13.0

* Total output of industry = 100.

In table 12:4 (immediately above) the proportions of output value of various industries for 1987 that are listed were fixed after making readjustments according to the new classifications of various industries in the national economy introduced in 1984. They are slightly different from the standards set before 1985. The figures for 1952 and 1957 were calculated in terms of the constant price of 1957. The 1965 figures were also calculated according to the constant price of 1957. The figures for 1978 and 1980 were calculated according to the constant price of 1970. The 1985 figures were calculated according to the constant price of 1980. The 1987 figures were calculated according to the current year price.

II.   CURRENT INDUSTRIAL STRUCTURE

1.   PROBLEMS IN THE EXISTING INDUSTRIAL STRUCTURE

Since 1979 China's industrial structure has gone through many positive changes, but many problems remain to be solved. The major problems are that:

(1)   *Agriculture has a Weak Foundation and Insufficient Capacity for Sustained Development.*

Since the introduction of reform, agricultural production, particularly grain production, has increased substantially but is very unstable. The material and technological foundation of agricultural production and the ability to resist natural calamities is poor and the capacity for expanding grain production is seriously restricted. Grain production in the past few years has been in a state of stagnation. Average per capita grain consumption in 1987 was 577 kg. This is only slightly more than enough. Owing to grave natural calamities, grain production in 1988 was lower than that of 1984.

After the rich harvest of 1984, cotton output fluctuated. By 1988 output was about the same as it had been in 1984. Forestry production, animal husbandry, sideline occupations and fishery production all increased, but their foundations remained very weak. China's agriculture needs fast development in order to meet immediate consumption demand and in order to meet the industrial sector's increasing demand for raw materials.

(2)   *The Internal Structure of China's Industry is Irrational*

Although the proportionate relationship between light and heavy industries is now appropriate, contradictions exist between the sector of light industry that uses agricultural products as raw materials and the sector that uses manufactured goods as raw materials. There are also acute contradictions within the heavy industrial sector. In most industries the technical and management levels are low and the consumption of raw materials is high. The machine-building and electronics industry, the largest industry in China, turns out large quantities of general products. But its high-grade precision products are not only inferior in quality, they are also inadequate in terms of quantity. Quantity of production is low compared with the same type of industries in developed countries. The level of technology lags behind by more than twenty years.

Basic industries are particularly weak. Metallurgical products cannot meet demand. Huge quantities of rolled steel are imported, close to twenty million metric tons annually in the past few years. In other words more than a quarter of the rolled steel required domestically is imported and there is still an acute supply shortage.

The problems of variety and quality are even more serious. Another problem is the backwardness of new industries. The micro-electronics industry, biological engineering industry and new materials industry that emerged with the advance of science and technology are very weak (some are non-existent).

(3)   Energy is in Short Supply

The strain on energy supply has continued unabated. It has been estimated that for the past few years there has been an annual shortage of 50 billion kW hrs of electricity. Each year generator installations have increased energy generating capacity by approximately 9 million kW. The capacity required just to meet increased demand is 12-15 million kW.

The shortage of power has led to many enterprises being unable to utilise fully their production capacity. To date the building of power plants to increase power producing capacity has usually depended on the central government. In the past few years 80% of investment made available for building power stations has been provided by the central government. Local government and enterprise investment has for the most part been used for the development of processing industries. But now the reliance on only the central government for power industry investment is recognised as resulting in only limited investment being made available for the purpose of increasing power supply.

(4)   Transport and Post and Communication Services Lag far Behind the Demand Placed on them by Economic Development

Infrastructure has become increasingly stressed. It is a situation that is incompatible with national economic development. Between 1949 and 1987 the total length of railway lines increased only 2.4 times while the volume of passenger and freight transport increased 10.9 and 25 times respectively. The overloading of transport is quite common. At present China has only 54.8 km of railway lines for every 10,000 square kilometres of land. Compared with the developed countries this figure is very low. It is even much lower than the figure for India. The quality of the transport lines is poor. Only 21.3% of the railway lines are double-track and only 22% of the highways are asphalt or residual-oil roads.

Communication services are underdeveloped. The number of telephones installed is only 0.8% of the world total. There is an average of 0.75 telephones for every 100 people. The ratio between the increase in the number of telephones and the growth of industrial production is 0.14:1. The result is a great deal of difficulty and inconvenience.

(5)   Commerce and Service Trades Remain Backward

China's commerce and service trades cannot keep up with the development of production and the people's rising standard of living. In 1987 the proportion of commerce in the gross social output value was 6.5%. This is much lower than under the First Five-Year Plan.

In many places in China people are confronted with the difficulties of travelling, accessing medical treatment, sending their babies to nurseries and sending their children to schools. The developing tertiary sector cannot meet demand. Services and commercial trading enterprises are particularly scarce in rural areas and in some cities services and commercial trading companies are over-concentrated in downtown areas. This has meant that in some cities in industrial areas, newly built residential areas and in the suburbs, services are not readily available.

2. INDUSTRIAL POLICY IN THE 1990s

Industrial policy in the 1990s is intended to further promote the industrial policy of the latter half of the 1980s. This policy focused on the development of energy (mainly electricity), transport and communications; the development of machine-building, electronic, iron and steel and raw and semi-finished materials industries; the development of agriculture; and the promotion of key industries and of the technological transformation of existing industries. (An industry is deemed to be a key industry if it occupies an important place in the national economy; if there is a huge demand for its products, both domestically and internationally; if the industry can promote the development of other related industries; and if the industry plays a crucial role in the development and/or adoption of technology. In the light of China's current economic situation, agriculture, transport, post and telecommunication services, the power industry, consumer goods industry, metallurgical industry, electronics and machine-building industries, automobile industry and the building industry are regarded as key industries.)

In order to fulfil the tasks of rationalisation and modernisation of the industrial structure in the context of the economic situation that is likely to continue in to the 1990s, attention will be paid to the following:

(1) The use of Industrial Policy for the Promotion of Economic Development and Reform

China's economic reform will take some time. To achieve optimum resource distribution, during the 1990s China will promote the role of the market while relying on correct centrally formulated industrial policy that will employ economic levers such as pricing, finance, taxation and credit to implement State intervention and regulation. Macro-economic control will be combined with micro-flexibility.

(2) To Promote Correct Handling of the Relationship Between Industrial Structure and Economic Growth Rate

China must solve the problems of its industrial structure while at the same time promoting economic development. The 1990s will continue to witness the replacing of the old system with the new. Although the new system will play a dominant role, the traditional system will also play its role. Also, because in China it is still possible to blindly seek a high growth rate, importance will be attached to correctly handling the relationship between industrial structure and economic growth rate. An appropriate growth rate will be centrally fixed to prevent the indiscriminate seeking of a high growth rate.

(3) An Industrial Policy that must Reflect the Demands of the Different Stages of Development of the Industrial Structure

China's industrialisation can be roughly divided into three periods—the early period, the middle period and the later period. The industrial structure of the early period is characterised by the dominant role played by the light and textile industries. The industrial structure of the middle period is dominated by the heavy and chemical industries with machine-building, power and other capital intensive industries playing a leading role. This will follow the development of basic industries and industrial infrastructure. The industrial structure of the later period is characterised by a high degree of industrial processing. Given China's existing economic situation, the industries for all three periods of industrialisation require development. And the country's agriculture has a weak foundation. Agriculture's basic industries and infrastructure are backward. In view of this situation vigorous development of the agricultural sector is also an important task to be accomplished in the 1990s.

(4)   To Control the Scale of Investment and to Readjust the Investment Structure

In order to secure stable growth of the national economy on the basis of increasing returns, efforts will be made to maintain a rough balance between total social demand and total supply. To this end it is necessary to control the scale of investment of the whole society. This must be done together with distributing investment in fixed assets and investment in circulating funds in accord with the need to promote rationalisation of the industrial structure. This will ensure priority of investment required for the development of key industrial sectors.

(5)   To Gradually Rationalise the Organisational Structure of Enterprises

The present organisational structure of Chinese enterprises is irrational. This problem has to be solved in the 1990s. First, it is necessary to achieve co-ordination among specialised departments to bring about a radical change in the backward state where an enterprise, whether big or small, is a self-contained unit. Co-ordination between enterprises must be realised. Second, attention must be paid to economy of scale. There is a need to reorganise those enterprises which should not be scattered or run on a small scale. The State undertakes overall planning of a small number of products which require large investment and are highly technology-intensive. The State organises their production on a large scale. Such products include automobiles, large-scale integrated circuits, programme controlled communication equipment, optical-fibre communication equipment and colour picture tubes. Third, it is necessary to encourage enterprises to enter into various forms of voluntary association. These associations can be carried out in the same industry or between industries. They can be in the form of scientific research and production, marketing, export, or in other forms.

(6)   To Strengthen Trade Management

Trade management is not designed to exercise direct control over enterprises. It is designed to formulate development plans for a particular trade and to investigate and study major economic and technological problems that may impede the development of that trade. Trade management also organises information and technology exchange and personnel training. Through these activities it coordinates the relations between enterprises and links the enterprise with relevant government departments. Usually trade management is conducted through trade associations which are non-governmental organisations voluntarily organised by the enterprises themselves. This work will be put on the agenda as an important item for the 1990s.

(7) To Accelerate Technical Transformation and Promote Technological Progress

A rational industrial structure will be built on the basis of advanced technology. The promotion of science and technology will be based on two approaches. First, efforts will be made to develop and popularise the results of scientific research which has desired economic effects and which brings quick returns. Second, major scientific research projects will be undertaken. These projects will be centred on key problems encountered in economic construction and social development.

As most Chinese enterprises have outdated equipment and backward technology, in the 1990s great importance will be attached to the appropriate technical transformation of existing enterprises. In order to alleviate the contradictions between the supply and demand of energy and raw and semi-finished materials, the existing enterprises will be transformed to conserve energy and to reduce the consumption of raw and semi-finished materials.

Practical plans for technological progress and for the technical transformation of industries will be mapped out. These plans will integrate technological progress, technical transformation, industrial readjustment and reorganisation of the existing enterprises. Funds for equipment updating and technical transformation will be concentrated to ensure that key projects benefit. This means that the technical transformation of industries, regions and enterprises that are the most important in terms of national economic development will achieve marked progress. Efforts will also be made to tighten control over the import of technical equipment; to put an end to the indiscriminate importing of equipment; to assimilate imported technology; and to develop import substitutes. Rules and regulations will be worked out to clearly provide for (under given conditions) the sharing of imported technology and expertise with other relevant enterprises. Greater advances will be made in the 1990s in speeding up the establishment and development of a technology market, promoting the close integration of scientific research and production and turning the results of scientific research into commodities.

(8) To Institute Correct Consumption Policy and Give Guidance to Consumption

The consumption policy of the 1990s will include (i) concentrating on improving the people's material and cultural life and (ii) raising the people's living standard on the basis of the development of production and guiding changes in consumption patterns.

As China has limited cultivated land and limited grassland, the consumption of animal food such as meat, poultry and eggs, cannot grow too fast and woollen and leather products must only be increased in an appropriate manner. As the strain on power supply will continue for a long time to come, the availability of household electrical appliances can only be sensibly increased. People's living conditions will continue to improve, but housing space should not be too large and building standard should not be too high. In the 1990s plain living, hard work, building the country and running all undertakings thriftily and industriously will be promoted, rather than the encouragement of excessively high consumption patterns.

CHAPTER 13

Fixed Asset Construction

In China fixed assets are divided into categories that accord with their different uses. The first category is productive fixed assets; the second is non-productive fixed assets. Productive fixed assets are used in direct material production or they are fixed assets necessary in terms of the provision of the conditions needed for material production. They include: productive equipment, power and transport equipment, factory buildings, warehouses and railways and roads. Non-productive fixed assets are those fixed assets that are not put into direct use in material production. They are mostly assets that are used for people's consumption. They include residential houses, stores, schools and hospitals.

I. FIXED ASSET INVESTMENT AND CONSTRUCTION

In the past the government has been the main investor in fixed asset construction, but since the introduction of economic reform, investment in fixed assets has been drawn from three sources: government investment, enterprise investment and individual investment.

1. GOVERNMENT INVESTMENT

This investment includes that undertaken by both central and local government administrations. Central government investment is arranged by the State Planning Commission, State special investment co-operatives and various other departments of the State Council. They use central capital investment funds, bank loans, self-raised funds, funds from abroad and other special funds. The scope of their investment includes major industrial energy bases; raw and semi-finished materials vital for the national economy; trans-regional key facilities for transport and communications; key machinery, electronics, light and textile industrial projects; key projects for harnessing major rivers; major agricultural bases and key shelter-forest projects; key newly-developed industrial projects; important scientific, technical, cultural and educational facilities; investment for the construction of national defence industries and construction projects for important installations; and support for construction in economically undeveloped regions.

Local government investment is arranged by the planning commissions of provinces, autonomous regions and municipalities directly under the central authority of counties. Local special investment corporations and various other departments of local governments use local capital construction funds, bank loans, self-raised funds, funds from abroad and other special funds.

The scope of their investment includes agricultural production, forestry, water conservation, energy, raw and semi-finished materials industries needed by the locality, local communications and transport facilities, machinery, electronics, light and textile industries, science and technology, education, culture, public health and urban public utilities and service utilities.

2. ENTERPRISE INVESTMENT

As the title suggests, this investment is that which is organised by the enterprise. The enterprise uses funds drawn from retained profits, depreciation funds, allocations for major overhauls, bank loans, funds from abroad and other funds raised with government approval. The scope of this investment includes updating and transforming projects and provision of necessary enterprise welfare installations. If there are surplus funds then investment on capital construction can still be carried out.

3. INDIVIDUAL INVESTMENT

Individual investment is carried out by residents and peasants in both urban and village contexts and consists of self-raised funds, loans and credits from the bank. The scope of this investment includes house building and the building of other structures and buying equipment, tools, appliances and draught animals.

4. THE RELATIONSHIP BETWEEN INVESTMENT BODIES

Government investment occupies the primary position among the investment bodies. Under past economic structure government investment mainly referred to central government investment, but in the period since 1978 the distribution of power over economic management between central and local government has been divided. In this context the financial and investment power of central and local government have been fixed with central and local government administrations having responsibility that accords with a specified division of labour.

In terms of enterprise investment the activity of enterprises in this area reflects the central concern of economic reform, i.e., that the enterprise become master of itself. Economic reform policy has including promotion of the practice of independent operation by enterprises that in turn must accept sole responsibility for their profit and loss. This has meant that enterprise investment power has also had to be expanded to the point where gradually, the enterprise will become the main investor in fixed asset construction. In this context the government will use economic levers, legal means and any necessary administrative means to guide enterprise decision-making. Meanwhile the enterprise is encouraged to develop lateral economic associations, particularly in the form of associated investment groups. The formation of these groups serves to promote a reasonable standard of economic scale.

The individual and the private economy are the necessary and beneficial supplements to the economy owned by the whole people. This is why the government encourages the development of individual investment. Development of the individual economy promotes production, extends employment and has been particularly beneficial in terms of increasing the stock of residential housing. The government is now formulating relevant policies and laws for the protection of the lawful interests of individual investors and for strengthening the guidance, supervision and management of individual investment.

5. THE SOURCE OF FUNDS FOR FIXED ASSET CONSTRUCTION

In the past, funds for fixed asset construction came from direct financial allocation. There was a single channel for funding. Now changes have been made with regard to the source of funds for fixed asset construction. These changes mean that funding is developing in the direction of multi-channel funding drawn from diversified sources. These sources include capital construction funds, bank loans, self-raised funds and funds from abroad.

(1) Capital Construction Funds

Capital construction funds are provided by both central and local administrations. In each case capital construction funds and financial expenses are managed separately. This is in line with the policy of ear-marking funds for specific purposes. The establishment of capital construction funds serves to maintain stability in terms of the source of funds for basic industries, for basic installations and for a number of major social development projects.

(2) Central Capital Construction Funds

These funds are composed of the following: funds that central departments have allocated for the development of key State energy and communication key construction projects; funds raised by central administrative departments through the collection of architectural tax; principal and interest recovered from loans drawn from State budgetary allocation for fixed asset construction; and fixed State financial allocations.

(3) Local Capital Construction Funds

Local capital construction funds are established by provinces, municipalities directly under central authority, autonomous regions, or cities that are separately listed and subordinate to the province. The Planning Commissions in the region organise the use of these funds in accord with the revenue and expenditure of the region.

(4) Bank Loans

These are loans that are to be used for fixed asset construction. They have been made available through utilisation of funds deposited in various State special banks and other State approved credit institutions. State special banks and credit institutions that extend loans for fixed asset construction include the following: The People's Construction Bank, The Industrial and Commercial Bank, The Agricultural Bank, The Bank of China, The China International Trust and Investment Corporation and The Everbright Industrial Corporation.

The use of bank loans to fund fixed asset construction has the advantage of using bank credit requirements as a means of disciplining enterprise investment behaviour. This is a means that is useful for effecting an improvement in the national economic benefit derived from investment. It is intended that bank loans will gradually become the chief source of funding for fixed asset investment.

Loan quotas for fixed asset construction listed by banks are to be listed under both the State credit plan and the State fixed assets construction plan. With the exception of special banks and trust and investment corporations approved by the State Council, other units are not allowed to handle fixed asset construction loans. An annual interest rate of 30% is levied on all fixed asset construction loans extended outside the State plan.

(5) Self-Raised Funds

These are funds raised by localities, departments and enterprises for the purpose of fixed asset construction. Since economic reform these funds have become a relatively important funding source. They have taken the following forms:

(i) Local self-raised funds. These funds include financial reserves left at the disposal of local authorities, including any financial surplus left from the previous year's fund allocation; financial charges and preparatory fees from the current year; local extra-budgetary funds such as additional product tax, additional income tax, additional urban public utility undertaking fees and additional agricultural tax; surplus funds from revenues used to offset expenditure by local administrative undertaking units; and key construction funds drawn from the local charges levied on key construction funds for energy and communications.

(ii) Enterprise self-raised funds. These funds include enterprise funds for developing production, welfare funds for staff and workers, depreciation funds, allocation for major overhauls, capital construction income and any surplus on contracting investment.

Control of excessive growth of investment drawn from self-raised funds is now a focus of effective national management of the economy. Improperly conceived and funded fixed asset construction projects that have not yet been undertaken, will not be listed in the plan adhered to by planning departments, will not be funded by banks and will not be given the necessary construction licence. Self-raised funds must be deposited in a special account held with the People's Construction Bank and can only be used after the deposit has been held for six months. An added requirement is that no less than 30% of circulating funds needed after the project for which fixed asset construction was undertaken, completed and put into operation, must be held by the enterprise.

(iii) Overseas self-raised funds. These are funds raised abroad and used for direct investment. They are raised from foreign government loans, international financial organisations and commercial loans from economic organisations or from individuals. The use of foreign funds for fixed asset construction can make up for insufficient availability of domestic funds and can be used to improve the technical and management level of enterprises. They can also be used to boost export capacity and so can boost the capacity of enterprises to earn foreign exchange.

In its bid to attract foreign funds for fixed asset investment the Chinese government has formulated preferential policy for the use of foreign funds and it has gradually developed foreign economic decrees. The government has striven to improve the climate for foreign investment.

II. MACRO-MANAGEMENT OF FIXED ASSET CONSTRUCTION

Macro-control of fixed asset construction is an important guarantee for the sustained stability and co-ordinated development of China's national economy. It requires implementation of effective regulation, control and management. The

13:1 INVESTMENT IN FIXED ASSETS

Unit: Rmb 100 million

	1981	1985	1986	1987
State Enterprises				
Capital construction	442.9	1074.4	1176.1	1324.1
Updating and transformation	195.3	449.2	619.2	742.6
Others	20.3	157.0	183.2	195.2
Collective units				
Town and country	31.6	128.2	146.4	182.3
Villages	83.7	199.2	245.4	298.4
Units owned by town and country residents				
Town and country	11.9	56.8	74.6	78.5
Villages	166.3	473.4	574.8	697.0
Total investment	952.0	2538.2	3019.7	3518.1

macro-level tasks to be achieved are (i) appropriate scale of investment through total volume management and (ii) a reasonable investment structure through structural management.

1. TOTAL VOLUME MANAGEMENT

The key problem for total volume management is the fixing of an appropriate scale of fixed asset investment so as to maintain a balance between investment demand and supply capability. Fixed asset construction must not only be decided by national economic demand, but also by the capacity of the national economy. A balance needs to be struck between investment demand and availability of State funds, goods and materials.

In order to effect target management of fixed asset investment, various types of administrative, economic and legal means are adopted by the State.

(1) Implementation of the Unified Plan Over Investment Scale of Fixed Assets

The State implements mandatory management over government investment in fixed assets. In terms of enterprise investment, the State implements guidance plan management usually through employing economic policy and economic regulatory means. Other appropriate forms of fixed asset investment are then facilitated through managing the scale of individual investment.

(2) Employing Economic Means to Control Scale of Investment

An important economic means of control is through the use of taxation. The State began collecting an architectural tax on fixed assets investment in 1983. A 10% architectural tax was levied on self-raised capital construction investment that is within the State plan and is used for updating and transformation projects. A 20% architectural tax is levied on project investment for updating and transformation projects outside the State plan and a 30% tax is levied on capital construction projects deemed to require strict control and not listed in the State plan.

(3) Establishing a Scientific Approach to Policy Decisions

Policy decisions for construction projects must only be made strictly in accordance with procedures for examination and approval based on full feasibility studies and after proper consultation. This system will prevent subjective assumptions on the part of policy-makers and so will serve to guard against major errors of judgement in policy-making.

(4) The Employment of Legal Means for Investment Management

The State has already mapped out and promulgated laws, rules and regulations concerning the management of fixed asset investment. The Investment Law is in the process of being studied and formulated. This law is an important part of putting fixed asset investment on a codified and routinised footing.

2. ADJUSTING THE STRUCTURE OF FIXED ASSET INVESTMENT

Readjustment of the basic direction of investment structure must focus on distribution of investment between departments and regions and between capital construction projects. It must also focus on technical updating and transformation in both the productive and the non-productive sectors of the national economy.

In accord with a policy of long-term adjustment of investment structure, the focus of investment should include: an increase in the material input for agricultural production; increased investment in basic industries and in basic installations such as those providing raw materials and energy and communications services; and investment in education and scientific study, including improving the scientific and technical level of workers' education.

(1) Curtailing Non-Productive Investment

Except for necessary tourist facilities and for the construction of residential housing on an appropriate scale, non-productive investment in large urban construction projects, especially hotels, guest houses, sanatoriums and office buildings should be curtailed. This is to ensure that funds will be available for productive construction and for increasing new productive capacity. For investment make-up of State enterprise capital construction during various planning periods.

13:2 STATE ENTERPRISE INVESTMENT IN CAPITAL CONSTRUCTION, UPDATING AND TRANSFORMATION PROJECTS

	Investment in capital construction Rmb 100 million	Investment in updating and transformation and other fixed assets Rmb 100 million
1st 5-year plan	588.4	23.1
2nd 5-year plan	1206.1	100.9
1963 - 1965	421.9	77.6
3rd 5-year plan	976.0	233.1
4th 5-year plan	1764.0	512.4
5th 5-year plan	2342.2	844.1
6th 5-year plan	3410.1	1920.2
1986	1176.1	802.4
1987	1324.1	937.9

13:3 STATE ENTERPRISE CAPITAL CONSTRUCTION INVESTMENT IN NEWLY BUILT PROJECTS, EXTENSION AND REBUILT PROJECTS

	Investment in newly built capital construction Rmb 100 million	Investment in extension and rebuilding projects Rmb 100 million
1st 5-year plan	271.6	309.2
2nd 5-year plan	694.9	443.1
1963 - 1965	220.5	179.4
3rd 5-year plan	532.9	389.1
4th 5-year plan	1005.4	658.4
5th 5-year plan	1291.0	910.8
6th 5-year plan	1591.9	1266.7
1986	549.9	569.7
1987	579.5	537.4

13:4 STATE ENTERPRISE INVESTMENT IN PRODUCTIVE AND NON-PRODUCTIVE CAPITAL CONSTRUCTION

	Productive capital construction	Non-productive capital construction	Housing construction
	Rmb 100 million	Rmb 100 million	Rmb 100 million
1st 5-year plan	394.5	194.0	53.8
2nd 5-year plan	1029.7	176.4	49.6
1963 - 1965	335.0	86.8	29.1
3rd 5-year plan	818.0	158.0	39.3
4th 5-year plan	1455.2	308.8	100.7
5th 5-year plan	1729.9	612.2	277.3
6th 5-year plan	1956.5	13.6	727.0
1986	712.2	464.0	189.4
1987	872.2	451.9	177.4

(2) Using Economic Means to Adjust Investment Structure

The State uses different interest rates in relation to the construction of such industries as the raw and semi-finished materials, energy and communications industries. These industries are given preferential treatment. This consists of a preferential annual interest rate of 2.4% for construction projects concerned with coal, for measures that will economise on energy, and for building materials. For projects such as power, excavation for oil, communications and civil aviation the rate is 3.6%. In addition, a preferential tax rate is being considered.

3. *CLASSIFICATION OF FIXED ASSET CONSTRUCTION*

Equipment, tools and appliances which do not need to be installed and purchased for the immediate use of a capital construction project, such as the purchase of automobiles, rolling stock, vessels, planes, prospecting equipment and construction machinery, cannot be listed as part of a capital construction project. And projects with total investment under Rmb 100,000 are also excluded from being categorised as independent capital construction projects.

In relation to updating and transformation projects, an independent design document (or project suggestion report) is required and must be approved. Projects such as the electroplate centre, heat treatment centre and forging and casting centre jointly built for specialised production by several enterprises and undertaking units or the joint central heating project jointly built for economising on energy, can only be counted as one updating and transformation project, but an enterprise or undertaking unit is permitted to engage in several updating and transformation projects at the same time.

It also must be remembered that an updating and transformation project with a total investment of less than Rmb 50,000 cannot be categorised as an independent project.

(1)   Classification of Fixed Asset Construction Projects in Terms of the Nature of the Project

These are divided into three types:

- ... A newly-built project. In order to attract this classification a project must begin from scratch.
- ... A rebuilt project. A project subject to updating and transformation carried out by the existing enterprise and undertaking unit.
- ... An extension project. A project that serves to extend the existing enterprise and undertaking unit or administrative unit with a view to augmenting output capacity.

(2)   Classification that Accords with Scale of Construction

These are divided into large, medium and small-scale construction projects categorised according to scale of construction. For example in coal-mining areas the category of large-scale relates to those projects with an annual output of over 5 million metric tons of coal, medium to those with an annual output of 2-5 million metric tons and small-scale are those with an output of under 2 million metric tons. When categorising power stations, installed capacity is used as a guide. For example over 250,000 kW would be categorised as large-scale, 25,000-250,000 kW would be medium-scale and less than 25,000 kW would be small-scale. In an iron and steel complex categorisation would be: output over 1 million metric tons, large-scale; 100,000 to 1 million metric tons, medium-scale; 100,000 metric tons would be considered to be small-scale. With reference to cotton textile factories the figures for categorisation would be: large-scale, equipment consisting of over 100,000 cotton spindles; 50,000-100,000 spindles, medium-scale and under 50,000 spindles, small-scale.

Construction projects that cannot be easily divided in accord with design capacity are divided according to project investment. The division standard used for these projects is: investment over Rmb 20 million, large-scale; Rmb 10-20 million, medium-scale and investment under Rmb 10 million, small-scale.

According to current regulations large and medium-scale productive construction projects must be examined and approved by the State Planning Commission and in the case of very large investments (over Rmb 200 million) there is the added precaution of these projects being examined by the State Planning Commission and by the State Council. The other construction projects (medium and small) are subject to decentralised examination and approval. This is done by the relevant localities and departments. It is a situation that is recognised as having served to promote local enthusiasm while at the same time leaving the State with direct control over key construction projects that are concerned with the national economy and people's livelihood.

(3)   Classification that Accords with Form of Lateral Association

An important content of economic reform has been the development of lateral economic associations. The basis of current management policy is the use of large and medium-scale enterprises as the backbone of production while taking quality and brand name commodities as the centre. The promotion of cooperation between scientific research and production is then to be added. Fixed asset construction based on lateral association between enterprises would promote this current approach to economic management.

Classification that accords with the form of lateral association can be divided into four types:

(i)   Productive association. This form then includes two sub-types. One is a productive association which involves joint investment in construction projects by parties practising unified accounting, but with independent management and independent responsibility for profit and loss. The other is a productive association that involves joint investment in construction projects by parties practising shared profits on the basis of ratio of investment and profits retained in accord with agreement.

(ii)   Resources development association. This is an association where resources are developed through joint investment by both the processing enterprise and the resource enterprise and where profits are shared in accord with agreement.

(iii)   Scientific research and production association. This is an economic association organised by industrial enterprises and scientific research units. The latter are to take technical results as investment. This investment is then combined with industrial enterprise production ability and expertise and profit is shared in accord with the agreement that has been made between the parties.

(iv)   Production and marketing association. This refers to association that unifies production and marketing through joint investment by industrial enterprises, commerce and foreign trade units.

4.   PROCEDURE WHEN UNDERTAKING FIXED ASSET CONSTRUCTION

When undertaking a fixed asset construction project the following eight stages must be followed:

(1)   A Project Report must be Forwarded

This is a report based on 'suggested' construction and it must be put forward for consideration in light of national long-term planning, trade planning and regional planning. Use of natural resources, distribution of production and market demand are also investigated at this stage.

For large scale projects the power to examine and approve a fixed asset suggestion report rests with the State Planning Commission. For other projects and for large scale cultural, educational and public health undertakings using locally raised investment, it rests with provinces, municipalities under the central government and autonomous regions.

(2)   A Feasibility Study

This study will assess the project in terms of its technological level, its structural and economic feasibility and on the basis of its alignment with policy.

(3) Compilation of a Design Task Report

The design task report is the basic document that fixes construction. At this point the accuracy of the task report should be within 10% of estimated investment cost. In the case of large and medium-sized projects and particularly in the case of foreign-funded projects and those that intend to import technology, when the design task report is presented it must have a feasibility study attached. Even when investment projects are using the State's foreign exchange or are borrowing foreign funds from a State level administration, it is still necessary to offer a design report for approval.

Large and medium-scale capital construction projects with lateral associated investment that is based on self-raised funds and where the concerned enterprises can provide for their own energy, raw and semi-finished materials, equipment, marketing, and necessary transport requirements, can seek approval of their design report from the relevant local authority.

(4) Listing in the Yearly Plan

The approved initial design construction project must be listed in the yearly plan. The contents of the yearly plan for fixed asset construction include the investment plan for fixed asset construction, the large and medium-scale project plan for fixed asset construction and the plan for newly-increased output capacity and newly-increased fixed assets. Construction projects that will last for more than one year should be divided and listed in terms of their duration.

(5) Preparing for Construction

Construction can only begin once all preparation requirements have been satisfied. These requirements include the steps above and they must also include fixing the construction period, arranging building materials, supply of construction machinery and if relevant, the requisition of land, levelling of the ground and the dismantling and moving of existing buildings and machinery.

During the process of construction, reasonable organisation of the construction process must ensue and construction must be checked. It must accord with design standards. Before being accepted for use in production large-scale and medium production projects must be examined and accepted by the State Planning Commission or by relevant government departments. In the case of the involvement of foreign interests, and particularly when a project has involved the import of complete sets of equipment, attention must be paid to the question of whether contract stipulations have been met.

CHAPTER 14

Industrial Materials and Equipment

I. THE PRODUCTION OF SEMI-FINISHED MATERIALS

China's semi-finished materials sector consists of three industries: the metallurgical, chemical and building industries. These three industries all depend directly on natural resources.

The semi-finished materials industries are all high energy consuming industries. In 1987 the total output of these industries amounted to Rmb 337 billion. This was 28.5% of the country's total industrial output value, but this proportion of national industrial output was achieved at the cost of 53% of the country's total energy consumption.

The semi-finished material industries are also investment intensive industries. In 1987 the original cost of the fixed assets of two of the three sectors of the semi-finished materials industries—the metallurgical and chemical industries—was Rmb 156 billion. This was 20% of China's industrial fixed asset cost. The average original cost of fixed assets for every worker in the metallurgical and chemical industries was Rmb 22,300. This is a figure that is 71% higher than the national industrial average.

1. THE METALLURGICAL INDUSTRY

(1) Metal Ore Resources

There are 1,760 locations in China with proven iron ore deposits. These are scattered over more than 600 counties in 27 provinces, municipalities and autonomous regions. Total iron ore reserves amount to 472 billion metric tons with industrial reserves estimated at 24.6 billion metric tons. China has seven large iron ore mining areas: Anshan-Benxi, East Hebei-Miyun, Panzhihua-Xichang, Ningwu-Luohe, East Hubei, West Hubei and Baotou-Baiyunobo. Iron ore reserves in these seven areas account for 65% of national reserves. After many years of development these mining areas have become the major bases of supply. But there are also significant iron ore deposits in Handan-Xingtai, Xuanhua, Central Shandong, Xinyu, Hainan, Shaoguan, Wuyang, Hanzhong, Jiuquan and Hami. These deposits are, or will also become, major iron ore supply bases.

A substantial weakness in terms of China's iron ore resources is that the iron content in the ore is low. It has an average iron content of 32.1%. This low grade ore accounts for 97.8% of the country's iron ore reserves.

China has abundant resources of auxiliary ores for the iron and steel industry. Among these main ores are magnetite and clay. China's proven resources of magnetite come to 2.8 billion metric tons. They top the world list of this resource. These ores are high quality ores. They consist of 46.5% first grade ore and 30.2% second grade ore. The geographic distribution of this ore resource is highly concentrated. Liaoning Province has 84% of deposits and Shandong Province a further 10%.

Proven reserves of clay minerals total 1.8 billion metric tons, silica ore 930 million metric tons, fluorspar ore 19 million metric tons, dolomite ore 8.4 billion metric tons and limestone ore 10.3 billion metric tons. These are all auxiliary minerals used in the development of the iron and steel industry.

China also has proven bauxite deposits that total 1.3 billion metric tons. Industrial reserves of bauxite amount to 484 million metric tons, ranking them eighth in the world. China's bauxite ores have high alumina content, the average content reaching 55%. The result is that only 4.2-4.5 metric tons of bauxite needs to be consumed for the production of each metric ton of aluminium, but China's bauxite does have a high silicon content. This means that it requires a very high smelting temperature and so large quantities of energy are consumed in the aluminium production process.

Gold resources are widely distributed in China. Of the country's 2,000 counties, gold has been discovered in more than 800 counties. Most of the gold mines are small rich mines. China also has tin deposits and there are rich deposits of a wide variety of non-ferrous metals, including tungsten, nickel and mercury. Tin output has been increasing at an annual rate of 5%, 60% of the tin that is mined is exported.

(2) The Iron and Steel Industry

Tremendous changes have taken place in China's iron and steel industry. After forty years of construction fourteen large iron and steel enterprises have been built together with over eighty medium-sized and small backbone enterprises. An iron and steel industry has been developed that has a production capacity of 60 million metric tons of steel annually.

By 1987 China's output of iron ore had reached 159 million metric tons. This was an increase of 220 times that of 1949. By 1987 the output of crude steel had reached 56.3 million metric tons, an increase of 356 times that of 1949.

In pre-Communist China 90% of iron and steel production capacity was concentrated in Northeast China, but since the 1950s the Chinese government has made an effort to change this irrational distribution of iron and steel production. Iron and steel plants in Anshan, Shanghai, Tianjin, Beijing, Benxi and Tangshan were expanded and the Taiyuan Iron and Steel Plant and the Maanshan Iron and Steel Plant were built together with other large iron and steel complexes in Baotou, Wuhan and Panzhihua.

By the end of 1987 14 large enterprises had come into existence. Each had an annual output of more than one million metric tons of steel. There were also medium-sized and small steel plants operating in all parts of country. They too had become and important part of in China's iron and steel industry. In 1987 the latter's crude steel output accounted for more than 20% of national output.

China uses several smelting techniques. Some of these have attracted worldwide attention. For instance the titanic magnetite method used by the Panzhihua Iron and Steel Company has a high titanium content that is rarely seen and blowing coal dust into blast furnaces in place of high quality coking coal (which was in short supply) was an important iron smelting technique developed in the 1960s by the Shoudu Iron and Steel Company. It is a technique that has now been exported to other countries.

China imports large quantities of rolled steel and iron ore. Although the country's steel output is fourth in the world, the average per capita crude steel output amounts to only 52 kg. To satisfy domestic demand for rolled steel China must import large quantities each year. From 1981 to 1987 a total of 79.8 million metric tons of rolled steel was imported. This amounted to 25% of domestic demand. The cost was $US25.9 billion. This amount represented 11.9% of the total imports for the 1981-1987 period.

China also imports iron ore and chromium ore. In 1985, 10.06 million metric tons of iron ore were imported, in 1986, 13.7 million metric tons and in 1987, 10.9 million metric tons. In 1985, 365,000 metric tons of chromium ore were imported, in 1986 385,000 metric tons and in 1987, 230,000 metric tons.

(3) Measures for the Future Development of the Iron and Steel Industry

The shortage of rolled steel supply is a considerable obstacle to China's further economic development. The iron and steel industry is confronted with three problems: a growth rate that has not matched the needs of economic growth; a product mix that is unsuited to changes that have taken place in production structure; and a quality of product that has not met the needs of technological progress. In order to solve these problems the Chinese government has decided to make the iron and steel industry an economic development priority.

By the end of this century the output of crude steel is expected to exceed 95 million metric tons and the rate of finished iron and steel products is expected to exceed 86% of total output. Special stress is to be laid on the development of alloy steel and on low alloy steel series which reflect China's natural resources. These include vanadium and titanic steel, niobium steel and rare-earth steel. It is intended that rolled steel production will make up more that 60% of total rolled steel output and that the capacity for ore mining will reach 250 million metric tons.

The following measures are to be adopted in order to achieve the above targets:

- Implementation of the contracting managerial responsibility system. The Ministry of Metallurgical Industry will ensure that each enterprise is responsible for production input and output. Enterprise responsibility will include responsibility for energy consumption, the output quality of major iron and steel products and the payment of profits and taxes to the government.
- Expanding and tapping the resources of existing enterprises. Using both domestic capital construction investment and foreign funds, stress will be placed on the transformation and expansion of existing plants instead of building new iron an steel enterprises.

... Actively fostering and promoting the development of local iron and steel industries. The State will enforce preferential policies towards local medium-sized and small iron and steel enterprises. It will do this in the areas of capital, taxation, credit and foreign trade. It will also actively promote the association of these enterprises with other trades and professions and it will open up more channels for raising construction funds as a means of promoting local industrial development.

... Speeding up technical transformation and promoting advanced technology allowing for China's actual production conditions, the iron and steel enterprises will make use of equipment that is of differing technical levels. But it is also expected that by 1990 more than 40% of the steel products of the key enterprises will be produced in accord with international standards. In terms of the technology of iron and steel production, the present use of extensive technology (relatively labour intensive based technology) will be replaced by intensive (capital intensive) technology.

(4)   The Development of the Nonferrous Metals Industry

After the founding of New China the country's smelting and processing capacity for all types of nonferrous metals increased rapidly. A number of large nonferrous enterprises were built.

(i)   The Aluminium Industry. Beginning from scratch, China has built eight major aluminium plants using Shandong, Zhengzhou and Guizhou as bases. In addition there are more than thirty medium-sized and small aluminium factories scattered in different parts of the country. The aluminium processing industry developed gradually in response to the needs of the defence industry. At present nearly 100 kinds of aluminium alloys are being widely used and there are more than 8,000 varieties of processed aluminium products. By the end of 1987 there were more than 370 aluminium processing plants with a total capacity exceeding 750,000 metric tons.

(ii)   The Rare-Earth Metals Industry. The rare-earth metals industry has become an independent industry (an industry distinct from mining, ore dressing, metallurgy and processing.) In 1987 the output of rare-earth metal mineral products reached 273,000 metric tons and rare-earth metal metallurgical products reached 26,007 metric tons. The production capacity of rare earth reached 18,000 metric tons (calculated in terms of oxides) and the output reached 15,000 metric tons. In addition to meeting domestic demand, rare earth, tungsten, molybdenum, beryllium and lithium products have been sold on the international market. In 1987 6,480 metric tons of rare earth was exported.

(iii)   Gold, Silver and Other Precious Metals. The precious metals industry has developed into an industry based on processing precious metals and their alloys and for the recovery of scrap materials. The precious metals produced by the enterprises under the China National Nonferrous Metals Industry Corporation are mainly extracted from polymetal ores. There are about 100 gold-mines and about 140 silver-mines and 40 metallurgical enterprises capable of retrieving gold, silver and other precious metals.

There is a wide geographic distribution of China's gold resources. The gold that has been discovered in more than 800 counties is mostly in small rich mines that are suitable for mining by local enterprises. In order to develop gold production, 18 provinces and autonomous regions have established gold companies. The China National Gold Corporation has been established and charged with carrying out the tasks of planning, prospecting, designing, exploiting and managing domestic gold production. It is also in charge of technological and economic cooperation with foreign countries. The latter includes the import of advanced equipment and cooperation with foreign enterprises engaged in opening mines.

(iv) The China National Nonferrous Metals Industry Corporation. The Corporation is an economic entity that is directly under the leadership of the State Council. Its role is to integrate production with marketing. It has 179 affiliated large and medium-sized production enterprises and 1.01 million specialised personnel who are engaged in geological prospecting, mining, ore dressing, metallurgy, processing, surveying, designing, construction and equipment manufacture. Its production interests include nonferrous metals, rare and scattered metal products, metallurgical products, processed products and semi-conductor materials. In 1988 the output of copper, aluminium, lead, zinc, nickel, tin, antimony, mercury, magnesium, and titanium exceeded two million metric tons. Products were exported to thirty countries. The Corporation's scientific research has also been very effective.

The Corporation has the China National Nonferrous Metals Import and Export Corporation, the China Nonferrous Metals Industry Corporation for Foreign Engineering Projects and the China International Nonferrous Metals Leasing Corporation Ltd under its control and it has established ten companies and offices in Hong Kong and abroad. The Hong Kong and overseas companies have been instrumental in promoting international trade in nonferrous metals, contract projects with foreign countries and the leasing of businesses at home and abroad.

2. THE CHEMICAL INDUSTRY

(1) Chemical Industry Ore Resources

There are 25 kinds of chemical industry ores listed on the national ore reserves table. There are very rich deposits of all the major chemical industry ores such as phosphorus, sulphur, potassium, boron, alumite, mirabilite, natural alkali and limestone. Among proven reserves, phosphorus ore exceeds 11.8 billion metric tons, with an average grade of 17%, and pyrite ore reserves amount to 3.3 billion metric tons, with an average grade of 18%.

(2) Development of the Chemical Industry

By the end of 1987 approximately 17,980 chemical enterprises had been established, including 430 key large and medium-sized enterprises and chemical enterprises established below county level. In 1987 the gross output value of the chemical industry was Rmb 83.6 billion. This was an increase of fifty times that of 1952. There were more than 20,000 types of chemical products. Seventy per cent of these were geared to the needs of agriculture, light industry and the textile industry. With the exception of high efficiency fertilisers, some chemical fibre lines, new varieties of pesticide, high grade dyestuffs, soda ash, caustic soda and some chemical intermediate raw materials which need partial import, the chemical products industry is able to meet domestic demand.

Between 1953 and 1987 increased chemical fertiliser production capacity came to 14 million metric tons and the increased synthetic ammonia production capacity reached 15.2 million metric tons. In 1987 the country's chemical fertiliser output reached 16.7 million metric tons (calculated in terms of 100% effectiveness or 82 million metric tons calculated in terms of standard content). Of this, nitrogenous fertiliser was 13.4 million metric tons and phosphate fertiliser 3.3 million metric tons. There are over a dozen varieties of chemical fertilisers including urea, ammonia nitrate, ammonia hydrogencarbonate, sal-ammoniac, ammonia water, liquid ammonia, ammonium sulphate, superphosphate, fused calcium-magnesium phosphate, phosphate of ammonia, potassium chloride, potassium sulphate, trace element fertiliser and human fertiliser.

By 1979 the output of chemical pesticides reached 537,000 metric tons. In the 1980s efforts have been made to develop high efficiency and low residue pesticides such as organic phosphate and carbonate. This has been done in combination with ceasing the use of high residue pesticides such as '666' and 'DDT'. In future low efficiency highly poisonous insecticides will be eliminated and considerable effort will be vested in studying and developing biological pesticides.

(i) Soda Ash and Caustic Soda Production. Another important task of the chemical industry has been to provide light and textile industries with chemical raw materials. These have been mainly soda ash and caustic soda. In 1987 the output of soda ash was 2.4 million metric tons and that of caustic soda 2.7 million metric tons.

(ii) The Petrochemical Industry. By 1966 China was able to produce ethylene and corresponding chemical raw materials and synthetic materials. In 1972 five sets of petroleum chemical fibre equipment and 13 sets of synthetic ammonia equipment with oil and gas as raw materials were imported. These went into operation around 1976. Then in 1978, four sets of ethylene equipment, four sets of synthetic ammonia equipment and two sets of petroleum chemical fibre equipment were imported, but it was not until the 1979 introduction of economic reform that the petrochemical industry experienced rapid development. The 1987 output of ethylene was 937,200 metric tons, synthetic fibre 982,000 metric tons, synthetic rubber 218,700 metric tons and plastics 1.5 million metric tons.

(iii) The Chemical Mining Industry. In 1987 14,866 million metric tons of phosphorus ore, 10,549 million metric tons of pyrite ore and 636,000 metric tons of boron ore were produced. The output of other minerals for the chemical industry, such as limestone and taxoite, met domestic demand. Future development stress will focus on phosphorus, pyrite and sylvite mines. Priority in terms of financial and material resources will be given to these mines when they have large deposits, high grade ore and good mining conditions. Improvements in prospecting and mining will also be undertaken and attention will be paid to such issues as reduction in transport costs and in the sources of pollution.

(iv) The Import and Export of Chemical Products. The China National Chemical Industry Import and Export Corporation is in charge of the import and export of China's chemical industrial products. As domestically produced chemical fertilisers, synthetic fibre, plastics and synthetic rubber, cannot meet the demands of economic development, huge imports are required each year. These have consumed large amounts of foreign exchange. In 1987 10.9 million metric tons of chemical fertilisers were imported, 1.1 million metric tons of various types of ethylene, 85,885 metric tons of synthetic fibre, 46,645 metric tons of synthetic rubber, 853,000 metric tons of soda ash, and 305,000 metric tons of caustic soda. The total cost of these imports was $US5 billion.

The proportion of chemical raw materials that are exported is high, while the proportion of fine chemical products exported is low. In 1987 China exported 514,000 metric tons of aluminium ore, 20,155 metric tons of aluminium products, 23,117 metric tons of tungsten ore, 337 metric tons of tungsten, 29,573 metric tons of antimony, 95,338 metric tons of zinc and zinc alloy and 15,894 metric tons of tin and tin alloy. These products do not earn much foreign exchange, consequently the deficit in the import and export trade of China's chemical products has been large. The deficit has stood at above $US2 billion since 1980. (It reached Rmb 3.1 billion in 1985 and Rmb 2.8 billion in 1987.)

3. THE BUILDING MATERIALS INDUSTRY

The building materials industry has developed considerably since the founding of New China. By the end of 1987 there were 63,674 building materials enterprises; of these 5,800 were large and medium-sized State-owned industries. The 1987 total output value of the building materials industry was Rmb 63 billion.

China's building materials industry is under the control of the State Bureau of the Building Materials Industry. There are more than 500 types of products. These are divided into three categories. The first category includes all kinds of building materials except rolled steel and timber. The second category includes all non-metallic minerals. The third category includes all new-type inorganic non-metallic materials and their products made by processing the raw materials of the above-mentioned two categories of product.

The first category of products are purely building materials. Part of the second and third categories of materials are building materials and the remainder are important raw materials for the metallurgical, chemical, machine-building, electronics and aeronautics industries.

(1)   *The New Building Materials Industry*

China's new building materials industry was established in the early 1960s and developed in the 1970s. Today there are more than 8,000 factories producing new building materials. The materials are managed by the China New Building Materials Corporation. It is an affiliate of the State Bureau of the Building Materials Industry.

(2)   *The Cement Industry*

China now has 4,600 cement plants. Fifty-seven of these are large and medium-sized plants. A small number of these plants have a 1970s level of technology, but many of them have only a 1950s level. During the Sixth Five-Year Plan period, production lines were imported (these lines were late 1970s and early 1980s level technology) and were used to equip the Jidong, Ningguo, Huaihai and Liuzhou cement plants.

In 1987 China's cement output reached 186.2 million metric tons. This was a 282 times increase over the 1949 output. Cement produced by large and medium-sized plants accounted for 25% of total output. Small plant production accounted for 75%.

During the first half of the 1980s the cement output of small plants increased by an average of 10 million metric tons annually. This played an important role in easing scarcity of cement and it supported local construction efforts such as building water conservation projects. However small cement plants often face the problem of backward technology, poor equipment, unstable quality of product and high energy consumption and they are often responsible for serious pollution problems.

(3) Production of Non-Metallic Minerals

Of the around one hundred types of non-metallic minerals that are used extensively throughout the world, China has eighty. Up to the end of 1985 the reserves of major non-metallic minerals prospected in the country were gypsum, 10.6 billion metric tons, ranked first in the world; bentonite, 630 million metric tons, second in the world; talcum, 89.7 million metric tons, asbestos, 55.2 million metric tons, graphite 108.5 million metric tons, these three ranked third in the world; phosphorus ore, second in the world; and pyrite and boron ores, first in the world. The deposits of porcelain clay, barite, siliceous earth, seolite and pearlite are all important in terms of quantity and China also has significant marble and granite resources.

The Non-metallic Minerals Department of the State Bureau of the Building Materials Industry controls non-metallic minerals and their products. There are now 280 state-owned non-metallic mines and plants. Thirty mines and twenty plants are engaged in the production of diamond, mica, asbestos, graphite, gypsum, talcum and bentonite.

Currently, foreign exchange earned through the export of non-metallic minerals and their products accounts for more than half of total foreign exchange earned through the export of building materials. Gypsum, lubricating oil, kaolin, graphite, precious stones and marble and granite are all sold on the international market.

II. THE CIRCULATION OF MATERIALS AND EQUIPMENT

Under China's present system of economic management, the circulation of materials and equipment refers to all means of production exchange activities that take place between enterprises and between sectors of the economy. Management of materials and equipment centres on the planning and supervision of the distribution and circulation of materials and equipment in a manner that promotes overall balance.

1. REFORM OF THE CIRCULATION SYSTEM

Since 1979 reform of the system for materials circulation has aimed to vitalise enterprise management through improved circulation and promotion of the use of the market.

To date reform of the system of materials circulation has consisted of the following measures:

(1) Reduction in the variety and proportion of goods and materials subject to mandatory planning and the expansion of the decision-making power of localities and enterprises. The past practice of planned distribution of major materials and equipment hindered circulation and efficiency. It blocked competition between enterprises. Since the introduction of economic reform the number of categories of goods and equipment subject to State unified distribution has been reduced (from 256 in 1978 to 27 in 1987) and the proportion of materials and equipment subject to central planning has fallen. For example, the proportion of steel subject to direct State allocation was reduced from 85.6% in 1978 to 46.8% in 1987 and the proportion of timber from 95.4% to 26.2%. Conversely, the proportion of materials and equipment left to the discretion of localities and enterprises has increased significantly. For example in 1987 rolled steel left to the supply and sales discretion of iron and steel plants totalled 17 million metric tons. This figure accounted for 38.6% of total national sales and it represented an increase of 30.5% or 4 million metric tons over the 1986 figure.

(2) Reform of the price of means of production. Reform has been promoted as a means of overcoming the previous prolonged ossification of prices. The price of important materials and equipment has been adjusted with many categories of items being released from direct government price control. From 1984 the planned price of materials and equipment such as coal, timber, pig iron, scrap steel, cement, caustic soda, soda ash, sulphuric acid, industrial ammonium nitrate, and some types of rolled steel, non-ferrous metals and tyres was increased and at the same time enterprises were allowed (within the range of 20% higher than State planned price) to set the price of their unbudgeted materials and equipment. In 1985 the 20% price range ruling was lifted and was replaced by open prices for that portion of materials and equipment allowed to be sold at the discretion of the enterprise. What then happened was that in 1987 ceiling prices were set for unbudgeted goods and equipment and in 1988 unified prices and monopoly management were introduced for a few types of rolled steel and non-ferrous metals which were in short supply.

It was through this form of price reform that the so-called 'double-track' price system was introduced. This system used both State-set prices and market prices. The 'double-track' price system is now recognised as having promoted production and circulation of materials and equipment. This is because it has played a particularly positive role in increasing production of materials and equipment that are in short supply.

(3) The development of various markets for means of production. This innovation was necessary if the new economic mechanism was to succeed in promoting policy whereby 'the State regulates the market and the market guides the enterprise'. Rolled steel markets, auto markets, coal markets, timber markets, used materials and equipment markets, idle equipment markets and markets for other means of production, have been established throughout the country. As a result barriers between regions, between administrative departments and ownership restrictions have been removed. Enterprises now have the right to sell and buy freely in these markets. Using the rolled steel market as an example, by the end of 1987 there were 182 markets in 151 big and medium-sized cities. According to statistics taken from 100 rolled steel markets, more than 7.4 million metric tons of rolled steel was sold in 1987 and 20.5% of this total was marketed directly by iron and steel plants.

(4) Various forms of co-operation and alliances established between different regions, departments and enterprises for the purpose of the exchange of materials and equipment. The expansion of co-operation and alliances has led to a considerable expansion in trans-regional and trans-trade exchange. In 1987 the amount of material and equipment exchanged through co-operation and alliances was valued at Rmb 41.2 billion or 13.7 times as much as the 1980 figure of Rmb 3 billion. During the ten years from 1978 to 1987 coal exchanged through such arrangements amounted to 274 million metric tons, timber 25.9 million cubic metres, cement 26.9 million metric tons, pig iron 8.5 million metric tons and coke 14.3 million metric tons. There are now more than 8,200 organisations for the exchange of materials and equipment.

(5) Trading centres established to provide a network for the exchange of materials and equipment. These centres have effectively boosted purchase and marketing of farm materials and equipment. Trading centres that provide outlets for unplanned materials and equipment have mushroomed. By the end of 1987 there were 395 centres scattered in 221 cities above the level of prefecture. They had a total turnover of Rmb 26.8 billion. These trading centres have combined with material and equipment companies, bazaars, and materials and equipment supply stations and shops, to form a national materials and equipment exchange network with nearly 37,000 trading outlets. This network has led to a substantial annual increase in the amount of materials and equipment that has been channelled into the countryside. The network has effected a break with the previous situation where the circulation of materials and equipment was limited to exchange between urban industrial enterprises. It must be concluded that the networking of materials and equipment has played an important role in promoting the development of the rural commodity economy.

It is clear that China's system of circulation of materials and equipment has begun to move from the old pattern where the State practised unified distribution and allocation to a new pattern of free flowing commodities. However there is still work to be done. Some of the problems still to be addressed are: the large amount and great variety of materials and equipment that continues to be subject to mandatory planned distributed by government departments; the resistance to change exhibited by regional and departmental administrations; the continued existence of numerous materials and equipment management procedures which scatter materials and resources and clog circulation; the need to overcome problems such as monopolisation of important goods, racketeering and the deliberate mark-up of prices.

The development of the national economy and reform of the economic structure calls for quicker and deeper reform of the circulation system for materials and equipment.

(6) Further reform of the system of circulation of materials and equipment. Further reform must focus on: strengthening macro-economic balance in terms of important materials and equipment; gradually narrowing the scope of mandatory planning; expanding the scope of guidance planning and market regulation; actively promoting the production of goods and materials that are in short supply; establishing integrated markets for means of production by relying on big and medium-sized cities; and guaranteeing the State's key enterprises.

The content of these reforms will be as follows:

(i) A further reduction in the variety and proportion of materials and equipment subject to mandatory planned distribution. Only a few types of goods, those that are deemed to be vital to the national economy and to people's livelihood, will continue to be subject to mandatory planned distribution. All other kinds of materials and equipment are to be either purchased by the State on contract or sold by producers to users under administrative co-ordination, or they are to be sold via free market trading transactions.

(ii) All State Council departments (not including military industrial departments) will be required to relinquish management of materials and equipment and this function will then be incorporated into the new Ministry of Materials and Equipment. This Ministry will then be responsible for overall planning and management of the national circulation of materials and equipment. The Ministry is an administrative organisation, but all the supply and marketing establishments under its jurisdiction will be enterprises.

(iii) Developing and perfecting the market for means of production, establishing markets for materials and equipment and improving market infrastructure, while at the same time establishing marketing rules and regulations and proper market order. In addition, under the 'double-track' pricing system ways are to be found for narrowing the gap between planned prices and market prices. This will serve to dampen speculation and profiteering based on taking advantage of price differences.

(iv) Formulating policies for the production of materials and equipment that are in short supply. These will include the establishment of a development fund; granting the Ministry of Materials and Equipment power to handle exports and imports independently in order to effectively regulate domestic supply and demand; promoting economic use of materials and equipment and the development of substitutes; and monopolising the management of those materials and equipment that are in very short supply.

(v) Expanding the network for circulation of materials and equipment, actively organising trans-regional co-operation for the exchange of equipment and materials and promoting business activities such as a futures trading, exchange of spot goods and compensatory trade between enterprises.

(vi) Improving the management of materials and equipment producing enterprises and increasing their vitality by making them economic entities which are independent in terms of management and in terms of being responsible for their own profit and loss.

(vii) Strengthening the power of the Ministry of Materials and Equipment and holding it responsible not only for overall planning and distribution, but also for developing and improving the market for means of production and for promoting circulation.

As the commodity economy develops and economic reform continues to unfold, China will gradually put all the means of production on a market footing that will allow the law of value and market supply and demand relations to regulate the flow of the means of production. But under present conditions, China can only follow the principle of deregulating most materials and equipment and controlling a few others, particularly those that are in short supply. The basic principle that is being followed is one of exercising more and stricter control over those means of production that are in short supply while deregulating goods whose supply can be expected to meet demand.

2. BUYING AND SELLING

(1) Buying and Selling Goods Covered by State Plans

Today, marketing of goods covered by State plans is conducted using either (i) transactions between productive enterprises and consumer units or (ii) transactions between capital goods circulating enterprises and consumer units.

Transactions between productive enterprises and consumer units are carried out in the following manner.

- ... Nationwide placement of orders. This is done through conducting two national orders placement meetings per annum. At these meetings the goods supply departments link producer and consumer departments and contracts for orders are signed.

- ... Regional placement of orders. For regions that have an abundant resource supply for the production of capital goods, but who also consume large amounts of goods, the amount allocated to other areas is fixed. The remaining resources will be left to the region for its own supply. These regions do not need to take part in national orders placement meetings. Use of their own regional resources strengthens contact between productive enterprises within the region and it alleviates transport pressure.

- ... Fixed supply. For units that produce fixed models of products, maintain stable production and consume large amounts of materials, long-term agreements are signed with materials producing enterprises. These agreements fix the supply relationship and are conducive to forging a close relationship between producer and consumer enterprises. They reduce the need for intermediate links and so simplify order procedures.

Transactions between capital goods circulation enterprises and consumer units take place on the following basis:

- ... Supply based on coupons. Goods in short supply can be supplied through ration coupons. The users of these goods are not subject to time limits or to limits in terms of place, variety and specification. They can choose what they need at capital goods handling departments. This form of exchange provides convenience for users and serves to expedite the circulation of capital goods.

- ... Supply that is checked and fixed in accord with need. For goods needed for production and maintenance purposes and for goods required by key programmes and users, there is no need to file applications level by level to obtain distribution quotas. After checking actual need local goods supply departments can simply supply users with the goods.

- ... Contracted 'one package' supply. For goods and equipment needed for production and construction, the goods supply departments can sign agreements or contracts with users for 'one package' supply and then supply the capital goods needed in line with the progress of production and/or construction.

(2) Exchange Relations

Exchange relations is the term used to cover transactions where producers and consumers establish a buyer-seller relationship on their own initiative. These take on the following forms:

- ... productive enterprises selling directly to units
- ... productive enterprises deputising capital goods circulation departments to sell their products; and
- ... productive enterprise and capital goods circulation departments who co-operate in marketing.

The venues for capital goods transactions are goods trading centres and goods and materials companies, department stores, supply stations and shops. Trading centres in large cities and large capital goods companies usually engage in batch transactions and futures trading. They serve the requirements of large production enterprises who trade in large quantities. Small and medium-sized capital goods companies, department stores, supply stations and shops scattered throughout urban and rural areas concentrate on the retail and wholesale spot trade. They meet the requirements of small and medium-sized users and any odd requirements that large enterprises may have. They act as purchasing and marketing agents for users by placing orders and facilitating consignments for shipment on the user's behalf. They also establish joint marketing agencies with productive enterprises, sell on credit, lease and even pawn idle equipment.

(3) Forms of Supply

After the establishment of a buyer-seller relationship, two forms of supply are available. These are either direct supply, or supply through intermediate links.

(i) Direct Supply. This means that the production enterprise directly transports goods to units. No intermediate link is used. This method applies to raw materials and fuel used in large quantities as well as large pieces of equipment and special goods. The method is used as a device for shortening circulation time, reducing transport losses and costs and reducing loading costs.

(ii) Supply Through Intermediate Links. When this means is used productive enterprises transport their goods to capital goods circulation enterprises. The latter then supply the goods to the consumers of the goods. This method is suitable for users scattered over a large area who require goods in small quantities or goods in common use where quantity cannot be easily set. In this case goods and materials circulation enterprises can purchase goods in large quantities and then supply them to users in small amounts. This process solves the problem of concentrated mass production and dispersed and gradual consumption. It serves to reduce stocks held by retailers.

(4) Import and Export of Capital Goods

In 1988 the State Council granted the Ministry of Materials and Equipment the power to handle the import and export of capital goods. This was seen as a means of strengthening the ability of the newly established Ministry to maintain a balance between supply and demand and to exercise overall control over the national supply of imported goods. The Ministry of Materials and Equipment subsequently established the China Capital Goods Import and Export Corporation to serve as a foreign trade window for the country's capital goods supply departments.

The China Capital Goods Import and Export Corporation is under the dual leadership of the Ministry of Materials and Equipment and the Ministry of Foreign Economic Relations and Trade. As a registered legal entity it is protected by Chinese law and has the power to hold business talks and to sign trade agreements or contracts with foreign business interests. It does this in line with Chinese government priorities and with reference to international conventions.

The other important central Chinese government organisation that is engaged in the import and export of capital goods is the Ministry of Foreign Economic Relations and Trade and its related foreign trade companies that operate under the direction of central government departments in concert with provinces, autonomous regions and municipalities.

CHAPTER 15

Provision of Energy, Transport and Communication Services

I. PROVISION OF ENERGY

1. ENERGY PRODUCTION

Policies adopted during the 1980s decade of reform have afforded priority to promoting energy production. As a result, since 1980 coal output has increased considerably, the production of crude oil and natural gas has shown a stable growth rate and hydropower production has increased rapidly.

In 1987 China's non-renewable energy, when converted into standard coal at the rate of 7,000 kilocalories per kg, equalled 891.2 million metric tons. This was 258.6 million metric tons more than in 1981 or an average annual increase of 48 million metric tons. In 1987 there was the fastest growth in energy output at any time since the founding of the People's Republic.

During the last three decades China's energy production has changed considerably. In terms of the output of primary energy converted into standard fuels, the proportion based on coal has constantly declined. It has declined from 96.7% in 1952 to 92.6% in 1987. Correspondingly, the proportion of oil, natural gas and hydropower has risen each year. Between 1952 and 1987 the proportion of oil rose from 1.3% to 21%; natural gas from a tiny amount to 2%; and hydropower from 2% to 4.4%.

It is currently estimated that in future the proportion of coal in energy consumption will continue to fall and the proportion of oil, natural gas, hydropower and nuclear power will rise. But even with these measures it must be recognised that for a fairly long period to come, China's energy consumption will centre on coal. The combination of China's considerable coal deposits, economic conditions, level of distribution and technology, means that this situation will only change slowly.

2. ENERGY SUPPLY AND DEMAND

With the increase in China's coal output in recent years, the considerable unmet energy demand has been somewhat relieved. But there are problems of distribution. For example, coal produced in Shanxi, Shaanxi, west Inner Mongolia, Heilongjiang and Guizhou cannot be shipped out due to poor transport facilities. This situation exists in the context of coal shortages in many areas, a shortage of oil products and a corresponding shortage in electricity supply. It has been estimated that in 1987 China was short of 70 billion kW hrs of electricity and 15 million kW of installed capacity. Energy shortage is a major obstacle to efficient and increased enterprise production.

A factor that resulted in a rapid increase in power consumption was that many localities and enterprises spent large amounts of funds on developing processing ability that was outside the State plan.

In 1986 and 1987, in an effort to solve the problem of power shortage, investment in the power industry was greatly increased and preferential policies were adopted in order to attract further funds from local governments and enterprises for the development of the power industry. During 1986 and 1987 efforts to increase installed generating capacity resulted in respective increases of 6.8 million kW and 8.1 million kW. This was the fastest increase in installed generated capacity since the founding of New China.

In order to relieve the strain on the supply of oil products, current energy export policy will be adjusted. This adjustment will gradually reduce the export of oil while continuing to discourage domestic oil consumption.

In order to guarantee the forecast quadrupling of GNP by the end of this century, China will need to consume 1.4 billion metric tons of standard coal and 1,200 billion kW of electricity. Whether this supply of energy can be guaranteed depends on policy on energy production and on the import and export of energy.

By the year 2000 China will still be researching and experimenting with the use of energy substitutes. This means that current energy production will be concentrated on the use of coal, hydropower, oil and gas resources and nuclear power. It is estimated that by the turn of the century coal output will have reached 1.3-1.4 billion metric tons; crude oil output, 200 million metric tons; natural gas output, 25 billion cubic metres; hydropower and nuclear power, 300 billion kW hrs - with each kW hr being equivalent to 340 g of standard coal, hydro and nuclear power output would equal 1.4 billion metric tons of standard coal.

This analysis of energy production suggests that China is in a position to produce enough energy to satisfy demand. But if this energy output is to be achieved, solutions must be found to current problems being experienced in relation to the prospecting for oil and gas resources, the transport of coal, and funding for the construction required for increased hydropower production. And there will be a need to find solutions to the problem of rational utilisation of resources and the problem of accessing the funds and technical expertise and equipment required for effective exploitation of resources.

3. SOLUTIONS TO ENERGY PROBLEMS

The per capita energy consumption of the Chinese people remains relatively low, but with economic growth and the improvement in people's living standard, the amount of energy needed is rapidly increasing. This of course means that there is a pressing need to increase energy production, but attention must also again be drawn to the point that due to low managerial and technological expertise, China's efficiency in energy utilisation is low. Energy consumption per unit of gross national product is not only higher than industrially developed countries such as Japan and the United States, it is also higher than developing countries such as India and Pakistan. This means that there is considerable potential for energy conservation. In 1980 China worked out a general policy for 'laying equal stress on energy exploitation and conservation'. This policy is to continue to be implemented as a means of solving current energy problems.

4. THE COAL INDUSTRY

China is rich in coal resources. Reserves are estimated at 500,000 billion metric tons. By the end of 1986, 859.7 billion metric tons of coal reserves had been verified and recoverable deposits had reached 845.9 billion metric tons.

China's coal reserves are widely scattered. Of China's thirty provinces and municipalities, Shanghai is the only one with no coal resources at all. Of the 2,300 counties in China, 1,400 have coal resources, with Shanxi, Inner Mongolia and Shaanxi having more than 10,000 billion metric tons of recoverable coal deposits. Coal from the Ikh Chao League mines in Inner Mongolia and from the Shenfu-Dongsheng Oilfield in Shaanxi Province contains less coal and sulphur ash and so is the type of coal that is most suitable for use by power plants.

Apart from the three provinces with especially large deposits that are noted immediately above, nine other provinces and autonomous regions have large recoverable coal deposits. Each of these reserves exceeds 1,000 billion metric tons.

The distribution of China's coal resources has promoted State development of large coal mines that ensure the production required by major areas and enterprises, but it has also been advantageous for various localities and townships to develop small and medium-sized coal mines in order to meet their own coal needs.

China's coal resources are concentrated in the West and North of China where inland river transport is not adequate. This has meant that the transport of coal has put enormous pressure on China's railways and harbours. It is clear that *China cannot solve its energy problem without solving its transport problems.*

(1) Development of the Coal Industry

China has a long history of coal mining. Even so, due to backward mining technology, in 1949 coal output was only 34.2 million metric tons. This meant that firewood served as the major energy source for both production and people's daily life (both urban and rural).

By the end of 1987 the State had made an aggregate investment of Rmb 82 billion in coal mining. This added an annual capacity of 607 million metric tons of coal and dressing and 177 million metric tons of coking coal. At the end of 1987 there were 10,553 State run coal enterprises (including 93 collieries under central planning). Their annual output totalled Rmb 25.7 billion.

China's most important coal production areas are:

... The Datong Mining Area. This area is located in the northern part of Shanxi Province. It includes fifteen pairs of coal pits, employs 119,000 workers and has a raw coal output of 29.2 million metric tons.

- ... Yanquan Mining Area. This area is situated in the eastern part of Shanxi Province. It has eleven pairs of coal pits, 77,000 workers and staff and a raw coal output of 14.3 million metric tons.
- ... Xishan Mining Area. This area is located in central Shanxi Province. It has eight pairs of coal pits, 75,000 workers and staff and a raw coal output of 12.6 million metric tons.
- ... Kailuan Mining Area. It is located in the eastern part of Hebei Province. It has ten pairs of coal pits, 135,000 workers and staff and a raw coal output of 18.5 million metric tons.
- ... Fuxin Mine. This mine is situated in west Liaoning Province. It has 17 pairs of coal pits, 88,000 employees and an annual output of 11.2 million metric tons of raw coal.
- ... Jixi Mine. It is situated in east Heilongjiang Province. It has 22 pairs of coal pits, employs 103,000 people and has an annual output of 13.5 million metric tons.
- ... Hegang Mine. This mine is located in north Heilongjiang Province. It has 13 pairs of coal pits and employs 103,000 people. It has an annual output of 14.5 million metric tons of raw coal.
- ... Xushou Mine. It is situated in north Jiangsu Province. It has 16 pairs of coal pits and employs 95,000 people. It has an annual output is 12.5 million metric tons of raw coal.
- ... Huaibei Mine. It is located in north Anhui Province. It has 12 pairs of coal pits, 127,000 employees and an annual output of 14.4 million metric tons of raw coal.
- ... Pingdingshan Mine. It is located in west Henan Province. It has 14 pairs of coal pits and employs 107,000 people. It has an annual output of 16.7 million metric tons of raw coal.

During the first half of the 1980s foreign funds were also used for the construction of coal mines. Mines developed through the use of foreign funds included the Huolinhe, Yiminhe and Yuanbaoshan open-cut mines in eastern Inner Mongolia. By the mid 1980s the largest Sino-foreign co-operative project in China was the Antaibao open-cut mine that went into production in September 1987. This mine involved a total investment of US$650 million. It has an annual output of 15.3 million metric tons of raw coal. It is one of the largest open-cut mines in the world.

(2) The Development of Local Coal Mines

Since 1979 China has introduced the principle of 'simultaneously developing large, medium-sized and small coal mines managed by the State, collectives and individuals'. At the same time it has also adopted a series of policies to encourage localities to develop coal mines. These measures include: allocating special funds from the State treasury's reserve for the development of local coal mines; raising the allocation prices of coal produced by local mines; encouraging township and village collectives to open coal pits; encouraging enterprises of different ownership systems and different trades to jointly run trans-regional coal mines; encouraging the masses to raise funds and open mines; and allowing individuals to invest in open coal pits.

In early 1986, aside from the 94 State-controlled mines with a total of 601 coal pits and a combined annual production capacity of 390.5 million metric tons, there were 1,684 local State-run coal mines with a total annual capacity of 176.9 million metric tons and more than 65,000 mines run by townships and individuals. Small coal mines now dot the country.

In 1987 local State-run coal mines produced 183.2 million metric tons of coal; township mines, 296.3 million metric tons; and individual coal mines, 28.4 million metric tons. They produced a total of 507.9 million metric tons, accounting for 54.7% of the country's total raw coal output for the year.

(3) Targets, Policies and Measures to be Adopted Before 2000

With an estimated need of 1.3 to 1.4 billion metric tons of raw coal before the end of this century, an annual increase in coal production of 30 to 40 million metric tons is called for. In order to fulfil this task the following policies and measures will be adopted:

- ... Increased investment in the coal industry. A policy of simultaneously developing large, medium-sized and small coal mines will be followed. In terms of construction, priority will continue to be afforded to the energy bases located in Shanxi, Shaanxi, west Inner Mongolia, Henan and Ningxia, as well as the coal mines in coal deficient areas in east and northeast China. Coal pits with particularly favourable conditions will be rebuilt or expanded.

- ... Operating State controlled mines under input and output contract arrangements. This is a policy that will encourage an increase in coal output while using less inputs.

- ... Supporting township coal mines. This policy will be based on an active and steady approach to the development of township coal mines. In line with this policy the State will continue to aid the development of township coal mines by providing materials and funds.

- ... Speeding up development of coal dressing and processing procedures. Quite rapid progress has been made in recent years in the area of dressing and processing coal. Liquefied coal and technology relative to coal burning have been developed and preliminary results have been achieved in experiments in the underground gasification of coal.

5. THE PETROLEUM AND NATURAL GAS INDUSTRY

(1) Oil and Natural Gas Resources and Distribution

China has an enormous oil-bearing area. According to an August 1986 appraisal of China's oil and gas resources, total oil reserves on land and on China's coastal continental shelves amounted to 78.8 billion metric tons while the natural gas reserves totalled 33,300 billion cubic metres.

Owing to past practices of 'attaching importance to oil while neglecting gas' and 'attaching importance to production while neglecting prospecting', the rate of verified reserves of both oil and natural gas is not high. But it is clear that the country's oil and gas exploitation potential is immense. There are verified oil and natural gas reserves in the Songliao Basin, in the Bohai Bay region and in Henan and Hubei Provinces and Sichuan Province is thought to have large natural gas reserves. As well, in recent years progress has been made in the prospecting and exploitation of off-shore oil and gas resources. These have included the Liyuhua 11-1 Oilfield at the estuary of the Zhujiang (Pearl River), the Wei 6-1 Oilfield in the Bac Bo Gulf, and the Suizhong 36-1 Oilfield in the Liaodong Bay. All of these reserves exceed 100 million metric tons.

China's oil resources are concentrated in northeast China and in the northern coastal areas. These are the areas that already have industrial development and transport and communication infrastructure and so a situation is created where conditions are particularly favourable for the development of both the petrochemical industry and the petroleum export industry.

Oil resources in northwest China are concentrated in the Xinjiang Uygur Autonomous Region. These provide a good basis for the development of this boundary area, while the development of the oil and gas fields in the South China Sea assists in addressing the shortage of energy resources in south China.

(2) Development of the Oil and Gas Industry

After liberation priority was given to development of the oil industry and a large number of army personnel were seconded to geological prospecting for oil. By 1959 the first high-yielding oil well was being drilled in Daqing, northeast China. In early 1960, in spite of difficulties with the economy, the State continued to commit manpower, materials and funds to prospecting and to the construction of the Daqing oilfield. As a result the construction of the large, rich Daqing oilfield was completed in just over three years.

By 1963 China's crude oil output had reached 6.5 million metric tons and basic self-sufficiency had been achieved. And then, one by one in the provinces and cities along the Bohai Bay, the Shengli, Daqing, Huabei, Liaohe and Zhongyuan oilfields were discovered. In 1978 oil production topped 100 million metric tons. Since 1980 particular importance has been attached to geological prospecting for oil and natural gas. Also during this period, the oil industry's management system was reformed. As a result of these two measures the country's oil output has grown steadily. In 1987 crude oil output reached 134 million metric tons and natural gas output 13.9 billion cubic metres.

(3) China's Main Oilfields

After thirty years of developing its oil industry, China now has the following large and medium-sized oilfields. These are oilfields with an output in excess of five million metric tons. They are:

- ... Daqing Oilfield. Situated in north Heilongjiang Province, this oilfield is the largest in China and it is also the largest base for export of crude oil. By 1987 its output had reached 55.6 million metric tons. It has 100,000 employees.
- ... Shengli Oilfield. Situated in north Shandong Province, this field is an important crude oil supply centre. Its crude oil output is 31.6 million metric tons and it has a workforce of 80,000.
- ... Liaohe Oilfield. This field is located in south Liaoning Province. It is the second largest oilfield in northeast China and is an important crude oil supply centre. Its crude oil output is 11.4 million metric tons and it employs 50,000 people.

... Huabei Oilfield. Located in east Hebei Province, it is a major crude oil supplier for Beijing and Tianjin. Its crude oil output was 8 metric tons in 1987, with 32,000 people employed.
... Zhongyuan Oilfield. This field is situated in east Henan Province. Its crude oil output totals 6.8 million metric tons. It has a workforce of 65,000.
... Xinjiang Oilfield. This oilfield consists mainly of the Karamay Oilfield in northern Xinjiang. It has a workforce of 50,000 people and produces 5.8 million metric tons of crude oil. Its output is used in northwest China.

6. THE POWER INDUSTRY

(1) Resources for the Development of the Power Industry

China is well endowed with resources which could be used for developing the power industry. Among these resources the reserves of coal and water are the most impressive, although China also has considerable nuclear resources for power generation. As an account of coal, oil and gas reserves has been given above, at this point it is only necessary to offer a very brief outline of China's water resources in relation to the power industry.

By 1987 only 5.3% of China's water resources had been exploited for use by the power industry. In theory China's hydropower water resource is estimated to be 5,800 billion kW hrs per year. This is a figure that includes an exploitable hydropower generating capacity of 1,900 billion kW hrs—71% concentrated in southwest China, 14% in central south China, 9.6% in northwest China, and 5.4% in north, east and northeast China.

Current use of power resources varies from region to region. This is due both to different levels of natural endowment and to different levels of economic development. The spread of China's power generating resources is as follows: southwest China is rich in water and coal resources and in overall terms is the richest area; north China has abundant coal reserves; northwest China is rich in hydropower resources, but is very poor in coal reserves; and east and northeast China are poor in coal and hydropower resources, but they are relatively very economically developed. It is this distribution of power generating resources that has promoted the decision that southwest, central south and northwest China should develop mainly hydropower, while north China concentrates on developing mainly thermal power. While developing coal-fuelled electricity, northeast and east China should develop nuclear power and should assist in meeting demand for power by transmitting power to other regions.

(2) Developing the Power Industry

The current adoption of large generating sets marks the adoption of a new level of technology in China's power industry. At liberation the generating capacity of China's largest thermal power generator was only 25,000 kW but since 1978 new generators have been introduced that have a power generating capacity ranging from 100,000 kW to 300,000 kW with a 600,000 kW generating set being installed at the Pingyu power plant in Anhui Province.

In the early years of New China the generating capacity of China's largest hydropower generator was 75,000 kW. This is a considerable contrast with the No 1 generating set at Longyangxia Hydropower Station which went into operation in October 1987. The Longyangxia generator has a capacity of 320,000 kW.

In the early years after liberation, in order to cope with long distance power transmission that has accompanied the adoption of large power generators and the construction of large power stations, 110,000 V, 220,000 V, 330,000 V and 500,000 V power transmission lines were built. Now the 10 million kW power grids in central, north, east and northeast China have formed a large power network of 500,000 V lines. This network is then to be further developed by the 1,080 km, 500,000 V DC power transmission lines being built from the Gezhouba Power Station in Hubei Province to Shanghai via Anhui, Zhejiang and Jiangsu Provinces.

Since 1978 efforts have been made to build power stations near large coal mines.

Aside from the construction of coal-fired and hydropower stations, nuclear power stations are being built at Dayawan in Guangdong Province and Qinshan in Zhejiang Province. The Qinshan nuclear power station has an installed capacity of 300,000 kW and it is intended that two 600,000 kW generating sets will be installed in the second stage of its development. The Dayawan Nuclear Power Station is being co-built with the Zhonghua Power Co of Hong Kong. It is to have an installed capacity of 1.8 million kW. Construction has begun.

Although the power industry has been developing very fast, it still cannot meet the ever-expanding demands made on it. In spite of a considerable increase in power generating capacity, there has been no fundamental change in terms of the power shortage in relation to demand. It is estimated that by the end of this century, China's power output will reach 1,200 billion kW hrs. In order to meet this demand a substantial increase in installed capacity will have to be added to China's power system. It is estimated that between 10 and 15 million kW of installed capacity will be needed each year in the decade 1990 to 2000. This situation has led to the need to adopt the following policies and measures.

... Preferential policies will continue to be implemented in order to encourage development of the power industry. Funds from various quarters will be pooled and localities and enterprises will be encouraged to spend non-budgetary capital on developing the power industry. And at the same time, electric power development funds will be collected from power consumers.

... Expansion of existing coal-power bases will continue together with the construction of new coal-power bases in coal producing areas and with reference to available water resources. Also large thermal power stations will be built in coal transporting centres and ports.

... Construction of hydropower stations is to be accelerated.

... Support for the development of small hydropower stations will continue. This support is necessary if growing demand for electricity in rural areas is to be met. And the construction of small thermal power stations in coal-producing areas that lie beyond the reach of large power grids is to be encouraged. This is to be done as a means of easing power shortages in remote areas.

In addition to State provision of electricity, localities are to operate their own power plants. In the future additional electricity consumed by newly built enterprises that have production subject to State allocation are to be supplied by power stations built by the State, but additional electricity required by other enterprises, municipal works and by agricultural production will have to be supplied by power stations built by localities. The division of work will be that construction of regional extra-large thermal power stations, large hydropower stations and nuclear power stations and trans-provincial key power grids will be organised by the State. Although these can also be built with funds raised by localities and departments. The profits and electricity generated would then be shared by the partners in line with their investment. Thermal power plants, hydropower stations and corresponding power transmission projects serving localities will be built by localities.

7. DEVELOPMENT OF OTHER ENERGY RESOURCES

China is very rich in solar energy, geothermal energy, wind energy, tidal energy, biological energy and excrement for the production of marsh gas. Many of these energy sources are renewable. However they are still being used only on a trial basis and on a small scale.

(1) Geothermal Energy

After years of prospecting some 3,300 areas of geothermal reserves have been discovered. Areas with high temperature geothermal resources are located in southern Tibet and in western Yunnan Province. Areas with medium and low temperature geothermal resources are located in southeast coastal areas, Shandong and the Liaodong Peninsula and geothermal water has been discovered in the North China Basin.

Recently use of geothermal energy has been expanding at a fast rate. For example 1.4 million metric tons of geothermal water was used per hour in 1985—a figure 8.4 times that of 1981. The Yangbajing Geothermal Power Station located 90 kilometres from Lhasa, is the largest of its kind in China. The No 1 station, with an installed capacity of 13,180 kW, has been operating and construction of the No 2 station, with an installed capacity of 12,000 kW, began in 1981. Two generating sets with a combined generating capacity of 6,000 kW went into operation in 1988. Upon completion, the No 1 and No 2 Yanbajing geothermal power stations will have a total installed capacity of 25,180 kW. They will obviously help to ease the power shortage being experienced in Lhasa.

(2) Solar Energy

With its vast territory China is in a position to use solar energy. Availability of solar energy gradually declines from the north to the south, concentrating mainly in the north and northwest and in Tibet. In these regions annual sunshine hours total 2,800-3,300. In north and northwest China, solar energy stoves and houses with solar energy equipment are already being popularised. Solar energy stoves developed in China are efficient and easy to operate. More than 5,000 solar energy stoves are being used in Qinhai Province, producing energy that is equivalent to 600-700 kg of stalks and each of the several thousand solar energy stoves being used in the Ningxia Hui Autonomous Region can save 1 metric ton of coal or 2.1

metric tons of firewood each year. It has also been estimated that each of the 1,000 solar energy stoves being used in the Tibet Autonomous Region save 1.9 metric tons of cowdung per year.

With the recent development of the urban and rural building industries houses using solar energy have developed quickly. According to incomplete statistics, in the first half of 1986, 300 solar energy using houses were built. Also, solar energy water heaters are now being popularised. Solar batteries that have been developed in China are being used not only for satellites but also for navigation markers, lighting and for rails in livestock sheds. China's largest silicon solar energy power station is a 5,000 watt station used by a stud sheep farm in Xinjiang.

(3) Marsh Gas

China is rich in crop stalks and human excrement. After fermentation these can be turned into marsh gas. Generated marsh gas contains 60-65% methane. Each cubic metre of gas generates 5,500-6,600 kilocalories of heat and this is gas energy that can be used by farmers for cooking and lighting lamps. In 1987 there were 3.5 million standard marsh gas pits in rural areas serving some 20 million farmers. These not only help to ease the energy shortage that exists in rural areas, but they also produced a large amount of quality fertiliser.

Recent years have seen a steady development of marsh gas as an energy source for use in China's cities. Some food processing factories, wineries and slaughter houses have used their waste material, waste water and human excrement to create marsh gas. According to statistics by the end of 1986 there were more than 1,000 large and medium-sized marsh gas pits in cities. Marsh gas that has been produced has been supplied to small marsh gas stations, small power stations and small power plants. To date 422 marsh gas power stations with a combined power capacity of 4,328 kW, and 822 marsh gas power plants with a combined installed capacity of 7,836 kW, have been established. These benefit more than 17,000 households and have helped to improve both energy supply and sanitation in rural and urban areas. They have also assisted in the disposal of garbage and waste in large and medium-sized cities.

(4) Wind Energy

Located in southeastern Asia, China experiences monsoons and hence has rich wind energy resources. Preliminary calculations estimate that the near-earth wind energy reserves reach 16 million kW. It has been estimated that in the southeast coastal areas the wind energy density reaches 200-300 watts per square metre. In this area usable wind is available for around 70% of the year.

In China research began on the construction of wind power stations in the 1960s and by the early 1980s some wind power stations had been put into operation. By the end of 1987 China's installed wind energy capacity had reached 4,500 kW.

(5) Tidal Energy

According to the second national survey conducted between 1978 and 1983, the theoretical reserves of China's tidal energy are 110 million kW. Current installed capacity amounts to 21.6 million kW.

Of China's total usable tidal energy resources, 88.6% is located in Zhejiang and Fujian Provinces. Use of tidal energy resources began in 1955 and by 1980 a number of experimental tidal power stations had been built including the Xiaoshashan Power Station (with an installed capacity of 200 kW), the Haishan Power Station (1,150 kW) and the Xiangshan Power Station (100 kW) in Zhejiang Province and the Rushan Power Station (with a designed installed capacity of 960 kW and 640 kW of generators in operation) in Shandong Province.

The Jiangxia Power Station in Zhejiang Province was completed in 1985. It has an installed capacity of 3,100 kW and is able to generate 10.7 million kW hrs of electricity per year. In terms of its installed capacity, it is next only to the Rance Tidal Power Station in France and the Annapolis Tidal Power Station in Canada.

II. TRANSPORT

1. THE DEVELOPMENT OF TRANSPORT SERVICES IN THE 1980s

By the end of 1987 the total length of China's transport network had reached 1,547,500 kilometres. This was an 8.3 increase over the figure for 1979. Total length of railways increased by 140%; highways experienced a 12.2 fold increase; inland waterways increased by 49.2%; and civil air routes experienced a 34.1 fold increase. In addition ocean shipping and pipeline transport, that had had to be developed from scratch, continued to develop well and the technological level of all transport facilities improved markedly.

Much of China's domestic transport is land transport, usually railway transport. Highways are used predominantly for short-distance transport of goods, including the transport of goods that have been off-loaded at railway stations.

Of total freight carried, waterways accounted for only 9.6%, but the present rapid development of ocean shipping and the need for long-distance transport of import and export goods has pushed the proportion of water transport higher.

Volume of transport has increased substantially, particularly since the 1979 introduction of economic reform policy.

15:1 GROWTH OF PASSENGER AND FREIGHT TRANSPORT

	Passenger volume (million people)	Freight volume (million metric tons/km)
1949	137.0	160.7
1952	245.2	315.2
1957	638.2	803.7
1965	963.3	1210.8
1978	2539.9	2489.5
1980	3417.9	5465.4
1985	6202.1	7457.6
1987	8610.3	9530.8

Figures listed in this table include railways run by localities and passenger volume and passenger transport recorded by non-transport departments are included in the post 1985 figures. Freight volume and turnover of freight transport originating from non-transport departments is included in the post 1980 figures.

For a long period after the 1956 completion of socialist transformation, State transport enterprises were responsible for the bulk of China's transport services, but since the beginning of the 1980s the principle of encouraging the State, collective and individuals to operate transport services has been implemented. It is this policy that has given rise to many different types of transport enterprises existing side by side and competing with each other.

(1)   State Transport Enterprises

Railways, civil aviation, pipeline transport departments, ocean shipping companies and navigation bureaus and special bus transport companies are State transport enterprises that are owned by the whole people. They are the main component of China's transport services. They possess the bulk of fixed assets and they are responsible for both passenger and freight transport. State investment has provided the capital for this section of the transport industry.

(2)   Collectively Owned Transport Enterprises

Collectively owned transport enterprises are usually engaged in water and highway transport. They have been established in accord with the principle of 'voluntary participation and mutual benefit'. They are under the guidance of the government.

(3)   Private and Individually Owned Transport Enterprises

Since 1979 the individually owned transport businesses that had virtually disappeared since 1956, have again been developed. By the end of 1987 the number of trucks owned by specialised transport households or groups of households had reached 420,000 and the total registered deadweight tonnage (dwt) of individually owned ships and junks had reached 3.41 million. The overwhelming majority of truck owners are farmers. They are making an invaluable contribution to transport services, particularly short-distance services. They have become an important supplementary force within the Chinese transport industry.

Privately owned transport enterprises have also been restored and developed under post 1979 economic reform policy. A case in point is the Changjiang (Yantze) Minsheng Company. It resumed business in 1984. At that time it had only two tugboats and four barges with a total capacity of 3,000 metric tons. By 1987 it had acquired more than 50 boats capable of handling river and sea transport. They have a total capacity of over 50,000 metric tons. The business scope of the enterprise has expanded from the Changjiang (the Yantze River) to the Zhujiang (Pearl River), from inland water transport to ocean shipping and from China to other countries. The company has now become China's first private shipping enterprise capable of managing inland, offshore and ocean shipping.

2.   RAILWAY TRANSPORT

(1)   Railway Construction

In the early post-liberation days China had only 22,000 kilometres of railways. These were mainly in northeast China and in the coastal areas. Over the past four decades, in line with the focus on national economic development and with the focus on promoting development of southwest and northwest China, together with the construction of key industrial and mining centres, attention has been paid to building railways in the interior and particularly to building railways to access major coal producing centres.

Today around 30% of China's railways are situated in Heilongjiang, Liaoning and Jilin Provinces and in the eastern sector of Inner Mongolia. The remaining 70% are in areas south of the Shanhaiguan Pass. These consist of three major north-south trunk lines. The first is the Beijing-Shanghai Railway, together with its branch lines. The second is the Beijing-Guangzhou Railway and the third runs from Datong in Shanxi Province to Zhanjiang in Guangdong Province. There are also three east-west thoroughfares. The first runs from Lianyungang in Jiangsu Province to Urumqi in the Xinjiang Uygur Autonomous Region and consists of the Lanzhou-Lianyungang Railway and the Lanzhou-Urumqi Railway. The second runs from Shanghai to Kunming, comprising the Shanghai-Hangzhou Railway, the Hangzhou-Nanchang Railway, the Xiangtan-Guiyang Railway and the Guiyang-Kunming Railway. The third stretches from Qinhuangdao to Lanzhou via the Beijing-Qinhuangdao Railway, the Beijing-Baotou Railway and the Baotou-Lanzhou Railway.

The railway south of the Shanhaiguan Pass has been formed around the three north-south thoroughfares and the three east-west trunk lines. These routes have been supplemented by other lines. While new railways have been constructed, efforts have also been made to upgrade existing lines. Some overburdened railways or sections have been, or are being, double-tracked and/or electrified.

(2)   Railway Management

The Ministry of Railways is now in charge of all railways. It directly manages State-owned railways and it gives technical and business guidance to local and special railways.

The management system used for the railways is now characterised by unified leadership and separate administration. In line with this principle railway administration has been divided into three levels. The Ministry of Railways is the highest management level. It exercises centralised leadership over State railways. Immediately below the Ministry of Railways there are the railway bureaus. They are responsible for railway operation and relevant capital construction and capital goods supplies within their regions. Below the railway bureaus there are railway branch bureaus. These branch bureaus are under the sub-regional transport organisations.

By the end of 1987 the railway bureaus had adopted the contract responsibility system. This meant that they contracted out some of the volume of railway freight and capital construction that they were responsible for. The term of the contracts used for this purpose was three years.

(3)   International Cooperation

During the 1950s China became a member of the Agreement on International Railway Through-Freight Transport signed by Albania, Hungary, the German Democratic Republic, Poland, Rumania, the Soviet Union and Czechoslovakia. From this time on China has participated in international rail cooperation through transport networks formed by these countries.

Since 1980 China has been developing a 'land-bridge' transport link that will handle international container traffic. Under this system freight can be carried to either Western or Northern European countries such as Germany, Switzerland, France, Austria, Italy, Finland and Sweden.

By the end of 1987 China had signed five loan agreements. These agreements totalled $US1.9 billion. Three of the agreements were with the World Bank for loans totalling $US685 million and two were signed with the Japanese Overseas Economic Co-operation Fund. They involved a total sum of 289 billion Japanese yen. All five loan agreements have provided funding for the development of China's rail systems.

3. HIGHWAY TRANSPORT

(1) Highway Construction

Highways now reach almost all counties, 90% of towns and 70% of villages. Over 80% of these highways are surfaced.

For administrative purposes China's highways have been categorised as State highways, provincial highways, county highways, town highways and special highways. State-run highways are national trunk highways that fan out from Beijing to form a network of highways that link all provincial and autonomous region capitals and municipalities directly under central government as well as big and medium-sized cities with populations of over 500,000. Then there are trunk highways that service major ports, major railway hubs and major industrial and agricultural base areas. After these highways there are highways that link various strategically important military areas and then there are intra-provincial highways and other trunk lines. Currently 70 highways are designated as State trunk lines with 12 that fan out from Beijing, 28 running from north to south and 30 east-west links. It is intended that by the end of this century all 70 highways will reach second-class highway standard.

(2) Highway Passenger and Freight Transport

Since 1980 there has been a rapid development of special households engaged in highway transport. This development has broken the single system of State ownership of the means of highway transport. By the end of 1987 the number of motor vehicles owned by specialised transport households had reached 420,000 and these were in addition to 4 million tractors owned by these households. Being small scale, widely dispersed and flexible, the specialised transport households have become an important part of China's passenger and freight transport system.

Aside from the significant contribution made by special transport households, particularly in rural areas, nearly all counties have established bus transport companies that provide transport services to more than 90% of villages and towns.

(3) Administration of Highway Transport

983 all highways were under the management of the Ministry of Communications, but since 1983 significant reform of transport management and administration has been undertaken. Since 1983 government transport administration

departments at all different levels have begun to separate their function from that of the management of transport enterprises. The focal point of transport administration has been moved from directly managing subordinate transport enterprises to overall management of the transport system. By the end of 1987 the majority of highway transport enterprises under the transport departments or bureaus of provinces or autonomous regions had had their management delegated to key cities and/or they had signed contracts with administrative higher authorities, the latter ensuring the relative autonomy of their management.

(4)   *Overseas Economic and Technological Co-operation in Highway Construction*

Since 1980 World Bank loans have been used to build Chinese highways and China has signed agreements with companies from other countries for joint construction of expressways.

Apart from domestic road building, China has also made efforts to participate in building highways abroad. For example the China Road and Bridge Engineering Company has signed highway-construction contracts with countries in Asia, the Middle East and the Pacific and in some cases it has also taken part in the construction of international airports.

4.   *TRANSPORT BY INLAND WATERWAY*

China's waterways are divided into several systems. These are the Changjiang (Yantze River) system, the Heilongjiang system, the Zhujiang (Pearl River) system, Haunghe (Yellow River) system and the Beijing-Hangzhou Grand Canal system. The Changjiang system is the largest system. The main navigable section of the system is 2,650 kilometres and is capable of accommodating 1,000-metric ton ships all year round. The section down from Hankou is navigable for 5,000-metric ton ships and the section downstream from Nanjing allows 10,000-metric ton steamers to pass.

Since 1980 the individual water transport business has developed rapidly. By the end of 1987 the number of individual households engaged in water transport was estimated to be 530,000 with 390,000 of these located in provinces, cities, villages and towns along the Changjiang.

By the end of 1987 China's dwt of ships for inland waterways had reached 10 million metric tons. Today most of the ships sailing inland rivers have diesel engines.

The Changjiang System is administered by the Changjiang Navigation Administrative Bureau and the Changjiang Shipping Corporation. The former is an agency of the Ministry of Communications. It takes overall responsibility for the administration and management of ports, waterway planning and development and the transport market and it gives business guidance to shipping administrations of the provinces along the Changjiang. The latter is a shipping enterprise that is also directly under the Ministry of Communications. It handles passenger and freight transport and ship maintenance. The transport businesses on tributaries of the Changjiang are managed by inland shipping enterprises of relevant provinces or cities.

The Heilongjiang System is managed by the Heilongjiang Provincial Navigation Bureau. This Bureau is under the dual leadership of the Ministry of Communications and the Heilongjiang Provincial Government.

Preparatory work is currently being undertaken for the establishment of the Zhujiang Navigation Bureau. This bureau will also act as an agency of the Ministry of Communications. It will be responsible for managing navigation and transportation along the Zhujiang River system and it will be responsible for coordinating and supervising planning and construction work relevant to the river system.

Navigation and transport along other river systems is under the management of relevant local governments.

5. COASTAL AND OCEAN TRANSPORT

(1) Shipping Companies

In the 1950s and 1960s marine transport was handled by the Shanghai Ocean Shipping Bureau in the north and the Guangzhou Ocean Shipping Bureau in the south. But in June 1979 the vessel the *Red Flag* made a maiden voyage through the Taiwan Straits and in the process opened up the 3,493 kilometre north-south transport artery. This is a sea artery extending from the port of Sanya on Hainan Island to the port of Yingkou in northeast China.

The major enterprises now involved in coastal transport are the Dalian Shipping Co., the Shanghai Ocean Shipping Bureau, and the Guangzhou Ocean Shipping Bureau. These three enterprises are under the direct control of the Ministry of Communications.

The major enterprise concerned with ocean shipping is the China Ocean Shipping Company. It is the largest State-owned international ocean shipping enterprise in China. It has more than 600 ships with a total carrying capacity of more than 14 million metric tons. The company is responsible for approximately 40% of total foreign trade volume.

In addition to the China Ocean Shipping Company, there is the China Foreign Trade Transportation Corporation under the direction of the Ministry of Foreign Economic Relations and Trade and, as of June 1988, there are 88 other international shipping companies. The fleets of these companies boast bulk carriers, sundry goods vessels, oil tankers, roll-on and roll-off ships, container ships and multi-purpose vessels. Some of the most modern vessels are equipped with advanced automatic piloting and satellite-guided navigation equipment.

The ocean shipping fleet that has been built up during the 1980s has changed the situation whereby Chinese imports and exports depended on chartered foreign ships. Now China serves third countries with cargo transported by Chinese freighters. In 1987 the volume of cargo transported for third countries amounted to more than 20 million metric tons.

(2) Shipping Agencies

The China Ocean Shipping Agency is responsible for procedures for foreign ships to enter and leave Chinese harbours and waters; for arrangements for navigating and berthing; for handling customs declarations, transferring, storing and insurance of cargo; and for recruiting seamen and assisting them with visa applications, finding any necessary medical assistance for seamen and replacing or repatriating seamen.

By the end of 1987 the China Ocean Shipping Agency had established 43 branches and eight representative offices. The latter were in over 150 countries and regions and were involved in through-transport, trade, industry, commerce, finance and insurance.

(3) Harbours

China's major sea ports are Dalian, Yingkou, Qinhuangdao, Tianjin, Yantai, Qingdao, Shijiusuo, Lianyungang, Shanghai, Ningbo, Shantou, Huangpu, Zhanjiang, Haikou, Basuo and Sanya. In 1987 these 16 ports handled 366.1 million metric tons of cargo and boasted a total of 63,089 metres of docks and 400 berths, including 191 berths for vessels of over 10,000 metric tons.

Of the 16 ports only the Qinhuangdao Harbour is directly under the Ministry of Communications; the others are under the dual leadership of the Ministry of Communications and their respective city governments, the latter shouldering the major responsibility for the ports.

Since 1980 coastal port construction, expansion and renovation has been a development priority. A large number of new harbours have been built in the period since 1980. Both domestic and foreign funds have been used for harbour construction. Foreign funding for harbour construction projects has usually been in the form of loans provided by the World Bank and by the Japanese Overseas Cooperation Fund.

6. PIPELINE TRANSPORT

Pipeline transport has been developed in reply to China's growth in oil and natural gas output. China's first long-distance crude oil pipeline ran from Xinjiang's Karamay oilfield to the Dushanzi Refinery. It was completed in 1958.

By 1987 China had 385 oil and gas pipelines. Their total length was 13,764 kilometres. They consisted of 59 pipelines for crude oil transportation, 135 pipelines for finished oil transportation, 152 pipelines for natural gas transportation and 39 pipelines for other gas transportation. Pipeline transport capacity has already exceeded crude oil output, but in the case of finished oil the transport capacity is much lower than output.

In 1966, 65.9% of crude oil was transported by rail and 25.3% by pipeline. By 1987 129 million metric tons of crude oil was transported by pipeline. This was almost all the crude oil extracted. China's finished oils continue to be mainly transported by rail and then by water transport. In contrast to transport of crude oil, pipeline transport of finished oils constitutes only a relatively small proportion of output. In 1987 13.4 million metric tons of finished oils and 8.3 billion cubic metres of natural gas were transported by pipeline.

Because China's crude oil contains a high content of wax and is of high viscosity, it is heated while being transported.

Pipeline transport is managed by the Pipeline Bureau. It is under the Ministry of Petroleum Industry. The Bureau has built and directly manages 71.4% of China's crude oil pipelines, while two-thirds of natural gas pipelines are constructed and managed by the Sichuan Petroleum Administration. It is mainly Sichuan's pipelines that transport China's natural gas.

7. CIVIL AVIATION SERVICES

(1) Reform of Civil Aviation Administration

China's civil air transport is managed by the General Administration of Civil Aviation (CAAC). In March 1980 the State Council decided that CAAC should be organisationally separated from the army and should come under direct management of the State Council.

The 1980 State Council decision, together with the directive that CAAC should follow the enterprise management form of organisation, marked an important turning point in the history of China's civil aviation services. After being administratively separated from the army, CAAC was put under the Beijing, Shanghai, Guangzhou, Chengdu, Xian and Shenyang regional administrations. But in 1985 the State Council approved CAAC's report on reforming this latter form of administration. Now CAAC follows the model of 'separating government administration from enterprise management, streamlining administration and delegating power downwards'. In practice this has meant that CAAC no longer directly manages air services. Its main responsibilities are now:

... formulating principles, policies, decrees and laws for the development of civil aviation undertakings:

... drawing up long-term plans, co-ordinating the development of various aviation enterprises through such economic regulatory means as taxation, pricing, credit and loans:

... managing foreign exchange and safeguarding national aviation rights and interests:

... examining and approving the establishment and dissolution of aviation enterprises, overseeing the management activities of aviation enterprises and setting all technical standards related to civil aviation; issuing management licences, airworthy certificates and technical licences: and

... Guiding air flight arrangements and investigating and handling air accidents.

Enterprise management has now been introduced to all airports. This has meant that all airports, other than the country's gateways, are to be open to all aviation companies. CAAC is to transfer their management over to their localities.

In line with the reforms that have been undertaken CAAC has established the following bureaus and companies: the Southwest China Administrative Bureau, the Southwest China Aviation Company and the Chengdu Airport Administration, the East China Administration Bureau, the China Oriental Aviation Company, the Shanghai Hongqiao International Airport Administration, the North China Administrative Bureau, the China International Aviation Company and the Beijing Capital International Airport Administration.

The China International Aviation Company is China's largest State-owned air transport enterprise. It has over 40 planes, including 30 Boeings, and flies 33 international and regional air routes. It has 23 representative offices spread throughout the world and it has established civil aviation ties with more than 100 countries and regions. The company has highly trained air crews and has the largest maintenance base in China. It also has advertising services, hotels and shops.

Domestic flights within China are now served by a growing number of aviation companies. By the end of 1987 China had 164 long, medium and short haul aeroplanes providing domestic flights within China (including an emerging domestic freight service currently centred in Beijing), regional airlines making flights to Hong Kong and international airlines flying to 31 cities in 24 countries. China has 83 airports. Thirty-four of these are large enough to accommodate Boeing 737s. There are also 11 airports under construction.

In 1987 China's air passenger transport volume was 13.1 million people carried, including 11.1 million people (84.6 %) carried on domestic airlines, 954,000 people (7.3 %) on international airlines and 1.1 million people (8.1 %) on regional airlines. Air freight volume totalled 299,000 metric tons.

(2) General Aviation Services

China's general aviation services are used for forest protection, fire prevention, aerial afforestation, aerial seed sowing, disease and pest prevention and treatment, weeding and fertiliser application, emergency aid, ice and snow control, aerial photography, selection of factory sites, forest surveys, air-mapping, geological surveying and mine prospecting.

General air services are managed by the General Administration of Civil Aviation. In 1987 CAAC had 238 special and multi-purpose planes capable of providing general services. In recent years new equipment and new technology have been adopted and new operations for the service have been developed. These include looking for geothermal water using new aerial remote sensing technology, prospecting for uranium, surveying geological structures, preventing and treating environmental pollution and carrying out soil surveys. In addition, services have been offered to Sino-foreign joint ventures prospecting for oil resources in offshore areas and in the Qadam Basin.

During the 1980s several localities and departments became interested in developing general air services and by the end of 1987 seven general air service enterprises had received general air service licences. The largest of these are the China Flying Dragon Special Aviation Company, the China Marine Helicopter Special Company and the Xinjiang Construction Corps Air Service Station.

(3) Imported Technology

To date, in the course of expanding air transportation and services, China has bought nearly 100 large passenger planes from the United States, Britain, France and Russia and has bought the Skylark, Super Wasp and American Camel helicopters. Equipment has also been leased from foreign aviation companies. For instance the Shanghai Aviation Company, organised by the Shanghai municipal government and the China Civil Aviation Service Company, has leased Boeing 737s and Boeing 757s from Australia's Ansett World Air Service Company.

In addition to aircraft imports and overseas leasing of aircraft, loans from the Kuwaiti government have been used to expand Xiamen Airport and a maintenance centre has been established jointly by China and the Lufthansa Company of Germany to improve China's ability to overhaul aircraft engines and components. Radar units and a control centre have also been provided by the Thomson-CSF company of France.

8. TRANSPORT PROBLEMS TO BE ADDRESSED

China's most serious transport problems are:
- ... inadequate rail transport capacity;
- ... limited harbours and limited dock and berth capacity, especially in relation to special purpose berths;
- ... a serious shortage of passenger trains and vessels; and
- ... an underdeveloped highway transport system.

Currently there is concern because the transport capacity for coal and other important materials is severely strained. Major trunk lines can only handle 50-70% of demand and energy resources and raw materials used in industrial production are seriously affected. Another area of considerable concern is harbour warehousing. The shortage of harbour warehousing has combined with low transport and distribution capacity to result in ships frequently being kept standing at anchor. Also passengers have often found themselves unable to purchase travel tickets. This has at times led to acute frustration and discontent.

It is predicted that the coal transport route from China's energy centre in Shanxi Province to other parts of the country and the east-west and north-south routes in the eastern part of China will face a growing transport shortage. And at the same time, with coastal regions entering the world market-place, the task of linking major coastal harbours will become more and more pressing.

In order to achieve the marked development required in transport facilities, construction funds are to be raised through various channels. Funds are to come from central authorities, local governments, enterprises and individuals. Foreign funds will also be used. Joint ventures, co-operative enterprises, loans and compensatory trade are to be adopted in order to attract foreign interest investment in China's transport enterprises. Funds raised for transport needs are to be spent on purchasing the large quantities of advanced Chinese and foreign equipment that will speed up the process of modernisation.

In order to keep pace with the overall situation in the national economy, a rational transport pricing system will be established. Profit from transport enterprises will then be made available for re-investment by the transport enterprises in projects that will promote their development.

III. POST AND COMMUNICATION SERVICES

1. POSTAL SERVICES

For a long time the State made very little investment in postal services. It was difficult for postal departments to attract funds and this had an adverse effect on the expansion and improvement of postal services. In 1986, in order to raise construction funds and to develop postal services, the government adopted a policy based on the self-development of postal services. Under the new policy 90% of profit generated from the provision of postal services is returned to postal departments to be used as discretionary development funds.

At the very beginning of China's programme for economic reform, a ZIP code system was introduced and since October 1988 it has been the practice not to deliver letters that are without a ZIP code. China's ZIP code system is a six digit system. The first two numbers represent the province, the third represents the postal zone, the fourth the county (or city) and the last two numbers represent the delivery district. Particularly large enterprises and institutions have their own special district numbers.

In November 1987 a domestic express mail delivery was introduced. This service operated between 196 large and medium-sized cities including Beijing, Shanghai, Guangzhou and Wuhan. The service provided a much more effective link between postal delivery agencies and the railway, airline and highway transport systems. It greatly shortened delivery times. By May 1988 this service had been extended to more than 1,970 cities and counties.

In a bid to quicken delivery, China's international mail delivery system has been divided into two services. There is the 'regular service' and the 'special need service'. The 'regular service' requires the customer to sign an advance contract with the post office. The contract stipulates number of deliveries required, time, destination and addressee. The 'special need service' allows the customer to either have mail promptly and simply handled by the post office within office hours, or on request, to have mail fetched from the sender. All types of documents and materials, monetary bills, computer data, engineering blueprints, trade contracts, passports, tenders and commodity samples can be sent using this method. By the end of 1987, 79 cities had introduced the international special need delivery service.

The business negotiated by Chinese post offices includes postal savings and postal remittances. In the early period after the establishment of New China, the post office undertook savings business, but this business was stopped in September 1953. Then in April 1986 post offices were again free to establish a savings business. The Postal Service Law now clearly lists postal savings as one of the main business activities of post offices. By the end of 1987 9,463 post offices had established savings businesses. By this time the total number of depositors had reached 53 million and the amount deposited had reached Rmb 3.8 billion.

In line with the division of labour between banks and post offices, funds remitted by the postal service are restricted to an individual's personal funds. Fund remittances between government organs and enterprises and between enterprises are handled by the banks.

2. TELECOMMUNICATION SERVICES

China's telecommunications network consists of two parts:
 ... the network for public telecommunications and
 ... the network for special telecommunications.

(1) Public Telecommunication Services

As its name suggests, the public telephone system offers local, long-distance and international services for public/civilian use. To speed up the expansion of the urban telephone service, the government has decided that profit made from the urban telephone service will not be turned over to the State. It will be used for expanding the telephone service and it has been decided that charges for installation of new telephones will also be used to this end.

In China today there are 0.75 telephones for every 100 people. By international standards this figure is very low, but it is a figure that compares favourably with the 1978 Chinese figure of 0.36 telephones per 100 people.

To speed up the expansion of the rural telephone service the Chinese government has been encouraging and helping townships, village and individuals to raise funds for the installation of telephones in rural areas. By the end of 1987 more than 47,000 telephone exchanges had been established in rural areas and 37,480 townships (over 72% of townships) had installed telephone exchanges.

In addition to urban and rural telephone services, China has, since the 1980s, also been developing a mobile communications system. This system has enjoyed rapid development. It has been established in Beijing, Shanghai, Guangzhou, Kunming and Qinhuangdao. Also, public mobile telephone networks have been under construction in the Beijing-Tianjin-Tangshan district and in the Changjiang and Zhujiang Deltas.

In the area of international calls, China has international telecommunication bureaus in Beijing and Shanghai. The 1987 completion of the Beijing International Telecommunications Bureau greatly increased international call handling capacity, while at the same time strenuous efforts were being made to establish a satellite communication network. In 1978 communication with foreign countries and with Hong Kong and Macao was usually via short-wave and open-wire facilities, but now more than 90% of international telecommunication services use international communication satellites.

(2) Special Telecommunication Services

The special telecommunications networks are those rented by the military, railways, communications, water conservancy and hydropower, broadcasting and television and petroleum departments of government. These systems are either rented from the post and telecommunications department or they are built by the departments for their own use.

The special railway telecommunications network is a very large independent system that extends to all large railway stations and workshops. Together with the public and military systems, it is one of the three largest telecommunications networks in China. It links railway stations, railway sections, railway sub-bureaus and bureaus, the Ministry of Railways and other organisations related to the operation of the rail system.

The water transport telecommunications network was established at the time that there was significant expansion in the use of water transport. This network is for both public and special use. It has four components: river bank and coastal radio stations, port or port area communication hubs, long-distance transport line circuits built by water transport departments and long-distance transport line circuits rented from the posts and telecommunications departments. The task performed by this telecommunications network is that of ensuring the safety of shipping, directing water traffic control and offering water transport communication. In addition to the water transport telecommunications network, riverbank and coastal radio stations and extra coastal shortwave radio-telephone stations also provide communication services for Chinese and foreign shipping.

The power system's telecommunication network is vital for the modern management of China's power grids. In the early 1980s a telecommunications network was established that serves to link the power grids of seven regions. It is intended that by 1990 these regional power grids will be linked to the Ministry of Water Resources.

The broadcasting and television network rents circuits from the post and telecommunications department and it has built its own microwave communications system.

The petroleum telecommunications network has been formed by renting satellite circuits and building microwave circuits along the oil pipelines. The system links Beijing with various oilfields. It forms a communications system that directs China's oil production.

3. DOMESTIC SATELLITE COMMUNICATION

Since the 1970s, when China began to develop satellite communication technology, a public satellite communication network has been established under the Ministry of Posts and Telecommunications and a special satellite communication network has also been established for use by broadcasting and television, meteorology, coal and petroleum departments.

Between 1978 and 1982 China held trial satellite transmission tests. These tests were made using German, French and Italian satellites. In 1985 China acquired three international communication satellite retransmitters. It was at this juncture that national satellite transmission of television programmes began.

At the same time as satellite transmission of television programmes was being established, ways and means of using communication satellites for the provision of public satellite circuits was being investigated. As a result, in 1986 earth stations for public communication in Beijing, Urumqi, Lhasa, Hohhot and Guangzhou went into operation and in the following year the number of satellite communication earth stations was increased to eight. Petroleum departments also built 15 such stations.

In April 1984, in order to build China's own satellite communication system, an experimental communication satellite was launched. This satellite was domestically made. Then in February 1986 another communication satellite was launched for experimental use and for use by those accessing the special communication system. In March 1988 a communication satellite capable of moving at fixed positions was successfully launched. Three of the four retransmitters on this satellite are currently used for transmitting television programmes and the fourth is used by the telephone service.

In future further expansion of domestic satellite communication will take place. It is intended that satellite communication will become the main means of promoting a modern Chinese communication system.

4. OPTICAL FIBRE COMMUNICATION

In China in the early 1970s optical fibre communication began to be studied and by 1974 quartz optical fibre was being successfully manufactured. By 1975 the successive emitting of semiconductor lasers had been realised and in the following year transmission of language and picture signals using optical fibre communication had been successfully executed. This transmission had relied exclusively on domestically produced components.

At first optical fibre communication was used for short distance urban communication. Later it was extended to long-distance trunk line use. A multimode short wave length experimental system was first used in the Shanghai urban area in 1979 and by 1982 a multimode short wave length system for urban telephone use had been established in Wuhan. The first China-made multimode long wave length system was commissioned in 1983 and by September 1988, 36 cities had adopted optical fibre communication technology and eight provinces had shown that they were capable of producing long-distance communication optical cable. To date Beijing city has laid 60 kilometres of optical cable for use by its urban telephone service.

Unless there is an unforeseen situation, domestic construction of coaxial cable communication trunk lines will be discontinued. In future optical cable communication trunk lines will be installed.

5. THE FUTURE DEVELOPMENT OF POST AND COMMUNICATION SERVICES

In future a continuous effort will be made to do away with monopolised State operation and management of these services. In the 1990s the State, localities, collectives and individuals will all be expected to participate in the development of communication services.

The Ministry of Posts and Telecommunications has been charged with planning the national communication network. The initiative of localities is to be used in the building of this network. The Ministry of Posts and Telecommunications will be responsible for international communication and for the building of trunk communication lines, but the construction of communication lines linking provincial government with prefectures, cities, counties and townships and with neighbouring provinces is to be undertaken by localities. At the same time the resources of the Ministry of Posts and Telecommunications, the Ministry of the Machine-Building and Electronics Industry, the Ministry of the Aeronautics and Astronautics Industry and other relevant departments and localities are to be pooled to develop communication services and to provide the equipment required for the expansion of these services. Efforts will also be made to import foreign funds, technology and equipment that can be used in the development of China's communication networks.

CHAPTER 16

The Electronics, Nuclear and Astronautics Industries

Since the founding of New China a number of new industries have been developed. Among the most important of these are the electronics, nuclear and astronautics industries. These are China's rising new industries.

I. THE ELECTRONICS INDUSTRY

In the past China's electronics industry depended on copying products produced elsewhere, but today it is an industry that designs its own products. It is an industry that combines both military and civilian production.

Centres of electronics production have now been established in eastern China with Shanghai and Jiangsu province as centres, in the north with Beijing, Tianjin and Liaoning Province as centres and in the southwest and northwest with Sichuan, Guizhou and Shaanxi provinces as centres. And there are now new electronics industry bases taking shape in the southern provinces of Guangdong and Fujian.

In 1987 the gross output value of the electronics industry was Rmb 35.8 billion. The electronics industry is producing a large quantity of products for national defence, development of the national economy and for people's everyday life. It has provided electronic equipment of such reliable quality that its products have been used for launching a carrier rocket into the Pacific, for launching a rocket from a submarine and for production of an experimental communications satellite.

1. ADMINISTRATIVE MANAGEMENT OF THE ELECTRONICS INDUSTRY

The Ministry of Machine-Building and Electronics Industries is in charge of the electronics industry. The Ministry's main function is to map out development of a rational production structure, to speed up the development of the electronics information industry and to promote integration of the machine-building and electronics industries.

From the time of the founding of New China until 1978 electronics factories were under the administration of the Ministry of Electronics Industry with other electronics factories affiliated to the Ministry of Astronautics Industry, the Ministry of Posts and Telecommunications, the Ministry of Radio and Television, the Ministry of Railways, the Ministry of Water Resources and Electric Power and the Chinese Academy of Sciences and various provinces, municipalities directly under the central government and autonomous regions. From 1979 departments concerned with the electronics industry have been gradually delegating their power over factory administration down to local authorities and they have been encouraging enterprises to enter into associations with each other through the establishment of companies, associated companies, associations and enterprise groups organised in accord with division of labour, channels of supply, scientific and technological cooperation and the market. What this has meant is that at the same time as factory administration has been decentralised, relevant central government ministries have become ministries that are responsible only for formulating principles, policies, laws, regulations and plans.

2. THE MANUFACTURE OF CONSUMER ELECTRONIC PRODUCTS

From 1979 China's output of consumer electronic products has increased at a rapid rate. In 1987, 19.3 million television sets were produced (including 6.7 million colour sets) together with 19.8 million tape recorders and 17.6 million radio sets. And in the case of the latter, the 1987 figure did not represent the production peak to date. In 1981 output of radio sets reached 40.6 million, a figure that was later affected by falling demand.

In the 1980s it was not only a substantial increase in quantity of production that marked the new era in China's consumer electronics industry; this period also saw a substantial improvement in production quality that came about with the increased specialised large-scale production of electronic products. By 1987 China's television sets and tape recorders and their components were being sold in large numbers on the international market. Technology and equipment was being exported along with finished products, with the latter having have made their way into markets in the United States, Japan, Britain and other developed countries.

3. MANUFACTURE OF COMPUTERS

China started to study the manufacture of computers as early as 1956. There was success in making a first small electronic tube computer in 1958 and the following year the first big electronic tube computer was produced. At this point China's computer technology was next only to that of the United States and the Soviet Union and was better than that of Japan and Britain. In the 1960s and 1970s second generation transistor digital computers were being produced and by the time the Sixth Five-Year Plan was being implemented, in addition to the Great Wall 0520 and Zijin-II series microcomputers, the 8030 medium-sized all-purpose computer series, the 2780 extra minicomputer series, the 2701 array processor and the computer laser with a Chinese character typesetting system were being produced. Also during this same period, the large 757 computer and the Yinhe (Milky Way) computer system (the latter capable of 100 million calculations per second) were manufactured.

By 1984 the number of large, medium-sized and small computers being manufactured had reached 354, but later domestic output declined somewhat due to the import of a large number of overseas manufactured computers. By 1987 the number of domestically produced computers had dropped to 229, but on the other hand, the output of micro-computers had risen annually. By 1987 it had reached 47,505 while the annual output of Great Wall 0520 CH computers had exceeded 10,000 and hardware and software for this model had found its way into the international market. By early 1988 the KSJ-HN 2220 micro 32 byte-extra minicomputer had passed a ministerial level technological appraisal.

4. TECHNOLOGICAL ADVANCES

In the early 1980s China entered the field of micro-electronic technology. In the field of integrated circuits, 5 micrometre line width circuits have gone into mass production and there are now more than 900 types of integrated circuit products. Also a breakthrough has been made in relation to making 3 micrometre line width circuits and efforts are currently being made to tackle the key problems associated with one micrometre technology. In terms of microprocessor circuits, two 8-bit processor series and one 4-bit processor series have been developed. While in terms of memory circuits, three power source 16 K dynamic storage and 4 K static storage circuits have been successfully manufactured and technological problems associated with making 64 K dynamic storage circuits and corresponding materials and equipment are being solved.

In the field of computers, in addition to the successful manufacture of various types of computers, work is proceeding apace in establishing computer networks and large data banks and in analog information processing and artificial intelligence development. In the field of communication technology, aside from the micro-wave communication lines, a domestically produced communication broadcasting satellite and a satellite ground station have gone into operation. An advanced level of technology has also been attained in the areas of radar remote control measuring, ground-measuring electronic equipment and rocket-carrying and ship-carrying electronic equipment.

In the application of laser technology, series products of laser devices that are in common use have been manufactured and some of these products have reached a level considered to be advanced in terms of international standards. These are the high stable frequency helium-neon laser, the precision photo-electric phase telemeter, laser polarised light components and one kW and two kW lasers. In industry lasers are now being used for precision parts boring, microwelding, numerically-controlled microwelding and numerically-controlled laser cutting and the laser collimation guide has been applied extensively in the building, ship-building and mining industries. All major measuring departments in the country have now established laser measuring systems and laser ranging technology has been applied in areas such as prospecting, design drawing and in the construction of communication projects and artificial satellites. It is thanks to the marked advance in the manufacture of plane-carrying sensors that remote sensing technology has been made capable of meeting the demands of all types of satellites. This is an advance that has also brought tremendous social benefit in terms of prospecting for natural resources, agriculture, forestry, water conservation, energy, communications and environmental protection and city planning.

5. DEVELOPMENT PRIORITIES FOR THE ELECTRONICS INDUSTRY

At present the technological level of China's electronics industry is not high enough. The capacity for new production is rather weak and the means of production for electronic products still does not have a very large market. In order to meet the demands of modernisation, the gross output value of electronics industry will be increased much faster than that of all other industries. It is intended that by the turn of the century major electronic products and production technology will have attained the level of the advanced countries of the late 1980s and early 1990s and that certain technologies will have reached the current advanced international level.

The electronic industry has been charged with the responsibility for serving all sectors of the national economy, with particular emphasis on the needs of key industries such as energy and communications. The production of electronics technology and equipment is to reflect the requirements of these industries and at the same time it is to develop the electronic equipment and technology required for servicing the coal and oil industries, water conservation projects, the railways, communications services, civil aviation, and the metallurgical, chemical, building materials, light and textile industries. This development would substantially increase the productive capacity of these industries and of the national economy.

In terms of development priorities, priority will be given to establishing electronics industry bases in eastern coastal areas. Help will be given to large and medium-sized key enterprises which have large scale production capacity and sound economic foundations. It is also intended that approximately a dozen export bases will be built.

Further development of the electronics industry will be through the importation of technology, establishment of joint ventures and the technological transformation of existing electronics factories and research institutions. Effort will also be made to accelerate the building of two micro-electronic technology development bases, one in the north and the other in the south.

With respect to product type, development stress will be laid on:
- ... producing integrated circuits;
- ... substituting domestically made colour television sets for imported sets;
- ... promotion of the use and servicing of computers and the use and servicing of communication facilities; and
- ... producing electronic products for export.

With respect to technology, development stress will be laid on the following five technologies:
- ... mass produced technology centred on auxiliary computer design and on auxiliary system manufacture and testing;
- ... micro-processing technology aimed at large-scale integrated circuits with 1-2 micrometre line widths;
- ... modern communications technology, mainly digital electronic techniques to be used for transforming existing traditional production techniques; and
- ... modern military electronic technology.

In order to promote development of the technologies listed immediately above, it will be necessary to build industrial development centres for the development of each of the five technologies.

It is intended that average annual growth rate for the electronics industry will more than 100% higher than gross industrial output value. In order to expand the export capacity of the electronics industry and the ability to participate in international market competition, the production system for export will be given priority. Priority will also be given to fostering key enterprises and to building export production bases.

II. THE NUCLEAR INDUSTRY

China's nuclear industry was established in early 1955. Both the 12 year plan for the development of science and technology (from 1956 to 1967) and the 10 year plan for the development of science and technology (from 1963 to 1972) listed the development of nuclear science and technology and the nuclear industry as a priority.

As early as January 1955, China began cooperating with the Soviet Union for prospecting for domestic uranium resources and it was with Soviet aid that China completed its first heavy water reactor and cyclotron in 1958. Meanwhile China went all out to design and build a number of uranium mines and hydrometallurgical plants.

In the 1960s the first batch of nuclear industrial enterprises was completed. This batch included a nuclear reactor and enterprises undertaking geological prospecting, mining for uranium, hydrometallurgical processing of uranium, enrichment of uranium, manufacture of uranium components, reprocessing of irradiation components, and manufacture of nuclear weapons.

In the late 1960s and during the 1970s nuclear science research was carried out and new industrial bases were built in interior areas. This meant that a complete nuclear industry had been established, one that reached from the geological prospecting and mining for uranium to the production of nuclear fuels and one that went from scientific research and design to the production and installation of equipment.

On 16 October 1964 China successfully exploded its first atomic bomb, making it the fifth country in the world to have nuclear weapons. It was after this explosion that the government decided to switch to developing the hydrogen bomb while at the same time accelerating the process of making atomic weapons. On 14th May 1965 a nuclear bomb was dropped from a bomber and exploded at a predetermined altitude and in a guided missile test held on 27 October 1966 a guided missile was successfully launched and a nuclear warhead exploded at a designated target and altitude.

On 17 June 1967 China successfully conducted its first nuclear bomb test: it had become the fourth country in the world to master hydrogen bomb technology. Then in December 1970 China's first nuclear submarine was launched, making China the fifth country in the world to launch its own nuclear submarine.

16:1 CHINA'S NUCLEAR INDUSTRY

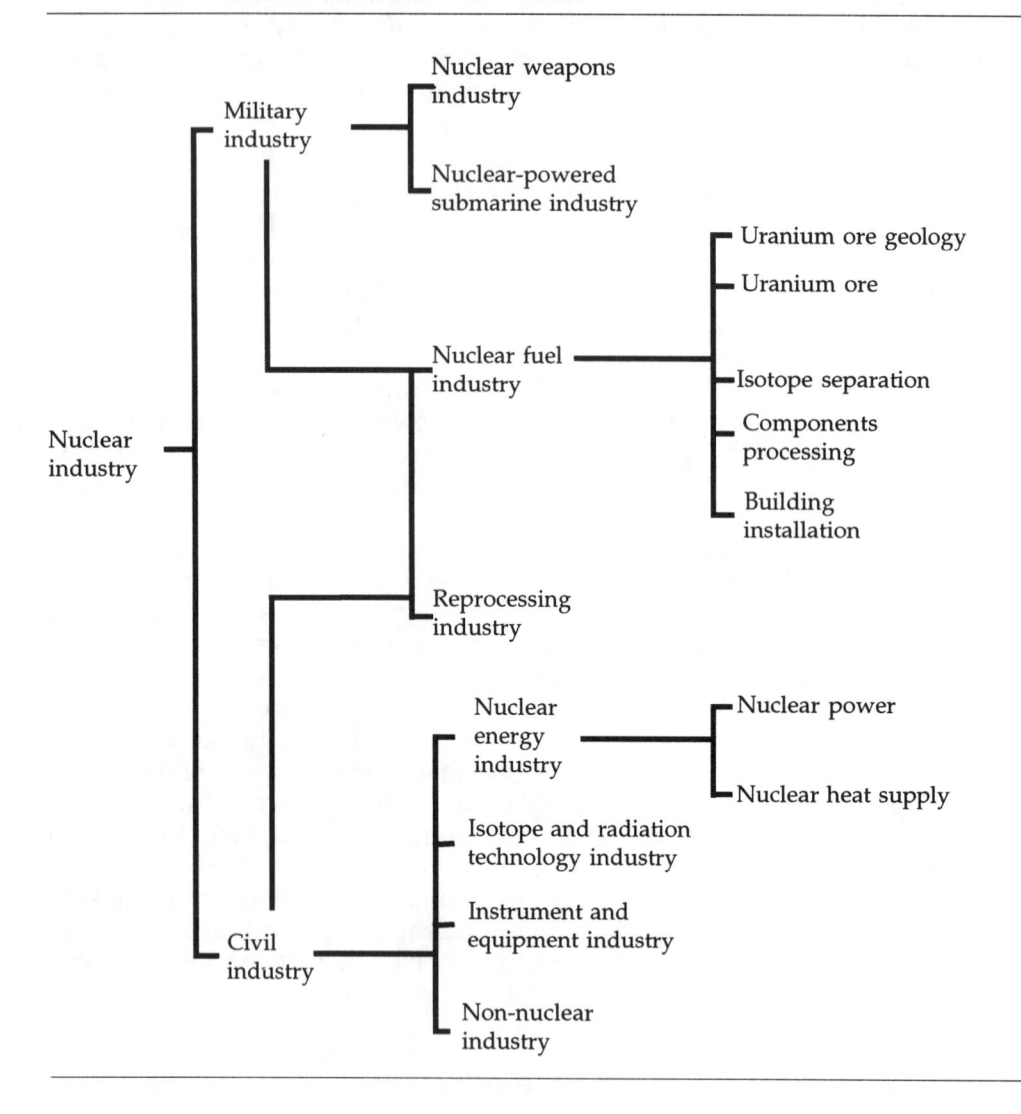

- Nuclear industry
  - Military industry
    - Nuclear weapons industry
    - Nuclear-powered submarine industry
  - Nuclear fuel industry
    - Uranium ore geology
    - Uranium ore
    - Isotope separation
    - Components processing
    - Building installation
  - Reprocessing industry
  - Civil industry
    - Nuclear energy industry
      - Nuclear power
      - Nuclear heat supply
    - Isotope and radiation technology industry
    - Instrument and equipment industry
    - Non-nuclear industry

During the 1960s and 1970s all types of nuclear tests were conducted. Tests were undertaken in the air, on the ground and underground. After the first underground nuclear test in September 1969 plans were drawn up for a series of underground nuclear tests which were completed by 1984. At present China has equipped its armed forces with nuclear weapons to be carried by all types of delivery vehicles.

1. THE APPLICATION OF ISOTOPE TECHNOLOGY

Over the past 30 years isotope technology has been applied to ever wider areas and has become an important technology with regard to the national economy.

It has been used in agriculture, medical science and industry.

(1) In agriculture isotope tracer technology has made contributions to pesticide residue detection, to the rational application of fertiliser, to the physiological and biochemical study of animals and plants and to the diagnosis of animal diseases. Statistics show that by the mid 1980s there had been considerable success in using isotope radiation 185 mutation to produce varieties of grain, cotton, oil-bearing crops, vegetables and fruit trees. China's contribution to this field now accounts for more than 30% of mutant crop varieties in the world.

The new varieties of crops have proved to be high-yielding, disease-resistant and good quality. This has meant that China now stands as a world leader in terms of the variety, quantity, planted area and economic return from crops bred using isotope radiation.

A number of provinces and municipalities have also adopted radiation as a method for preserving grain, meat products, fruit and mushrooms. Radiating potatoes and onions with cobalt-60 has achieved good results in terms of product freshness. Radiating tussah eggs with isotopes in order to stimulate production of tussah silk has also been successful.

(2) In terms of medical science there has been integration of isotope technology with other nuclear technology. This has resulted in nuclear medical science which has become an important branch of China's medical science. About 200 methods for diagnosis using such technology are now in clinical use. Important achievements have been gained in the treatment of malignant tumours, research in basic medical science using radioactive medicine, the making of synthetic crystalline insulin and in the study of the theory of acupuncture analgesia.

(3) In industry, isotope tracer technology was significantly advanced during the 1970s. It is now used in water conservation and in the petroleum, metallurgical, chemical, machine-building and electronics industries. Success has been achieved in solving the problem of steam bubbles in continuous steel casting; in detecting reservoir leakage and in ensuring the stability of dyke foundations; in observing sand and mud movement in river ports and reservoirs; in detecting holes in underground oil pipelines; and in examining sealed receptacles and semi-conductor appliances.

2. COMBINING MILITARY PURPOSES WITH CIVILIAN PRODUCTION

Over a long period of time the nuclear industry was regarded as a military industry with all its products serving only military purposes. But in June 1986 the Ministry of Nuclear Industry was put under direct leadership of the State

Council. It was to be managed in the same manner as other industries. It was at this point that the industry developed in the direction of combining military purposes with civilian production.

In 1988 the Ministry of Nuclear Industry was dissolved and the China National Nuclear Industry Corporation was established. The latter is under the Ministry of Energy Resources. The Corporation has the status of an independent legal and economic entity.

Since 1980 a new policy has been adopted in terms of development of the nuclear industry. While ensuring military use first, developmental stress has switched to serving the national economy and people's daily life. This has opened up a broad road for the development of the nuclear industry. In light of this new policy, in 1986 general principles for readjusting the nuclear industry were put forward. These principles are:

... to reduce production for military purposes,

... to readjust the pattern of production, and

... to readjust both product mix and the ranks of people working in the industry.

After readjustment, the nuclear industry, while giving priority to the research and manufacture of nuclear weapons, will strive to develop relevant high technology for the good of the national economy. For example geological work connected with uranium will centre on looking for ores, bearing in mind that high-grade ores will produce good economic returns. But at the same time, priority afforded to military requirements will ensure that nuclear weapons continue to be steadily improved and that China will continue to study and manufacture a new generation of nuclear weapons, conduct research on a new generation of nuclear-powered submarines, improve scientific and technological services for existing nuclear weapons and transfer strategic nuclear weapons technology to conventional arms.

To date more than 1,000 types of product in ten categories have been developed by the nuclear industry and in future, development will take on the following four aspects.

(1) Vigorous efforts will be made to develop nuclear energy. This will assist in solving the problem of acute shortages of electricity. It is intended that the contract system will be introduced in the building of nuclear power stations and, in line with the principle of relying on domestic nuclear fuels, efforts will be made to supply nuclear fuels to meet the requirements of nuclear power generation.

(2) Nuclear technology will be popularised. This will include the application of reactors, accelerators and radioactive isotopes in all branches of the economy. Meanwhile, in conjunction with existing science and technology and with a number of new branches of learning, new technologies and new industries will be developed. These will include nuclear medical science, nuclear agriculture, nuclear environmental protection, nuclear analysis and survey technologies, nuclear tracer technology, nuclear automation technology, development of the nuclear radiation processing industry and nuclear electronic instruments manufacture.

(3) Advanced non-nuclear technologies that have been developed and applied in the course of building up the nuclear industry will be transferred to civilian industrial concerns. This will promote the development of civil industrial

technology. Such technologies would include fusing agent extraction, ion exchange, heat pump evaporation, special processing, low temperature super conduction, remote control and remote measuring technologies.

(4) The nuclear industry involves many types of production work and so its capacity in terms of geological prospecting, mining, scientific research, design, manufacture of equipment and instruments and building installation and construction, should be used for civilian purposes. In future the industry will provide all-round technical cooperation and engineering services for the energy industry, for urban and rural construction, for light industry, for the food industry and for public health and environmental protection.

III. THE ASTRONAUTICS INDUSTRY

The development of China's astronautics industry can be divided into two periods. The first period was from the mid-1950s to the mid-1960s. During that decade work focused on establishing the industry and on establishing and improving scientific research in terms of guided missiles. In scientific research stress was placed on the development of ballistic ground-to-ground missiles. This period was also the time when the material and technological basis was laid for the development of a carrier rocket. The foundation for China's independent strategic nuclear counter-striking force was established during this period.

The second period began from the mid-1960s and extends to the present. During this period the first artificial satellite was launched. This was on the basis of China's research and manufacture of carrier rockets.

After more than 30 years of development the astronautics industry is a industry with a nationwide network of coordinated scientific research and production. It has skilled scientific research and production workers capable of undertaking research, design, trial manufacture, experiment and production of all types of artificial satellites, carrier rockets, strategic guided missiles and tactical guided missiles.

1. ROCKET MANUFACTURE

China's astronautics industry started with the manufacture of rockets and guided missiles. In June 1964 there was a successful launching of the first domestically manufactured medium and short-range carrier rocket and from July to October of the same year repeated experiments were carried out on launching the same rocket model. They were successful.

In the late 1960s research and manufacture began on medium and long-range rockets and on continental multi-stage carrier rockets. By April 1970 a satellite had been launched for the first time. The Long March No 1 three-stage carrier rocket sent a 300 kg artificial satellite into near-earth orbit.

In the early 1970s there was success in the manufacture of carrier rockets. The Storm No 1 and the Long March No 2 carrier rockets, capable of sending 1,500 kg and 2,000 kg artificial satellites into near-earth orbit, were manufactured. In July 1975 the former was used to send an experimental satellite weighing more than one metric ton into predetermined orbit and in September 1981 it accurately sent a group of three space physical survey satellites into close orbits. It also successfully launched the country's first return satellite in November 1975.

In the early 1980s China manufactured the Long March No 3 three-stage large carrier rocket. On 8 April 1984 the rocket was used to launch an earth static orbit experimental communication satellite. This successful launch demonstrated that the rocket had the capacity for sending a 1,430 kg satellite into shifting orbit with an apogee of 36,000 km. Also by using a high energy and low temperature liquid hydrogen and oxygen engine, it had for the second time solved the technical problem of hydrogen and oxygen engine ignition under conditions of weightlessness. It demonstrated that China had joined the advanced countries of the world in terms of carrier rocket technology.

On 18 May 1980 China successfully launched a long-range carrier rocket into the Pacific Ocean and then on 12 October 1982 a carrier rocket was launched from a submarine into a predetermined ocean area. This was China's first solid fuel rocket to be fired from a submarine.

2. DEVELOPMENT OF ASTRONAUTIC TECHNOLOGY

In April 1970, after more than four years of effort, the Dongfanghong No 1 satellite (the country's first artificial earth satellite) was successfully launched and then in March 1971 the Shijian No 1 satellite (the second artificial satellite) was launched. The latter was an experimental satellite used to test the power supply system of solar batteries, temperature control systems, the properties of electronic components and parts operating in space for a long period of time and to measure various types of physical parameters in space. Shijian No 1 operated in space for eight years. It provided valuable experience for the future design of long-service satellites.

On 26 November 1975 for the first time, a remote sensing return satellite was launched. It worked normally in space and returned to earth three days later. Since that time two artificial earth satellites and two scientific experimental satellites have been launched and recovered according to plan. The accurate recovery of satellites in densely populated areas shows that China has made new breakthroughs in orbit control technology, retro-rocket, heat protection technology and recovery technology.

On 20 September 1981 for the first time, a rocket was used to launch a group of three scientific experimental satellites. Two of the three satellites were physical survey satellites which used a solar cell panel, active temperature control and other up-to-date technologies. They were used to obtain comprehensive space survey data. The successful launching of these three satellites showed that China had mastered the technology of launching a number of satellites using one rocket.

On 8 April 1984 an earth static orbit experimental satellite was successfully launched. The launching was a gigantic and complicated engineering project involving the work of five systems, i.e., the satellite itself, the carrier rocket, the launching site and the ground monitoring and satellite communication station. The satellite itself then had ten systems: the structure, the energy system, control and communication systems, a remote measuring system, remote control, tracing, antenna, and temperature control systems and the apogee engine.

On 1 February 1986 China launched its first practical communication broadcasting satellite. On 20 February the satellite reached its geostationary position at longitude 103 degrees east over the equator. The tests for retransmission of broadcasts, television and communications using the satellite all proved successful. Then on 6 October in the same year, a general land survey satellite was launched using a Long March No 2 carrier rocket. After five days of operation the satellite returned to earth at its scheduled time, route and landing site. The satellite had obtained clear photographs and useful information, including providing valuable scientific information relevant to use of natural resources.

On 5 August and on 9 September 1987 the Long March No 2 carrier rocket was used to launch and recover China's 9th and 10th remote sensing return satellites. Use had been made of the two satellites for conducting an experiment on space micro-gravity, 12 experiments on materials and 68 experiments on space biology. The experiments on such projects as superconduction of specific materials and on refractory alloy, all achieved satisfactory results. The biological experiments obtained information on variations and changes in plants, germs and low order animals.

By the end of 1987, 21 different types of artificial satellites had been launched. These included technological experimental satellites, scientific research satellites, space remote sensing satellites and a communications broadcasting satellite.

16:2 SATELLITES SUCCESSFULLY LAUNCHED

		Launch date	Conditions of operation	Remarks
1	Dongfanghong No 1 satellite	24/4/70	Broadcast music `East is Red'	Satellite weight 173 kg perigee 439 km
2	Shijian No 1 satellite	3/3/71	Sent scientific experimental data to earth	Perigee 266 km apogee 1,826 km
3	Technological experimental satellite	26/7/75	All instruments on satellite work normally	Perigee 186 km apogee 464 km
4	Remote sensing return satellite I	26/11/75	All systems on satellite work normally	Returned to earth on schedule after operating for 3 days
5	Technological experimental satellite	16/12/75	Satellite works normally	
6	Technological experimental satellite	30/8/75	Satellite works normally	
7	Remote sensing return satellite II	7/12/76	Satellite works normally	Returned to earth accurately

SATELLITES SUCCESSFULLY LAUNCHED (cont'd)

		Launch date	Conditions of operation	Remarks
8	Remote sensing return satellite II	26/1/78	All systems worked normally	Returned to earth accurately
9	Shijian No 2 satellite	20/9/81	All systems worked normally constantly sending data back to earth	Three satellites launched from one rocket
10	Shijian No 2 A satellite	20/9/81	All systems worked normally	Three satellites launched from one rocket
11	Shijian No 2 B satellite	20/9/81	All systems worked normally	Three satellites launched from one rocket
12	Remote sensing return satellite IV	9/9/82	All systems worked normally	Returned to earth after operating for 5 days
13	Remote sensing return satellite V	19/8/83	All systems worked normally	Returned to earth according to plan
14	Experimental satellite	29/1/84	Gained important results	
15	Experimental communication satellite	8/8/84	Equipment worked normally	Satellite reached geostationary position at longitude 125 degrees over the equator
16	Remote sensing return satellite VI	12/9/84	All systems worked normally	Returned to earth accurately
17	Remote sensing return satellite VII	21/10/85	Obtained land survey material	Returned to earth accurately

SATELLITES SUCCESSFULLY LAUNCHED (cont'd)

	Launch date	Conditions of operation	Remarks
18 Practical communication broadcasting satellite	1/2/86	All systems worked normally	Satellite reached geostationary position at longitude 103 degrees east over equator
19 Remote sensing return satellite	6/10/86	Obtained land survey material	Returned to earth accurately
20 Remote sensing return satellite	5/8/87	Conducted scientific survey, conducted experiment on micro-gravity	Operated for five days and returned to earth as planned
21 Remote sensing return satellite	9/9/87	Conducted scientific survey with 34 experimental devices	Returned to earth according to plan after operating for eight days

3. INTERNATIONAL EXCHANGES

When developing satellite technology, China has followed the principle of independence and self-reliance, but at the same time there has been an active promotion of technological exchange with other countries.

In 1982 the Seventh Ministry of Machine-Building Industry was reorganised and renamed the Ministry of Astronautics Industry. This latter Ministry then began to establish ties with other countries. The Ministry established ties with more than 40 countries and regions, came into contact with several hundred research institutions, companies and factories abroad and promoted both governmental and non-governmental visits.

China has signed agreements on scientific and technological cooperation and exchange in the field of astronautics with Germany, Italy, the United States, France, Britain and Japan and has explored questions of cooperation with Brazil and with other developing countries. China has also actively participated in activities organised by the International Telecommunication Union, the International Space Navigation Federation, the United Nations Committee on the Peaceful Use of Outer Space and with other international organisations.

In the field of space technology co-operation with other countries is conducted through the China Great Wall Industrial Corporation. Affiliated to the Ministry of Aeronautics and Astronautics, the Corporation acts as an independent foreign trade company. It has its own legal entity and it handles both import and export of relevant industrial products and technology. The Corporation is responsible for conducting research and production of satellites for other countries. It offers them satellite launching services and co-operation in the field of space technology. The Corporation is based in Beijing, with branches in Shanghai, Guangzhou, Shenzhen, Dalian, Jinan, Chongqing and Tianjin and with representative offices in the United States, Western Europe and the Middle East.

China's astronautics industry not only provides domestic services, it also serves other countries. On 10 March 1987 it was announced that China would provide return satellite services for foreign customers. Two models of satellite, the FSW-I and the FSW-II, have been used for this service. They have respective load capacities of 300 kg and 500 kg.

International users can rent the Chinese satellite or they can put their own devices onto it with a view to conducting load tests in space. Between 1987 and 1988 China provided the latter service for four French and German companies. By the end of 1987 forty companies in fifteen countries had asked China to launch satellites on their behalf.

SECTION IV

RURAL PRODUCTION

CHAPTER 17

Agriculture

I. AGRICULTURAL PRODUCTION

1. REFORM OF THE AGRICULTURAL SECTOR

After liberation China's agricultural production developed quickly. However serious set-backs were suffered in the late 1950s and the interruptions of the Cultural Revolution period adversely affected agricultural growth. Taking 1952 as 100, the country's index of gross agricultural output value in 1978 was 210.2. The growth in the intervening 26 years had been 110.2% with an average annual increase of 2.9%. Although this growth rate is slightly higher than most developing countries have experienced, it is not a rate that has been adequate in view of the demand for agricultural products generated by domestic economic construction and by the people's consumption needs.

By 1978 average per capita grain consumption was 319 kg, cotton 2.3 kg, oil-bearing crops 5.5 kg, pork, beef and mutton 9 kg and aquatic products 4.9 kg. These figures show that there had been only a small increase in consumption since the release of the 1957 consumption figures. Increase in peasants' income had been restricted by limited production growth. Average net income for each peasant in 1978 was only Rmb 133.6

Most peasants were restricted to merely keeping themselves adequately fed and clothed. The life of peasants in some areas was very difficult. It was against the background of this situation that the December 1978 Third Plenary Session decision was taken to adopt, in principle, the Decision of the Central Committee of the Communist Party of China on Some Questions Concerning the Acceleration of Agricultural Production (Draft).

Since 1979 adoption of the draft on Agricultural Production, measures for promoting growth in agricultural production have included:

(1)   Substantially Raising the Purchase Price of Agricultural Products

Compared with 1978, the 1987 purchase price of the country's agricultural products has experienced an average annual increase of 7.9%. Since 1979 peasants have been allowed to purchase and sell agricultural products and restrictions on the purchasing and marketing prices of a range of agricultural products have been lifted.

(2)   Adoption of the Contract Responsibility System

This system linked remuneration to output. It is a system that has had a far-reaching and profound impact on agricultural production. The establishment and popularisation of this system resulted in the household contract responsibility system. The typical form that this system takes is one where land is contracted to a peasant household and draught animals and medium-sized and small farm implements are purchased and privately owned by the household. After paying agricultural tax, fulfilling the task of selling an assigned quota of products to the State and contributing to the public reserve fund, the peasant retains the remaining income. This system clearly defines relations of interest between the State, the collective and the peasant household and it provides effective incentive for peasant production.

From the winter of 1984 further measures were taken to promote the output-related contract system. First, the land contract period was extended from the originally stipulated three to five years to 15 years and a land and fertiliser grading system was established and peasants were encouraged to carry out long-term land improvement. Second, the problem of adjusting land tenure in accord with population increase or decrease was addressed and third, contracted land scattered over different areas was, where possible, consolidated into one holding. Fourth, the transfer of land use right, with or without compensation, was allowed. This was done as a means of promoting land use by skilled land-tillers. And fifth, efforts were made to develop socialised services for the support of agricultural production. Peasant households require seeds, crop protection, irrigation and drainage facilities, storage facilities, processing, transport and marketing services and there is a need for stress to be laid on public welfare services that individual households are unable to provide.

(3)   Readjustment of the Rural Production Structure

The guide lines of one-sidedly stressing grain production were changed. Development of a variety of agricultural products was promoted (crop farming, forestry, livestock raising, fisheries and sideline production) and secondary and tertiary industries in rural areas, mainly township enterprises, were developed. The latter offered a solution to the problem of effectively using surplus agricultural workers while at the same time accumulating funds for agricultural development.

(4)   Increased State Input into Support for Agricultural Production

The State systematically expanded the production capacity of industry that serves agriculture and imported an appropriate amount of chemical fertilisers and other agricultural means of production. The latter served to compensate for insufficient domestic production. In 1987 the total amount of chemical fertiliser applied reached 19,993 million metric tons (calculated in terms of effective components), the gross motive power of agricultural machinery reached 248.4 billion watts and the total amount of power consumed in rural areas reached 65.9 billion kW. This represented an increase over 1978 consumption of 126.2%, 111.4% and 160.3% respectively.

(5)   Popularising the application of agricultural science and technology

Stress was laid on popularising the adoption of improved crop varieties, dryland farming, water-saving irrigation, crop plant protection, epidemic prevention for poultry and livestock and other advanced practical techniques. At the same time co-operation between scientific research, education and popularisation was strengthened and grass-roots service organisations were established forming a network of accessible technical services.

The measures outlined above played an important role in promoting peasant creativeness, providing peasant production incentives, improving the technical foundation of agricultural production and speeding up the development of agricultural production. In 1987 national gross agricultural output value totalled Rmb 467.6 billion (current year price), showing an increase of 76.8% over 1978 (calculated in terms of comparable price), with an average annual growth rate of 6.5% or 2.2 times the average annual growth rate experienced from 1953 to 1978.

The relatively fast growth of agricultural production resulted in a corresponding increase in the country's average per capita consumption of farm produce and in peasants' net income. In 1987 per capita consumption of major agricultural products was 377 kg of grain, an increase of 18.2% over 1978; 4 kg of cotton, an increase of 73.9%; 14.2 kg of oils, an increase of 158.2%; 18.5 kg of pork, beef and mutton, an increase of 105.6%; and 8.9 kg of aquatic products, an increase of 1.6%.

Together with the rapid growth in agricultural production, diversity of agricultural production also increased markedly. The proportion of crop farming in gross output value of agricultural production dropped from 76.7% in 1978 to 60.7% in 1987, while the proportion of forestry, animal husbandry, fishery and sideline production increased from 23.3% to 39.3%, an increase of 10 percentage points. The effect of this increased diversity is that the productivity of limited farmland has increased and hilly land, grassland and water resources have been developed and used.

In addition to increased diversity in agricultural production, rural production as a whole has also diversified. The proportion of agricultural production in the gross output value of rural areas dropped from 68.6% in 1978 to 49.6% in 1987, while that of rural industry, the building industry, transport and commerce rose from 31.4% to 50.4%, an increase of 19 percentage points. These figures show that rural production has changed in terms of its structure. It has changed from being mainly agricultural production to being mainly non-agricultural production.

2. CROP FARMING

In China crop farming is the most important type of agricultural production. Crop farming is divided into grain crops for consumption and industrial crops for production. Grain crops include grain (rice, wheat, maize, sorghum and millet), beans and potatoes. Industrial crops include cotton, oil-bearing crops, sugar-yielding crops, hemp and flax, cured tobacco, silkworm cocoons, tea and fruit production. The area planted to the two types of crops (consumption and industrial) makes up approximately 90% of the total area used for crop farming. The remaining 10% of land area used for crop farming is used for crops such as melons, vegetables, fodder and green manure. In the past grain production has been stressed. It was a policy that one-sidedly emphasised grain production at the cost of neglecting industrial and other crops. This was a policy that meant that land resources were not either fully or rationally used.

From 1979 all administrative levels of the government have adopted a series of economic policies and technical measures intended to promote the speedy development of industrial crops while maintaining steady growth in grain production. These measures have been:
(1)   Readjusting the areas sown to grain and those sown to industrial crops in such a manner that crops accord with local conditions and make rational use of

land resources. In the following nine years, the area sown to cereals decreased by 9.3 million hectares (a figure that includes some places that have inappropriately decreased grain production area). Areas released from grain production have been used for expanding industrial crop production. The ratio of area sown to cereals in terms of total area sown to crops fell from 80.3% in 1978 to 76.8% in 1987, while the ratio of industrial crops rose from 9.6% to 14.3%.

(2)   Substantially increasing per unit area crop production output. This has served to ease the tension between using land for cereal crops and using land for industrial crops. By popularising improved varieties, improving cultivation technique, increasing chemical fertilisers applied and strengthening field management, in many localities the per unit area output has steadily increased. Calculated in terms of area sown, average per hectare yield of cereals came to 3,630 kg in 1987, an increase of 43.2% over the 2,535 kg 1978 figure. It represents an average annual increase of 4.1%. Cotton yield reached 870 kg in 1987, an increase of 93.3% over the 450 kg 1978 figure and the per unit area output of oil-bearing crops and sugar-yielding crops also increased substantially during the same period.

(3)   Where appropriate, grain has been imported from abroad. This has been a policy aimed at alleviating pressure on domestic grain production. From 1979 the State systematically increased the amount of grain imported. For five consecutive years the net import of grain exceeded 10 million metric tons. In 1982 net grain import reached a peak level of 14.9 million metric tons. This is a policy that has supported the domestic development of industrial crops.

In 1984 gross grain output reached 407.3 million metric tons, an increase of 33.6% over the 1978 grain output. It was an annual growth rate of 5% and the average grain output per person reached 396 kg, a figure approaching the world average. At the same time, the output of industrial crops also rose continuously. Gross output of cotton reached 6.3 million metric tons, an increase of 189% over 1978 and the output of all other industrial crops also increased substantially. But peasants in some areas found it difficult to buy the raw materials needed for grain or cotton production and they lacked suitable facilities for storage, transport and processing. These areas lagged far behind in production and income. And there was another very serious problem. With the implementation of policy that fixed the purchasing price for agricultural products higher than the marketing price, State expenditure for subsidising the price difference for agricultural product had climbed.

In 1985 the government sought to effect a further adjustment in rural production. The unwanted result was that areas sown to grain and cotton decreased considerably. In 1985 areas sown to grain decreased by 4 million hectares in this one year alone and peasants' material input into their grain and cotton fields also decreased. This situation inevitably led to a decline in per hectare yield. For grain a decline of 135 kg and for cotton 105 kg. It was quite clearly the simultaneous drop in the sown area and the per unit area output that resulted in an enormous reduction in gross output of grain and cotton. In 1985 gross output of grain was 379.1 million metric tons. Gross output of cotton was 4.1 million metric tons. This was a drop of 28.2 million metric tons and 2.1 million metric tons, or 6.9% and 33.7% respectively.

The unexpected reduction in grain and cotton output aroused nation-wide attention and concern. Measures were immediately put in place to remedy the situation. In 1986 area sown to grain and per unit area output began to increase. Compared with 1985, the 1987 area sown to grain increased by 2.4 million hectares and per hectare yield increased by 150 kg. Gross grain output rose to 404.7 million metric tons, but it was still 2.6 million metric tons lower than the 1984 yield.

In 1986 the area sown to cotton dropped further, but it began to increase in 1987 and by 1986 the per hectare yield of cotton had begun to rise. Gross cotton output in 1987 reached 4.2 million metric tons, but was still well behind the 1984 output figure.

Nevertheless, between 1979 and 1987 average annual growth rate for all grain and industrial crops (with the exception of jute, bluish dogbane and cured tobacco) was higher than that of the previous 26 years. The 1987 total output value of crops was Rmb 283.8 billion (current year price). This represented an increase of 54.6% over the 1978 figure (using comparable prices), or an average annual growth of 5%. It was a much higher growth rate than the 2.2% of the previous 26 years.

17:1 INCREASE IN OUTPUT OF GRAIN AND INDUSTRIAL CROPS

Unit: 10,000 metric tons

	Grain	Cotton	Oil-bearing crops	Sugar-cane	Tea-leaves	Cured tobacco
1952	16392	130.4	419.3	711.6	8.2	22.2
1957	19505	164.0	419.6	1039.2	11.2	25.6
1965	19453	209.8	362.5	1339.1	10.1	37.2
1978	30477	216.7	521.8	2111.6	26.8	105.2
1980	32056	270.7	769.1	2280.7	30.4	71.7
1984	40731	625.8	1191.0	3951.9	41.4	154.3
1985	37911	414.7	1578.4	5154.9	43.2	207.5
1986	39151	354.0	1473.8	5021.9	46.1	137.4
1987	40473	424.5	1527.8	4736.3	50.8	163.6

3. STATE FARMS

State farms are distributed in the vast rural areas and frontier regions of the nation's 27 provinces (excluding Taiwan) and autonomous regions and they can also be found in the suburbs of Beijing, Tianjin and Shanghai. As State-owned agro-economic entities, these State farms not only supply huge quantities of agricultural products, including grain, rubber and processed products, with their advanced production techniques and equipment, they play a demonstration role. This means that they promote the modernisation of agricultural production.

China's State farms were established in the early period after liberation and by 1987 State farms had 8 million workers and staff members, 8.3% of the total number of workers and employees in State enterprises. In 1987 State farms under the Department of State Farms and Land Reclamation were the largest agricultural production entities in China.

As a result of the adoption of economic reform policy, from the beginning of 1979 State farms have experienced their own process of reform. State farm reforms have consisted of:

... development and coexistence of diverse forms of ownership;

... universal implementation of the contract responsibility system with remuneration linked to output; and

... changes in farm leadership and management.

In the past the collective and individual economic activity of the State farms made up only a very small proportion of their production. This is no longer the case. Now certain pieces of land have been earmarked for use by families of workers and staff members who engage in household sideline production and sell their products. At the same time workers and staff who had professional skills have been allowed to 'retain their posts without drawing pay' while they engage in household full-time or part-time commodity production.

Since 1979 most State farms have reformed their original collective enterprises by gradually adopting the economic responsibility system, delegating full management decision-making power to collective enterprises and developing a diversified economy that accords with local conditions. After experimenting with this situation for some time, a rational division of labour grew up where State, collective and individual economies support and closely co-operate with one another to achieve joint development.

From 1983, inspired by the household output-related contract system used in rural areas, State farms introduced a household output-related contract responsibility system. State farm practice became that of contracting major production and management targets and the task of selling main products to households which then delivered a fixed amount of profit tax, depreciation charge, management fee and welfare fund contribution to the State farm. Households take care of their own production expenses. The State farm then no longer issues wages to workers and staff, but, though not receiving wages, workers have been allowed to retain their before contract wage grade entitlements and their entitlement to unified wage increases. After completing their delivery obligations and after deducting production expenses, contracted households keep all remaining income for their own use.

As a result of the popularity of the household output-related contract system, a large number of family farms have been established. These family farms are an economic entity managed by a household under the leadership of a State farm and their management integrates with the overall management of the State farm. They differ from a household output-related contract production entity in their relationship to the State farm and they differ in that they have more land and so are larger. The term of their contracted use of State land is longer. These family farms have large and medium-sized farm machinery and implements and other means of production that they have purchased. By the end of 1987 the number of family farms under the Department of State Farms and Land Reclamation had grown to 1 million with a labour force of 2 million, of which 1.7 million were workers and staff members. They accounted for 32.5% of total number of workers and staff under the Department of State Farms and Land Reclamation.

The success of the post reform decentralised management structure is reflected in State farm productivity figures. Calculated in terms of a constant price of 1980, gross industrial and agricultural output value of State farms under the Department of State Farms and Land Reclamation reached Rmb 21.4 billion in 1987: an increase 2.5 times that of 1978.

In addition to supplying food grain and grain for livestock breeding for the 11.4 million people attached to the nation's land reclamation enterprises, State farms delivered 4.6 million metric tons of commodity grain to the State. This tonnage was the same as the total amount of grain shipped to Beijing, Tianjin and Shanghai.

The percentage of marketable grain rose from 30.5% in 1978 to 52.1% in 1987, a rise substantially higher than the average level for rural areas. State farms also supplied significant quantities of cotton, rubber, poultry, eggs, milk, wool and other marketable farm produce. Losses were made prior to 1979, but by 1987 profits were being made. In 1987 total profit was Rmb 1.3 billion with taxes paid to the State amounting to Rmb 912 million. State farms also purchased 67,700 large and medium-sized tractors, 18,200 combine harvesters, 21,800 trucks, and a substantial amount of chemical fertilisers and irrigation and drainage equipment.

4. FORESTRY

China's forested area totals 115.3 million hectares. It accounts for only 12% of total land area.

In 1978 the output value of the forestry industry was Rmb 4.8 billion (current year price), accounting for only 3.4% of gross agricultural output value. The backwardness of forestry production has led to the acute shortage of timber and other forest products. Because the forestry industry cannot meet the demands made by national economic development, there has been further degradation of China's ecosystem. This has had an adverse effect on both agricultural production and people's living environment.

In order to speed up the development of forestry production, the Central Committee of the Chinese Communist Party and the State Council adopted a series of measures. These have been:

- strengthening forestry legislation, stopping indiscriminate felling of trees and rigorously enforcing forest management and protection;
- fixing the ownership of forests, marking out private mountain plots and establishing a responsibility system to encourage peasants to plant trees in mountain areas;
- launching an afforestation campaign, encouraging the planting of trees in town and country and planting shelter belts;
- readjusting the price of timber, tightening control of the timber market and cracking down on all illegal activities in forestry;
- stabilising the allowed amount of timber to be felled, increasing the import of timber and pulp and raising the timber utilisation rate;

- ... adjusting the structure of the forests, vigorously promoting the establishment of tree plantations for economic value, promoting fast growing species of trees and developing diversified production that will increase economic returns; and
- ... closing forested hills in order to protect trees and promoting afforestation, using planes to speed up the planting of barren hillsides.

These measures have already achieved marked results. Between 1979 and 1987 more than 36 million hectares of land were planted with trees, over 20 billion trees were planted on roadsides and by the side of fields, houses, rivers and ponds and 1.1 million hectares of farmland were covered with trees. After eight years of hard work the first phase shelter belt project has been completed on more than six million hectares of land in Northwest China, the northern part of North China and the western part of Northeast China. From 1986 work has been proceeding apace on the 10 year second phase of this shelter belt project and rapid progress has also been made in planting trees and growing grass in other areas of the Northeast. Successes have also been achieved in the northern desert areas where sand control has been effected and oasis areas have been expanded.

It is clear that afforestation has a positive ecological effect, but fast growing trees and trees of economic value also bring high economic returns. In addition to the two million hectares of fast growing trees that have been planted, by 1986 trees to be used for economic return had been planted on four million hectares of land. These are trees that produce fruit, nuts and industrial raw materials. The output of dried dates, walnuts, chestnuts, raw lacquer, peppers, aniseed and all types of woody oil-bearing plants has also increased considerably. In 1987 the economic value of all forestry products amounted to Rmb 22.2 billion (current year price), an increase of 71.9% over the 1978 total, representing an average annual growth of 6.2%. Proportion of gross agricultural output value had risen to 4.7%.

5. ANIMAL HUSBANDRY

In the past China's animal husbandry production has developed slowly. The output value of livestock breeding in 1978 was Rmb 20.9 billion (current year price), accounting for only 15% of gross agricultural output value. This was a figure that was not compatible with the rich resources for animal husbandry available in China and with society's growing need and demand for animal products.

The 1978 animal husbandry situation was attributable to many factors. Aside from factors existing in the agriculture sector as a whole, such as an irrational management system and low purchasing prices, the main problems were:
- ... Too much stress laid on increasing the number of pigs in a situation where pigs consume large amounts of grain. Attention was paid to the number of stock kept and the number of pigs marketed was neglected.
- ... Insufficient attention paid to raising herbivorous animals such as cattle and sheep and insufficient attention paid to raising poultry.
- ... Most grasslands were overtaxed by livestock raising with little attention being paid to improvement of resources.
- ... Under-utilisation of other sources of livestock feed such as oil-cakes and stalks.

... And an irrational approach to the nutritional aspect of feed hampering the fast growth of livestock and poultry.

In light of these problems the contract system, with remuneration linked to output, was introduced in animal husbandry and selling and marketing prices for animal products were readjusted. And from 1979 a host of new techno-economic measures were adopted in order to promote the development of animal husbandry. These measures consisted of the following:

(1) The production structure for animal foodstuffs was adjusted. While maintaining an appropriate increase in pig numbers, efforts were made to make better use of grassland resources and to increase the number of herbivorous animals and low grain consuming animals. Efforts were also made to raise the ratio of beef, mutton, poultry and rabbit in total meat output and to increase the output of eggs, milk and other animal products.

In 1987 national output of pork reached 18.3 million metric tons, an increase of 52.2% over the 1980 output, while the output of beef and mutton reached 1.5 million metric tons, an increase of 111.6% over 1980. The growth of the output of poultry and rabbit was, like beef, higher than that of pork. The growth of milk and eggs was even faster during this period. In 1987 milk output was 3.8 million metric tons, an increase of 18% over that of 1980 and egg output was 5.9 million metric tons, 130% higher than 1980.

(2) The assessment standard for pig raising was changed. While stress had been laid on the number of pigs in stock at the end of a given year, the emphasis was now placed on number of pigs slaughtered. And the feeding cycle was shortened. This was done through popularising mixed feed and other advanced techniques. In 1987, 261.8 million pigs were slaughtered, an increase of 100.7 million over 1978. And at the same time, the meat production rate of pigs was raised. The average amount of pork produced from each pig increased to 70.1 kg as against 53.3 kg in 1979.

(3) The number of draught animals and sheep was steadily increased. In pastoral areas the number of cattle, horses and sheep was increased through grassland improvement and rotation grazing. Other fodder resources were also improved. By the end of 1987 121.9 million head of cattle, horses, donkeys, mules and camels were in stock, 28 million head more than in 1978. This was an increase of 29.8%. The number of sheep in stock at the end of 1978 was 169.9 million. In 1981 the number reached a peak of 187.7 million and then for four successive years it dropped. In 1985 a new low of 155.9 million was reached. In 1987 sheep numbers increased to 180.3 million with the number of wool-producing sheep estimated at 102.7 million, accounting for 56.9%. Output of wool was affected by these changes in the number of sheep. The nation's wool output in 1978 was 148,000 metric tons and increased to 215,000 metric tons in 1982. It dropped to 189,000 metric tons in 1985 and rose again to 222,000 metric tons in 1987. Wool output increased by 49.7% in nine years, with an average annual increase of 4.6%.

In the period 1979 to 1987, average output of animal foodstuffs for each person rose steadily. In 1987 the output value of animal husbandry products was Rmb 106.6 billion (current year price). This is an increase of 122.8% over the 1978 figure. Also in 1987, average animal foodstuffs such as meat, eggs, milk and aquatic products per capita exceeded 38 kg. Promotion of animal husbandry has increased animal protein and other nutrients in people's diets and has built up their physique.

6. FISHERIES

In 1978 fishery output value came to Rmb 2.2 billion (current year price) accounting for 1.6% of gross agricultural output value. National output value of aquatic products was only 4.7 million metric tons. With the exception of a few fishing areas, the domestic shortage of aquatic products far surpassed that of pork, eggs and poultry.

The main causes of low aquatic production were:
- ... fishing without paying attention to fish breeding;
- ... excessive fishing in off-shore and inland waters leading to depletion of resources;
- ... off-shore beaches and inland rivers not being sufficiently used, leaving large expanses of water that is suitable for breeding either not used or poorly utilised; and
- ... poor management of fisheries and an irrational purchasing and marketing system for aquatic products.

In view of these problems departments concerned with aquatic resources adjusted their policies. They adopted the following measures:
- ... restricting off-shore and inland fishing;
- ... stipulating a period during which fishing is banned;
- ... improving breeding and cultivating techniques and importing new breeds and increasing mixed baits to raise the per unit area output of cultivation;
- ... encouraging increased investment in cultivated aquatic products;
- ... developing deep-sea fishing and opening new channels of fishing as a means of supplementing insufficient off-shore fishing resources;
- ... reforming the system of fishery management for State and collective enterprises;
- ... promoting the contract managerial responsibility system as a means of providing production incentive;
- ... making use of surface water to develop family fish breeding and breeding in rice fields, popularising intensive pond breeding and high density breeding, strengthening technical guidance and social services; and
- ... integrating production and marketing, reducing intermediate links and increasing the portion of aquatic products purchased by the State at negotiated prices and at market prices.

These measures brought tangible results and made it possible for fisheries to manage the difficult 1979-1981 period of readjustment. In 1982 output of aquatic products was restored. It passed the 1978 level. In 1984 it rose to 6.2 million metric tons and in March 1985 the government relaxed its policies for the acceleration of aquatic product development. The government also relaxed its control of prices of aquatic products. Market regulation was introduced. From 1985 the output of aquatic products increased substantially. In 1987 output climbed to 9.5 million metric tons. As a result of this large increase in output, the output value of fisheries rose to Rmb 22.5 billion and proportion of gross agricultural output value rose to 4.8%.

II. AGRICULTURE AND FOREIGN ECONOMIC RELATIONS

1. TECHNO-ECONOMIC CHANGE AND COOPERATION WITH OVERSEAS COUNTRIES

Since the introduction of economic reform policy, China's economic and technical exchange and cooperation with other countries has been substantially increased resulting in the following policies:

(1) Promotion of exchange and training of personnel and of cooperative experiments and research. Agricultural and forestry departments and relevant scientific research and educational institutions have sent specialised personnel abroad for research, advanced studies and to conduct joint research and foreign experts have been invited to come to China. They have given lectures and guidance.

(2) Importing technology, instruments, equipment and management expertise. This has been done with a view to raising the level of domestic agro-economic technology. Present realities and the ability for assimilation have been considered. The government has attached great importance to the practical effect of importing advanced foreign technology and management expertise. This has resulted in technology, equipment and management expertise imported from abroad during the 1980s promoting good production results. These imports, together with popularisation of attendant ideas, have included covering crops with plastic to provide large-scale hot-house cultivation of vegetables; the use of freeze-dried semen and artificial insemination for domestic animal breeding; embryonic implantation of cattle and sheep; remote sensing testing analysis in agriculture; spray irrigation of farmland; mechanised poultry and livestock raising; and processing of mixed feed.

Together with the import of agricultural technology, equipment and expertise, China has been exporting advanced agricultural techniques that have been adopted by other countries. These include rice hybrids, organic fertiliser, methane energy, fresh water fish raising, biological nitrogen fixation, irrigation and water conservation, biological control and veterinary acupuncture. China's rice transplanter, combine harvester and other agricultural machinery have also been well received abroad.

(3) Exchanging fine strains of animals and plants. Scope for exchange is extensive and involves grains and industrial crops, vegetables, fruit and timber trees, fodder grass, green manure, flowers, poultry, animals and fish. Foreign countries have shown a particular interest in hybrid rice, the soybean of Northeast China, 'Meishan' pig and freshwater fish. Using exchange agreements, China has imported large numbers of good strains of animals and plants. Subsequent hybrid varieties of stock resulting from the union of imported strains with domestic strains have been systematically popularised.

Agricultural techno-economic exchange and cooperation between China and United Nations organisations and national regional associations has also developed rapidly. Since the 1980s, China has participated in increasing numbers of exchanges and cooperation in agricultural techniques organised by international organisations. And at the same time, China has organised a number of international symposiums on agricultural economic techniques. Trusted by the United Nations Food and Agriculture Organisation and other international organisations, China has held many training classes on methane production, freshwater fishing, silkworm raising, hybrid rice and veterinary acupuncture.

2. FOREIGN TRADE AND THE USE OF FOREIGN FUNDS

(1) Foreign Trade

Export of agricultural products and processed products makes up a large proportion of total volume of exports. In most years from the 1950s to the 1970s, the proportion reached more than 70%. Since the 1980s, with the sharp increase in the export of manufactured goods using minerals as raw materials, the proportion of export of agricultural products and agricultural processed products has declined, but absolute volume of export has risen annually. In 1986 the country's export volume of agricultural products reached $US5.2 billion and the export volume of processed products using agricultural products as raw materials was $US8.5 billion. This was an increase of 93.3% and 148.1% respectively over the 1978 figure, an average annual increase of 8.6% and 12%. In terms of total volume of exports, the proportion of agricultural products was 19.3% and that of processed products using agricultural products as raw materials was 31.3%. Exported agricultural products were mainly live pigs, live poultry, frozen beef and pork, aquatic products, rice, soybean, vegetables, fruit, tea leaves, goat skin, cotton and silk. Exported processed products using agricultural products as raw materials, included tinned food, cotton yarn, cotton cloth, silks and satins, woollen goods, blankets, carpets and clothing.

As a means of supplementing domestic production and as a means of enriching varieties, grain, sugar, coffee, cocoa, natural rubber, timber, wool, edible vegetable oil and pesticides were imported. In 1987 the products with a large import volume were wheat, 13.2 million metric tons; maize, 1.5 million metric tons; sugar, 1.8 million metric tons; natural rubber 350,000 metric tons; timber, 6.5 million cubic metres; wool, 151,000 metric tons; and pesticides, 10,000 metric tons.

(2) Use of Foreign Funds

With constantly increasing opening to the outside world, the amount of foreign funds used by China have steadily increased. These funds have been used for scientific research, education, production and agricultural construction. Between 1981 and 1985, foreign funds used by departments under the Ministry of Agriculture totalled over $US2 billion. Since 1986 the use of foreign funds in agriculture has increased further. The World Bank has offered long-term, low-interest loans for agricultural development and financial aid loans for agricultural development projects have also been provided by the United Nations Food and

Agriculture Organisation, the World Food Programme, the International Fund for Agricultural Development, the European Community, Canada, Germany, Australia, Japan, the United States, Belgium, Sweden, Kuwait and Denmark. The use of foreign funds for agricultural projects falls into four categories:

- ... Production projects aimed at raising the level of production. These projects account for 40% of agricultural projects using foreign funds.
- ... Scientific and technological projects aimed at raising the scientific and technological level and the training of personnel. This use accounts for 8% of funds.
- ... Aid rendered gratis aimed at solving basic production problems and at improving the lives of people in poverty-stricken areas. This accounts for around 9% of foreign funds used.
- ... And commercial projects using foreign funds in the form of joint ventures, cooperative enterprises and compensation trade. These account for more than 40% of foreign funds used in agriculture.

3. AGRICULTURAL AID TO OTHER COUNTRIES AND OVERSEAS JOINT VENTURES

(1) Agricultural Aid

Since the 1950s, China has offered aid to friendly third world countries. The scope of this aid has gradually increased.

Between 1979 and 1986 164 foreign agricultural aid projects were conducted, 92 in crop farming and animal husbandry and the remainder in forestry, fisheries and land reclamation. Among the countries which received aid, 38 were in Asia, 118 in Africa and the remainder were in the South Pacific and Latin America. China has also helped a number of African countries to develop methane-generating projects and students from third world countries have been assisted through training classes and through being able to study in China. China has also donated large quantities of grain and other consumer products, as well as agricultural means of production, to countries in Africa and South Asia stricken by natural calamities such as drought, floods and locust attacks.

In order to promote the work of foreign agricultural aid, the agricultural and forestry departments of most provinces, centrally administered municipalities and autonomous regions have established foreign aid offices. Foreign aid organisations under the former Ministry of Agriculture and Forestry have been expanded into the Corporation of International Cooperation in Agriculture, Animal Husbandry and Fisheries and the Corporation of International Cooperation in Forestry. The economic responsibility system has now been introduced into foreign aid projects and free aid is being gradually replaced by low-interest or interest-free loans.

(2) Overseas Joint Ventures

During the 1980s China undertook various agricultural projects abroad. These have included engineering construction projects, labour service cooperation, training personnel and establishing joint ventures in other countries.

Since 1981 China has explored new fields of cooperation with nearly 40 countries. These fields have included fishing, forestry and animal husbandry. The projects have been used for the development of deep-sea fishing, joint exploitation of forests and the establishment of joint ventures for grazing ground, breeding farms for aquatic products and facilities that promote agricultural production and processing.

China has established some sole Chinese-funded fishing enterprises through purchasing fishing permits or, when cooperating in fishing ventures, has assisted in fishery development. On several occasions the marine fishing fleet has been sent to the waters of countries in Africa, North America, the Middle East and Oceania to engage in fishing and other operations. In 1986 the marine fishing fleet had 33 vessels that caught over 40,000 metric tons of fish with 7,000 metric tons being used to supply the domestic market.

Overseas forestry ventures have reflected the domestic need for temperate zone coniferous timber, hardwood and other kinds of timber for the plywood industry and furniture, building and shipbuilding industries. To this end sole Chinese ventures and joint ventures have been established in South America, Oceania and Africa where a suitable climate exists for the exploitation of temperate zone forests. These ventures have provided reliable timber imports.

III. FUTURE PROSPECTS FOR AGRICULTURAL DEVELOPMENT

1. EXISTING PROBLEMS

The major problems in agriculture are:

(1) An acute shortage of agricultural products. Gross output of agricultural products has increased substantially since the beginning of the 1980s. But in spite of this situation, average per capita output of major agricultural products is still very low. Average grain output per person is lower than world average and the gap in the output of meat, milk, eggs, aquatic products and fruit is even larger. In the 1980s farmland was reduced by some 450,000 hectares annually and the production of grain and other crops has been increasingly threatened by shortage of farmland. Meanwhile, population increase has been rapid.

(2) The level of agricultural production is relatively low. This situation is demonstrated by the fact that the per unit area output of grain, cotton and oil-bearing crops is higher than world average, but still falls far behind that of agriculturally developed countries. The rate of fodder return in animal husbandry is around one-third lower than in developed countries. In most areas agricultural production still relies chiefly on manual labour and draught animals. Although the amount of chemical fertiliser applied to each hectare of land reached an average of 208.4 kg, approaching the level of agriculturally developed countries, the proportion of nitrogenous fertiliser, phosphate fertiliser and potassium fertiliser is not at all rational, making it impossible to substantially increase production.

(3) Scientific research, education and the popularisation of advanced agricultural technology are rather backward. Research in basic agricultural science is rather weak with many results of scientific research not being applied to production. It is estimated that science and technology play only a 30% role in

increasing agricultural production. Agricultural education is backward and organisation of the popularisation of agro-techniques is by no means perfect. Agricultural labourers have a low level of education.

(4)   The market mechanism is immature. The relationship between the purchasing of agricultural products and the marketing system and prices is not a rational one. Peasants who engage in the production of grain, cotton and other major agricultural products make profits that are too low and so development of the production of vital agricultural products is adversely affected.

2.   FUTURE MEASURES TO BE ADOPTED

(1)   A steady improvement in economic performance through sustained growth in the rural economy and productivity dependent increases in peasant income.

(2)   Agricultural production to be developed to the point where the needs of all people are comfortably met. In order to satisfy a comfortable standard of living, average per capita grain output will need to reach 400 kg or possibly 425 kg. Average amount of meat available for per capita consumption should exceed 25 kg and eggs, milk and aquatic products should bring total animal foodstuffs consumed to 50 kg. This food pattern would increase the proportion of people's nutritional needs drawn from animal foodstuffs. Attention should also be paid to increasing processed agricultural products.

(3)   Substantially raising the modernisation level of agricultural production. The major operations in crop farming, forestry, animal husbandry and fisheries are all to be mechanised. The proportion of farmland ploughed by tractors and that sown by machines should reach 70% and 60% respectively. Areas irrigated by mechanical means and electrically-operated facilities should account for more than 60% of irrigated areas. The amount of chemical fertiliser applied should total 32 million metric tons, an increase of more than 60% over the 1987 figure. Consumption of electricity, oil, pesticides and plastic sheeting for the protection of agricultural crops in rural areas should also be substantially increased.

(4)   Planned guidance of the agricultural labour force to promote transfer of surplus labourers into non-agricultural production. By the end of the century the number of people employed in township enterprises will total 170-200 million. This situation, plus employment in other non-agricultural undertakings, will promote higher rural labour productivity. Efforts must be made to speed up the building of rural townships and township infrastructure.

Future policies and measures must rely on the intensive development of natural resources and rural production. In future it will be basic agricultural policy to make the utmost effort to develop, utilise and protect cultivated land, grassland, hilly areas and water resources fit for production of aquatic products. Land-saving crops must be developed and grain-saving aquatic breeding should be steadily improved. Agricultural production should be based on high and stable output, good product quality, high efficiency and low consumption of raw materials. To this end the following measures should be adopted:

(i)   New sources for obtaining agricultural funds should be opened up. From 1989 these sources will include collecting agricultural development funds from extra-budgetary capital construction investments; collecting charges for improvement in grain production techniques from departments concerned; collecting a grain consumption tax from foodstuff production enterprises that receive their grain supply at State prices; using the income from increased township enterprise tax for agricultural development; using all tax income from individual rural businessmen, private enterprises and the regulatory tax levied on individuals; and allocating a certain proportion of World Bank loans to agricultural development. In addition, from 1991 the government plans to substantially increase budgeted investment in agricultural capital construction projects. Also, through the regulation of economic levers, peasants will be encouraged to increase input for agricultural production and a system of collective peasant labour will be restored and improved. Each agricultural labourer will be required to spend at least 15 work days on obligatory labour, mainly on water conservation projects.

(ii) Attention will be paid to improving circulation within the rural commodity economy. In line with the principle of exchange of equal values between the agricultural and industrial sectors of the economy, the 'scissors' price difference between industrial and agricultural products, which is still too large, will be gradually narrowed. Peasants' enthusiasm for increasing the production of marketable agricultural products will be encouraged by increasing the benefits from agricultural production, particularly from grain and cotton production.

Rational price parities between agricultural products should be established as early as possible so that profit obtained from different kinds of products will be balanced. This will promote coordinated development of the production of different types of products.

In order to protect the interests of consumers, the purchasing and marketing prices of major agricultural products should be systematically rationalised.

(iii) Scientific research and agricultural education should be promoted. Attention should be paid to raising the quality of the agricultural labour force. This should be done with the aim of promoting intensive management of agricultural production. Scientific and technological progress should have pride of place in the development of agricultural production. Reform of the system of agricultural science and technology and the technical service system should be accelerated.

(iv) In areas where township enterprises flourish and in areas where there is more land and less population, the development of specialised households engaged in crop farming or aquatic production should be encouraged. On the basis of raising land productivity and the rate of fodder return, economy of scale should be considered. This would solve some production problems arising from implementation of the household output-related contract system.

(v) More effective economic, administrative and legal measures should be adopted to keep the country's total population below 1.25 billion by the end of this century. Particular stress should be placed on controlling the above-plan increase in the rural population.

(vii) Taking up good farmland for building industrial enterprises, communication facilities and urban and rural housing must be avoided. Efforts must be made to ensure that the area of farmland used for building purposes is smaller than newly reclaimed farmland. The decrease in average per capita farmland must be controlled and a consistent effort must be made to improve the ecological environment while developing agriculture.

(viii) Promotion of foreign economic relations and the expansion of agricultural international exchange and cooperation. Exchange and cooperation between governments, non-governmental organisations and international organisations should be strengthened. While developing domestic agriculture, importation of agricultural products and agricultural means of production that are in short supply domestically should be encouraged. And agricultural exports should be vigorously promoted. Aid to friendly third world countries should continue and improvement in the quality and economic performance of aid projects should be promoted. China should actively import and make use of diverse forms of foreign funds and should apply advanced technologies, equipment and management expertise drawn from foreign countries.

CHAPTER 18

Township Enterprise Production

I. TOWNSHIP ENTERPRISES

China has a population that exceeds 1 billion and 80% of this population live in the countryside. They produce predominantly through the use of manual labour. This is a situation that means that modernisation policy must focus on the countryside. It must enable China's farmers to become wealthy as soon as possible. There must be a change in the situation where the rural population engaged in agricultural production constitutes the majority, to one where the rural population engaged in non-agricultural production is the majority. China's rural economy must become an integral part of a highly developed national commodity exchange sector. If this task is not fulfilled, China's modernisation will not succeed.

Township enterprises have played a particularly important role in developing the rural economy. The enterprises are classified according to economic sectors. They include agriculture, industry, construction, transport, commerce, catering and service trades and of these, industry represents the main grouping. It includes township-run enterprises, village-run enterprises, enterprises jointly run by farmer households and individually run enterprises. Township and village enterprises are the largest of this group. Since 1978 township enterprises have developed quickly. They represent one of the major achievements of rural reform.

1. THE POSITION OF TOWNSHIP ENTERPRISES IN THE NATIONAL ECONOMY

The rapid development of township enterprises has meant that previously insignificant rural household sideline production has now become an economic force that occupies an important position in the rural economy and indeed in the national economy. By 1987 there were an estimated 17.5 million township enterprises with a fixed asset value of Rmb 123.3 billion and a workforce of 88 million people. Total output value was Rmb 476.4 billion, accounting for 20.9% of national output value and 50.5% of gross rural output value. For the first time township enterprise output value was greater than total agricultural output value. Township industrial output value was Rmb 324.4 billion. This was a figure that represented 23.5% of national industrial output value.

Many of the products of township industries account for a substantial portion of the national industrial output value for that product. For example, in 1987 figures township production of raw coal represented 31.9% of national coal output, cement 25.5%, machine-made paper and paperboard 37%, garments

46%, brick and tile and small and medium-sized farm tools over 90%. Township construction workers represented 57% of all construction workers and housing area completed accounted for 43% of the national total. Taxes returned to the State by township enterprises accounted for 8.2% of State revenue and 10.4% of the various types of taxes collected. The export volume of township enterprises made up 12.7% of the national total.

2. THE HISTORY AND COMPOSITION OF TOWNSHIP ENTERPRISES

Township enterprises were originally collective enterprises run by people's communes, production brigades and teams. After 1978, with reform of the rural economic structure, farmers' jointly run enterprises and individually managed enterprises began to be established and by the end of 1984, the Chinese government had decided to rename commune production brigade operated enterprises and call them township enterprises.

People's commune production brigade operated enterprises had originated from rural sideline occupations. A survey conducted in 1954 revealed that there were more than 10 million full-time and part-time handicraft workers who produced an output value that exceeded Rmb 2 billion. When the people's communes were established in 1958 an edict was issued that 'the people's communes must run industry in a big way'. As a result of this edict a large number of commune-brigade-run enterprises were established taking up excessive rural labour power, but during the economic readjustment of the early 1960s a large number of the commune-brigade-run industries were suspended so as to guarantee a sufficient labour force for agricultural production. In 1963, after economic readjustment, the number of commune industrial enterprises was reduced. There had been 260,000 commune-brigade-run enterprises in 1958. By the end of 1963 this number had been reduced to 11,000 and commune industrial output value dropped from Rmb 6.2 billion to Rmb 420 million with this latter level being maintained for the next two or three years.

By 1966 there was a call for some small factories to be run by collectives in communes and this resulted in the gradual re-development of commune-brigade-run industries. In the early 1970s, in order to speed up agricultural mechanisation, a batch of what was called 'five small industries' were established i.e., small chemical fertiliser, machinery, iron and steel, coal, and cement industries. During the decade of the Cultural Revolution commune-brigade-run industries were regarded as leading to rural workers 'ignoring their proper occupation' and as 'taking the capitalist road'. Even so, by 1976 the output value of commune industries had still managed to reach Rmb 24.3 billion.

After 1978 the government promoted the development of commune enterprises by strengthening its guidance and support for them. With the introduction of the rural contract responsibility system and the attendant increase in agricultural productivity, it was possible for a section of the rural labour force to switch to industrial and other undertakings. This situation created conditions that promoted the development of township enterprises.

In the period 1978 to 1983 total output from township and village run enterprises increased at an average annual rate of 16.6%. In 1985 the government clearly stated that developing township enterprises was the inevitable course for revitalising China's rural economy and it put forward a guideline that contained a call for 'active support, reasonable planning, correct guidance and strengthened management'. Subsequently, in 1987 the total output value of township enterprises increased 4 times over 1983 output value, increasing at an average annual rate of 41.3%. This increase far outpaced any previous speed of development.

Since 1978 great changes have taken place in terms of the structure of enterprise ownership and in terms of composition of township enterprise production.

In terms of changes in ownership, in 1978 there was still no enterprise jointly run by farmer households and there were no individually run enterprises. At this time all enterprises were run either by the township or village collectives. After 1984 enterprises jointly run by farmer households and individually managed enterprises developed rapidly. In 1987, of the total output value of township enterprises, the output value of township and village enterprises accounted for 67.9%, that of enterprises jointly operated by farmer households 8.9% and that of individually managed enterprises 23.2%.

In terms of total industrial output value of township and village enterprises, the proportion of light industry increased and that of heavy industry declined and services provided by rural enterprises increased markedly, particularly in the area of transport.

3. SIZE OF TOWNSHIP ENTERPRISES

Township enterprises are usually small. There are a few enterprises with a workforce of over 1,000 people and an output value that reaches Rmb 100 million, but these are in the minority. In 1987 township enterprises had an average workforce of 57 workers and an output value of Rmb 434,000; village enterprises had an average 20 person workforce and output value of Rmb 121,400; enterprises jointly managed by farmer households, 7.8 workers and an output value of Rmb 35,800; individually run enterprises, 2.1 workers and an output value of Rmb 7,480. Because the number of individually managed enterprises accounted for 84.2% of the total (even though enterprise output value is low), it accounts for almost 25% of total output value.

4. OPERATION AND MANAGEMENT OF TOWNSHIP ENTERPRISES

In policy terms the administrative organs that exercise management of and give guidance to township enterprises are the Ministry of Agriculture and below the Ministry, township enterprise bureaus. The bureaus are directly under provincial, city level or county administrations.

Then, aside from the above administrative management of township enterprises, in townships and villages there are economic federations. These include economic commissions and industrial companies. Enterprises are required to return a prescribed proportion of their profits to the economic federation, but production, supply and marketing and human, financial and material resources are under enterprise control and it is the enterprise that assumes sole responsibility for profit and loss.

Household enterprises that are jointly managed and individually owned enterprises have to pay a prescribed quota of tax, but they enjoy full autonomy in terms of enterprise operation. These enterprises have a strong market orientation and attendant sense of competition. Township enterprises are given no tasks under State mandatory planning and they do not receive State investment or State supplied materials. Their production, supply and marketing are market regulated.

Because they are small, household enterprises that are jointly managed and individually owned enterprises have a simple internal management structure. This means that their rate of work efficiency is high. Their distribution system is closely linked with performance: when enterprises are well managed, individuals receive more income, and vice versa. If the enterprise is closed, its workers have to go home and again become farmers. Therefore, compared with State-owned enterprises, township enterprise workers tend to display a higher level of enthusiasm.

5. SOURCE OF FUNDS FOR TOWNSHIP ENTERPRISES

In the initial stage of their development township enterprises drew investment funds from the collective economic accumulation of the people's communes. With the expansion of the enterprises and the changes in economic and management methods, their source of funds became diversified. The present major source of funds are the enterprises' own accumulated funds and bank and credit co-operative loans.

In the past few years financial departments have supplied township enterprises with Rmb 70-80 billion per year. This has become their main source of funds even though there has been joint investment, non-government loans and labourers bringing funds with them for use as enterprise investment. In addition the shareholding system is now being tried out in enterprises.

18:1 FUNDING OF TOWNSHIP AND VILLAGE ENTERPRISE EXPANDED PRODUCTION

Unit - Rmb 1 million.

	1978	1980	1985	1986	1987
Enterprise profit used for expanding production	3080	4700	7940	8020	10010
Bank loans drawn	2200	5610	27780	40830	57810

With the rapid increase in the amount of bank loans, it became possible for the government to guide the development of township enterprises through credit policy. In 1987 banks and credit co-operatives implemented a policy of both guaranteeing and controlling credits: supporting export-oriented enterprises which produce products that find a ready market; supporting the technical transformation of enterprises; and of strictly controlling loans to third-class enterprises which yield poor economic results.

II. THE ROLE OF TOWNSHIP ENTERPRISES

1. *TRANSFORMATION OF THE COUNTRYSIDE FROM A SELF-SUPPORTING AND SEMI-SUPPORTING ECONOMY INTO A COMMODITY ECONOMY*

From 1949 to 1979 China followed the erroneous policy of 'taking grain as the key link'. This was a policy that limited satisfactory development of farming, forestry, animal husbandry, sideline occupations and fisheries.

Past policy meant that the 800 million farmers were confined to a limited amount of land to grow grain to feed the people. As a result, labour power and natural resources could not be utilised to the full and agricultural productivity was very low and less than a third of agricultural products were exchanged for peasant income. Between 1957 and 1978 an estimated 70% of agricultural products were produced for the farmers' own consumption. For the most part the rural economy remained a 'natural' economy.

The rapid expansion of township enterprises promoted the development of the division of labour in the countryside and caused industry, transport, commerce and construction to separate themselves from agriculture and become independent departments of production. The expansion of township enterprises changed the single-product economic structure that had been dominated by crop cultivation. It promoted the development of a rural commodity economy.

In the past few years, profound changes have taken place in the structure of the rural economy. From 1980 to 1987 the proportion of agricultural output value in terms of total output value dropped annually, while the proportion of non-agricultural output value rose annually. In terms of agricultural output value, the proportion of output value of crop cultivated declined, while that of forestry, animal husbandry, sideline occupations and fisheries rose.

18:2 CHANGES IN THE STRUCTURE OF THE RURAL ECONOMY

Unit as %

	Gross value of rural products	Output of agricultural production	Total Value of rural production	Total value value of rural construction, transport, commerce and catering trades
1980	100	68.9	19.5	11.6
1985	100	57.1	27.6	15.3
1987	100	49.6	34.8	15.6

CHANGES IN THE STRUCTURE OF THE RURAL ECONOMY

	Total value of agricultural production	Output value of crop cultivation	Output value of forestry and fisheries	Output value of animal husbandry and sideline occupations
1980	100	71.7	5.9	22.4
1985	100	63.0	8.7	28.3
1987	100	60.7	9.5	29.8

In 1980 total volume of agricultural and sideline products purchased and total value of transactions at urban and rural fairs totalled Rmb 107.8 billion. This figure represented 56% of the year's total agricultural output. The 1987 figure was Rmb 352.7 billion. It represented 75.4% of the year's total agricultural output value.

2. *ACCUMULATING FUNDS FOR AGRICULTURAL MODERNISATION*

China has a large population but limited land for cultivation. Under the past single-product economic structure, agricultural production developed very slowly. Moreover, with the 'price-scissors' difference between industrial and agricultural products, agriculture was denied any chance of accumulating investment funds that would be available to further its own development. This meant that it was difficult to improve and expand agricultural production.

Modernisation of agriculture requires substantial investment funds. According to the experience gained in some counties in southern Jiangsu, the initial mechanisation of every hectare of cultivated land requires approximately Rmb 4,500. Calculated according to this formula, the nation's 100 million hectares of land will require Rmb 450 billion of investment funding in order to meet initial mechanisation requirements. It is impossible for the State alone to provide such a large sum. This means that the countryside must be primarily self-reliant in terms of accumulating funds for its own development. Statistics indicate that between 1980 and 1987 total net profit invested by township enterprises amounted to Rmb 98.1 billion and that between 1980 and 1987 funds invested by township and village enterprises for the direct support of agriculture amounted to Rmb 9.8 billion.

The more developed township enterprises are, the more funds are available for the support of agriculture. For example in Suzhou city in Jiangsu Province, between 1979 and 1984, township industries spent Rmb 450 million on supporting agriculture. This sum was four times higher than the State's investment in agriculture in this area.

18:3 PROPORTION OF TOWNSHIP AND VILLAGE ENTERPRISE PROFITS USED FOR THE SUPPORT OF AGRICULTURAL PRODUCTION

	Net profit invested Rmb 1 billion	Funds used in support of agriculture Rmb 1 billion
1980	9.5	2.3
1981	10.0	1.7
1982	10.4	1.4
1983	10.5	1.4
1984	9.8	0.7
1985	13.1	0.9
1986	16.1	0.7
1987	18.9	0.9

3. PROVIDING JOB OPPORTUNITIES FOR THE SURPLUS RURAL LABOUR FORCE

China's population has grown very fast. In 1987, of the nation's 1.08 billion people, 857 million were in the countryside. This was an increase in the period since 1952 of 88% and 70.3% respectively.

In 1987 rural China had a labour force of 390 million (a 113.8% increase over the 1952 figure) and China has 100 million hectares of cultivated land. In terms of cultivated land there has been no area increase, rather, there has instead, during the past 30 years, been a decrease and, even if this reduction in cultivated land is not factored in, the per capita share of cultivated land in the countryside was 0.55 hectares in 1952 and only 0.26 hectares in 1987.

According to the present level of the productive forces, it is entirely possible for each rural labourer to be responsible for one hectare of cultivated land. This means that there actually are a huge number of surplus rural workers in the countryside. How to provide job opportunities for this surplus workforce and how to make full use of the rural labour resource is a problem that urgently requires a solution.

In light of China's actual conditions, the problem of turning the agricultural population into a non-agricultural population should be solved by the locality concerned. The agricultural population should flow into the following three areas:

... into forestry, animal husbandry and fisheries—a shift within agricultural production:

... into cities and industrial and mining areas:

... into township enterprises.

It is estimated that by the year 2000, China's rural labour force will have reached 450 million people. Labourers that can be absorbed by crop cultivation can be expected to exceed 30% of the total labour force, those absorbed by forestry, animal husbandry and fisheries less than 20% and those absorbed by cities and industrial and mining areas less than 10%. The remaining 40% (an estimated 180 million labourers) will need to be absorbed by township enterprises, particularly by township industries.

In 1987 there were 88 million people, 22.6% of the total rural workforce, working in township enterprises, nearly 60 million people more than in 1978. If the State had had to be responsible for providing employment for this number of workers, it would have needed an investment of Rmb 2,000 billion.

18:4 INCREASE IN NUMBER OF WORKERS AND STAFF EMPLOYED BY RURAL ENTERPRISES

Unit 1 million

	Township enterprises	Village enterprises	Joint enterprises	Individual enterprises
1978	12.6	15.6		
1983	15.7	16.7		
1984	18.8	21.0	5.2	7.0
1985	21.1	22.2	7.7	18.8
1986	22.7	22.7	8.3	25.6
1987	24.0	23.2	9.2	31.6

It is clear from the above table that the number of workers and staff in township enterprises mainly increased during the 1984-1987 period and that the number of workers and staff in individually run enterprises saw the largest increase.

A major feature of China's rural policy is to encourage farmers to leave the land, but not to leave the village and to enter factories, but not the cities. This is a policy that does not need State investment, but which is beneficial to a balanced distribution of population and to the rational distribution of the productive forces.

4. *INCREASING FARMERS' INCOMES AND IMPROVING THEIR MATERIAL AND CULTURAL LIFE*

Since 1978 the growth rate of farmers' per capita net income has outpaced that of urban workers. The result is that the living standard of farmers has been substantially improved. Apart from the growth of agricultural production and the rise in prices for agricultural products, the expansion of township enterprises and the increase in farmers' household sideline occupations have been important factors in improving the rural standard of living.

Statistics show that in 1987 wages drawn from township enterprises totalled Rmb 73.6 billion. This was an average of Rmb 835.7 for each township enterprise worker. In the same year the per capita net income of farmers totalled Rmb 463 billion (or Rmb 329 billion more than in 1978). This was an average of Rmb 85.9

for each farmer. At this time the wages of township enterprises accounted for 26.1% of the net increase in farmers' incomes.

In areas where township enterprises are reasonably developed 80% of farmers' incomes come from these enterprises. And township enterprises have also promoted the growth of household sideline occupations. They have indirectly increased farmers' incomes and allowed them to become rich within a relatively short period. In terms of per capita income, in the past ten years the structure of farmers' households has undergone considerable change. In 1978 farmers' households with an average per capita net income of over Rmb 400 accounted for only 2.4% of total farmers' households while farmers' households with an average per capita net income of less than Rmb 150 made up 65%.

It has also been the case that with the increase in income, the farmers' consumption pattern gradually shifted from one of having enough to feed and clothe themselves to one of living a well-off life. In 1978, only 12.5% was used for housing, articles for daily use and cultural life. By 1987 these figures had changed to 63.8% and 31.4%.

Township enterprises have not only increased farmer's personal incomes, they have also contributed to enriching their cultural life. Between 1989 and 1987 township and village enterprises' net profits amounted to Rmb 10.3 billion. This profit was used for the development of rural education, culture, public health, physical culture and other collective welfare undertakings. It was also funding that promoted the construction of rural market towns. Over 10,000 market towns took shape, serving as local economic, political and cultural centres.

5. ACCELERATING THE INDUSTRIAL MODERNISATION PROCESS

Some 70% of township enterprises are industrial enterprises. Their growth is very significant in terms of expediting industrial modernisation.

First, being small in scale, township industries require less investment and yield quick economic returns. Also, by relying on the strength of farmers and effectively using rural natural and labour resources, these enterprises promote industrial development that accords with local conditions.

Township development has not required investment by the State, but has accumulated funds for modernisation and for the State. Statistics show that between 1978 and 1987, township enterprises remitted Rmb 83 billion of taxes to the State. This amount represented 16.3% of net added State revenue.

Secondly, township enterprises have promoted realisation of the national goal of economic development. Using the figure for 1980, by the end of this century, China's total industrial and agricultural output value will have quadrupled.

Thirdly, division of labour and co-ordination between urban and rural industries has served to promote development of specialised industrial production.

Some cities have space restrictions. This has meant that when developing and extending their production many enterprises have followed the practice of extending product and spare parts production to rural areas. This is a practice that has not only supported township industries, it has also enabled urban enterprises to yield higher economic returns. In this context the Beijing General Washing Machine Plant can be taken as an example. This company has entrusted township enterprises with production of 98% of its components and parts requirements for production of the Bailan brand washing machine. In the past five years its output has increased almost 31-fold without an increase in the number of personnel and without the expansion of factory buildings. This situation has been cited as the 'Bailan road'.

Today co-ordination and a division of labour between urban and rural industrial enterprise is quite common. About 70-80% of township industries in Beijing, Shanghai and Tianjin have rendered services to urban industries. After distributing components and parts, an urban industrial enterprise releases some of its personnel and financial resources for the development of new products and for the production of high-grade, precision and sophisticated industrial products. Clearly this situation is of great significance in terms of speeding up industrial modernisation.

Fourth, the growth of township industries has improved industrial distribution and has broken the long-standing pattern whereby cities develop industries and rural areas develop agriculture. By combining industry with agriculture, and by combining cities with rural areas, China has taken a path that has particular Chinese characteristics.

6. PROMOTION OF FOREIGN ECONOMIC RELATIONS AND TRADE AND INCREASING FOREIGN EXCHANGE INCOME

With the expansion of township enterprises, a number of township enterprises, particularly those in coastal areas, have been processing materials that have been supplied by foreign businessmen. These enterprises have been assembling parts supplied by clients, undertaking joint ventures with foreign business interests, undertaking compensation trade and co-operative production and they have been processing in accord with buyers' samples. According to statistics, by 1987, 2,400 township enterprises were Chinese-foreign joint ventures and co-operative enterprises and 15,000 township enterprises were engaged in processing and assembly using supplied materials and co-operative agreements.

Though incomplete, statistics show that in 1987, township enterprises produced over 7,000 varieties of goods and had among their ranks 18,000 export-oriented enterprises that exported to 140 countries and regions. As noted, a number of export-oriented centres and enterprise groups have congregated in coastal provinces and cities and it is these centres and groups that have become the back-bone of township enterprises earning foreign exchange through exports. Statistics show that in 1987 township enterprises earned $US5 billion through product export and service charges and $US400 million through processing and assembly using supplied materials.

In 1988, in order to promote township enterprise commodity export, the State Council approved the Regulations on Some Policies Concerning Promotion of Township Enterprises' Foreign Exchange Earnings Through Export. This document was jointly formulated by the Ministry of Agriculture, the State Planning Commission, the Ministry of Foreign Economic Relations and Trade and the Ministry of Finance. The document granted preferential taxation treatment, retention of foreign exchange earnings, bank loans, and bonuses for workers and staff, to export-oriented township enterprises. At this point too, the trade-industry-agriculture associated export commodity production centre leading group was established. This centre was charged with formulating a development plan and major policies for the promotion of foreign exchange earnings through the export of township enterprise products.

III. THE FURTHER DEVELOPMENT OF TOWNSHIP ENTERPRISES

In China's rural areas there are huge resources that have not yet been rationally utilised. This means that there are good prospects for the development of agriculture, forestry, animal husbandry, sideline occupations and fisheries and for township enterprises.

A tentative assessment made by the Ministry of Agriculture estimates that by 1990 township enterprises will have absorbed a labour force of 110 million whose output value will have totalled Rmb 540 billion. Further estimates suggest that by the end of this century, township enterprise will have absorbed 170-200 million workers, i.e., 40% of the total rural labour force and that their output value will have amounted to Rmb 1,360-1,500 billion or 70-75% of total rural output value. It is with these figures in mind that it has been recognised that special attention must be paid to the following two problems.

1. THE RELATIONSHIP BETWEEN NON-AGRICULTURAL INDUSTRIES AND AGRICULTURE

The proportionate development of non-agricultural industries and agriculture, particularly grain production is a new problem that requires special attention. With a population of over 1 billion, the success of agricultural production, particularly grain production, is crucial. To stabilise agriculture the State has adopted a series of policies and measures:

(1) Not only should a part of township enterprise profit be used for agriculture, but township enterprises should increase their input into agriculture in such a manner that growth in agricultural production is sustained and consolidated.

(2) The promotion of the development of a number of industries that serve agricultural production, such as those that improve farm machinery, field management, the prevention and control of animal and plant disease and insect pests, and the storage of farm produce.

(3) The provision of social insurance for staff and workers (for example, a pension scheme).

(4) The promotion of circumstances whereby labourers in non-agricultural industries break away from agricultural production. This should be done so that farm production becomes concentrated in the hands of farm households that are good at agricultural production. The promotion of skilled management of agricultural production is necessary and too the creation of better conditions for specialisation.

(5) Less cultivated land should be occupied. Township enterprises will gradually be concentrated in rural market towns and industrial buildings will be constructed. The number of small-scale enterprises would increase and planned use of town space would be promoted.

(6) It will be necessary to prevent the spread of pollution. No-one is to be allowed to destroy the ecological environment.

2. THE RELATIONSHIP BETWEEN SPEED OF DEVELOPMENT AND TOWNSHIP ENTERPRISE EFFICIENCY

Total output value of township enterprises increased at a rapid rate. Between 1980 and 1986 total output value of township enterprises increased at an average annual rate of 24.6%. But now the economic return on township production has dropped markedly.

Between 1980 and 1986 the profit rate on output value increased at an average annual rate of 15.6% and the profit rate on funds decreased at an average rate of 14.6%, but in 1986 there was an even greater drop than in 1985. In 1986 there was a drop of 24.4% in terms of profit rate in proportion to output value and 26.9% in terms of profit rate in proportion to invested funds. Using sales costs figures, though labour consumption decreased, the growth of material consumption was higher than the rate in the decrease in labour consumption. Total costs rose. Enterprise budget deficits and the number of enterprises operating in the red climbed considerably. In 1980 there were 17,000 enterprises which were recording losses. Their deficits totalled Rmb 150 million. In 1986 the figure for the number of enterprises in the red jumped to 75,500 with a deficit totalling Rmb 1.4 billion. This experience means that it is important to be able to control growth rate and improve economic returns during the future course of township enterprise development.

In accord with current policy of 'paying close attention to benefits, raising quality, co-ordinating development and stabilising growth', it has been advised that the enterprises should be:

... Moving from the previous extensive development mode based on increasing input to using science and technology in order to achieve an equal emphasis on intensive and extensive based development.

... Moving from paying attention to growth of output value to paying attention to quality of product and to stressing economic, social and ecological benefits.

... Moving from a reliance on the domestic market to an emphasis on export markets. In short, seeking to use both the domestic market and world markets.

... Moving from decentralised management of enterprises to specialised co-ordination of production and to the development of various forms of enterprise production based on the scientific management that is necessary in a modern enterprise.

All of these areas can be summarised as a required shift from an extensive approach to an intensive approach to township enterprise development. Other necessary requirements of this process are listed as follows:

... separation of the function of government from that of the enterprise;
... further perfecting the management contract responsibility system and further separating ownership from management;
... improving the system of job responsibility;
... actively promoting the share co-operative system and opening up township enterprise fund sources; and
... giving administrative guidance through rationally readjusting product distribution in line with local conditions.

Township enterprises throughout the country will continue to be divided into five regional types:

(1) Enterprises in suburban areas of large and medium-sized cities. These enterprises both rely on and serve the cities. They actively integrate with urban enterprises that are often much more technologically developed.

(2) Enterprises that sustain export through import. These are often located in coastal areas. They are likely to develop labour-intensive and processing industries and to expand their export earnings.

(3) Pastoral and semi-pastoral areas that will develop local natural resources and process animal by-products.

(4) Agricultural production areas that will develop multi-purpose processing industries using agricultural and sideline products as raw materials. It is expected that these industries will integrate agriculture, industry and commerce and that they will streamline crop production and animal breeding and processing.

(5) Mountainous and hilly areas that will develop their mineral and biological resources.

Enterprise specialisation will be promoted through associations between enterprises. Enterprise conglomerates and groups can be established. These conglomerates and groups can make use of production advantages and can combine scientific research with production. Also, by making full use of advantages in terms of supply and marketing, township enterprises will foster and benefit from market information networks. And by focusing attention on enterprise management and administration, the quality of their products will be raised. Production of low quality products should be eliminated and a quality inspection system should be established. Meanwhile close attention should be paid to safety in production and the prevention and control of pollution.

SECTION V

FOREIGN INVESTMENT

CHAPTER 19

Foreign Economic and Technical Cooperation

I. OPEN DOOR POLICY

China has had an open door to the outside world since 1979. From this time on it has been State policy to develop foreign economic and technical cooperation. With economic reform came Chinese government recognition that socialist modernisation needs to utilise two resources—domestic resources and foreign resources and that it needs two types of market—a domestic market and a foreign market. This recognition has meant that, while adhering to the principle of 'equality and mutual-benefit, striving for actual effect, with diversified forms and co-development', China has for the last decade, been developing foreign economic and technical cooperation. The form that this has taken includes the use of both direct and indirect investment, import of technology, projects based on foreign contracts, labour service cooperation, investment abroad and production cooperation.

To date the main forms adopted for the use of foreign investment have been (1) absorption of direct foreign investment and (2) borrowing from foreign sources.

1. DIRECT FOREIGN INVESTMENT

Absorption of direct foreign investment has taken the following forms:

(1) Sino-foreign Joint Ventures

These are foreign companies, enterprises and other organisations or individuals who join with Chinese companies, enterprises or organisations to establish joint ventures in which each party enjoys profits and each party bears the business risks. The undertakings must accord with the Law of the People's Republic of China on Chinese-foreign Joint Ventures. The companies are equity joint ventures with limited-liability. They have the status of a legal person (entity). They have been the most usual channel for China's absorption of direct foreign investment.

(2) Sino-foreign Cooperative Enterprises

These are contractual ventures that operate according to the principle of equality and mutual benefit. In these ventures China has provided the land, factory buildings, labour services and equipment, facilities and technology. The foreign investor provides funds, technology, equipment, management experience and raw and semi-finished materials. Cooperative arrangements are flexible and they adapt well to Chinese conditions. This has meant that they have enjoyed encouraging development in recent years.

(3)   Sole-foreign Invested Enterprises

These enterprises have been invested in and operated solely by the foreign investor. The foreign businessman has operated the enterprise on an independent basis and the foreign investor has assumed responsibility for profit and loss. Profit belongs to the foreign investor. China provides land, raw and semi-finished materials and factory buildings for these enterprises and, in accord with State stipulations, collects reasonable expenses. For its part, the foreign enterprise must abide by relevant Chinese policy, laws and decrees and must pay tax to the Chinese government.

(4)   Compensation Trade

Compensation trade refers to credit sales of technology, equipment and raw and semi-finished materials by the foreign investor. The Chinese interest uses the technology, equipment and raw and semi-finished materials as principal and using the product it produces, or other products, repays the credit sale in instalments. This is a special use of foreign investment. It is a credit sale that is repaid by barter. It is also a form of exchange that effectively fuses commodity trade, technology trade and credit services. This form of foreign investment has been most welcome, especially in relation to investment in national defence, military industries and mineral resource exploration.

(5)   Leasing Arrangements

Leasing arrangements are a special form of raising funds. The Chinese side rents technologically advanced foreign owned mechanical equipment. In practice, the renter (usually it is a Chinese leasing company) solicits mechanical equipment according to the need of its Chinese customer and then rents the equipment for use by the customer. In terms of the law, the situation is that the renter (the Chinese leasing company) has temporary ownership over the mechanical equipment while the Chinese leasing company customer has the right to use of the equipment. All parties are regarded as independent legal entities.

(6)   Processing Supplied Materials and Assembling Supplied Parts

This is a cooperative form of foreign investment use. The Chinese side accepts funds, technology, equipment, parts and components and raw and supplementary materials provided by the foreign partner. The Chinese side then processes or assembles these into products. It must do this in accord with the specifications demanded by the foreign interest. The finished product is made available to the foreign interest. The Chinese side earns processing fees.

At the end of the day the foreign equipment that has been supplied is refunded to the foreign interest using the processing fees due to the Chinese party.

China is rich in labour resources and so making use of foreign investment in this manner is a very suitable approach. This form of investment is one that has been successful in developing foreign processing and assembly production along China's coastal regions.

(7) Co-Development

Co-development is the term used to cover co-prospecting and co-mining of China's oil, coal, iron and other energy and mineral resources. The foreign investor provides the funds, technology and equipment.

Co-development has usually been divided into two stages. The first stage has been the geophysical prospecting stage where expenses are paid by the foreign interest and the second stage has been the prospecting development stage that operates through inviting bids for joint investment in development of the resource. It is in the second stage that the Chinese side selects its foreign co-operator, but it is only those who joined the first stage who are entitled to bid.

After entering commercialised production the Chinese side retains a fixed proportion of earnings (minus operating costs).

2. FOREIGN LOANS

Foreign funds have been borrowed in the following forms:

(1) Government Loans

Often loans from foreign governments have been transferred by that government to the foreign interest involved in a given project. These funds are to be used as credit funds for commodity export for which the Chinese government, after consultation with the foreign government, has signed a contract. The Chinese government has then been responsible for repayment of loan principal and any interest due. Usually these loans have been interest-free or they have carried medium or low rates of interest.

(2) Loans from International Financial Organisations

These loans have been provided by international financial organisations including the World Bank, the International Monetary Fund, the International Development Association and the International Agricultural Development Fund.

(3) Bank Loans

These loans have been borrowed from foreign private banks or from international banks. They are also called commercial loans. If China's State-owned enterprises have sought loans from foreign banks, they have been required to report to the Chinese government for approval and then the Bank of China has assisted them with their business negotiations.

Foreign invested enterprises can contact foreign banks by themselves if they want to borrow from foreign banks and the Chinese government will not interfere in their business dealings.

(4) Bond Issues

This is a process of obtaining funds through issuing bonds to foreign countries. The international bond market is used and the funds of the host country or an international currency recognised by both parties is used to assess the face value of the bonds.

(5) Export Credit

Export credits are subsidised loans extended to China by the banks of a commodity exporting country. The loans have been negotiated with the support of the exporting country's government. These loans have been in the form of either seller's credit or buyer's credit.

II. MANAGEMENT, EXAMINATION AND APPROVAL PROCEDURES APPLIED TO THE USE OF FOREIGN FUNDS

1. MACRO-MANAGEMENT OF FOREIGN INVESTMENT

Macro- management of foreign investment has aimed to guide foreign investment input, to offer rational control over the scale of foreign investment use, to improve investment climate and to coordinate the interests of both central and local authorities. The intention has been to provide flexibility, to promote diversified management measures for foreign investment and to gain maximum benefit from the investment. To this end the State Council has established the Leading Group for Foreign Investment Works.

The Leading Group has the responsibility for effecting national coordination and management of foreign investment use. The Group is in the charge of a relevant member of the State Council and its membership includes responsible personnel drawn from the State Planning Commission, the Ministry of Foreign Economic Relations and Trade, the Ministry of Finance, the People's Bank of China, the Ministry of Labour, the Ministry of Personnel, the State General Administration of Customs, the State Administration of Industry and Commerce and the State Administration of Exchange. The Group exercises considerable authority.

With regard to planning, examination and approval of foreign investment use, the Leading Group has made clear and definite divisions of labour among relevant ministries. Similarly it has made clear and definite divisions of labour with regard to the management of foreign-invested enterprises, the supply of raw and semi-finished materials and the balance of foreign exchange. It is in this way that China's foreign investment management has been and will be highly effective in addressing both China's national interests and the interests of international investors.

2. MICRO-MANAGEMENT OF FOREIGN INVESTMENT

Based on their own situation, provinces and cities have established their own service centres to attend to the needs of foreign investors.

Within the scope permitted by Chinese law, regulations and contracts, foreign business interests have been given enough decision-making power over their productive operations to allow them to engage in successful economic opera-

They have had full decision-making power in the fields of business policy decisions, labour and wages, the raising of funds and over the circulation of commodities. They have also been given preferential consideration when it comes to the supply of energy and the supply of raw and semi-finished materials.

3. EXAMINATION AND APPROVAL PROCEDURES

All foreign business interests seeking to invest in enterprises in China have had to undergo a procedure of examination and approval for their project. It is through these examination and approval procedures that the central government has been able to realise macro-management of foreign economic enterprise investment.

(1)   Examination and Approval of Sino-foreign Joint Venture Enterprises

When establishing a joint venture, the Chinese company must report its intention to the Ministry of Foreign Economic Relations and Trade and it must seek authorisation for its intended joint venture project.

Authorisation is gained through the following process:

(i) Presenting a suggestion report on the project (also referred to as the report for establishing the project) to the relevant and responsible department. The department will then report on the project and ask for examination and approval by the relevant planning department.

Projects involving relatively large amounts of investment funding (i.e., above norm investment funding) must seek and obtain approval of the State Planning Commission together with the Ministry of Foreign Economic Relations and Trade, the Ministry of Finance and the management departments of the relevant province, autonomous region or municipality directly under central authority.

Projects with a smaller amount of intended investment (below norm funding) and projects not involved directly in production (and so not needing to be fitted into a national production balance), can have their projects examined and approved by the authorities of provinces or autonomous regions or by municipal authorities when the city is under central authority or is separately listed, is one of the 14 coastal open cities, or is designated as a Special Economic Zone. In addition, these projects may also have their ventures approved by relevant ministries and bureaus of the State Council.

Once approval for the intended venture has been sought and obtained, a feasibility study can be undertaken.

In a situation where a foreign interest in a joint venture has found it difficult to find a Chinese partner for an intended joint venture project, it can forward a suggestion report to the Chinese Ministry of Foreign Economic Relations and Trade or it can use the services of the trust, investment and consultant companies of China. A foreign interest can also seek help through China's offices in foreign countries, while commodity exhibitions and investment symposiums offered by the Chinese government also provide promising paths for initiating joint venture investment.

(ii) Presenting a Report on the Feasibility Study. After approval has been given for the intended joint venture project, both sides must jointly complete a report based on their feasibility study. This report must include an analysis of general feasibility of the project and it must include the manner in which the technological

and economic aspects of the joint venture project are to be implemented. Examination and approval of the report on the feasibility study then parallels the process undertaken when seeking examination and approval of the suggestion report.

Once the report on the feasibility study has been approved, partners in the joint venture are free to hold further discussions on implementation of their project and they are free to sign formal documents including agreement documents, contracts and articles of association.

(iii) Seeking Examination and Approval of Contracts. Articles of association are fixed through the use of consultation and once they have been fixed, they are formally signed by the parties to the joint venture. The Articles are in three copies and the Chinese party must then take the responsibility of sending them, and all documents concerning the establishment of the joint venture, for examination and approval by relative administrative departments.

As in the case of suggestion and feasibility reports, if the intended project is not above norm in terms of funds to be invested or is a non-productive project and so does not need central State approval, contract approval can be sought from provincial, autonomous region or municipal level government.

Together with the suggestion and feasibility study reports, documents presented for approval at this juncture are the agreement, contract and articles of association (all formally signed by an authorised representative of the parties to the joint venture) and the approval documents for the suggestion and feasibility reports. Name of the chairman, vice-chairmen and directors of the joint venture enterprises must then also be presented.

(iv) Receipt of an Approval Certificate. Examining and approving departments must give an official written reply to an application for establishment of a joint venture enterprise within three months. This period begins from the point of receipt of complete documentation of the joint enterprise application.

Having gained administrative approval for a joint venture, parties to the project will receive an approval certificate.

Projects that fall below the investment funding norm (or that are non-productive in nature) that have been processed by relevant provincial, autonomous or municipal governments (the latter including municipal governments under central authority and those of separately listed cities) must be in receipt of an approval certificate from the relevant administrative department of these governments. Projects that have been processed by central government ministries and bureaus receive an approval certificate from the Ministry of Foreign Economic Relations and Trade while projects approved for location in the 14 coastal open cities or Special Economic Zones receive their certificate from the relevant government of the province, autonomous region or municipality in the area where the enterprise will be situated.

After approval certificates that have been signed and issued by provincial, autonomous region or municipal governments must be registered with the Foreign Investment Administration of the Ministry of Foreign Economic Relations and Trade together with a photocopy of the approval certificate for the joint venture enterprise, the suggestion report and the report of the feasibility study, the list of the board of directors, and a duplicate of the officially written reply from the examining and approval body commenting on the examining and approval documents lodged with regard to the joint venture.

All documents must be written in Chinese and in addition documents can be written in an agreed foreign language. Documents will only be considered to be authentic if they have been signed by authorised representatives of the interested parties to the Sino-foreign joint venture.

(v) Receipt of a Business Licence. Within one month of receiving an approval certificate, the joint venture must be registered with the department for industry and commerce of the province, autonomous region or municipality where the enterprise is to be located.

After approval of the State Administration of Industry and Commerce, a business licence is issued to the joint venture enterprise. From this point on (i.e., the date of issue of the business licence) the joint venture has been formally established. It can undertake legitimate production activities and it is protected by Chinese law.

(2) Examination and Approval of Sole-foreign Invested Enterprises

In April 1986 the Law on Foreign Enterprises was promulgated. The law set out the procedure for sole-foreign investment enterprise (i.e., foreign enterprise) operation in China. The following was stipulated:

(i) A foreign investor interested in operating a foreign enterprise in China must forward a written application to the department charged with the responsibility for foreign investment in the province, autonomous region or municipality (when the latter is directly under central authority, a separately listed city, or a coastal open city) where the proposed enterprise is to be located. And if the foreign interest seeks to operate in a Special Economic Zone, a written application must be lodged with the management committee of the local Special Economic Zone.

Applications are examined and approved by the Ministry of Foreign Economic Relations and Trade or by an authorised organ of the State Council and it is the Ministry of Foreign Economic Relations and Trade that issues the necessary approval certificate.

(ii) The written application that must be submitted by a foreign interest must include the following: variety, specifications, uses and functions of products to be produced; intended production scale; total investment; geographic location of the factory; number of staff and workers; time allowed for factory construction; source of raw materials; market for product; number of years that the interest is intending to operate the enterprise; and any other matters deemed by the foreign investor to be in need of explanation.

(iii) After application approval it is the foreign interest that must handle registration procedures and that must obtain relevant documents and an approval certificate. Documents must be lodged with the administrative department of industry and commerce at the place where the foreign enterprise is to be located. When administrative approval of the foreign project has been obtained, a business licence will be issued to take effect from the day of issue.

(iv) It is also the foreign investing interest that must take responsibility for opening an account with a bank and for handling such matters as taxation and foreign exchange. The two latter matters are to be taken up with the taxation department and the department for exchange management and the foreign investor's business licence must be presented when dealing with these matters.

III. AREAS FOR FOREIGN INVESTMENT

In the interest of effectively optimising industrial structure and protecting the interests of both Chinese and foreign investors, and in the interest of improving cooperative efficiency, China has established explicit areas in which foreign investment is to be either encouraged, limited or forbidden.

1. AREAS WHERE FOREIGN INVESTMENT IS TO BE PROMOTED

The following areas are to be encouraged:
(1) Foreign investment in new equipment and new materials that can be produced and are adaptable to both domestic and overseas markets, but which cannot currently be domestically produced.
(2) Investment in projects that can be readily adapted to foreign market requirements. Such investment may improve quality of products already produced, open new markets for Chinese products, expand export and so increase foreign exchange earnings.
(3) Investment in technically advanced products that can improve output capacity of industry and improve technical and economic benefit.
(4) Investment in the construction of energy, communications and transport services and in raw and semi-finished materials industries.

2. AREAS WHERE INVESTMENT IS TO BE LIMITED

(1) Foreign investment is to be limited in the following areas

- ... Investment in areas of production that have already been domestically developed or that have already benefited from imported technology in a way that domestic demand can now be satisfied.
- ... Investment in products that are not domestically competitive and cannot be exported.
- ... Investment purely for profit with no offer of advanced technology and which does not generate foreign exchange.
- ... Investment in projects that simply import and assemble products using production line methods to produce goods that are to be sold on the foreign country's domestic market. In other words, production that seeks only to take advantage of cheaper production costs, without providing benefit for China.
- ... Foreign investment in producing China's special arts and crafts and traditional products.
- ... Investment in other items stipulated by the State.

(2) Foreign investment is to be forbidden in the following areas

- ... areas of State security,
- ... areas deemed to be detrimental to national economic and social development, and
- ... investment in projects that pollute the natural environment, destroy natural resources and those that are harmful to people's health.

CHAPTER 20

China's Foreign Investment Experience

I. FOREIGN INVESTMENT PROMOTES DEVELOPMENT

Since the July 1979 promulgation of the Law on Chinese-Foreign Joint Ventures, over 200 foreign economic laws and regulations have been passed. These have offered considerable advantage to foreign investors. Over time these laws and regulations have been combined with the streamlining of the administration of foreign investment. A substantial amount of relevant infrastructural development has also taken place.

The Procedures of the State Council to Encourage Foreign Investment that were promulgated in October 1986 clearly set out preferential policies to be applied to foreign business interests investing in export-oriented, foreign-exchange generating and technically advanced enterprises. These preferential policies apply to taxation, customs tariffs and land use fees.

Up to the end of 1987 China had absorbed foreign investment from 40 countries and regions with over 10,000 foreign-invested enterprises having been approved, including 4,600 Sino-foreign joint ventures, 5,190 cooperative enterprises and 183 solely foreign invested enterprises. Forty-four contracts for off-shore oil prospecting projects had also been signed. Total value of these foreign investment agreements was in excess of US$22.8 billion with US$8.6 billion actually invested.

There are already over 4,000 foreign invested enterprises in production. They are distributed among China's most important economic development industries, including the energy, communications, metallurgy, electronics, chemical and textile industries.

Encouragement of foreign investment in China has led to the import of technically advanced equipment and modern management experience. It is through the use of foreign funds for operating foreign invested enterprises that internationally advanced technology, equipment and management experience promotes technical and management knowledge and provides for the technical renovation of older existing enterprises.

Foreign investment has provided a powerful boost to the economic development of Chinese provinces and cities. For example over the past nine years, foreign investment worth US$5.5 billion has been used by Guangdong Province. This investment has provided over 800,000 sets of technical equipment and more than 1,600 imported production lines.

In the period up until June 1987 the agreed value of foreign loans borrowed by China had reached US$31.1 billion: US$22.8 billion of this amount has been used. Sixty per cent of the funds have been used for infrastructural investment in areas such as railway transport, increased port handling capacity, programme-controlled telephones and in the development of crude oil and iron and steel production. China's experience in the practice of open door policy has been correct. Present use of foreign investment is beneficial and the potential for further foreign investment is most encouraging.

Successful examples of joint venture enterprises include the following.

1. THE CHINA OTSUKA PHARMACY CO LTD

This company is a joint venture between the China Pharmaceutical Engineering Co and Japan's Otsuka Pharmaceutical Co Ltd. It is China's first pharmaceutical producing joint venture enterprise. The joint venture contract was signed in August 1980 and the enterprise was constructed and in operation by February 1984.

The company imported a whole set of new advanced foreign technology and integrated it with existing technology. The result is a production line that integrates automatic and semi-automatic equipment.

The company's main product is various types of transfusion products contained in 500 ml polypropylene plastic vessels. At first the company was producing 6 million bottles per annum. Three and a half million of these were produced for the domestic market and 1.5 million were for re-export to Japan.

The company's profits have increased year by year. In 1985 a net profit of Rmb 2 million was recorded. In 1986 net profit was Rmb 3.4 million and in 1987 it was Rmb 4.1 million. Since 1987 further extensions to the enterprise have doubled its production output capacity. Annual output now reaches 12 million bottles of 500 ml transfusion packages. Four million of these are re-exported to Japan.

The company's product is now used by over 160 of the main hospitals in Beijing, Tianjin and Shanghai and also in hospitals scattered over many other provinces, municipalities and autonomous zones. But only eight months after the company had gone into production, it became clear that the company's product intended for the domestic market was being stockpiled rather than being made available for use. A solution to the problem was sought. The Tianjin Medical Purchasing Station adopted a series of marketing measures. Batch after batch of special personnel were organised by the company to call on hospitals and promote the use of the infusion packages and to instruct on their correct use. The problem was then solved.

In order to guarantee quality of product, the enterprise has a strict system of examination. When recruiting workers only culture and intelligence are taken into account and once recruited, level of worker responsibility and ability is tracked using the company's computer system.

Over 70 types of raw and semi-finished materials are required by the company in order to produce in line with its capacity and if the problem of local availability of raw and semi-finished materials cannot be solved, there will be a need to rely on foreign provision of these materials. This reduces the company's ability to earn net foreign currency profit and it is the reason that a policy of giving priority to the purchase of raw and semi-finished materials available on the Chinese domestic market has been adopted.

When preparations were being made for the construction of the joint enterprise, a special raw materials group was established. This group has been active in situations such as the one where the Beijing Yanshan Petro-chemical Industry General Company produced polypropylene resin, but it did not have the technical capacity required for producing polypropylene suitable for medical use and so it did not produce the type that was required by the China Otsuka company. After two years of study and experimentation by China Otsuka and Yanshan Petrochemical, the type required by China Otsuka was successfully produced. By 1987 the local content of raw and semifinished materials used by China Otsuka had already risen from 21% to 80%.

New production targets set by this joint-venture company are based on the observation that China's annual domestic consumption of 500 ml transfusion packages alone was estimated to be 500 million packages in 1987 with China Otsuka providing 8 million of this total number used. Current production was then described as 'a drop in the ocean' and it was decided that China Otsuka will construct a new factory.

2. SHANGHAI VOLKSWAGEN LIMITED

Shanghai Volkswagen Limited is a joint venture between China and Germany. It is one of the biggest Sino-foreign joint machine-building ventures. The partners involved in Shanghai Volkswagen are the Chinese companies Shanghai Tractor and Automobile Industry Co, China Automobile Industry Co and the Shanghai Trust and Consultant Co of the Bank of China and the German company Volkswagen Ltd. Total investment is valued at Rmb 400 million: 40% of investment is in fixed assets. There has been a fifty-fifty division of investment between China and Germany.

Shanghai Volkswagen opened for business in September 1985. Three years later it had a staff of 2,095, including 35 foreign staff and workers. The company is governed by the Executive Management Committee under the leadership of a board of directors. The Executive Management Committee is composed of four members. Chinese members fill the positions of general manager and executive manager for personnel and German members have the positions of executive manager of commerce and executive manager of technology.

The company has received favourable treatment from the Shanghai Municipal Government. The Government allocated special funds for rebuilding a highway, extending water works and waste water treatment facilities and ensuring power supply for the company, while for its part, the company has successfully cooperated between its partners to allow the import of German automobile manufacturing technology for renovation work on the existing Shanghai Automobile Factory. The renovation work began in 1986 and is expected to be completed around 1990. When completed the company will have a production capacity of 60,000 Santana limousines. It is also expected that by January 1991 an engine plant will have been constructed that will have an annual output of 100,000 engine sets. In the period May 1985 to 1987 the company produced 29,000 limousines, (28,000 were Santanas and 1,000 were other car models).

Both the Chinese and German interests in the company have agreed that localisation is a goal that the company will follow. While localisation is an obvious goal for the Chinese interest, the German interest in localisation requires further explanation. To this end the German executive manager of technology is quoted as stating that:

> ***Our interest is not in short-term profit.*** *We want to pay attention to the sustained long run development of Shanghai Volkswagen. [He then went further.] Localisation is the common interest of both China and Germany. We should promote the export of low cost localised cars and the export of localised parts and components for assembly so that **we can occupy the Southeast Asian market**...*

Localisation is a difficult process. First of all the technical level of the original Shanghai car industry only corresponded with the international technical level of the 1950s. This leaves a considerable jump before the enterprise can produce at the internationally recognised technological level of the 1980s. Moreover, this problem is exacerbated by the automobile industry's use of a relatively large number of trades. Second, there are still problems in terms of enterprise organisational management and policy and in the supply of funds. This second problem is now being addressed through the establishment of the Localisation Community of Shanghai Santana Limousine. This organisation has been established by Shanghai Volkswagen and has resulted in boosting the cooperative relations that have been negotiated by Shanghai Volkswagen with 132 other factories in China.

The third set of problems are those concerned with product quality and the need to provide satisfactory after-sales service. These problems are also being addressed by Shanghai Volkswagen.

In line with the practice of German Volkswagen, Shanghai Volkswagen takes after-sales service as a part of product quality. To this end 34 maintenance and repair stations have been established in various areas in China and now these stations are also to be established in small and medium-sized cities. The centres provide repair equipment, meters and instruments free of charge for the stations. In addition, well-equipped mobile maintenance cars have also been put into service. They are centred in Shanghai and Beijing. A central fitting warehouse has also been established. It is recognised that maintenance and repair facilities serve to boost the reputation of the Santana limousine.

While importing advanced foreign managerial experience and method, the company has paid attention to digestion, absorption and establishment of managerial methods suitable for production in China. In spite of a serious shortage of funds, it has been decided by both the Chinese and German interests in the company that funds must be allocated to building a training centre equipped with advanced facilities. This has been done as a part of the localisation project.

In the initial stage of its operation the company lacked suitably trained personnel. Engineering and technical personnel only accounted for 5% of total staff and workers and was much lower than the level of these personnel in domestic automobile manufacturing enterprises in China. The company adopted a series of measures, including inviting a number of skilled engineering and technical personnel from various localities to work for the company. Some 200 university graduates were recruited during the two years 1986 and 1987. Now the number of engineering and technical personnel and specialised personnel employed by the company accounts for over 30% of the workforce.

In order to develop and modernise China's car industry, Shanghai Volkswagen has formulated the following policies:

... importation of advanced technology,

... preference for localisation of content, and

... use of economy of scale for organisation of production.

Then in order to realise a production figure of 180,000 cars by 1996 and to have a new model Santana, a new factory is to be built.

II. CHINESE OVERSEAS INVESTMENT

In the period 1979 to the end of 1987, 385 non-trade enterprises were approved by the Chinese Government. These enterprises were to operate in foreign countries and in the Hong Kong and Macao regions. Their investment totalled US$1.8 billion, with Chinese investment accounting for around US$620 million, 35% of total investment. There are over 200 of these enterprises now open for business, mostly in the Hong Kong and Macao regions. The others are in developing countries. They involve many trades, including industrial processing, production and assembly, contract building projects, restaurants and tourism, consulting services, banking and insurance, communications and transport, fisheries, forestry projects, mining and medical and public health projects.

It is in the interest of safeguarding China's international reputation that overseas investment intended by domestic companies must be examined and approved. Present government regulations decree that all projects with investment funds of US$3 million or more must be examined and approved by the Department of Foreign Economic Cooperation under the Ministry of Foreign Economic Relations and Trade. Projects with investment of under US$3 million are examined and approved by relevant departments of the State Council and relevant local governments.

The guidelines for Chinese investment overseas are that investment should duly consider both actual need and mutual benefit and that the scale should be medium and small so that production based on little input, short cycle and quick benefits is possible. China-made equipment, materials and technology should be adopted as the investment contribution made by the Chinese side. Ideally these should join with capital as the Chinese share in the project.

In order to encourage overseas investment by Chinese enterprises, the Chinese government has adopted the following measures:

1. PROVIDING PREFERENTIAL LOANS

Investment companies which operate resource development or productive projects and require more investment can apply for a preferential loan from the State (in both foreign exchange and Renminbi currencies). This loan would be in addition to their own funds.

2. TAX REDUCTION AND EXEMPTION

Tax on profits recovered by overseas invested enterprises will be exempt for the first five years of operation. The date that the business began operating is the starting date used, regardless of whether or not China has signed an agreement with the resident country for the avoidance of double taxation. Products drawn from a resource development project will enjoy the same customs tariff treatment and subsidy as long as they are a part of the State plan.

3. RE-EXPORTING PRODUCTS

If producing a product needed for domestic use and/or required by the domestic market, overseas invested enterprises can apply to have their product listed by the State. Import of their product will then be given preference. But products which are to be limited in terms of importation will have to obtain an import licence. Products taken by the Chinese interest as a form of profit are allowed to be transported back to China and they can then be marketed by the Chinese interest.

Future emphasis for overseas investment by Chinese interests will include: resource development (including forestry, mining and fisheries); processing, production and assembly and enterprise integration of technology (the latter usually referring to new technology introduced into developing nations); transport and communication services; banking and insurance; and consultancy services where an economic return is available.

III. TECHNOLOGY IMPORTS

Large scale import of technology into China began in 1979. In the period 1979-1987 a total of over 18,000 items of technology were imported. These involved the signing of nearly 30,000 contracts and over US$20 million in investment.

In terms of technical imports, business transacted in the light and textile industries was worth $US4.6 billion and business transacted in the machine-building and electronics industries was worth US$4.3 billion. In the raw and semi-finished materials and energy industries the total was US$3 billion.

The import of batches of foreign technology has played an important role in promoting industrial modernisation. Large-scale technical import projects involved foreign exchange totalling US$9.7 billion and included technologies relevant to energy development, the electrical and machine building industries, transport and communication services and the production of raw and semi-finished materials. Imported products included 300,000 kW and 600,000 kW power generating sets, 500,000 v direct current and alternating current transmission transformer equipment, programme-controlled telephone switchboards, manufacturing technology for artificial satellite ground station equipment and manufacturing technology for large-scale slab casting. These are imports that have served to overcome gaps in domestic technology.

The use of imported technical equipment for renovating existing domestic enterprises is another important element of China's import programme. Over recent years 27,527 technical-import contracts have been signed. These contracts were in relation to the technical transformation of existing domestic enterprises. An amount of US$12.4 billion was involved.

Expanding exports is recognised as a means of reducing imports and a means of further promoting China's entry into the world market. Provinces and cities like Shenyang, Tianjin, Shandong, Jiangsu and Dalian have digested and absorbed imported technology. They have used this technology to develop 7,000 types of new products and many of these products have already entered the international market. For example, technology imported for ship-building has resulted in the export of ships made in China.

In the period 1978 to 1986, after technical transformation projects on old enterprises had increased production, it was estimated that there had been a relevant output increase of Rmb 110.7 billion and that tax and profits worth Rmb 25.7 billion had been created. This meant that tax and profit accrued had already outstripped total investment. Total investment had amounted to Rmb 23.3 billion.

The current situation in relation to technical imports is promising, but problems and difficulties still remain. For example some departments and enterprises have imported merely for immediate use. They have not considered any further in-depth development that could result from their import of technology. Also the pace of localisation has been too slow. It gets bogged down in a vicious cycle of import-use-import again. Some departments and enterprises needed to import only a part of the key equipment and technology that they required, but they imported it all. Plans are being formulated to iron out these problems.

As a developing nation, China needs to import technology in a selective and planned manner. There are only limited foreign exchange funds available for the import of technology. Clearly, negative behaviour connected to the import of technology must be overcome. Projects that can be accomplished using domestic resources must not use imported products. Technical imports for the whole nation should be carried out in an orderly manner. They must be selective and planned and they must be in line with the State's long-term plan for the national economy.

In future attention must be paid to importing soft-ware and necessary key equipment and attention must be paid to importing not on the basis of individual enterprise requirements, but on the basis of industry requirements. When it comes to importing for technical renovation of old enterprises, emphasis should be placed on importing technology that economises on energy, raw and semi-finished materials and on generally reducing production costs. Technology that should be encouraged is technology that is capable of improving production mix, developing new generations of products, promoting production quality and competitiveness on the international market and technology that can be reasonably distributed.

In line with the selective and planned import of technology, preferential treatment will be given to projects that digest, absorb and localise imported technology. Product tax (value-added tax), import customs tariffs, foreign exchange management, domestic loans for cost of scientific and technical development and for distribution of goods and materials, will all favour such projects.

1. MANAGEMENT OF TECHNOLOGY IMPORTS

Management of technical imports can be divided into two categories: industrial management and projects management.

(1)   Industrial Management

This involves the managerial departments of different levels of government who are charged with organising and formulating the principles, policy, programmes, plans, decrees, laws and regulations for technical importation. They do this with regard to nationwide macro-coordination of the economy.

Management departments formulate decrees that will protect the mutual interests of both the Chinese and foreign interests concerned with technology imports and they provide policy that ensures macro-coordination in terms of foreign exchange and balance of domestic investment for imports.

Managerial departments are also in charge of examination, approval and registration of large-scale import projects (projects involving US$5 million and over in investment) and they are in charge of organising, inspecting and supervising the implementation of technical import policy. These departments are also responsible for surveying, studying and assessing the experience gained in the course of key technical import projects that have been implemented.

(2)   Projects Management

Management of projects concerns the organisation and management of a specific project. It covers the whole process from project proposal, examination and formulation to foreign contacts and negotiation and the process of reaching production stage and the subsequent digestion and absorption of the imported technology.

Project management can be divided into the following four stages:

- Examination and approval from the planning commission or the relevant responsible department
- Formulating the technical import scheme and preparing a feasibility study.
- Bidding and negotiating on the price to be paid for the imported technology. (This includes extensive enquiries concerning the relevant price paid in the international market place, bidding to select the best clients and going abroad for inspection of the technology to be purchased and finally undertaking technical and commercial negotiations.
- And signing the import contract. Signing the contract may well involve organising specialised personnel to travel abroad for training, inviting foreign technical experts to come to China to supply technical guidance, and ensuring that the technology intended for import is technology that is suitable for use under Chinese conditions.

Macro-management departments concerned with the import of technology include the State Planning Commission, the Ministry of Foreign Economic Relations and Trade and the State Science and Technology Commission. The State Planning Commission is responsible for examining and approving technical import projects. The Ministry of Foreign Economic Relations is responsible for examining and approving contracts for technical import projects and the State Science and Technology Commission is responsible for organising scientific and technical institutes established for the purpose of undertaking feasibility studies relevant to technical import projects.

IV. TECHNICAL EXPORTS

While importing technology, China has striven to promote trade based on technical export. Although arriving comparatively late on the world technical export scene, agreements based on the export of domestic technical expertise have been concluded. These have included the transfer of computer software to Japan's largest computer group; the transfer of a modern system of welding technology to Sweden; export of technology based on blast furnace coal powder spraying and tipburn hot blast stoves to the United Kingdom and Luxembourg; and the design and manufacture of plate-fin exchanger technology exported to Germany.

Technical export trade has also been promoted by preferential policies implemented by the State. These have allowed enterprise retention of foreign exchange earnings and the provision of credit funds. As a result, technical exports for 1987 amounted to $US160 million which was a three-fold increase over total technical exports for the period 1979 to 1986.

V. PROVISION OF FOREIGN AID

1. FOREIGN AID

The principles governing China's aid are outlined in the Eight Principles of Foreign Economic and Technical Assistance. These Principles were proclaimed by the late Premier Zhou Enlai when he visited Africa at the beginning of 1964. The Principles are:

(1) The Chinese government offers foreign aid in accord with the principle of equality and mutual benefit. Aid is considered to be a form of mutual assistance.
(2) When providing foreign aid, the government strictly respects the sovereignty of the recipient country. It does not attach any conditions and asks for no special privileges.
(3) China will provide economic aid in the form of loans without interest or with a very low interest rate and the government allows long repayment periods if they are needed. As much as possible, the government reduces the burden on the recipient country.
(4) The aim is to provide foreign aid and not to create dependence. The aim is to assist the recipient country to gradually take the road of self-reliance and independent economic development.
(5) The project that China offers aid for should be a project that uses limited investment but provides quick economic gain. It is this type of investment that will result in the recipient country increasing its income, allowing it to accumulate its own investment funds.
(6) China will provide equipment, goods and materials that are of good quality and will negotiate their price in accord with the price paid in the international market place. The government guarantees replacement of equipment, goods and materials provided if they do not conform with agreed specifications and quality.
(7) When providing technical aid, the Chinese government guarantees that the personnel of the receiving country can understand the technology provided.
(8) Construction experts sent by the Chinese government to the recipient country are to enjoy the same material treatment as the experts of the recipient country.

Aid is given either in the form of loans or in the form of non-reimbursable funds or technology. Technical aid can be divided into several categories. It is either complete set equipment aid, general technical aid, goods and materials aid or spot exchange aid. Complete set equipment aid is the most used form.

2. ADMINISTRATION OF FOREIGN AID

Policy decisions in relation to foreign aid are made by China's central government. The Department of Foreign Aid is a department under the centralised Ministry of Foreign Economic Relations and Trade.

When aid is given it is based on the needs of the recipient country and it is set through consultation at government level.

Usually, when loans are the form of aid given by the Chinese government, they are interest free. When loans have been provided for complete set projects, it is usual for the term of the loan to be for a period of 5-7 years, with the period being lengthened if required. This is done through negotiation. In some cases the period before repayment is required can be as long as ten years. The country that is in receipt of aid can repay its debt using its export commodities or using a convertible currency.

When aid has been given in the form of materials and spot exchange aid, repayment terms will be fixed according to the relevant situation. In the case of difficulties at the time that repayment falls due, after government to government negotiation, repayment is often delayed.

When complete set projects have been provided, the Chinese side is responsible for design of the project, providing whole or part of the equipment and building materials required for the project, providing personnel for organising and guiding construction, installation of equipment and trial production runs and providing necessary technical aid in the course of project construction. On-the-spot training should be given to personnel from the recipient country.

From the founding of New China until the end of 1987, China has provided economic and technical aid to more than 90 countries and regions. More than 1,200 projects have been completed. These projects have covered a wide range of areas including industry, agriculture, water conservation, communications, telecommunications, culture, education and public health. The aid given has hastened the development of the economies of the recipient countries.

CHAPTER 21

Open Coastal Areas and Special Economic Zones

I. COASTAL AREAS

After the founding of New China, existing industries in coastal areas were transformed and developed. It is the coastal areas of China that have a long history of economic, technological and cultural exchange with the outside world. Shanghai, Tianjin, Dalian, Qingdao, Guangzhou, Xiamen and Ningbo were all major industrial and commercial cities in old China. Now they are areas that account for over 60% of the country's industrial output value. They are also areas with a population density that reaches 336 persons per square kilometre. This is three times the national average.

The population of the coastal area now exceeds 400 million or 41.2% of China's total population. They live in an area that covers 1.3 million square kilometres or 13.5% of the country's territory.

Most industrial enterprises in the coastal area have relatively high labour productivity and economic returns. They boast profitable businesses, relatively high levels of science, technology and education, and relatively well developed transport and communication facilities. Since 1979 it has been the coastal areas that have been at the forefront in terms of benefiting from open-door policy.

21:1 COASTAL AREAS OUTPUT
Rmb 100 million

	Output value of industry and agriculture	Output value of industry	Output value of agriculture	Total volume of retail sales
National output	18489	13813	4676	5820
Coastal area output	10586	8428	2158	2937

All figures are for 1987

1. OPENING COASTAL AREAS

In 1979, in a bid to gain maximum benefit from the existing industrial infrastructure of coastal areas, the State Council conferred special powers in relation to foreign economic transactions on Guangdong and Fujian provinces. At the same time it decided to establish four special economic zones--Shenzhen, Zhuhai, Shantou and Xiamen. These were the first major experiments in opening to trade with the outside world.

In April 1984 the State Council decided that a further 14 coastal cities and Hainan Island should be opened to outside interests.* And at the same time, the State Council extended the area of the Xiamen Special Economic Zone from the Huli district to the whole city. Then early in 1985 it was announced that the Changjiang (Yantze River) Delta would be opened together with the Zhujiang (Pearl River) Delta and the Xiamen-Zhangzhou-Quanzhou area in south Fujian Province. These were to be open economic areas.

In April 1988 the government approved both the establishment of Hainan Province and the plan to turn the province into the largest special economic zone in the country. Meanwhile, the State Council also made the decision to further expand coastal economic open areas to include the Liaodong Peninsula, the Shandong Peninsula and part of the counties and cities of the Tianjin Municipality and Hebei, Zhejiang, Jiangsu, Fujian and Guangxi Provinces. Now from north to south there is a strip that is open to the outside world.

2. STRATEGY FOR DEVELOPING COASTAL AREAS

In March 1988 the Second Plenary Session of the 13th Central Committee adopted a resolution on the strategy for economic development of coastal areas. The strategy called on these areas to gear their products to international markets and to take steps to develop an outward-looking economy.

In line with this strategy the economically developed coastal provinces and municipalities were advised that they must take full advantage of their rich labour resources and low production costs. They were advised that they must use these advantages to develop processing and export of high-quality, competitive, labour-intensive and labour and technology intensive products. The coastal industrial cities and special economic zones were instructed that they must play a leading role in the implementation of this policy.

Lateral economic ties between coastal areas and the interior must be vigorously promoted. Policy that promotes the transfer of technology, management expertise and labour skills to inland areas will promote the economic development of the coastal areas and at the same time will effect the economic development and modernisation of central and western China.

II. EXPERIMENTS IN REFORM: THE DEVELOPMENT OF GUANGDONG AND FUJIAN PROVINCES

Both Guangdong and Fujian Provinces have rich natural resources and a subtropical climate. Guangdong borders on Hong Kong and Macao and Fujian faces Taiwan. Both provinces have foreign trade ports that have a long history and both

---

* *The 14 coastal cities were - Dalian, Qinhuangdao, Tianjin, Yantai, Qingdao, Lianyungang, Nantong, Shanghai, Ningbo, Wenzhou, Fuzhou, Guangzhou, Zhanjiang and Beihai.*

are well-known home towns for overseas Chinese. The latter being recognised as being helpful in drawing foreign funds and overseas Chinese remittances that can be used for the promotion of economic and technological cooperation and exchange.

In order to exploit the full scope of the provinces' resources, in September 1979 the Chinese government decided to apply special policies and flexible measures to both provinces. The central government began a policy of holding the two provinces responsible for their own finances. This is a policy that met with considerable success. Guangdong Province has been delivering Rmb one billion to the State treasury every year. Central government policy that allowed the province's foreign exchange earnings to be divided between centre and province (on a 3 to 7 ratio in favour of the province) has done much to enhance Guangdong's ability to purchase both overseas technology and domestic products that are in short supply. In the case of Fujian Province, the central government has provided a fixed amount of subsidy each year. This subsidy has remained unchanged for five years and increased financial income in the five years has been retained by the local government.

With implementation of special policy and flexible measures, the two provinces have increased their exports and each year they have increased their income. They have invested their increased income on expanding their infrastructure and so have improved their investment environment. This has resulted in the further promotion of economic development.

In 1988, on the basis of the experience of the two provinces, the central government decided to extend the local financial responsibility system further. In the case of Guangdong Province, a basic amount was fixed as the amount to be remitted to State treasury. This amount was to increase 7% annually for a period of three years. The State Council also decided that the two provinces should undertake experimental reform policies that would provide valuable experience for the whole country.

In the first half of 1988 both provinces drew up plans for reform experimentation. Guangdong Province put forward reform measures that, in the field of finance, included steps to develop a monetary market, enterprises being allowed to issue bonds, expansion of the foreign exchange market, establishment of foreign exchange regulation centres in big and medium-sized cities and allowing foreign loans to be accepted with only provincial government approval. In the field of foreign economic relations and trade, the power of local government in relation to examination and approval of foreign-funded projects and in examining, approving and engaging in export, was expanded. Under these new arrangements, local government was also allowed to delegate power for concluding foreign trade transactions to qualified production enterprises. In relation to the labour wage system, increase in total amount of wages was attached to a comprehensive economic growth index covering the whole province and the total amount of wages for both workers and staff of an enterprise (including allowances, subsidies and bonuses) was linked to economic performance.

For its part Fujian Province put forward a policy of relaxing control over the use of foreign funds and at the same time expanded the power of local government in relation to the examination and approval of foreign-funded projects. It also expanded the power of local authorities in terms of managing and engaging in export transactions and expanded their power to examine, approve and engage in import transactions. The province delegated power to conclude foreign trade transactions down to qualified enterprises or enterprise groups and it promoted the use of loans involving foreign funds or foreign exchange loans for the establishment of enterprises or for undertaking technical transformation of existing enterprises. The province increased the powers of the Fujian Foreign Economic and Technological Cooperation Company of China for contracting engineering projects abroad and for exporting labour. In addition Fujian Province announced its intention to adopt preferential policies for economic and trade cooperation with Taiwan. This was done to encourage Taiwan business interests to establish enterprises in Fujian.

III. POLICIES FOR THE ESTABLISHMENT OF SPECIAL ECONOMIC ZONES

The establishment of special economic zones was based on making use of foreign funds, the import of advanced technology and the use of overseas enterprise management experience.

The special economic zones differ from overseas free trade areas or export processing areas in that they are all-encompassing economic areas where industry, commerce, agriculture and housing construction are developed. These economic zones differ from other development areas within China because they operate in line with policies that are especially designed for them. These policies offer flexible economic measures and a special system of economic management.

In special economic zones policy provides for preferential treatment in relation to customs duties, income tax and land use. These are policies designed to attract foreign investment either in the form of joint operation investment or solely foreign-funded investment. The zones accommodate joint ventures, cooperative enterprises and wholly foreign-funded enterprises and they offer a management system based on administrative committees and various service organisations established to facilitate and promote investment by foreign interests.

In the zones there is an emphasis on processing for export. Production is geared to the international marketplace. To this end the already very low 15% rate of income tax for enterprises can be reduced to 10% if the output value of an enterprise's export product reaches 70% of total output value for a given year.

In 1984 the State Council decided to experiment with special economic zone policy in Guangdong and Fujian provinces. The Shenzhen and Xiamen special economic zones were put under direct State planning and more flexible policies were adopted toward the zones with the intention of making them more attractive to foreign investors. This meant that while the zones are still a part of Guangdong and Fujian Provinces, they also enjoy provincial level economic management powers. In all central government plans separate planning targets are set for the zones. The aim is that these areas will have economic systems that operate in accord with international practice.

In the zones foreign-funded enterprise administrative bureaus have been established. The function of these bureaus is to examine and approve the establishment of foreign-funded enterprises. They are able to reply to applications from foreign interests in a short period of time and so have added to the improved foreign-funded enterprise services that include service companies, material supply companies, foreign exchange regulation centres, foreign-funded enterprise associations and various other service organisations. A number of foreign banks have also established branch offices in special economic zones and quite a few foreign economic agencies have established representative offices in the zones.

IV. OPEN COASTAL CITIES

The open coastal cities are located in China's most economically developed areas. The cities have good harbours. They are the cities that have the best foundations for industrial development. The production technology and equipment used in their enterprises is superior to that used by similar enterprises in other parts of China.

With the exception of Beihai and Wenzhou, all the open coastal cities have built economic and technological development districts. These are China's forward bases for the import of advanced technology and they are centres that focus on the development of international export trade. The infrastructural facilities of these development districts have been completed. The districts are governed by laws and regulations that amount to a highly efficient administration that in turn creates a favourable climate for investment and further economic development.

Owing to the differing natural, geographical and historical conditions of the open cities, the economic development of each city has had its own characteristics. The cities can be divided into four categories:

- ... Those cities that have a solid industrial foundation and a strong technologically trained labour force. These are China's old industrial base cities and foreign trade ports. They have developed as economic centres over a long period of time.
- ... In the second category there are the cities that have a relatively good industrial base and so can expect rapid development. These are to be the new rising industrial cities and they are also cities that are important as agricultural production bases.
- ... The third category consists of cities that have good transport facilities. These are also cities that play a vital role in the national communications network.
- ... In the fourth category there are cities that are essentially port cities. They are cities that have not yet developed as industrial centres. To date they are cities with poor infrastructural facilities, but they do have very rich natural resources and good harbours. This means that they are cities that have good development potential.

Development of the open coastal cities is based on making full use of the special policies that have been allowed by the central government while giving full play to the relative economic and infrastructural advantages that the cities enjoy. At present the developmental focus is on technological transformation of existing enterprises and on establishing medium-sized and small enterprises that require less up-front investment while being capable of returning relatively high profits. But at the same time, the development of knowledge-intensive and technology-intensive enterprises is also being promoted in these cities.

Preferential treatment is to be given to foreign interests seeking to invest in the open cities. In fields such as taxation, land use, customs duties and remittance of profits overseas, special concessions will be given, but they are not to be given to the same extent as they have been given in the special economic zones.

In order to attract foreign investment, open coastal cities have adopted a series of measures aimed at simplifying investment project examination and they have established service organisations such as investment service centres, consultancy service companies, material supply companies, personnel exchange service centres, foreign exchange regulation centres and lawyers' offices and accountants' offices.

V. COASTAL OPEN ECONOMIC AREAS

1. ECONOMIC CHARACTERISTICS AND DEVELOPMENT STRATEGIES

The Zhujiang (Pearl River) Delta, the Changjiang (Yangtze River) Delta and the South Fujian triangle area were opened up in 1985. They are now well established areas that have the following characteristics:

First, all three areas are richly endowed. They have mild climates, ample rainfall, abundant and highly developed agricultural production. They also have good transport facilities and the Zhujiang Delta and the South Fujian triangle area are home town areas for many overseas Chinese. This is a situation that is conducive to creating close economic and technological ties with the outside world.

Second, in all three areas an export-oriented economy has been established based on township enterprise production. The township enterprises are divided into two types; (i) enterprises which use rich local labour resources to develop processing with supplied materials and samples and compensation trade, and (ii) enterprises which import advanced technology and equipment and gradually establish a number of enterprise groups which have substantial strength in production and export.

Third, through transforming traditional modes of agricultural production by promoting mechanisation, intensive production methods and the application of agricultural science and technology, the vast countryside of the three areas, while raising the per unit area yield of agricultural products, has developed export-oriented agriculture and has established more than 300 large export production bases for agricultural and sideline products.

Fourth, the development of township enterprises has not only employed all the agricultural surplus labour force of the Zhujiang Delta, but has also attracted part of the rural labour force from Jiangsu, Zhejiang and Fujian provinces and from the Shanghai Municipality. An open labour market has taken shape.

In order to carry out the development strategy planned for the coastal areas, open coastal areas will implement the trade-industry-agriculture policy. This policy is intended to develop the processing industry in accord with export trade requirements while developing agriculture and other raw material industries. The open coastal areas will import technology and they will use technical transformation to update enterprises and products, promoting exports and increasing foreign exchange earnings.

2. POLICY MEASURES

The policy measures in force in the coastal economic development areas include:

(1) Expansion of the power of the governments of provincial cities and of certain counties so that they have power to examine and approve use of foreign funds for technical transformation of existing enterprises and for building new factories.

(2) Relevant departments of the State Council and of provincial governments (or municipalities directly under the central government) supporting and making priority arrangements for projects that facilitate technical transformation of key industries and enterprises.

(3) Income tax collection from foreign-funded enterprises at an 80% discount on existing tax regulations. This discount will apply to foreign-funded enterprises in open cities and county towns that are productive or scientific research enterprises. Whether or not local income tax is reduced or forgiven will be then be the decision of the relevant provincial (municipal) government.

(4) Equipment and building materials imported by foreign-funded enterprises for production or management purposes and raw materials, components, parts and accessories and packaging materials imported by these enterprises for the purpose of production for export will be made exempt from customs duties, from import and export tax and from added value tax. This will be done upon presentation of documentary proof. Products then exported by these enterprises will be exempt from export duties and from unified industrial and commercial tax.

Aside from the three development areas noted above, in 1988 the central government included the following as coastal economic development areas: eighteen coastal cities in the counties and districts of Shantou, Jiangmen, Maoming and Zhanjiang cities and Huiyang prefecture: the Liaodong Peninsula, Jiaodong Peninsula and 72 cities and counties along Bohai Bay that are in Tianjin Municipality and Hebei Province: Ningde and Xiapu Counties in the northeast of Fujian Province: six coastal cities and counties in southern Guangxi Zhuang Autonomous Region. As China's open door policy develops, there will be further expansion of the coastal open economic areas.

It is intended that new high tech industries will be developed in the Changjiang Delta area to the point where, in the future, technological progress will account for 50-60% of industrial growth in the area. In the Zhujiang Delta economic development area the future development focus will be on promoting key sites for industrial development and on the export of fresh food products to Macao and Hong Kong. New rising industries and agricultural export production and processing bases are to be the focus of future development in the South Fujian Triangle.

VI. PROSPECTS FOR ECONOMIC RELATIONS BETWEEN HONG KONG AND THE HINTERLAND

Hong Kong is a centre of international trade. It is a centre of finance, shipping and information and it is also a city that plays an important role in the economic development of China's hinterland.

Hong Kong is a vital link in economic contact and exchange between China's hinterland and Western countries and it is the largest distributing centre for China's trade. And at the same time, the hinterland of China supports Hong Kong's economy. The two economies are closely tied. Hong Kong and China's hinterland are interdependent.

Since the late 1970s, when China adopted the policy of opening to the outside world, economic relations between Hong Kong and the hinterland have been expanding. Relations have progressed from import and export trade alone to a great variety of economic exchanges, including import and export trade, loans, direct investment, processing with supplied materials and samples, compensation trade, transfer of technology and transmission of information. From the late 1970s onward, economic ties between Hong Kong and the inland areas, especially the coastal areas, have substantially increased.

Cooperation between Hong Kong and the inland areas will be of considerable benefit in terms both areas needs when trading in an increasingly competitive international market. First, Hong Kong can take advantage of the relatively low cost of labour offered by inland areas, especially the southeast coastal areas. Processing with supplied materials and samples and compensation trade can be developed and labour-intensive industries can be moved to the hinterland. Goods produced can be sold on the international market. Second, in the field of science and technology, particularly in the field of hard science and technology, Hong Kong can assist the inland areas. Hong Kong and the hinterland could increasingly cooperate in science and technology. Third, Hong Kong can play the role of an international monetary centre and in so doing raise funds for economic development of the inland areas.

In short, extensive economic and technological cooperation between Hong Kong and the hinterland would be to the advantage of both. Hong Kong's sustained economic growth would be further promoted and Hong Kong can assist the hinterland so that it is in a position to play an increasing role in world trade.

Editor's Conclusion

No one who has read this book could be left in any doubt over the complexity and extent of policy initiative and administrative restructuring that the process of reforming a centrally planned economy requires. The difficulty of the task of orchestrating economic reform is obvious.

The process of economic reform extends far beyond the policy dilemmas involved in lowering production costs and increasing productivity through the reorganisation of the internal management of production enterprises and the provision of individual worker incentives. In order to effectively move a centrally administered economy toward market integration a 'routinised' legal and administrative structure must be established and developed.

The routinisation that is an integral part of the reform process makes extensive and seemingly insatiable demands on the administrative structure of the reforming society. The process of 'modernisation' that in China has become inseparable from the process of reform, requires the impersonal formalisation and codification of a large proportion of economic and social interaction and this situation in turn demands a considerable expansion of the existing legal structure. The Chinese government has undertaken this task in the manner outlined in chapter six—The Economic Legal System. Early in the reform decade, in July 1979, it was decreed that a discrete economic court system be established and the system of administrative courts was added in 1986. The economic courts hear disputes (mostly between enterprises) over the enforcement of economic contracts and can order compensation for loss or damage caused by infringement of economic rights in the spheres of production and distribution. For their part the administrative courts are responsible for cases where a litigant has refused to comply with a disciplinary decision issued by a government administrative body. Both the economic court and the administrative court systems have responsibilities that differ from those of China's existing civil and criminal courts and both have been developed in response to the demands made on China's legal system by the process of reform.

The economic reform project is by definition a process that takes place in the context of immature market integration and in the absence of a developed capital market. The latter is presented by reform theorists as the end stage of the reform of a centrally administered economy. The consequence of immature market integration is a lack of effective market disciplining of an increasingly decentralised system of economic decision-making. It is this situation that demands that the process of economic reform take place within the ambit of a 'modern' legal structure that is capable of facilitating central government use of the economic levers. During the reform period it is the levers of credit, price and taxation that provide the vehicles for impressing national economic policy on decentralised enterprise decision-making. They replace the previous system of direct centralised administrative management while at the same time functioning as a substitute for the discipline that an immature market is unable to provide.

Since the introduction of its programme of economic reform the Chinese government has found that it has constantly needed to adjust its credit, pricing and taxation policy. And now, in line with the present focus on eliminating corruption, promoting 'clean and honest government' and 'deepening' reform, the government is again stressing that credit must be extended only in accord with formalised and impersonal government rules and regulations that reflect central government investment priorities, that the pricing system must be 'rational' and that tax must be levied fairly and impersonally. The government is arguing that it is only when an economy operates in a fair manner that competition is promoted and the best enterprises are encouraged and that it must be recognised that it is the use of impersonal routinised rules and regulations that will ensure a fair system.

But China's reform experience has also demonstrated that even when the newly expanded legal system has reached the point where it is 'an important means for effecting economic adjustment', the reform process requires that it be extended still further. As the content of this book makes clear, China's legal system has been made responsible for facilitating such wide ranging matters as the effective promotion of environmental protection; rules and regulations covering such diverse areas as rural grain production, markets and land use, the introduction of postal zip codes, the issuing of business licences that can be granted or revoked in accord with government policy and enterprise behaviour and arrangements that are able to ensure the secure purchase of housing by individuals and the equitable sale of land use rights. It has included policy that has promoted government approved foreign investment and most recently has even included the introduction of formalised arbitration procedures between individual industrial workers and their employing enterprise. But even these measures are not the end of the matter. As the process of reform continues new regulatory needs have appeared. New problems have constantly come into view and these have often included structurally embedded problems that are stubbornly resistant to immediate administrative redress.

As noted in the chapter with the all-encompassing title of Housing, Real Estate Administration, Urban Planning and Environmental Protection (chapter eleven), China's first post reform environmental law was promulgated, on a trial basis, as early as September 1979. It was then followed by laws to prevent pollution of water and air, control urban noise, protect wild animals and safeguard the ocean environment. But the passing of laws has not by itself been enough to control pollution. The passing of laws is a first and very necessary stage in an ongoing process where the implementing of environmental regulations has often proved to be difficult and is sometimes impossible. It has often been difficult to identify enterprises, groups or individuals who can be held responsible for environmental pollution. The cause of environmental degradation is very often embedded in past industrial policy that cannot be immediately changed. For example factories have been built on environmentally inappropriate sites and there is the wide-spread and continued use of obsolete equipment.

China's planners are currently giving priority to housing reform and reform of land use rights. They have promoted both measures as a means of (i) promoting the routinisation of use rights and (ii) funding infrastructural development. Housing reform is based on arrangements that encourage individuals to contract for the purchase of their housing requirements as an alternative to the expectation that housing will be provided through either State enterprise or direct government administrative allocation. It is policy that in many cases has been slow to find acceptance among China's workers, but it is also policy that when it has included a sweetening wage subsidy has promoted the process of effecting payment of a greater proportion of a worker's 'real' wage in cash form and this in turn is a process that is recognised as being central to 'modernising' enterprise/worker relations. It is policy that assists the government to lay the groundwork for its future plan to divest the large State enterprises of their considerable welfare responsibilities. In immediate terms housing reform provides an avenue for the centrally directed mobilisation of the substantially increased bank savings of individuals and when implemented in the manner that is intended, it would, without drawing on government funding, effectively provide a useful source for the funding of further much needed infrastructural investment.

For its part land use compensation was expected to (i) promote formal and secure peasant land use tenure and (ii) to ensure a stable State income from real estate which could be used to upgrade China's inefficient urban infrastructure. Land use reform has aimed to convert the practice of free use of land to one where compensation is paid. It is not a process that is to be perceived as the introduction of a system of land ownership. As noted in chapter eleven, in China 'all institutions and individuals have a right to land use, but they do *not* have a right to ownership of land'. Land use compensation has been carefully and correctly presented as a formal and routinised system of land use rights. But even with administrative rules and regulations in place, there have been problems. For example there has been a considerable illegal trade in the transfer of land use rights. One aspect of this trade is that many urban land users, particularly State enterprises and institutions, have been found to have sold or transferred land use rights and to have received significant compensation. The problem is that in many cases they have not sought the necessary government approval for these sales and they have not passed on the monies received. Apart from urban planning and environmental infringements that have resulted, including significant encroachment on land designated for agricultural production, government coffers have been denied funds due to them. Chinese governments, both central and provincial, have publicised their estimated loss of millions of yuan annually and have repeatedly cautioned that land-use rights can only be traded on the official market and have mounted anti-corruption campaigns that have included a focus on the illegal trading of land use rights. But in a situation where the financial interests of enterprises and institutions have been in competition with the government's financial interest, the illegal sale of land use rights has continued. The development of routinised legally enforceable rules and regulations has not been enough, even when it has been accompanied by the publicised loss of 'public' funds, repeated cautions and anti-corruption campaigns and an 'in-depth' publicity and education campaign focusing on the legal system. But in spite of the problems that have been and that are now being experienced in relation to implementing a wide-spread system of contracted residential occupancy of urban housing and both urban and rural land use rights, the Chinese government has continued to promote and develop a formally recognised and secure system of housing and land use tenure.

In the agricultural sector where formal recognition of land use rights dates back to the first half of the 1980s, there continues to be recognition of the need for long term land use tenure. This is because long term land tenure is seen as necessary insurance against 'the plundering use of land resources' and now even the possibility of a permanent lease of land is under discussion. The latter measure is intended to not only avoid the insufficient input of agricultural requirements such as fertiliser and pesticides ('the plundering use of land resources'), but also to promote infrastructural development within the agricultural production sector together with the types of diversified agricultural projects that have been discussed in chapter seventeen, for example the production, storage and processing of aquatic and animal food products.

Two further issues currently under discussion in relation to agricultural land use rights are (i) the provision of 'ample rights' for peasant land users and (ii) the ever increasing problem of loss of productive agricultural land to uses such as 'building industrial enterprises, communication facilities and urban and rural housing'. This is a problem foreshadowed in the last pages of chapter seventeen. In relation to the provision of 'ample rights' for peasant land users, it is currently being argued that rural land use rights should include the peasant households being able to legally transfer and sell land use rights and being in a position to mortgage land use rights. Though it is then immediately noted that such measures would rely on further strengthening and standardisation of the formal legal recognition currently afforded land use rights. In relation to (ii), the problem of loss of agricultural productive land to industrial use and to housing construction, in chapter seventeen it has been estimated that during the 1980s 'farmland was reduced by some 450,000 hectares annually'. This is a situation that is continuing. Indeed it has been accelerating.

The recent acceleration of the destruction of farmland for use by industry and housing is due to what is being described as a real estate investment boom. Though it is recognised that this boom is centred on the coastal areas and in the south, it has affected most areas of China. At the moment there is a situation described as 'the hectic selling of land, enclosing of land, and setting up of development zones'. This is recognised as a problem that is going hand in hand with and has been exacerbated by the building of 'high-class commodity homes' on new land sub-divisions while the construction of 'ordinary housing' is being relatively neglected. The extent of the problem becomes apparent when we note that it is estimated that in 1992 the Guangdong Provincial government earned around 45% of its annual development revenue from the lease of land. In many areas the land income has already become one of the most important and stable fund resources for improving backward urban infrastructure.

Legal provisions in relation to land use have gone some way to promoting security of land use tenure for peasant household producers, have funded urban infrastructural development and have promoted foreign investment. But in a situation where provincial and city governments have come to depend on land lease arrangements for a significant proportion of their income it is taking more than rules and regulations to ensure that significant tracts of farmland are not lost, that urban planning and environmental concerns are not floated and that prudent foreign investment projects are fostered. In spite of recognition of the damage being done and in spite of the recent imposition of central government administered rules and regulations, we can expect that it will take more than legally enforceable policy to stop the unwanted unplanned trading of land use rights and so the effective dampening of China's current real estate boom.

Many of China's provinces have established land use procedures and legislation as a means of encouraging foreign investors. They have recognised that foreign investors are attracted by a climate of security and predictability of land tenure. Indeed this policy has been seen as having so much potential that the number of economic zones established by provinces has now led to considerable central government concern and to policy that calls for the rationalisation of existing zones. Nevertheless, and even though China's central government has noted that too many provincially instigated economic zones are continuing to be established, the setting aside of centrally sanctioned specified areas such as the open coastal cities and special economic zones in the manner outlined in the last chapter of this book has been very successful. In the special economic zones security of land use has been provided together with tax breaks and the simplification and clarification of administrative procedures and for the most part this policy has functioned to attract foreign investment that is in accord with Chinese government priorities. For example domestic enterprises establishing in economic zones have been encouraged to undertake contract production for foreign invested companies. The goal has been to participate in earning export currency and to acquire scientific expertise while at the same time providing technical training for workers and exposing them to new forms of labour discipline. As noted in the chapter on foreign investment experience (chapter twenty), the argument is that 'foreign technologies can play a significant role in optimising China's industrial structure and promoting industrial modernisation' and this modernisation process includes the promotion of worker skills (particularly organisational skills) and discipline. In this context foreign invested enterprises are cast in the role of technology suppliers and worker educators and it is in return for this service that they were given access to the significant profit advantage that they draw from the low cost of Chinese workers' labour time.

There is little or no disagreement over the observation that simplified 'modern' administrative procedures, including security of land lease arrangements and taxation breaks have enhanced the attraction of China's low cost of Chinese workers' labour time and that this situation has afforded considerable benefit to China's modernisation project. But it is also quite clear that not all of the results of these policies were adequately predicted. Apart from the issue of the overheated real estate market and the flouting of environmental protection and urban planning there is the situation where China's opening to the outside world has led to a new economically driven regionalism: a regionalism promoted and shaped by China's current and increasing integration into the world economy.

In terms of China's further development, the Chinese government's response to this growing new regionalism has been twofold. On one hand it has promoted policy that will effect a 'gradual' opening up of areas inland along the coast and rivers and on the other hand it has promoted policy whereby lesser developed areas in China's central and western regions are encouraged to offer support for the relatively fast track development taking place in southern China and along the Eastern seaboard. The opening first of the Yantze River (Changjiang) Delta and Pearl River (Zhujiang) Delta economic development areas discussed in Open Coastal Areas and Special Economic Zones (chapter twenty-one) has been followed by the more recent opening of the Yantze River valley region incorporating areas adjacent to both the lower and middle reaches of the river. It is an area that extends from the city of Wuhan in Hubei Province to Shanghai's Pudong Development Area. This is the practical face of policy intended to encourage investment, particularly foreign investment, inland along China's longest river system.

The discussion in chapter twenty-one gave a clear outline of the central government's intention to attract foreign investment into Fujian Province and particularly into Guangdong Province. In the case of Fujian Province this intention has provided the potential for the province to become China's next rapidly growing economic region (after the Guangdong/Hong Kong region and the Shanghai city and hinterland region) and in the case of Guangdong Province it is an intention that is already being realised. Indeed there is every reason to expect that in the 1990s the increasing interdependence between the economies of Hong Kong and Guangdong Province will expand, increase and become more developed and diversified. What remains to be seen is whether the increasing investment by Hong Kong, Japanese and Taiwan interests in southern and eastern China will provide a starting point for their investment in other regions of China. But in the meantime the Chinese government is implementing policy that effectively promotes a division of labour between southern and eastern China and the provinces located in central and western China.

An example of China's developing regional division of labour is the current form of cooperation between southern and east coast development and the provinces in China's central and western sectors. This cooperation has taken the form of the recently constituted 'central-southern economic and technological coordination zone'. The zone consists of the provinces of Guangdong, Hunan, Hubei, Hainan and Guizhou and the autonomous region of Guangxi. It is intended that it will facilitate joint projects that link industrial, agricultural, resource and material production. In practice it has meant the beginning of the construction of a hydroelectric power station jointly planned by Guangdong Province, the State Energy Investment Company and the Guangxi and Guizhou regions and has included an aluminium production base that is to be built in Guizhou Province.

It is quite clear that China's programme for economic reform has achieved much and that it promises to achieve much more.

The economic policies adopted by the Chinese government during the 1980s have already succeeded in delivering a substantial increase in both industrial and agricultural production and in improving the living standard of the majority of the Chinese people. But as noted in the introduction to this book, China's first decade of reform did not succeed in even-handedly implementing the promise of 'a common prosperity for all'. As Ma Hong correctly predicted in his preface to this book—with the deepening of reform the difference in residents' income will become more marked. Ma recognised that while reform policy will promote the increasing modernisation of industrial production and that policy would be implemented that is intended to redress the uneven development of industrial commodity production, manual labour will continue to be the predominant form of productive means in rural areas. He then noted that the unevenness of regional development that was already being experienced in the late 1980s, expressed his concern over this unevenness and then perceptively foreshadowed the extent of the new regionalism now clearly evident in the fast track development of southern and eastern China. Ma concludes that 'this situation means that changes will take place over a fairly long period of time... [and so] the formation of an advanced commodity economy will [also] take some time.' It is an assessment of China's first decade of reform that in light of the Chinese government policy and administrative initiatives outlined in this book, must lead us to agree with his conclusion.

In administrative terms China's first decade of reform fostered and promoted the routinisation of many areas of Chinese economic and social life and at the same time confirmed the comprehensive and complex nature of the process of reforming a centralised economy. The Chinese legal structure was considerably extended, a large number of rules and regulations covering a diverse set of needs and concerns were promulgated and formal and impersonal avenues of exchange were established. But above all, China's policy and administrative experience during the 1980s has provided a graphic illustration of the organisational effort and political wisdom required to successfully promote the reform of a centralised economy, particularly when this is a project that has been combined with the political need to maintain the image of 'a common prosperity for all'.

Kate Hannan

Index

administration of individual industry and commerce 131–4
administration of industry and commerce 123, 128, 130
administrative judicial courts 97
advertising 135–6; Regulations on Advertising 135
Africa 289, 290, 327
Agreement on International Railway Through-Freight Transport 249
Agricultural Bank of China 50, 51, 114, 139, 213
Agriculture – animal husbandry 284–6; household contract responsibility system 277–8 (also see contract responsibility system); crop farming – grain and industrial crops 279–83; fisheries 286–7; foreign trade, technology and funds 287–90; forestry 283–4; popularising science and technology 278–9; Agricultural Development Plan 107
Albania 249
aluminium industry 226
Anhui Province 10, 240, 243
Annapolis Tidal Power Station (Canada) 247
Ansett World Air Service (Australia) 255
Anshan (coal deposit, iron and steel plant) 223, 224
Antaibao open cut (coal) mine 240
Arbitration Commission of the State Administration for Industry and Commerce 103
astronautics technology and industry 269–74
audit/auditing 23, 34, 114
Australia 51, 52, 247, 279, 289; CITIC Australia Pty Ltd – Melbourne 54; Portland Aluminium Smelter (Australia) 54; Sydney 52
Austria 250
automobile production and assembly 4–6, 60, 64, 133, 141, 208, 209, 231, 321–3

Bac Bo Gulf 242
Bank of China 33–8, 41, 50, 51–2, 114, 139, 213, 313, 321; Shanghai Trust and Consultant Company of the Bank of China 321
bankruptcy 86, 91, 155–7, 171; Bankruptcy Law – State Enterprises 90

Baotou (coal deposit, iron and steel plant) 224
Basuo (sea port) 253
Beihai (city) 329, 333
Beijing 10, 51, 52, 99, 147, 181, 186, 189, 190, 224, 243, 249, 250, 254, 255, 257, 258, 259, 260, 261, 274, 281, 304, 320, 322
Beijing Capital International Airport Administration 254
Beijing General Washing Machine Plant (the Bailin Road) 303
Beijing No.1 Machine Tool Plant 147
Beijing Yanshan Petro-chemical Industry General Company 321
Belgium 279, 289
business licence(s) (administration of) 125–6
Bohai, Bohai Bay 192, 241, 242
bonds – domestic bonds 45–8, State Economic Construction Bonds 45–6, State Treasury Bonds 46–7, 48; enterprise stocks and bonds 145, 152; international bond market 314 (also see stock market development)
bonus payments to workers 6, 85, 142, 144, 147–8, 162, 167, 168–70; Circular on Issuing Bonuses (for state-owned enterprises) 169
Brazil 273
Britain, British, London 52, 56, 57, 262, 273, 327
Bureau of Urban Planning 187
business licence(s) 43, 57; issuing licences 125–6, 133; licences for foreign invested enterprises 317

Cairo 52
Canada 54, 247, 289; Celgar Pulp Mill, British Columbia 54; CITIC Vancouver 54
Capital Iron and Steel Company 148
Cathay Pacific Airways 54
cement plants 229–30
Changjiang (Yantze River) 248, 251, 342; Changjiang Delta 258, 330, 342; Changjiang Minsheng Company 248; Changjiang Shipping Corporation 251
Chengdu (city) 254; Chengdu Airport Administration 254
China Capital Goods Import and Export Corporation 236

China Civil Aviation Service Company 255
China Council for the Promotion of International Trade 106
China Flying Dragon Special Aviation Company 255
China Foreign Trade Transportation Corporation 252
China Great Wall Industrial Corporation 274
China Housing Development Corporation 181
China Housing Problem Research Society 180
China International Aviation Company 254
China International Trade Arbitration Commission 105
China International Trust and Investment Corporation (CITIC) 53, 54, 213; China International Trust and Investment Corporation Hong Kong (Holdings) Limited [CITIC (HK) Limited] 54; CITIC Australia Pty Ltd 54; CITIFOR Inc – Seattle 54
China Land Society 180
China Marine Helicopter Special Company 255
China National Chemical Industry Import and Export Corporation 228
China National Gold Corporation 227
China National Nonferrous Metals Industry Corporation 226, 227
China National Nuclear Industry Corporation 268
China New Technology Pioneering Investment Corporation 50
China New-type Construction Materials Corporation 120
China Nonmetal Ore Industrial Corporation 120
China Ocean Shipping Company/Agency 252, 253
China Oriental Aviation Company 254
China Otsuka Pharmacy Co. Ltd., 320–1
China Pharmaceutical Engineering Company 320
China Real Estate (Development) Association 180, 181
China Road and Bridge Engineering Company 251
China Statistical Monthly Report 117, China Statistical Excerpts 117, China Statistical Yearbook 117
Chinese Academy of Sciences xi, 261
Chinese Communist Party xii, 149, 199, 200, 204, 277, 283
Chonqing (city) 45, 121, 274; Chonqing Iron and Steel Company 144
city planning 186–92, 263; Bureau of Urban Planning 187; Regulations on City Planning 177, 180, 186
civil aviation (development and administration of) 254–64
coal industry and resources 239–41; coal mining areas 239–40; local coal mines 240–1
Commercial Bank of China 114
commodity economy 4, 5–11, 107
Communications Bank 50, 52, 57
computer manufacturing 262–6
Constitution 94, 95, 99, 132, 180
contract responsibility system (industrial enterprises) 147–9 (also see agriculture, household contract responsibility system)
Corporation of International Agriculture and Forestry 289
Corporation of International Cooperation in Forestry 289
cooperative legal advisory offices 101
Cultural Revolution xv, 91, 165, 201, 268, 277, 285, 296
Customs Law 92
Czechoslovakia 249

Dalian (city) 120, 180, 189, 253, 274, 325, 329; Dalian Shipping Company 252
Datong Mining Area 239
Daqing Oilfield 242
Dayawan Nuclear Power Station 244
Decision to Implement Cash control in State Organs 38
Department of Foreign Aid 328
Department of Foreign Economic Cooperation 323
Department of Land Registration 179; Department of Land Use Planning 179
Department of Policies and Statutes 179
Department of Real Estate 178
Department of Scientific and Technological Publicity and Education 179
Department of State Farms and Land Reclamation 282, 283
Department of Supervision and Inspection 179
Department of Urban Planning 178–9
Deng Xiaoping xv, 5
Denmark 190, 289
deposit reserve rate 28, 31
Development District Administration Committee 180
Dongfang Motor Vehicle Industrial Associated Corporation 120
Dongfang Power Station Complete Set of Equipment Corporation 120
Donghai (sea) 192
double-track price(s) xii, 61–3, 231
Dushanzi Refinery 253

East China (Aviation) Administration Bureau 254
economic contracts (administration and arbitration) 128–31; Economic Contract Arbitration Authority 129; economic contract law 93, 123, 130
Economic Law Concerning Overseas Interests 92
economic legal system 91–106; economic arbitration 103–6; Economic Judicial Court 97, 98; Regulations on the Arbitration of Disputes Over Economic Contracts 103, 104
economic planning (national) 107–21; economic forecasting 119
Eighth Five Year-Plan (1991-95) 108
electronics industry (development of) 263–5
enterprise classification 137–42
Enterprise Law 145, 148, 156
Enterprise Party Committee (work of) 149; role of enterprise director 148–9, 151
enterprise registration 124–6
enterprise welfare system 171–2
environmental protection policy 192–6, 263; China's General Station of Environmental Monitoring 194; Environmental Protection Law 184, 190; State Environmental Protection Bureau 193
European Community 289
Everbright Industrial Corporation 213
export credit 314

Fifth Five Year Plan (1976-80) 108, 203, 204, 217, 218
financial market between banks 54–5
Finland 250
First Five Year Plan (1953-57) 17, 18, 91, 108, 143, 186, 199, 200, 201, 203, 204, 207, 217, 218
Fisheries Law 92
fixed asset investment (macro-management of) 215–21; fixed asset depreciation fund 154
foreign aid (provision and administration of) 327–8
foreign exchange certificates 33–4
foreign exchange control 36–8; Foreign Currency Exchange Centres 49; State Administration of Exchange Control (SAEC) 35–7, 49
foreign government loans 313
foreign investment (procedures for the use of) 314–8; examination and approval of contracts 316; tax reduction 324
foreign trade arbitration 105–6; Foreign Trade Arbitration Commission 105
Forestry Law 92

France/French 247, 250, 259, 273, 274; Paris 52; Thomson CSF Company – France 255
Fujian Province 10, 53, 247, 261, 330-3, 341
Fujian Foreign Economic and Technological Cooperation Company 332
Fujian Investment Enterprise Company 53
Fuxin Mine 240

Gansu Province 10,11
General Administration of Civil Aviation (CAAC) 254, 255
geothermal energy 245
German, Germany 250, 259, 273, 274, 289, 321, 322, 327
German Democratic Republic 249
Grand Canal 250
Grasslands Law 92
Great Leap Forward 201
Great Wall Computer Group Corporation 120, 262
Gross National Product (GNP) 199, 200, 238
Guangdong Province, Guangzhou (city) 11, 45, 121, 190, 249, 254, 257, 258, 259, 261, 274, 319, 329, 330-2, 340, 342
Guangzhou Ocean Shipping Bureau 252
Guangxi (Guangxi Zhuang Autonomous Region) 10, 330, 335, 342
Guizhou Province 10, 226, 238, 261, 342

Harbin Power Station Complete Set of Equipment Corporation 120
Haihe river system 192
Hainan (island) 330, 332
Hangzhou (city) 186, 249
Hankou 45, 242, 251
Haunghe (yellow river) system 189, 251
Harbin 121
Heavy-duty Motor Vehicle Industrial Associated 120
Hebei Province 10, 233, 240, 242, 330, 335
Hegang Mine 240
Heilongjiang Province, Heilongjiang (river) system, 10, 238, 240, 242, 249, 251
Henan Province 10, 240, 241, 243
Hong Kong 33, 34, 35, 36, 37, 38, 52, 53, 54, 97, 106, 183, 227, 255, 258, 323, 331, 342; Hong Kong (development of hinterland) 335–6
housing (urban) 175–80; privatizing housing 177–81; Regulations on the Management of Urban Private Houses 180
Huaibei (mine and oilfield) 240, 242, 243
Huanghai (sea) 192
Huanghe (Yellow) river system 189, 251
Huangpu (river, port) 189
Hubei Province 10, 24, 155, 233, 241, 342
Hunan Province 10, 11, 342

Hungary 249
Huolinhe (open cut coal mine) 240

Ikh Chao League (coal mines) 240
Implementation Procedures Concerning the National Taxation Policy 81
Income Tax Law Concerning Foreign Enterprises 92
India 239
Industrial and Commercial Bank of China 50, 51, 139, 213
industrial structure 199–210
inflation (causes and impact of) 77–8
Inner Mongolia, Hohot 10, 237, 240, 241, 249, 259
insurance (domestic) 56; insurance market 57; People's Insurance Company of China 55, 57; Provisional Regulations on the Management of Insurance Enterprises 57 (also see labour insurance)
Interim Regulations on Banking Management 92
Interim Provisions on Corporation Registration 123
Interim Provisions on Job-waiting Insurance for Employees of State-owned Enterprises 171
Interim Provisions on Price Control 92
Interim Regulations on Administration of Urban and Rural Individual Industry and Labourers 123
Interim Regulations on Foreign Trade Management 91
Interim Regulations on Housing Tax 180
Interim Regulations on Joint-state-private Industrial Enterprises 91
Interim Regulations on Private Enterprises 117, 123, 133
Interim Regulations on the Selling and Transfer of the Use Right of Urban State-owned Land 180
Interim Regulations on the Use of Cultivated Land Tax 180
Interim Regulations on the Use of Land for Construction by Chinese-foreign Joint Ventures 183
Interim Regulations on Urban Land Use 92, 182; Interim Regulations on Urban Land Use Tax 180, 182
International Development Association 313
International Development Fund 313
International Fund for Agricultural Development 289
International Monetary Fund (IMF) 313
International Space Navigation Federation 273
International Telecommunication Union 273
Investment Bank of China 50, 52

iron and steel industry (development of) 244–6
iron ore (deposits and reserves) 223
isotope technology 267
Italy 250, 259, 273

Japan, Japanese 35, 105, 238, 273, 289, 320, 342; Japanese Overseas Economic Co-operation Fund 250, 253; Tokyo 52
Jiangxi Province 10, 155
Jiangsu Province 10, 240, 261, 300, 301, 325, 330, 335
Jiaodong Peninsula 335
Jiefang Motor Vehicle Industrial Associated Corporation 120
Jilin Province 10, 249
Jinan (city) 274
Jixi Mine 240

Kailuan Mining Area 240
Karamay Oilfield 243, 253
Ka Wah Bank 54
Kunming 258
Kuwait 255, 289

labour contract system 160–4; Regulations Concerning the Contract Labour System 160
labour insurance 170–1
labour protection (safety) 172–3; Regulations on Accident Reports of Injuries and Deaths 172; Safety and Technical Regulations for Construction Installation Workers 172; Stipulations on Strengthening Worker Safety 173
labour market 163–4; labour recruitment 161–2; labour service companies 162–3
Land Administration Law 180
land use (compensation and rights) 182–6, 339; Land Administration Law 180; State Bureau of Land Administration 178, 179, 184
laser technology 263
Latin America 289
Law Governing Civil Procedures 91, 96, 98, 133
Law Governing Criminal Procedures 92, 98
Law Governing Economic Contracts 91, 93
Law Governing Sanitary Production and Handling of Food 92
Law of Local People's Congresses and Government 95
Law of the People's Courts and Procuratorates 91, 96
Law on Accounting 92
Law on Agrarian Reform 91
Law on Chinese-foreign Joint Ventures 183, 306, 312, 319

Law on Foreign Enterprises 92–3
Law on Joint Ventures Using Chinese and Foreign Investment 92–3
Law on Medicine Management 92
Law on Mineral Resources 92
Law on Sino-foreign Cooperative Enterprises 92
Law on Technical Contracts 91
Law on the Prevention and Control of Air Pollution 92
Law Protecting Wild Animals 92, 193
Legal System Working Committee 93
lawyer(s) 99–103; Provisional Regulations Concerning Lawyers 94, 95–6, 101
Leading Group for Foreign Investment Work 314
Liaodong Peninsular 245, 335; Liaodong Bay 242
Liaohe (river) 192; Liaohe Oilfield 242
Liaoning Province 10, 155, 224, 240, 242, 249, 261
Liaohe (river) 189
limited liability companies 133
Lufthansa Company 255
Luxemborg 52, 327

Maanshan Iron and Steel Plant 224
Macao 33, 34, 36, 37, 38, 52, 53, 54, 97, 106, 183, 258, 323, 331
Ma Hong xi, xiv, 1, 342, 343
Major Overhaul Depreciation Fund 155
Management Measures for Environmental Protection and Capital Construction Projects 194
Maritime Arbitration Commission 105, 106
Maritime Law 92; Maritime Courts 96
Measures on the Management of Housing Construction 180
Measures on the Management of Land Used by Foreign Funded Enterprises 184
Measures to Collect Enterprise Regulating Tax 82
Measuring Law 92
metal ore resources 223–4
Micronesia 54
Middle East 251, 274, 290
Ministry of Aeronautics and Astronautics 260, 261, 273, 274
Ministry of Agriculture and Forestry 289, 304, 305
Ministry of Civil Affairs 57
Ministry of Coal Industry 120
Ministry of Commerce 5
Ministry of Communications 250, 251, 253
Ministry of Construction 178, 179, 180, 187

Ministry of Energy Resources 268
Ministry of Finance 21, 22, 24, 26, 86, 182, 304, 314, 315; Ministry of Finance's Report Concerning the Second Step to Carry Out Substituting Tax for Surrendered Profit 82
Ministry of Foreign Economic Relations and Trade 252, 304, 314, 315, 316, 317, 323, 326, 327
Ministry of Justice 99, 100, 101
Ministry of Labour 314
Ministry of Machine-building and Electronics Industry 260, 261, 273
Ministry of Materials and Equipment 233, 235, 236
Ministry of Metallurgical Industry 120, 225
Ministry of Nuclear Industry 267
Ministry of Personnel 314
Ministry of Petroleum Industry 119, 253
Ministry of Posts and Telecommunications 259, 260
Ministry of Radio and Television 261
Ministry of Railways 120, 249, 258, 261
Ministry of Water Resources 259, 261
monetary policy 27–32; cash control 38–9; credit 39–43; deposit reserve rate 28; exchange rate 34–6; foreign exchange control 36–8; loan interest rate 28–9; Provisional Regulations Concerning Cash Control 39; Provisional Regulations on Banning Bills and Securities in State Currency From Leaving and Entering the Country 35; Regulations Concerning the Control of Foreign Exchange 49 (also see foreign exchange control – State Administration of Exchange Control (SAEC)

Nanhai (sea) 192
Nanjing (city) 186, 191, 251
national budget (preparation of) 20–6
National People's Congress – NPC (see People's Congress)
Ningbo (city) 121, 180, 253, 329
Ningxia (Ningxia Hui Autonomous Region) 10, 241, 245
Noise Standard for the Urban Regional Environment 194
Nonferrous Corporation 120
North America 290 (also see United States)
Notice on the Levying and Exemption of Taxes on Houses and Residences Owned by Chinese-foreign Joint Ventures 180
nuclear industry 265–9
Number of Questions Concerning Speeding Up Industrial Development 143

Ocean Environmental Protection Law 193
oil and natural gas resource distribution and production 241–3

open coastal cities, open cities 51, 52, 315, 316
open door policy 82, 83, 312–18, 329, 335; co-development 313; compensation trade 312; direct foreign investment 311–12; leasing 312; processing and assembly 312–13; sole-foreign invested enterprises 312
opening coastal areas 329–32

Pacific 251, 262, 270, 289; Oceania 290
Panzhihua (coal deposit and steel plant) 224, 225
Pakistan 239
People's Bank of China (People's Bank) 28, 38, 39, 49, 50, 51, 54, 57, 139, 314
(National) People's Congress 21, 23, 25, 91, 92, 93, 94, 95, 110, 119, 132, 193
People's Construction Bank of China 50, 52, 114, 139, 213, 214
People's Court(s) 96–9, 105
petrochemical industry (development of) 228–9; Petroleum Corporation 120
People's Insurance Company of China 55, 57
Pingdingshan (coal) Mine 240
Plan for the Rehabilitation and Development of Land 107
Poland 249
postal services (development and administration of) 256–7, 260; Postal Service Law 257
Prevention and Treatment Law for Air Pollution 193
Prevention and Treatment Law for Water Pollution 193
'price-scissors' 69, 74, 282, 289, 300
price subsidies 78–9, 213
pricing (reform of) 59–76; price of new products 80; State Price Information Centre 73; State Pricing Administrative Bureau 63
'primary stage of socialism' xiv, 1, 2, 7
Principles of Foreign Economic and Technical Assistance 327
Procedures of the State Council for Encouraging Foreign Investment 319
Provisional Measures to Collect Waste Discharge Fees 194
Provisional Regulations Concerning Insurance of Staff and Workers of State-owned Enterprises Waiting for Re-employment 155
Provisional Regulations Concerning the Bankruptcy of Collective-owned Industrial Enterprises 155
Provisional Regulations Concerning the Collection of Income Tax from State-owned Enterprises 82

Provisional Regulations for Encouraging Foreign Investment 92, 184
Provisional Regulations on Budget and Final Accounts 91
Provisional Regulations on Promoting Economic Association 92
Provisional Stipulations on Large Associated Industrial Enterprises to Draw Up Plans Independently 92, 120, 144
Provisions for Urban and Rural Construction 180

Qadam Basin (oil resources) 255
Qingdao 120, 189, 329
Qing Dynasty 51
Qinghai Province 10, 245
Qinghuangdao (sea port) 253, 258
Qinshan Nuclear Power Station 244
Quality Standard for Sea-water 194
Quality Standard for the Atmospheric Environment 194
Quality Standard for the (inland) Water Environment 194

Rance Tidal Power Station (France) 247
rare-earth metals industry 226
real estate (administration of) 178–82; Real Estate Economics Research Association 180
re-export 324
Regulations on Some Policies Concerning Promotion of Township Enterprises' Foreign Exchange Earnings Through Export 304
Regulations on the Work of Directors of Industrial State-enterprises 148
Regulations on the Registration and Administration of Legal Entities 123
Regulations on the Work of the Grassroots Organizations of the Communist Party in Industrial Enterprises 148
Regulations on the Work of Workers' Congresses 148
renminbi currency 32–9
rocket manufacture 269–70; Long-march No.1 and No.2 carrier rockets 269, 271
Rumania 249
rural credit cooperatives 55, 139, 298

satellites – domestic satellite communication 259; imported satellite ground station equipment 324; satellite insurance 56; satellite technology and services 252, 270–4
Science and Technology Commission 50, 313, 326
Second Five Year Plan (1958-62) 108, 165, 200, 201, 202, 203, 204, 217, 218
second (state-enterprise) tax replacing profit stage 145–6

separation of (state-enterprise) ownership from right of management 146–8
Seventh Five Year Plan (1986-90) 108, 200
sewage, sanitation and pollution 190
Shaanxi Province 10, 237, 241, 253
Shandong Province, Peninsular 226, 242, 245, 325, 330
Shanghai 10, 45, 53, 57, 186, 188, 189, 190, 234, 254, 257, 258, 261, 274, 281, 283, 304, 320, 329, 335; Shanghai/Pudong Development Area 341; Hongqiao International Airport (Shanghai) Administration 254; Yangshupu Waterworks (Shanghai) 188
Shanghai Aviation Company 255
Shanghai Electrical Integrated Corporation 120
Shanghai Ocean Shipping Bureau 252
Shanghai Volkswagon Limited (Santana Limousine) 321–3; Shanghai Tractor and Automobile Industry Company 321
Shantou (sea port) 253, 330
Shanxi Province 10, 237, 239, 240, 241, 249, 255
Shenfu Dongsheng Coalfield 120, 239
Shengli Oilfield 241
Shenyang 121, 155, 187, 254, 325; Shenyang Anti-explosion Appliances Factory 155
Shenzhen 121, 190, 274, 332; Shenzhen Special Economic Zone 49, 106
Shoudu Iron and Steel Company 225
Sichuan Province 10, 144, 241; Sichuan Petroleum Administration 253
Singapore 52
Sixth Five-year Plan (1981-85) 108, 188, 194, 200, 203, 204, 209, 210, 220, 217, 218, 229, 254, 262
socialist commodity economy 4–5
Song Hua Jiang (river) 192
Songliao Basin 241
South America 290
Southeast Asia 54
South Fujian Triangle 344, 345
Southwest China Administrative Bureau 254
Southwest China Aviation Company 254
Soviet Union 241, 249, 265
special economic zone(s) 49, 51, 52, 106, 180, 315, 316, 317, 330, 332–3, 341, 342
State Administration of Exchange Control (SAEC) 36, 37, 38, 49, 314
State Administration of Industry and Commerce 103, 123, 124, 126, 129, 134, 135, 180, 314, 317
State Bureau of the Building Materials Industry 229; China New Buildings Materials Corporation 229, 230
State Council 20, 21, 22, 23, 25, 26, 32, 33, 36, 37, 38, 39, 50, 52, 53, 55, 57, 80, 82, 86, 92, 93, 94, 95, 103, 105, 106, 108, 115, 116, 118, 120, 123, 124, 126, 131, 132, 133, 142, 144, 145, 148, 160, 169, 173, 183, 184, 193, 211, 214, 219, 227, 233, 235, 283, 304, 314, 315, 317, 330, 331, 335
State Credit Management Bureau 48
State Energy Investment Company 342
State General Administration of Customs 314
State Planning Commission 108, 109, 110, 113, 114, 115, 118, 119, 120, 187, 211, 219, 220, 221, 304, 314, 326
State Statistical Bureau 67, 116, 117, 118
Stipulations Concerning Radioactivity 194
stock market (development of) 48–9
Suzhou (city) 186, 301
Sweden 250, 289, 327
Switzerland 250

Taiwan 183, 252, 281, 330, 332, 342; Taiwan Straits 252
Taiyuan Iron and Steel Plant 224
taxation system 81–7; Procedures Concerning National Taxation Policy 81
technical imports 324–6; technical exports 327
telecommunication services (administration and development of) 257–60
Ten-year Plan for the Development of the National Economy (1976-85) 107
Thailand 54
Third Five Year Plan (1966-70) 108, 202, 203, 204, 217, 218
Third Plenum (December 1978) 15, 17
'Three Integration' Employment System 159–60
Tianjin Province 10, 45, 180, 186, 225, 243, 253, 261, 274, 281, 283, 320, 325, 335
Tibet, Lhasa, 10, 56, 245, 246, 259
township and village enterprises 295–307; township enterprises (funding of) 298; township enterprises (management of) 297–8; township enterprise workers 302; rural industrial modernisation 303–4; role of township enterprises 299–300; surplus rural labourers 301–2
trade fairs (urban and rural) 127–8
trademarks 134–5; Trademark Law 91, 123, 134; Trademark Office 134
transport services (development and administration of) 27–56; city roads 190, 238, 239; highway transport 250–1; pipeline transport 253; railway transport 248–50; water transport 251–3 (major sea ports 253)
Trial Measures Concerning the Management of Extra Budgetary Funds 26

United Nations 288; United Nations Committee on the Peaceful Use of Outer Space 273; United Nations Food and Agricultural

Organisation 288; United Nations 1958 Convention for Recognizing Foreign Arbitration Awards 105
United States 53, 54, 238, 262, 274; Seattle 54, Washington State 54 (also see North America)
Urban Noise Control Law 193

wages 164–7; wage funds 164; wage subsidies 167–8 (also see bonus payments); Provisional measures for the Management of the Wage Fund 164
Wenzhou (city) 329, 333
Western Europe 274
wind and tidal energy 246–7
Workers' Congresses (in state-owned enterprises) 150
World Bank 52, 251, 253, 288, 292, 313
World Food Programme 288
Wuhan (city) 120, 186, 234, 257, 342

Xiamen 53, 121, 329, 330; Xiamen Special Economic Zone 330; Xiamen International Bank 50, 53
Xian (city) 45, 121, 254; Xian Power Machinery Manufacturing Cooperation 120
Xinjiang (Uygar Autonomous Region) 10, 57, 233, 240, 244, 246, 249; Xinjiang Construction Corps Air Service Station 255; Xinjiang Construction Corps Agricultural and Animal Husbandry Insurance Company 57; Xinjiang Oilfield 243
Xishan Mining Area 240
Xushou Mine 240

Yangbajing Geothermal Power Station 245
Yanquan Mining Area 239
Yantai (sea port) 253, 329
Yiminhe (open-cut coal) Mine 240
Yingkou (sea port) 253
Yuanbaoshan (open-cut coal) Mine 240
Yunnan Province 10, 144, 245

Zhao Ziyang xiv
Zhengzhou (city) 191, 226
Zhejiang Province 10, 244, 247; Zhejiang Power Station 244
Zhongxin Enterprise Bank 50
Zhongyuan Oilfield 242, 243
(Premier) Zhou En Lai 327
Zhujiang (Pearl River), Zhujiang (river) system, 192, 242, 248, 251; Zhujiang Delta 258, 330, 335, 336; Zhujiang Navigation Bureau 252
Zhonghua Power Company 244

DATE DUE

11/6/95	11/15/95		
SJD	12/14/96		
Due			

DEC 2 0 2007

Demco, Inc. 38-293